THE HISTORY OF
THE MOST RENOWNED AND VICTORIOUS
PRINCESS ELIZABETH
LATE QUEEN OF ENGLAND

Classics of British Historical Literature

JOHN CLIVE, EDITOR

William Camden

———

THE

History of

THE MOST RENOWNED AND VICTORIOUS

Princess Elizabeth

LATE QUEEN OF ENGLAND

Selected Chapters

EDITED AND WITH AN INTRODUCTION BY

WALLACE T. MacCAFFREY

The University of Chicago Press

CHICAGO AND LONDON

ISBN: 0-226-09218-6 (clothbound); 0-226-09219-4 (paperbound)
Library of Congress Catalog Card Number: 74-115682
The University of Chicago Press, Chicago 60637
The University of Chicago Press, Ltd., London
© 1970 by The University of Chicago
Published 1970
Printed in the United States of America

DA 350
.C17
1970

Shi

Contents

CONTENTS

Series Editor's Preface

This series of reprints has one major purpose: to put into the hands of students and other interested readers outstanding—and sometimes neglected—works dealing with British history which have either gone out of print or are obtainable only at a forbiddingly high price.

The phrase Classics of British Historical Literature requires some explanation, in view of the fact that the two companion series published by the University of Chicago Press are entitled, respectively, Classic European Historians and Classic American Historians. Why, then, introduce the word *literature* into the title of this series?

One reason lies close at hand. History, if it is to live beyond its own generation, must be memorably written. The greatest British historians—Clarendon, Gibbon, Hume, Carlyle, Macaulay—are still alive today, not merely because they contributed to the cumulative historical knowledge about their subjects, but because they were masters of style and literary artists as well. And even historians of the second rank, if they deserve to survive, are able to do so only because they can still be read with pleasure. To emphasize this truth at the present time, when much eminently solid and worthy academic history suffers from being almost totally unreadable, seems worth doing.

The other reason for including the word *literature* in the title of the series has to do with its scope. To read history is to learn about the past. But if, in trying to learn about the British past, one were to restrict oneself to the reading of formal works of history, one would miss a great deal. Often a historical novel, a sociological inquiry, or an account of events and institutions couched in semifictional form teaches us just as much about the past as does the "history" that calls itself by that name. And, not infrequently, these "informal" historical works turn out to be less well known than their merit deserves. By calling this series Classics of British Historical Literature it will be possible to include such books without doing violence to the usual nomenclature.

In the history of British historiography, William Camden occupies an important place among those who, guiding themselves by classical models, made the important advance from antiquarianism to the writing of history proper. For students of Elizabethan England, his *History* will always remain an invaluable and indispensable source. But it would be a mistake to delimit his appeal in this way. As one reads Professor MacCaffrey's introduction and is led on to the annals themselves, one receives a strong sense of the essential continuity of historiographic problems over the centuries. It has been said that the great Thucydides himself contributed to his own reputation for objectivity by repeatedly calling himself nonpartisan. Camden, for his part, is convinced that by letting the facts speak for themselves, the glorious achievements of Elizabeth's reign will duly emerge. He does his best not to let his conscious prejudices influence his selection and presentation of these facts. But, as Professor MacCaffrey demonstrates, he wrote with certain assumptions and predispositions too deeply ingrained to be cast aside. And they inevitably color his narrative.

Does this not have a familiar ring? Any writer of recent history, and more particularly any writer of anything that might be put under the heading of "official" history, finds himself in the same boat. It is a sobering thought that perhaps, three centuries hence, some of our present-day "objective" histories may appear in a series similar to this one, with their pride and prejudice duly put in place by means of an editorial introduction.

All this should not lead us to underestimate Camden's achievement. He helped to shape the form and tradition of British historiography at a time when such an effort involved all the hazards and difficulties of a pioneering attempt. There is something genuinely moving about the way in which in his preface he pays tribute not only to the dignity of history, but also to "that ingenuous Freedom of Speech joyned with Modesty which becometh an Historian." And all those who have tried to write history themselves, or are thinking of doing so, will salute him across the ages as they read of his "searching and turning over whereof whilst I laboured till I sweat again, covered all over with Dust, to gather fit Matter together, (which I diligently sought for, but more rarely found than I expected.)"

JOHN CLIVE

Editor's Introduction

William Camden's *Annals of Queen Elizabeth* is surely one of the most neglected of the major English histories. It has been more than two hundred and fifty years since the last printing of this book (an English version in 1706 and a Latin edition in 1717). This is all the more surprising since Camden's is the earliest authoritative history of this much-studied reign and still a prime source for an understanding of it. Moreover, it is a book signally important in the development of English historical writing. It stands at the very close of the ancient tradition of the English chronicle, but it has many original elements which make it a pioneer work in the whole tradition of modern historical study.

Perhaps the very fact that it is a hybrid, compounded of two different traditions, is responsible for its lack of continued popularity. Although in form it resembles the Tudor chronicles of Hall or Holinshed, in tone and content it is quite different, and it is addressed to an audience more learned and more sophisticated than that reached by the popular writers. It lacks the colorful description, the picturesque detail, and the melodramatic narrative which they adopted. On the other hand Camden had not mastered the technique of continuous narrative to which a modern reader is accustomed, and the rather clumsy organization in which each chapter corresponds to a calendar year confuses and distracts his audience at times. Finally, the work, written in Latin, comes to us through translators in a stiffly austere style which, while it reflects the author's tone of mind, demands large drafts upon our sympathetic imagination to sustain our interest.

There is much to say about the work, but first the man himself requires attention. Camden's career ran a smooth and undramatic course, yet its circumstances are very relevant to understanding his achievement. Born in 1551 in the first flush of the Edwardian Reformation,[1] he was a native Londoner, whose father, an immigrant from the Midland town of Lichfield, was a member of the painters' company, while his mother came of a Cumberland family of somewhat higher social status. The family circumstances must have been modest; it is possible that Camden spent some time in Christ's Hospital, the great London orphans' school. He did certainly attend St. Paul's School, founded a generation earlier by Dean Colet and dedicated to a rigorous humanist education.

The young Camden was lucky in finding a patron to provide for the next phase of his career—entry into Oxford. This was Thomas Cooper, a notable antiquary, later Bishop of Lincoln, but then a fellow of Magdalen College and head of the college school. It was under his protection that Camden went to the University in 1566. Cooper was unable to advance Camden at Magdalen, but the young man's luck held when he found a second patron in Dr. Thomas Thornton of Pembroke. When the latter obtained a canonry at Christ Church, he took his protegé with him, and Camden seems to have regarded this foundation as his own college. But, oddly enough, he probably never took a formal degree although he remained at the university until 1571.

Camden did not find the permanent settlement in the university which he may have hoped for, but once again he attracted the attention of a patron—this time of two, the brothers Gabriel

---

1. For biographical information on Camden the most readily available source is the entry in the *Dictionary of National Biography* (by Sir Edward Maunde-Thompson). This is based on the Latin life of Camden in Thomas Smith, *V. Cl. Camdeni et illustrium virorum ad G. Camdenum epistolae* (London, 1691). Much of the matter in Smith's life is incorporated into Edmund Gibson's preface to his edition of *Britannia* (London, 1695). Other useful accounts are the biographical article in Henri Bayle, *General Dictionary, Historical and Critical* (London, 1736), 4:61–68, and in Anthony à Wood, *Athenae Oxonienses* (London, 1815), 2:339–50.

and Godfrey Goodman, of whom the former was Dean of Westminster. They apparently provided him with money and with books, and the next few years, between 1571 and 1575, were probably spent in travels through England on which he collected geographical and historical information. This was part of the raw material for his great survey of England, published in the next decade. In 1575 Dean Goodman was able to appoint him second master in Westminster School, the recently refounded school attached to the Abbey. There Camden spent the next twenty years, first as a teacher, and after 1593, as headmaster. He took his teaching seriously and published in 1597 a new Greek grammar which long remained a standard introduction to the language for English schoolboys.

But he found time during the years at Westminster for other activities as well. The years of teaching hindered the continuation of his antiquarian research, and his work flagged. But his abilities were recognized by other scholars with similar interests. When Ortelius, the great Flemish geographer, visited England in 1577, he was introduced to Camden, and his enthusiastic urging inspired the young scholar to renewed effort. In 1586 the appearance of the great survey of England, *Britannia*, established Camden's position as a major European scholar and one of England's famous men.

These years brought not only fame but modest fortune as well. In 1589 Bishop Piers of Salisbury granted him a sinecure prebend in Salisbury cathedral, a post which he was licensed to hold without meeting the usual requirement of being an ordained clergyman. In 1597 the courtier, Sir Fulke Greville, poet and patron of letters and a royal favorite, secured him appointment to the College of Heralds as Clarenceux King at Arms. This gave him a respectable income and a dignified post with duties which were highly congenial and not too onerous. The heralds were ceremonial officers of the court, required to attend at great public occasions. But they had a more important function, since it was also their business to grant coats of arms to families newly seeking them and to confirm the continuing rights of those who already boasted them. In the intensely rank-conscious world of late Tudor England there was an unceasing scramble to cross the dividing line which separated gentlemen (the "common sort of nobility," as Camden called them)[2] from the mere yeoman or freeholder. The necessary passport was the heralds' certificate. To function as the issuing officers for such vital social documents required not only a profound genealogical expertise, but also a nice sensitivity towards the most delicate shades of social distinction.

The rest of Camden's career was one of content and fulfillment. While he worked hard at his job as a herald, he found time for successive revisions of the *Britannia* and for the great labor of the *Annals* along with a number of lesser works. He had the means to buy a house at Chislehurst in Kent, accessible to London but far enough from the bustle of the capital to give him the seclusion which he needed for his scholarly tasks. From 1609, when he bought this house, until his death in 1623, he spent increasingly long periods of time in Kent. In 1622 he had the satisfaction of setting up a handsome endowment for Oxford's first lectureship in history and in nominating the first holder of the chair.

Camden was honored in death by burial in Westminster Abbey, where his marble effigy, its hand resting on a copy of *Britannia,* may still be seen. His life had been a quiet and unadventurous one and, in a conventional sense, unambitious. He had never sought entry into court circles; his preferments had come unasked. He had declined the prestigious offices of a Master of Requests, as well as the honor of knighthood. Camden had accepted without demur the established order in which he lived; he conformed to the religion established by law and accepted the hedging restrictions of the hierarchical official world in which he moved. But he had found the leisure he needed to complete the intellectual tasks he set himself. He had also gained entry to a society of educated aristocrats who offered him both stimulus and response. Lastly, while he had lived close to the world of high politics and the men who ruled England, he had not lost the freedom and detachment which differentiated the observer from the participant. All this experience was to count heavily when he came to write the history of his own times.

2. *Britannia,* clxxxiv. This reference and all following references to this work are from Edmund Gibson's edition (London, 1695).

But if his official career had been that of a loyal and un-ambitious civil servant, his intellectual life had been a lively and venturesome one which took him deep into a "sort of learn-ing that was then but just peeping into the world."[3] Camden's intellectual ambitions had led him to a kind of study which was then novel and fresh—indeed, original. His intellectual explorations were part of a grand enterprise, shared by several generations of scholars, which was illuminating the past in startling ways. But the form which most of his work took is now, if not obsolete, at least old-fashioned, and it is not easy to give it a label familiar to twentieth-century ears. It is quite proper to refer to Camden as a historian but more precise to call him an antiquary. This is a term which has come to have an ambiguous meaning since the eighteenth century. It has come to imply an amateur as opposed to a professional and perhaps to suggest a rather undiscriminating and intellectually undisciplined en-thusiasm for the past. Such strictures certainly do not apply to the antiquaries of the sixteenth and seventeenth centuries. They were clearly the professionals of their age, highly trained in the skills of their calling, discriminating and clear-sighted as to the questions they sought to answer and rigorous in the standards they set themselves in their investigations.

To understand the nature of Camden's work one has to glimpse some of the complexities of his cultural inheritance.[4] Like all scholars of his generation he was grounded in a mastery of the classical languages. For most of them this mastery was the necessary preliminary to those philosophical or literary studies which they saw as the focal point of all humanistic culture. Their interests in classical learning were not in its historical, but in its contemporary relevance. It was not curiosity about the past but concern for the present and future moral well-being of men which led them to their studies. They saw the works of the classical authors as authoritative and inspiring guides to the moral development of contemporary men, which was for them

3. Gibson's life of William Camden in the Introduction to *Britannia*, sig b^v.
4. For general accounts of English scholarship in the sixteenth century see F. O. Levy, *Tudor Historical Thought* (San Marino, Calif., 1967); F. S. Fuss-ner, *The English Historical Revolution 1570–1640* (London, 1962); T. D. Kendrick, *British Antiquity* (London, 1950).

the raison d'être of all their labors. But a minority of scholars—increasing in numbers since the fifteenth century—had gradually become interested in antiquity for its own sake, for historical rather than philosophical ends. Many of these men found the prime attractions of classical learning to lie not in its literary or philosophical writers but in the topographers and geographers, such as Strabo or Ptolemy, who had left behind detailed physical descriptions of the Imperial Roman provinces. These antiquaries had begun with the task of reconciling the ancient descriptions of Europe with the political geography of the sixteenth century. But their interests had broadened rapidly to include many other aspects of ancient life—law, social customs, language—interests which, in the terminology of modern specialization, were at once historical, geographical, and anthropological. In Camden's hands these were to broaden out to include not only the written descriptions left behind by classical writers but also the material remains of the past, its ruined monuments, so visible yet so little noticed, or the buried wreckage, coins, and inscriptions which the labors of ditch-diggers or ploughmen threw up to modern notice. Since most of these scholars concentrated their efforts on some particular region of the Roman Empire, they soon took on more than a tinge of local or patriotic pride. Ortelius urged Camden "to acquaint the world with Britain, that ancient island."[5] And when Camden's task sometimes overwhelmed him, he took heart in the remembrance that it was for the glory of his country that he labored. As he himself was to say, he sought "to restore Britain to its antiquities and its antiquities to Britain."[6] The rediscovery of Britain's ancient past would secure her an honorable place among the nations of Europe. It would establish the connection between modern England and the common ancestor of all civilized realms, the Roman Empire.[7] This was the great task which Camden took up and which resulted in the publication, in 1586,

5. *Britannia,* Mr. Camden's Preface, sig dii[r].
6. *Britannia,* ibid.
7. See the essay by Stuart Piggott, "William Camden and the *Britannia,"* in *Proceedings of the British Academy* 37 (1951): 199–217; and F. J. Levy, "The Making of Camden's *Britannia," Bibliotheque d'Humanisme et Renaissance* 26 (1964): 70–97.

of the first edition of *Britannia*. Its full title in translation was *Britain, or a chorographical*[8] *description of the most flourishing kingdoms of England, Scotland, and Ireland, and the adjoining islands from the most profound antiquity.*

The work that had to be done when Camden took up his task was enormous, but the ground was by no means unprepared. Interest in producing a chorographical description of England was no longer new. There had been a few partial attempts as early as the mid-fifteenth century. More recently in Henry VIII's reign, John Leland had won royal patronage for a planned survey on a national scale which he proposed to publish. Leland worked hard at the collection of information, primarily geographical and topographical in character, but it was still a mass of unpublished notes when madness ended his working career. But the notes remained and were to prove a major source for Camden's own work.[9]

In the mid-sixteenth century, interest in chorographical study continued to grow. One of Camden's predecessors among the Heralds, Robert Talbot, made the first attempt to identify the places mentioned in the Roman geographical account of Britain —the *Antonine Itinerary*. Other writers attempted general descriptions of the country; two were published before 1580, both impressionistic and discursive. The first such work on a single county was William Lambarde's *Perambulation of Kent* (1576), while John Hooker printed a description of his native Exeter about 1575. It was not until 1598 that John Stow brought out his classic survey of London. Most of these men were close friends and associates of Camden and generous in their assistance to his efforts. Besides these eminent figures there were lesser men scattered through the whole country who were eager and helpful collaborators. And Camden enjoyed not only the professional collaboration of other antiquaries but also the friendship and sympathetic interest of wider circles of Elizabethan

---

8. *"chorography*—The art or practice of describing, or of delineating on a map or chart, particular regions or districts, as distinguished from geography, taken as dealing with the earth in general, and (less distinctly) from topography, which deals with particular places, as towns, etc." (*New English Dictionary*).

9. For a full account, see Kendrick, *British Antiquity*.

intellectuals, including the group centered upon Sir Philip Sidney. There was thus a cordially receptive atmosphere for Camden's new work.

The general stirring of interest in Britain's remote past had opened up several vexing questions. Most particularly there had been a generation of fierce debate about the whole question of British origins. For centuries past no one had doubted the account given by Geoffrey of Monmouth in his twelfth-century *History of the Kings of Britain.* This book enshrined two great national myths, those of the Trojan Brutus and King Arthur. The former ascribed the foundation of British society to Brutus, a great-grandson of Aeneas, who had fled to the island from the Mediterranean and in 1108 B.C. had overcome the giants who then inhabited it and given his name to his new homeland. Geoffrey followed up with a long catalogue of quite imaginary kings who reigned down to Roman times. The centuries following Roman withdrawal were filled in a similar fashion with another great body of mythical material. Geoffrey's elaborate account of Arthur and his knights in which, among other achievements, the king is portrayed as the conqueror of all western Europe, formed the basis for the efflorescence of the Arthurian legend in the cycles of chivalric romance. In Britain these two myths were treasured for obvious patriotic reasons. Through Brutus Britain was linked with the origins of classical civilization, particularly with the founder of Imperial Rome, the Trojan Aeneas. In Geoffrey's Arthur the island possessed a national hero equal in stature and fame to Charlemagne, and a proud imperial achievement. Britons could feel assured that their past equalled in splendor that of their continental neighbors.

The Brutus story had come under attack from Polydore Vergil,[10] the Italian servant of Henry VII, who in his history of England published in 1534, questioned it because of the complete lack of verification in any ancient author. This had led to an outburst of patriotic rage and to some serious discussion of the question; a few scholars began to doubt the Brutus story, but most writers, popular or learned, still clung defensively to it. Polydore had also raised some uneasy doubts about the au-

---

10. See Denis Hay, *Polydore Vergil; Renaissance Historian and Man of Letters* (Oxford, 1952).

thenticity of the Arthur legend, again pointing out the lack of verifying authority, and this too led to angry denunciation and continuing debate. In short, confidence in the received tradition about Britain's remoter past was severely shaken, and this in turn led to even more fundamental issues. Not only was the substance of the tradition under fire, but more important, central questions of methodology began to emerge. What were the standards by which the authenticity of any account of the remote past could be judged? How were men to choose among the competing versions of British antiquity which were now put forward? How could certainty of knowledge about these matters be reestablished?

This was the background against which Camden commenced his work on *Britannia*. At least a part of his labors of collection had been accomplished by Leland and others; he had eager and numerous collaborators. Acrimonious but not unfruitful discussion had opened up central questions about British history, and it was fairly clear that much of the received canon about the remoter past would have to be recast.

Camden's labors on the *Britannia* were probably begun in the early 1570s, after he had left Oxford, and could be continued, once he was at Westminster, only during the school vacations. They took him on arduous journeys over the abominable roads of the sixteenth century to almost every part of England and Wales. In 1582 he went to York by way of Suffolk, returning through Lancashire. Later, after the first edition was out, he was on the road again—to Devonshire in 1589 and Wales in 1590. Six years later he visited Salisbury and Wells and in 1600 made a six-month trip as far north as Carlisle. These journeys were made so that he might engage in on-the-spot investigations of all possible traces of antiquity—ruins, inscriptions, excavated artifacts (such as coins), local legend, the courses of Roman roads—and in the collation of this evidence with what the written sources, ancient or medieval, could tell him. Camden was among the first to realize the potential uses of archaeological material and pioneered a new kind of scholarship by using this evidence to complement the written sources. His later editions of *Britannia* included plates of coins (with explanatory texts) and reproductions of ancient inscriptions, especially from the area of Hadrian's wall. (His use of coins led him to discover the existence of a pre-Roman coinage in Britain.) His work in pre-Roman, Romano-British, and Anglo-Saxon materials imposed yet another labor on him. Latin and Greek served well enough for classical texts or medieval documents, but the investigation of Celtic or Anglo-Saxon matters meant the mastering of two additional languages. Welsh was at least a living, although not a scholarly, tongue; but Anglo-Saxon was long forgotten, and its rediscovery had just begun. In all these tasks Camden built on the work of his predecessors and collaborators, but he brought to the final accomplishment a wider and far more perceptive imagination and a stronger understanding of the problems to be dealt with.

The first result of these labors came in 1586 when the first edition of *Britannia* appeared in London in a modest octavo dedicated to Lord Burghley. Four more London editions were out by 1600. Each new edition contained additions and revisions, and the last had some plates in it. The final edition in Camden's lifetime was the great folio of 1607, handsomely equipped with maps and plates of coins and inscriptions. These editions, as well as the foreign ones at Frankfort (1590 and 1616), were intended for a learned and an international audience. But in 1610 the author supervised a translation into English which was printed again in 1637. The *Britannia* continued to reappear after Camden's death in a series of new editions, the last of which came out in 1806. Later editors supplemented and corrected the text in the light of new evidence. By the opening of the nineteenth century the work was superseded by the host of individual county histories which had by then appeared. And thereafter the historico-topographical survey pioneered by Camden gradually faded as a mode of historical writing. The genre is now so unfamiliar that its very form and content require a word of explanation for the modern reader.

Britannia is divided into two rather different parts. The first and shorter section is more familiar to modern experience since it is a chronologically arranged survey of British history from earliest times to the Norman Conquest. There is a minimum of narrative; the author's main purpose is to give a full account of all the sources of information (which are liberally excerpted) and a critical consideration of the problems which they raise.

In tackling the prickly question of British origins, Camden displays imaginative originality. He deals with the Brutus myth fairly and gently but conclusively dismisses it by quietly assigning it to the genre of founding myths, which "disguise the truth with the mixture of a fable and bring in the gods themselves to act a part . . . thereby to render the beginnings either of a city or of a nation, more noble and majestical."[11] This cool anthropological insight seems commonplace to our age; in his own time it was fresh and startling. He follows up his dismissal of Brutus by suggesting that Britain was peopled by immigrants from the nearby shores of the continent and that the ancient Britons were of the same race and culture as the Gauls. He adduces evidence of language, religion, and social customs to support his case. Brutus was to survive for almost another century among popular and patriotic writers, but Camden now offered in place of a plausible myth a structure of anthropological and historical theory which could be proved or disproved by precise investigation of all the evidence available. His work was a key episode in an intellectual revolution which radically altered Englishmen's perception of their own past.

He handled the remaining sections on Roman and post-Roman history in much the same way. (He is the first English writer to use the term "middle ages" to distinguish the interval between Roman antiquity and recent times.)[12] Arthur is casually mentioned, but Camden's main reliance is on the chronicles which give contemporary accounts of events, which can be checked one against another, and against continental sources. Only in dealing with the Norman Conquest does he abandon this approach, giving us a fragment of the general history of Britain which he had once contemplated. Breaking away from quotation and criticism of his sources, he gives us a brief and straightforward narrative in his own words.

With the Normans he ends the first portion of *Britannia.* What follows is a series of short essays meant to serve as background to the detailed county-by-county survey. Some deal with

11. *Britannia,* ix.
12. See Camden, *Remains concerning Britain,* 5 (London, 1623).

historical geography, recounting the different divisions of Britain since pre-Roman times; others explain the origin and present structure of the ranks of nobility; and a final essay unravels the mysteries of English law-court organization for the uninitiated continental.

The whole remainder of *Britannia* treats successively each county in England and Wales. Cornwall is the first county dealt with "in imitation of Strabo, Ptolemy and the most ancient geographers, who in their descriptions always begin at the most western parts, as first from the great meridian."[13] How each section is arranged can be told in the author's own words. "In my treatise of each county I will shew with as much plainness and brevity as I can who were the ancient inhabitants, what was the reason of the name, what are the bounds of the county, the nature of the soil, the places of greatest antiquity, and most eminent at present; and lastly, who have been dukes or earls of them since the Norman Conquest."[14]

What results is a kind of guidebook, but one designed for a special kind of traveler, since its information is largely historical. (Here Camden differs from his predecessor, Leland, who clearly intended a work more geographical and topographical in character.) *Britannia* is cast in a form of historical writing which, instead of the familiar technique of narrative, uses a systematic description of places. For each locality we are provided with a bundle of geographical, topographical, but above all, historical, data. With these clues, the traveler, as he moves (figuratively or literally) from town to town, is made to see not only what meets the eye but also those indelible, but hitherto illegible, lineaments of the past which the antiquary can call back to our vision. The total effect is of a richly detailed mosaic, for the modern taste, perhaps a bit too complex for the eye to take in with ease. But in an age when men lived much more circumscribed within the bounds of family and countryside, this kind of history, which showed them the past in the familiar guise of their own parish and county and in the persons of their own ancestors made it all the more vivid to their imaginations. It stimulated local and family pride; it gave a new and dignified

13. *Britannia*, cxcvi.
14. *Britannia*, ibid.

dimension to their familiar world by linking it to the majesty of classical and medieval antiquity.

For fellow professionals the work offered a new but well-developed model for all antiquarian study. The critics of the old tradition had hitherto enjoyed mounting success in breaking it down, but efforts to authenticate a newer and better account of antiquity had only imperfectly succeeded. Camden went far toward perfecting these partial achievements. By seeking out all possible evidence, by comparing and combining it, and by rejecting what was anachronistic or simply—by common-sense standards—improbable, he arrived at a description of the British past which scholars must either accept or else disprove by the same careful methods which Camden himself used. His own modesty about his errors and his continuing efforts, in successive editions, to correct, improve, and enlarge helped to win acceptance both for his conclusions and for his method.

The appearance of five editions of *Britannia* within fourteen years is sufficient evidence for the book's popularity, even in its Latin original. In fact, increased interest in antiquarian matters had led to the first formal organization of antiquaries at about the same time as the publication of *Britannia*; in this Camden had a leading part. The first Society of Antiquaries had an obscure history and a short life, but a few facts are quite certain.[15] About the year 1585 a group of interested gentlemen began to meet weekly at Derby House (the Heralds' office) to read papers to one another on antiquarian topics. Some of these papers are extant (and in print)[16] and deal with just such subjects as we might anticipate—the origins of nobility and gentry, of real property, of castles and cities, or with funeral customs or the measuring of land. Proceedings had to be in English, for the members were amateurs rather than scholars, although two of the moving spirits were Camden himself and the great antiquary of London, John Stow. Another leading light was Sir Robert Bruce Cotton, once a pupil at Westminster School and now a close collaborator of Camden. He was now far advanced in gathering his great collection of documents, the first of its kind, and later the core

15. See Joan Evans, *A History of the Society of Antiquaries* (Oxford, 1956).
16. Many are printed in Thomas Hearne, *A Collection of Curious Discourses* (London, 1720), and in Joseph Ayloffe's enlarged edition (1771).

of the British Museum's manuscript collection. Other members, several score in number, included many important figures in court and official circles. Significantly, it was about 1608, just when Camden bought his house in Kent and began to live away from London that their meetings ceased. In 1614 an attempt was made by Camden and others to resume meetings, but James I's distrust of such discussion (which he thought too political in character) quashed these hopes. It was not until the middle of the next century that the Society of Antiquaries was to be firmly established.

In 1607 Camden put the finishing touches on his final edition of *Britannia*; in the following year he began work on the second great achievement of his career, *The Annals or History of Queen Elizabeth*.[17] As he himself tells us in his preface,[18] he was first urged to this work by the Lord Treasurer Burghley, Elizabeth's great minister, who about 1597 put his own papers and those of the Queen at Camden's disposal. But Burghley died the next year, and Camden's enthusiasm waned. It was not until 1608 that he began seriously to work, and it was 1615 before the first half (up through 1588) was published. The rest of the work, to the end of the reign, was finished by 1617, but Camden refused to allow publication in his lifetime. The second part first appeared at Leyden in 1625 and in London in 1627. An English translation of the first part came out in 1625 and of the second in 1629. A complete edition in English followed in 1630 and another in 1635. There were more editions a generation later, in 1675 and 1688 (with a new translation). The last appearances of the *History* in print were in 1706, when (again retranslated) it formed part of White Kennet's general history of England, and in 1717, when the Latin version was reedited.

The problems Camden faced in his new venture were quite different from those he dealt with in *Britannia*. That work was

17. Its full title in Latin is *Annales rerum Anglicarum et Hibernicarum regnante Elizabetha*. In English the title is *The Annals or the History of the most renowned and victorious Princess Elizabeth late Queen of England containing all the most important and remarkable passages of state, both at home and abroad (so far as they were linked with English affairs) during her long and prosperous reign*. In later editions (from 1675) the word *Annals* disappears.

18. *History*, Author to Reader, p. 3 below.

concerned principally with places and institutions and with a remote past. He now had to tell a story of human actions fresh in men's memory and at a time when many of the principal actors in those events were still alive. This meant that he must exercise quite different skills in the arrangement and presentation of the material and very delicate judgments in the interpretation of it. There were, it is true, plenty of models to look to. The English medieval chronicle tradition was ancient and distinguished, and since the invention of printing it had evolved into a very flourishing genre. Chronicles of English history written in the native tongue were steady best-sellers in the Tudor publishing world. Much of the Tudor chroniclers' work was uncritical copying of their medieval predecessors, but they were not unaffected, as the century went on, by the new critical standards set by Italian historical writers, and they show increasing concern about critical use of sources. Nevertheless, they stuck closely to the annalistic form and wrote to please the taste of a large and not very discriminating audience.

Their books were strongly patriotic and Protestant in tone, lively in description, and occasionally bold enough in political comment to invite the censorship of the Privy Council. There was increasing interest in contemporary history. Polydore Vergil had included Henry VII's and part of Henry VIII's reign in his work. Edward Hall devoted himself entirely to the last century and a half—from Richard II to the second Tudor, with a great emphasis on the latter reign. The Elizabethan chroniclers paid much attention to recent events and by successive editions, each with recent material added, kept their histories up to date.[19]

Their sources for contemporary events were largely what was

19. See Edward Hall, *The Union of the two noble and illustre fameles of York and Lancaster* (London, 1548); Richard Grafton, *An Abridgement of the Chronicles of England* (London, 1562, 1563, 1564, 1570, 1572); idem, *The Chronicle at large and meere history of the affayres of England* (London, 1568, 1569); Raphael Holinshed, *Chronicles* (London, 1577, 1587), 2d ed. edited by Thomas Hooker et al.; John Stow, *A Summarie of Englyshe chronicles* (London, 1565, 1566, 1570, 1574, 1575, 1590); idem, *The Summarie of English chronicles. Lately collected and published, now abridged and continued* ... (London, 1566, 1567, 1573, 1579, 1584, 1598, 1604, 1607, 1611, 1618); idem, *The Chronicles of England, from Brutus to this present year of Christ, 1580* (London, 1580, 1592 [2d ed., under title *The Annals of England faithfully collected* ...], 1600, 1601, 1605, 1614, 1615, 1631).

general public knowledge, although they probably had some inside information from court. Their books were loosely and simply constructed with a separate chapter for each year so that additional chapters could easily be tacked on when a new edition brought the work up to date. The contents were by no means merely political. In their indiscriminate enjoyment of natural calamities, scandal and gossip, and of the mysterious or unnatural, they rivaled the modern popular press.

Camden, a scholar by training and experience, had a radically different conception of his work, but he by no means ignored the model they offered. Most importantly he adopted their annalistic form. This placed his work in the familiar English tradition, although he could (and did) cite the classical authority of Tacitus to justify his choice. But in most essential aspects Camden sets himself a much more difficult and sophisticated set of goals than those of the popular annalists. His use of Latin signified his gravity of purpose as well as the fact that he was addressing an international and learned audience.

Moreover, Camden in his preface ("The Author to the Reader") sets himself high goals of scholarly principle. Although the work is to celebrate "the memory of that Princess (which amongst Englishmen ought ever to be grateful and sacred)"[20] and its writing is a patriotic duty, he seeks to achieve an impartial detachment of tone and entirely to exclude his own prejudices or partialities from the book. This was to be a work which was to do more than entertain, more than stimulate patriotic feeling, more indeed than merely pay tribute to the late queen; it was to have the weight, dignity, and didactic value of the great classical histories, such as those of Tacitus or of Polybius to whom the author admiringly refers.

To accomplish this goal Camden, faithful to his antiquarian background, turned to his evidence, above all, to the state documents which were the immediate record of debate, decision, and action by the makers of national policy. These must be used, he asserts, with the greatest possible care lest the historian's own prejudices obscure the light of truth which is somehow manifest in the prime evidence for historical events. But he is aware that

20. All the quotations in this and the next paragraph are from *History*, Author to Reader, p. 8 below.

there are awkward obstacles in the way of such clinical detach-ment. The documents themselves (as he hints in his comments on Burghley's papers) do not always yield that ore of certain fact, that "real truth of passages," presumably lodged in them. The historian cannot exclude his own judgment when the evi-dence is sometimes partisan in character. In the final analysis, the historian must rely on his own moral sense to keep him free of prejudice, unmoved by hope of reward, and untouched by personal affection or dislike. These are far-reaching, though not wholly unattainable, goals. How far does Camden achieve them in his book?

So large a question must be answered piecemeal by exploring particular problems. Perhaps the easiest to begin with is that of sources. Camden himself tells us much on this score, although not so clearly as we could hope.[21] In 1597 Lord Burghley made available his own voluminous papers and those of the royal archives. Camden writes rather vaguely of his examination of these documents, but how far he used them he set to work seriously a decade later is not made at all clear.[22] He writes more explicitly of his use of Cotton's collection and seems to say that most of his material came from those papers. The Cottonian manuscripts certainly contain a great part of the key documents for Elizabethan political history and are still prime evidence for the historian. But apart from having had access to such docu-ments Camden had been a privileged—and "inside"—observer of many events of the reign. His personal observation went back at least to 1572 when, barely 21, he attended the Duke of Nor-folk's trial. He had also known personally many of the greater personages of state or their intimates, some of whom were still alive when he wrote. In short, he enjoyed an unusually favorable position as a historian with ready access to full and authoritative information.

Camden realized his advantages and fully exploited them. He took his documentary sources very seriously and adhered closely to them. He makes frequent use of direct quotation and para-phrases even more widely. He does not follow his practice in

21. We cannot answer very fully questions about Camden's sources until we have a scholarly, annotated edition, at present altogether lacking.

22. *History,* Author to Reader, p. 3 below.

Britannia of citing his sources in the margin, and since we lack a modern annotated edition, it is not possible to identify the sources for each passage; but it is safe to say that behind every statement of fact stands some specific authority, written or oral. In his scrupulous respect for authentic and direct supporting evidence for every assertion he puts forward, Camden provides a model for modern historical practice. No previous English historian, writing of his own times (with the honorable exception of Bede), had given so painfully self-conscious adherence to such principles.

In following these principles Camden specifically repudiates the practice of classical historians who used fictitious speech, put in the mouths of principal protagonists, in order to explain motives and actions and to carry the narrative forward. Camden prefers the actual words of the actors themselves. But this principled fidelity to sources, however praiseworthy, has also some patent shortcomings. Camden himself admits that he has not pried into "the hidden meaning of princes."[23] This of course means that he has gone no further than the face value of the documents he deals with. In sixteenth-century circumstances this is a real disadvantage, since politicians (fearful of the interception of their letters) were very wary in putting to paper anything but their most cautiously official views, and it is very uncommon to find the veil of discretion which conceals their private views and feelings drawn aside. One can applaud Camden's resolve not to make any assertion which is not solidly founded on his sources, but since these sources are so official and often so disingenuous in character, the resulting account is stiffly formal and sometimes quite artificial. Camden is not above the occasional turn of phrase which hints at more than he can say, but his discretion almost never wavers even though in his position he must have had much inside knowledge of the court.

Camden had access to an abundance of varied and authoritative material, but how widely did he conceive the scope of his finished work? He declares that the proper business of the historian is war and policy, but he insists on the need for at least some ecclesiastical history and, a little apologetically, proposes

23. *History,* Author to Reader, pp. 5–6 below.

to include some small matters "which if they please not one, may yet delight another to know."[24] In practice he goes farther than this and provides a fair amount of rather unsystematic information about social and economic issues. He notices with fair regularity all measures of social control—such as the regulation of personal dress or the prevention of public disorder. A little more attention is given to fiscal matters[25] and to the reform of naval and military arrangements.[26] Trade receives full emphasis. The fortunes of the new overseas companies are fully reported; so are the negotiations over English merchants' rights on the continent. Drake's voyages get thorough coverage. Apart from these grave matters, Camden cannot resist occasional reports of sea monsters, earthquakes, or the eccentric behavior of the Thames tides. The variety of these topics bears witness to a certain perceptiveness in Camden. He is dimly aware that war and policy—the history of the state—do not sum up the whole English historical experience in these years. But he is not able effectively to absorb this information into the mainstream of his historical account.

Indeed, Camden never wholly solved the great problems of arranging even his strictly political materials. He was aware that there was a problem; the title page of Book I announces it will include "all the most remarkable things which happened in England, Scotland, France and Ireland." Camden clearly saw that the history of England under Elizabeth would not be intelligible without sizeable infusions of other national histories (including that of the Low Countries after 1572). But how was he to set out this huge and tangled complex of separate yet related national narratives? His somewhat unimaginative answer was to use the annalistic form. Events were to be summarily packaged within the limits of each calendar year. As we have noted, he had in doing this the weighty authority of Tacitus and the almost universal practice of his English predecessors.

As far as English domestic affairs went, this arrangement proved reasonably workable. They had, on the whole, a spasmodic rather than a continuous rhythm. The great episodes—the

24. *History,* Author to Reader, p. 6 below.
25. *History,* (1688 ed.), pp. 56–57.
26. Ibid.

rebellion of the Northern Earls, the Norfolk and Essex trials, the Armada—were each self-contained, relatively isolated, and manageable within the confines of a single or adjacent annals. Camden's technique in handling episodic narrative is skillful enough, subdued in style but lucidly structured. And since, in his eyes, each one of these episodes was another phase in a splendid but self-annunciatory theme—the successive Elizabethan triumphs over foes foreign and domestic—there was no need for interpretation and little for explanation. Each episode spoke for itself; the self-evident contains its own demonstration without any need for addition by the author.

But his technique falters when he has to deal with such matters as the disorderly and unchecked flow of Scottish events—purposeless, shapeless, seldom reaching a halting place and never a solution. Faced with the events of 1567—the year of the Darnley murder, the Bothwell marriage, and the deposition of Mary—he abandons the annalistic form altogether and lumps within that year's chapter Mary's whole history since her French marriage in 1558. After her flight from the kingdom in 1568, Scottish affairs demanded his constant attention, but the formless struggle of incessant faction defied any attempt at dramatic unity. Less still was it possible to arrange these endless factional fights within the narrow bounds of the annal. Camden then falls back on the strategy of discontinuous narrative; each annal contains another fragment of narrative history, its length arbitrarily determined by the calendar. The reader's attention is distracted by the interruption of the narrative and his understanding of the significance of events is blurred by the lack of focus.

It is in his handling of such long, disorderly sequences that some of Camden's limitations display themselves. They are not wholly limitations of understanding. He perceives that a record of sequences of events and of the interplay of personalities does not exhaust the range of historical explanation. He is aware of the larger and less tangible forces which shape the movement of historical events. He sees the abiding constraints of circumstance and the long-range interests which they create. He understands, for instance, the strategic necessities which made vital for England a manageable Scotland and a submissive Ireland and which exercised steady pressure on all English policy towards those states. He sees the grave long-term risks which would arise from either French or Spanish domination of the Low Countries, and which lay behind the labyrinthine negotiations over the Anjou marriages. But he is not able to manage his material in such a way as to subordinate the particulars of his narrative to the presentation of these greater and overarching themes. Discontinuous narrative is, of course, a stumbling block, but there are deeper causes at work than a flaw in technique. There is the larger question of Camden's overall conception of his work.

The book is conceived as a monument to the achievement of Queen Elizabeth and her government. This purpose he seeks to accomplish not by praising her merits but, more obliquely, more delicately, by laying out the record of her reign. To him that record is self-evident; its very recital will command the admiration of the world and of posterity. What Camden does not quite grasp is that the record by itself, unadorned by interpretation or examination, is intellectually unassimilable by his readers. The relentless flow of historical fact informs their minds without illuminating their understanding. Mere chronological arrangement is inadequate without some other ordering principle by which to fit together the bewildering array of data. In the introduction Camden takes some note of this situation and makes an attempt at providing some historical perspective by his account of the Queen's career up to her accession. The narrative is crisp and succinct, and he is bold in his judgments of people and events. The contrast between this short introductory chapter and the main text is all the more striking, for we are left without adequate perspective to evaluate Elizabeth's achievement as compared with those of her predecessors or her contemporaries.

Nor is there an attempt to explain to us the nature of the problems which confronted the queen during her career as a ruler. There is no central matrix of questions which, by providing a governing principle of organization, would hold together the diverse themes treated by Camden or the multiplicity of fact reported by him. It is hard to judge the cause of this failure. In part, harsh circumstances forced itself upon him. The events were too recent, the issues too warm, and the survivors (or the descendants of the great actors) too touchy to allow him much freedom of judgment. Under the threat of censorship, or even of persecution, a neutral presentation of the record was both a defensible position and an honourable stance. But apart from these tactical considerations, Camden's timidity arose from his own principles as an historian, from too great respect for the record. He is unwilling to impose upon it his own judgment or interpretation lest in doing so he damage the integrity or obscure the truth of history.

This brings us to a major problem in any critical estimate of Camden—his conception of the historian's role. In his statement to the reader he very self-consciously sets out to detach himself as writer from the history he is recounting. "Mine own judgment I have not delivered according to prejudice or affection; whilst writing with an undistempered and even mind; I have rather sifted out the sense and opinion of others; and scarcely have I anywhere interposed mine own, no, not by the bye, since it is a question whether an historian may lawfully do it."[27]

This is a bold claim, more likely to arouse scepticism among the self-conscious—and self-doubting—historian of the twentieth century than among Camden's contemporaries. But there can be no doubt that he took his own prescriptions seriously. He labored carefully to exclude his own explicit judgments from the text and to achieve an austere impartiality. This task is a difficult one since the work is by no means neutral: its avowed purpose is to pay tribute to the wisdom of the queen's judgments and the justness of her actions. The technique is artful and yet simple. The voice which speaks in the book is not Camden's but that of the historical record. The whole justification of Elizabeth's policy is made to flow directly from the evidence itself by direct quotation and by careful paraphrases. Although he always indicates (by the use of italics or of quotation marks) that he is quoting verbatim, he never identifies the source of the quotation (nor of his frequent paraphrases). When there is a difference of opinion on policy to record, he often (though not always) presents both arguments, as for instance in the decision to make an alliance with the Dutch in 1585.[28] Rhetorically the effect of this method is extraordinarily successful. The tone is always

27. *History*, Author to Reader, p. 6 below.
28. *History*, pp. 204–6 below.

coolly impersonal; the arguments, presented with a rigorous economy of words, are arrayed with starkly logical simplicity. There is an absence of any persuasive eloquence by the author. The result is a grave objectivity which, at its best, lends to the argument an almost irresistible force and seems to preclude any other understanding of the facts. Even when Camden is making explicit moral assessments of individuals, as in his annual batch of obituaries, he conveys the impression of a general public judgment rather than a merely personal one—the voice of posterity rather than of William Camden. It is an extraordinary feat; Camden has succeeded in simultaneously achieving two very different goals. He has successfully maintained his author's aloofness and the integrity of his materials while producing a weightily persuasive defense of the Elizabethan regime.

But Camden's claim to impartiality has to be judged at other levels than that of composition and rhetoric. The twentieth-century reader will certainly ask how far the historian's unconsciously assumed social and political values color his view of the past. In Camden's case it is not very hard to ascertain these values. They were uncomplicated, firmly held, and shared with most of his friends and associates in the higher reaches of the Tudor establishment. Like his patron, Lord Burghley, he was a profound conservative in his reverence for the established hierarchical social order and for its accredited representatives, and in his distaste for any opposition, overt or covert, to it. One sees a sidelight of this attitude in his frequent mention of sumptuary legislation, laws designed to regulate dress so as to make it correspond with social rank.

There is perhaps a special quality to Camden's conservatism. He moved in an intellectual world marked by a certain disillusionment and more than a touch of bitterness. The first generation educated under the auspices of English humanism, the students of the 1540s, entered their maturity full of a hopeful idealism. But their children—the generation of Philip Sidney, of Francis Bacon, and of Camden himself—were heirs of disappointment and of frustration. The opportunistic compromises of the Elizabethan government, at home and abroad, and the brutal struggle for place and power within the court begot disillusionment and a certain cynicism. In Camden there are at least hints of this Tacitean attitude. There is in his commitment to the Elizabethan establishment a certain weariness, a certain lack of enthusiasm and warmth, something of the slightly embittered, slightly cynical resignation to a world of grim but inescapable political fact which one sometimes senses in Burghley and his royal mistress. There is in Camden certainly a sense that the achievements of the regime were hard won and fragile, and the struggle for order a never-ending one. There is nothing of the over-dramatic view subsequently held of the Elizabethan age— as an era of constructive beginnings, a harbinger of permanent progress to come.

But at least on one great issue of his age Camden can fairly be called a liberal. He did not share the blinding partisanship which most of his contemporaries, Protestant or Catholic, felt towards those differing in religious opinion from themselves. His own Protestantism was beyond question; he probably failed to obtain an All Souls fellowship in his student days because of it; but his distaste for Catholicism was secular in character. He disapproved of its adherents as dissidents to the religion established by law rather than as men spiritually delinquent. His treatment of Catholics throughout his work is cool and dispassionate, refreshingly free of the prevalent rancor although totally unsympathetic to their views.

Consistent with this point of view is his treatment of the Puritans. Here, for once, he casts aside all impartiality and bursts into sputtering indignation. Writing of the ribald Puritan pamphleteer, Martin Marprelate, he begins, "And certainly never did contumacious impudency and contumelious malapertness against ecclesiastical magistrates shew itself more bold and insolent."[29] He goes on to denounce the Puritans as seeking to cut asunder "the very sinews of ecclesiastical government and her royal prerogative." These men threatened the civil order and thus trespassed upon the limits of Camden's *politique* tolerance. To Camden, of course, these limits of tolerance rested on reason and not prejudice since, as he saw it, ordered social hierarchy and obedience to constituted authority were laid down in the order of nature. Camden's limits of tolerance are not iden-

29. *History,* p. 331 below.

tical with those of the twentieth century, but it is important to emphasize again that among his contemporaries, in an age of virulent and unbridled ideological hatreds, he stands apart by his dispassionate good temper and by a cool clarity of vision.

These are great virtues—rare in his age—but the bounds of his tolerance do suggest something important about the limits of the book. Camden views the world about him from within the walls of the Elizabethan establishment, and he never doubts the verities which it upheld. This deep assurance is of course reflected in the method and the tone of the book. There is no real need for an apologia when the very record of events justifies the regime in the understanding of all rational men. For posterity there is considerable value in so self-assured a contemporary account; we hear the authentic, unselfconscious voice of the inner Elizabethan political world. But we should be cautious about being overpersuaded by an author who, for all his virtues, is so little self-critical of his own social values and of the social order around him.

There is one more test to which Camden's claims to impartiality must be submitted. Is there any evidence that his writing was tailored to benefit the reputation of any particular historical personage? Did he play favorites himself? Was he swayed by any outside pressures to tamper with the historical record? The latter charge was certainly levied against him within a few years after his death, perhaps in his lifetime. It was alleged that he had whitewashed the character of Mary Queen of Scots and that he had done this at the bidding of her son, King James I.

The facts are far from clear. Certainly James was exceedingly sensitive about his mother's history, particularly about the allegation that he might be David Rizzio's son, and the awful charge that Mary had connived in her husband's murder by the Earl of Bothwell, just before she married the latter. When in 1607 the French historian De Thou (Thuanus) published the second part of his *Universal History* including an unflattering account of Mary's conduct, James was very angry and commanded Camden to draw up a set of corrections to be sent to the Frenchman. Later the story got about that Camden had provided De Thou with the source material for this part of his work and that after James's outburst the French historian had reproached his English colleague for having dealt dishonestly. There is no evidence to support this story, and the surviving correspondence between the two historians makes it highly improbable.[30]

But whether or not Camden's own book was affected by royal intervention is another question. The late seventeenth-century historian Gilbert Burnet, writing about 1685, repeats a story which he had heard.[31] According to this account, James had summoned Camden before the publication of the first half of the *History* and ordered him to submit it for censorship to the Earl of Northhampton (a favorite of James and a survivor from the Elizabethan court), and that Northampton had cut out some matter and revised other portions. The truth of this story is impugned by Camden's own drafts (now in the British Museum) which give us a good idea of the work in its various stages of preparation and which can be compared with the printed version. There is no indication of changes between the earlier drafts and the final manuscript, which presumably Northampton would have seen—nor between that manuscript and the printed work.

Of course Camden was perfectly aware of the problem which he faced when he started work in 1608, since the De Thou affair had already taken place. His position was a very delicate one. Camden was the servant of a vain and touchy royal master whose displeasure could be very severe and who could, of course, prevent the publication of the book. (He had, just about this time, forbidden any more meetings of the Society of Antiquaries.) Luckily James's concerns about this particular book were pretty much limited to the treatment of his mother—and particularly of her reign in Scotland. No objection was raised, for instance, to Camden's forthright condemnation of Henry VIII for avarice, tyranny, lust, and extravagance.[32] And even in Mary's case it was principally the years 1565–68 which excited the king's interest. Her later career in England, especially her trial and execution, attracted less of the royal attention. Camden

30. See Bayle, *General Dictionary*, 4:61–68; Camden's own letters and his criticisms of Thuanus, in Smith, *Epistolae*. See also *DNB* article.

31. See Gilbert Burnet, *Reflections on M. Varillas History of the Revolutions* (Amsterdam, 1686), p. 25; and idem, *Defense of the Reflections* (Amsterdam, 1688), p. 60.

32. *History*, (1688 ed.) The Introduction, sigs A i^r; B^r.

uses the official English record for these events; his tone is judicial but not unsympathetic to Mary. He is careful to match the government's accusations by reporting the defense made by the Scottish queen and by her supporters, and the balance is by a slight but clear margin in her favor. Camden must have pretty clearly understood the limitations which he must observe when he set to work on the *History*.

The particular problem which Camden faced with regard to Mary Stuart was that of sources. There were two major contemporary authorities for Scottish events in the 1560s. One was George Buchanan, whose *Detection of the Queen of Scots* was written in 1570. Buchanan, the greatest Scottish scholar of his generation and tutor to the young James, was passionately anti-Marian. The other account was that of John Leslie, Bishop of Ross, whose *Defense of the Queen of Scots* was published in various editions from 1569 onwards. Leslie was an eyewitness, since he was a member of the Scottish Privy Council in the 1560s. But he was also a servant of the queen (her agent in England during the first years of her exile) and as strongly pro-Marian as Buchanan was hostile.

But Buchanan's account was discredited by no less an authority than the king himself, to whom the historian was said to have admitted his faults in falsely aspersing Mary Stuart.[33] Therefore, as Camden himself tells us, he preferred to use other sources, which had earlier been suppressed in England—a reference to Leslie's book. Using this material, Camden lays the blame for most of Mary's unwise actions on her half-brother, James, Earl of Moray, regent after her downfall. He does not follow Leslie in emphasizing Mary's faithful adherence to Catholicism. But what he does achieve is a picture of James's mother as a princess tossed about by fortune and a victim of "ungrateful and ambitious subjects." He also makes very clear James's undoubted rights of inheritance to the English throne. Camden could fairly claim that he had made as little concession to royal pressure as possible. He had chosen to reject a source discredited not only by the king's evidence but also by Buchanan's own alleged death-

33. *History*, p. 60 below.

bed repudiation. Camden could justly claim that his account of Mary was as solidly based on the best contemporary evidence as any part of his book.

But if Camden made the best case he could for the Queen of Scots, he went out of his way to paint the blackest possible picture of another Elizabethan figure—Robert Dudley, Earl of Leicester. He never fails to report the most discreditable allegations about the favorite. It is true that he reports without confirming, but he leaves the reader—to give but a sample—with the suspicion that Leicester arranged the murder of the Earl of Essex in order to marry the widowed countess, and that he attempted the assassination of the Duke of Anjou. Leicester was certainly an intensely unpopular man among his contemporaries and the subject of a widely-circulated and very libelous book, *Leicester's Commonwealth* (1581). Camden knew many of the earl's friends, including his nephew, Philip Sidney, but we must suppose that his judgment on the favorite was more influenced by the views of Lord Burghley. Burghley had a lifelong antipathy for Leicester, which was shared by many of his more conservative associates in the Elizabethan political world. Camden probably reflects the views of those stiffly conventional circles who never ceased to regard Leicester as an untrustworthy *arriviste*. Here, more than in Mary's case, Camden may be reasonably accused of succumbing to personal bias.

To sum up Camden is not an easy task. This Tudor civil servant, so conventional and correct in his attitudes, so orthodox in his social outlook, was also one of the most original and perceptive scholars of his age. He rose to the conception and the execution of historical writings which rested on a rigorously disciplined use of the record. In this way Camden shared importantly in a large and continuing intellectual revolution by which man's conception of his own past would radically change. The *History* stands alone, an authoritative and considered account of a great age of English history, but not a book which was to be imitated by later writers. But in the *Britannia* Camden opened the way for the next important development of English historical writing, for the great scholars of the late seventeenth and early eighteenth century whose perceptive editing of English medieval records would lay a foundation for all modern historical scholarship in England.

Textual Note

The text of Camden used here is that of 1688. The translation in that edition is the same as that used in its predecessor of 1675; the translator is unknown. Selected groups of years have been chosen to form this abridged edition; about a third of the entire text is presented. The first group of years deals with the beginning of the reign; the second with the late 1560's; the third covers the period leading up to Mary Stuart's execution and to the Armada and includes the annal for 1588. The annal for each year included is complete without omissions. The spelling has not been modernized, and the seventeenth-century practice of capitalizing nouns has been retained. Camden quotes from or paraphrases his documentary materials copiously and indicates this either by italicization or by quotation marks. It is often not clear whether he is quoting directly or slightly altering the original document by turning all sentences into "that—" clauses. I have treated all such passages as direct quotations.

WALLACE T. MacCaffrey

THE HISTORY OF
THE MOST RENOWNED AND VICTORIOUS
PRINCESS ELIZABETH
LATE QUEEN OF ENGLAND

I

The Author

to the Reader

Above eighteen Years since William Cecyll, Baron of Burghley, Lord High Treasurer of England, (when full little I thought of any such Business) imparted to me, first his own, and then the Queen's Rolls, Memorials and Records, willing me to compile from thence an Historical Account of the first Beginnings of the Reign of Queen Elizabeth: with what Intent I know not, unless, while he had a desire to eternize the Memory of that Renowned Queen, he would first see an Introduction thereinto by my Pains in this kind. I obeyed him, and not unwillingly, lest I might seem either to neglect the Memory of that most Excellent Princess, or to fail his Expectation and (which I prized as dear as them both) the Truth itself. For in these Papers, if any where, I had confident Hopes to meet the real Truth of Passages lodged, as it were, in so many Repositories.

But at my very first Entrance upon the Task, an intricate Difficulty did in a manner wholly discourage me. For I lighted upon great Piles and Heaps of Papers and Writings of all sorts, reasonably well digested indeed in respect of the Times, but in regard of the Variety of the Arguments very much confused. In searching and turning over whereof whilst I laboured till I sweat again, covered all over with Dust, to gather fit Matter together, (which I diligently sought for, but more rarely found than I expected,) that Noble Lord died, and my Industry began to flag and wax cold in the Business. Not long after that Incomparable Princess also rendered her celestial Soul to God: when I stood in expectation for some time, full of Hope that some other Person, haply some one of that great number of Learned men who through her Favour and Bounty did abound both with Wealth and Leisure, would render her this due and deserved piece of Gratitude. But when I certainly found that some, who were best able, could not for their more weighty Employments, and others (I know not for what causes) fairly desired to be excused; I buckled myself afresh to my intermitted Study, and plied it harder than before. I procured all the Helps I possibly could for writing it: Charters and Grants of Kings and great Personages, Letters, Consultations in the Council-Chamber, Embassadours Instructions and Epistles, I carefully turned over and over; the Parliamentary Diaries, Acts and Statutes, I thoroughly perused, and read over every Edict or Proclamation. For the greatest part of all which as I am beholden to that most Excellent Gentleman Sir Robert Cotton, Knight and Baronet, who hath with great Cost and successful Industry furnished himself with the choicest things relating to History and Antiquity; (for he readily and willingly gave me Light and Direction in my Business from his own Light and Knowledge of things:) so, Reader, if I shall in any thing profit or delight thee in this Undertaking, thou art deservedly obliged to give him Thanks for the same.

Mine own Cabinets and Writings I also searched into: who though I have been a studious Regarder and Admirer of venerable Antiquity, yet have I not been altogether careless of later and more modern Occurrences; but have myself seen and observed many things, and received others from credible Persons that have been before me, men who have been present at the transacting of Matters, and such as have been addicted to the Parties on both Sides in this contrariety of Religion. All which I have in the Balance of mine own Judgment (such as it is) weighed and examined, lest I should at any time through a beguiling Credulity incline to that which is false. For the Love of Truth, as it hath been the onely Incitement to me to undertake this Work; so hath it also been my onely Scope and Aim in it. Which Truth to take from History, is nothing else but, as it were, to pluck out the Eyes of the beautifullest Creature in the World; and, in stead of wholesome Liquour, to offer a Draught of Poison to the Readers Minds.

All such things therefore as use to obscure and prejudice the Light of Truth I resolved to remove. Ignorance, and (which spring from thence) doubtfull Uncertainty and flat Falsity, I have to my power dispelled by the bright Lustre of uncorrupt Faithfulness shining forth in those Monuments and Records, which are beyond all Exception: and peradventure I have attained by them no less Knowledge of those Affairs than some others who have been long and deeply versed in State-matters. Prejudices I have shunned, forasmuch as it taketh away a man's Judgment, and doth so blind the Minds of men in matters both of Religion and State, that like dim Eyes they can behold nothing clearly. As for Danger, I feared none, no not from those who think the Memory of succeeding Ages may be extinguished by present Power. And let such remember, that never any were severe and cruel towards Writers for keeping to the Truth, but they have heaped Dishonour upon themselves, and Glory upon the other. The Hope of any Gain hath not drawn me aside. To set the Dignity of History to Sale, to me (who have been ever well contented with a mean Estate) always seemed base and servile. Suspicion either of Affection or Disaffection can here have no place. For of all those that I am to mention I know scarce one by whom I have received any Benefit or Advantage, not one from whom I have received any Injury: so as no man can reckon me amongst those that are either obnoxious, or malicious. Such as are living I have said but little of, either in their Praise or Dispraise. By inveighing against the Enemies of my Countrey, to aim at the Commendation of a good Commonwealths-man, and at the same time get the Repute of a bad Historian, I held a thing ridiculous. This I have been careful of, that, according as Polybius directeth, I might have an Eye to the Truth onely. Neither shall any man (I trust) find lacking in me that ingenious Freedom of Speech joyned with Modesty which becometh an Historian. That Licenciousness accompanied with Malignity and Backbiting, which is cloaked under the counterfeit Shew of Freedom, and is every-where entertained with a plausible Acceptance, I do from my Heart detest. Things manifest and evident I have not concealed; Things doubtfull I have interpreted favourably; Things secret and abtruse I have not pried into. "The hidden Meanings of Princes (saith that great Master of History) and what they secretly design to search out, it is unlawfull, it is doubt-full and dangerous: pursue not therefore the Search thereof." And, with Halicarnassaeus, I am angry with those curious inquisitive people, who will needs seek to know more than by the Laws is permitted them.

As for other matters: although I am not ignorant that Affairs of War and Policy are the things proper to History; yet Ecclesiastical Matters I neither could, nor indeed ought to omit. (For Religion and the Commonwealth cannot be parted asunder.) But forasmuch as the Writer of the Ecclesiastical History may justly challenge those things as belonging to himself; I for my part have not touched them but with a light and chary Hand. And whereas it standeth with the Rules and Dignity of History, to handle Businesses of greatest Weight and Importance, and not to enquire after small matters; I have not insisted upon small things: yet some such there are, which if they please not one, may yet delight another to know. Circumstances I have in no wise omitted, that not onely the Events of Affairs, but also the Reasons and Causes thereof might be understood. That of Polybius I like well: "Take away from History Why, How, and To what end, things have been done, and Whether the thing done hath succeeded according to Reason; and all that remains will rather be an idle Sport and Foolery, than a profitable Instruction: and though for the present it may delight, for the future it cannot profit." Mine own Judgment I have not delivered according to Prejudice or Affection, whilst writing with an undistempered and even Mind, I have rather sifted out the Sense and Opinion of others; and scarcely have I any-where interposed mine own, no not by the Bye, since it is a Question whether an Historian may lawfully doe it. Let every man, for me, have his free liberty to judge according to his Fancy. Speeches and Orations, unless they be the very same *verbatim*, or else abbreviated, I have not medled withall, much less coined them of mine own Head. Short Sentences I have seldom interlaced, nor adorned my Discourse with those animadverting Observations which the Grecians aptly term ΈΠΙΣΤΑ'ΣΕΙΣ, whilst I have solely and closely made it my Business to inform the Mind. Digressions I have avoided. Words of form I have used: Matters belonging to Topography and Genealogy I have not neglected, nor yet Chronology; following the Series and Order of Time as near as might be, and beginning the Year, as our Chroniclers of old have used to doe, from the first of January.

My Work I have intitled by the Name of Annals, in regard I have disposed every thing in its proper Year: for I have learn'd of Tacitus, that Weighty and remarkable Occurrences are to be digested by way of Annals; and that the principal Business of Annals is, to preserve Vertuous Actions from being buried in Oblivion, and to deter men from either speaking or doing what is amiss, for fear of after-Infamy with Posterity. Besides, a courser and curter Style (such as mine here is) is proper and peculiar to things that are writ by way of Annals.

Upon these Foundations I set myself to writing, with this Intention and Design I went forward, and in composing, polishing and perfecting my Undertakings I resolved to spend my whole Pains at spare times, and to bequeath them by my last Testament to that honourable Person Jacobus Augustus Thuanus, who hath, with singular Commendations of his Fidelity and Moderation, begun an History of his own Time. And that, lest one so much respected by me (as indeed all Strangers are) should, as one unacquainted in a foreign State, be at a Loss in the Affairs of our Countrey.

But in this my Purpose I was (I know not by what Fate) prevented, and a great part of these *Annals* were sent over to him some Years before, whilst they lay yet shadowed in the first Lineaments, and were scarce well begun, disfigured with Blurs and Dashes, full of Chinks and Patches here and there cobbled together, as they slipped from my hasty Pen, and very ill handled by the Transcriber. Out of these, by taking away some things, changing and adding others, he hath inserted some few Passages in the Eleventh and Twelfth Tomes of his History, but indeed by his grave and solid Judgment well rectified and refined. But whereas he, according to the Proportion of his Work, (for he undertakes an Universal History of his Time,) hath picked out onely a few Passages concerning England and Ireland, and omitted very many things which may delight, and haply concern, our Countrey-men to be acquainted with; and I myself have heard that the Knowledge of our Affairs is earnestly desired by Foreigners, and that not without some Check and Reproach of our Remisness in communicating them; I again set my Shoulders to the Work which I had for some time discontinued, I read it all over again, considered of it anew, many things I added, and somewhat polished the Phrase of it, howbeit without any curious trimming or bravery of pleasing words. For it is enough (I think) for me, if, like a Picture ill drawn with weak and faint Colours, I place it in a good and advantageous Light.

Yet after all, whether I should publish it or no, I rested altogether doubtfull. But the truth is, those Censures and Prejudices, that Hatred and Backbiting, which I foresee advance their Ensigns and sound the Charge against me, have not so much discouraged me, as my Love to the Truth, my Affection to my Countrey, and the Memory of that Princess (which amongst English-men ought ever to be gratefull and sacred,) have born me up against those men who, having shaken off their Allegeance towards their Prince and Countrey, cease not with Hearts full fraught with Malice and Spleen, by their scandalous Books published in foreign Parts, to wound the Reputation of the one, and the Glory of the other; and at this very Instant (as they stick not to own) are ready to leave unto Posterity in a large Volume a Monument of their Lewdness and Dishonesty. For my part, I desire nothing more than that I may be like myself, and they like themselves. Posterity will render to every man his due Honour.

What the Loftiness of the Argument requireth, I confess, and am sorry, I have not reach'd to; yet have I willingly bestowed what Pains I was able. Myself I have neither in my other Writings nor yet in this any ways satisfied. Nevertheless I shall esteem myself fully recompensed for my Labour, if by my ready Willingness to preserve the Memory of Things, to relate the Truth, and to train up the Minds of men to Honesty and Wisedom, I may thereby find a Place amongst the petty Writers of great Matters. Whatsoever it be,

To God my Countrey and Posterity,
at the Altar of Truth, I dedicate
and consecrate it.

II

The First Year of Her Reign, Anno Domini 1558

The Death of Queen Mary having been certain hours concealed, the first news thereof was brought to the Bishops and Nobility in the Parliament-Chamber, (for the Estates of the Realm were assembled a little before in Parliament.) They, out of singular Grief, for a time stand mute: yet comforting one another, they soon gather heart again; and mingling Mirth with Mourning, lest they should seem either to sorrow for her which was to succeed, or to joy for her which was dead, they run themselves to the publick Cares of the State, and with general Consent decree the Lady Elizabeth to be proclaimed true and lawfull Heir to the Crown, according to the Act of Succession of the 35th year of Henry the Eighth. Soon after, those of the Lower House being assembled, Heath, Archbishop of York, Lord Chancellour of the Realm, with Sighs and Sobs signifieth unto them, "That their most Excellent Queen is by untimely Death taken away both from Religion and Commonwealth; that every of them had taken such inward Grief thereat as it exceeded all Consolation, were it not that Almighty God had of his mercy towards the English Nation preserved the Lady Elizabeth, the other Daughter of King Henry, alive. Of whose most undoubted Title to the Succession seeing there is none that can, none that ought, to doubt, the Prelates and Peers had with one voice and mind decreed (in case they would assent) presently to proclaim her Queen." Scarce had he spoken the word, when all from all sides cried and recried, "God Save Queen Elizabeth, Reign She most long, Reign She most happily." And forthwith the Parliament breaking up, they proclaimed her in the greater Palace of Westminster, and immediately after in Cheapside, the chief Street of the City of London, Queen of England, France and Ireland, Defendress of the Faith, and that with happy Acclamations and most joyfull Applause of the People, and certainly with a most prosperous and auspicious beginning: neither did the People ever embrace any other Prince with more willing and constant mind and affection, with greater observance, more joyfull applause, and prayers reiterated, whensoever she went abroad, during the whole course of her Life, than they did her.

She being now 25 years of age, and taught by Experience and Adversity, (two most effectual and powerfull Masters,) had gathered Wisedom above her age: the first proof whereof she gave in chusing her Counsellours. For into her Privy Council she took

> Nicholas Heath, Archbishop of York, before mentioned, a man of great wisedom and modest disposition;
>
> William Powlet, Marquess of Winchester, Lord High Treasurer of England;
>
> Henry Fitz-Allen, Earl of Arundel;
>
> Francis Talbot, Earl of Shrewsbury;
>
> Edward Stanley, Earl of Darby;
>
> William Herbert, Earl of Pembroke.
>
> Edward Lord Clinton, Lord Admiral of the Sea; and William Lord Howard of Effingham, Lord Chamberlain;
>
> Sir Thomas Cheiney,
> Sir William Peter,
> Sir John Mason,   Knights;
> Sir Richard Sackvill,
> and Nicholas Wotton, Dean of Canterbury:

all which were of Queen Mary's Council, and of the same Religion with her. To these, with a certain moderation and temperature, according to the respect of the Times, she joyned of her own,

> William Parr, Marquess of Northampton;
>
> Francis Russell, Earl of Bedford;
>
> Edward Rogers;
>
> Ambrose Cave;

Francis Knolles; and

William Cecyl, who had been Secretary to King Edward the Sixth, an exceeding wise man, and as good as many: and within a while after,

Nicholas Bacon, to whom she committed the keeping of the Great Seal:

all these embracing the Protestant Religion, and in no place under Queen Mary. Whom, as others substituted ever after in their rooms, she tempered and restrained in such sort, that they were to her most devoted, and she was always her own free woman, and obnoxious to none.

In the first beginning of her Reign she applied her first Care (howbeit with but a few of her inwardest Counsellours) to the restoring of the Protestant Religion, which both by her Instruction from her tender years, and by her own Judgment, she verily perswaded her self to be most true, and consonant to the Sacred Scriptures, and the Sincerity of the Primitive Church; and to restore the same she had with a settled and constant resolution determined in her mind. Then with the rest of her Council she adviseth, That the Ports should be shut up; That the Tower of London should be committed to some man of approved fidelity; That a new Commission should be sent over to Thomas Earl of Sussex, Lord Deputy of Ireland (who kept Ireland in awfull duty, so that it was never more quiet and peaceable, with three hundred and twenty horse, and eight hundred and sixty foot, lying there in Garrison;) That the commissions also to the Juridical Magistrates should be renewed, (lest the Term or Juridical Assembly, which was then holden, should be broken up,) with a Clause added, That they should not bestow any Office; That new Justicers and Sherifs should be appointed in every County; That Money should not be transported in exchange into Countries beyond the Seas; and that Preachers should abstain from Questions controverted in Religion. And for foreign matters, That Embassadours should be sent to the Princes of Christendom, to signifie unto them the Death of Queen Mary. To the Emperour Ferdinand therefore is forthwith sent Sir Thomas Challoner with Letters, wherein the Queen with her own hand gave him to understand, "That her Sister was dead; that she by God's goodness did by right of Inheritance and

Consent of her Subjects succeed her in her Kingdoms, and desired nothing more, than that the ancient Amity betwixt the House of England and Austria might not onely be kept, but also increased." To the Spaniard in the Netherlands is sent the Lord Cobham with Instructions to the same purpose; and also with a Commission, whereby the Earl of Arundell, Thurlby Bishop of Ely, and Doctour Wotton, Commissioners lately sent by Queen Mary to treat a Peace at Cambray, are made Commissioners anew in the Queen's name: And with them is joyned in Commission William Lord Howard of Effingham. Sir Henry Killegrew also is privily sent to win the minds of the German Princes, out of their affection to the purer Religion; D. B. to the King of Denmark, and Armigill Waad to the Duke of Holstein.

King Philip understanding of the Death of Queen Mary his Wife, fearing lest he should lose the Strength and Title of the Kingdom of England, which were to him of special use, and that the Kingdoms of England, Ireland and Scotland, would by Mary, Queen of Scots, be annexed unto France, dealt seriously, by means of the Count of Feria, (whom he had sent to visit both his sick Wife, and the Lady Elizabeth,) with Queen Elizabeth about a Marriage to be contracted with her, promising to procure a special Dispensation from the Bishop of Rome. This much troubled her, that the most potent Prince of Europe, and one that had very well deserved of her, should be rejected by her, when of his own voluntary motion he sought to her for Marriage: which to her seemed the part both of an unwise and an unthankfull woman. This also troubled the French King, who could not but misdoubt France, if by this new Marriage England should fall again to the Spaniard his Enemy. He laboured therefore all he could at Rome, by the Bishop of Angoulesme, that no such Dispensation might be obtained, forasmuch as Queen Elizabeth was thought to favour the Protestant Doctrine, yea, was pronounced as Illegitimate. But these things he did very closely, lest he might seem to incense the English, matters being not yet fully compounded betwixt them. The Count of Feria, to effect this Marriage, beateth into the Papists heads every-where in England, "That they have no other means to uphold the Catholick Religion, and maintain their ancient Honour; and this Marriage being neglected, he cannot but pity England, as being exhausted of her Wealth, needy of Military men, ill strengthened with Fortresses and Holds, as ill provided of warlike Munition, and as if the Counsellours of the Land were void of Counsel." And certainly the State of England lay now most afflicted, imbroiled on the one side with the Scottish, on the other side with the French War; overcharged with Debt incurred by Henry the Eighth and Edward the Sixth; the Treasure exhausted; Calice and the Country of Oye, with great Provision for the Wars, lost, to the great Dishonour of the English Nation; the people distracted with different Opinions in Religion; the Queen bare of potent Friends, and strengthened with no Alliance of foreign Princes.

The Queen, when she had in her mind more advisedly considered of this Marriage of a woman with her deceased Sister's Husband, judged it *ex rationis paritate,* that is, by the like reason, prohibited by Sacred Authority, as is the marriage of a man with his Brother's Widow, and therefore unlawfull, notwithstanding the Pope's Dispensation. And she perceived that by contractinge such a Marriage by Dispensation, she could not but acknowledg her self to be born in unlawfull Wedlock, whom her Father King Henry had begotten after he had put away Queen Katharine of Spain, for that she was his Brother's Widow. Which Wedlock, notwithstanding, the Universities of Christendom and a Synod at London had approved to be most just by the Law of God, as that with Queen Katharine to be unjust, and altogether undispensable. Her Suitour therefore King Philip she putteth off by little and little, with a most modest answer, and honest and maidenly shamefac'dness, but in very deed out of scruple of Conscience. But when he instantly pressed her by many Letters, and she admired and rejoyced to imitate the manners and behaviour of so great a King joyned with most modest gravity and grace, most beseeming his Royal Majesty, ever and anon extolling the same; forth stepped certain Courtiers, which declaimed against the Spaniards as a People puffed up with Pride: and some of her inwardest Counsellours, fearing lest her mind, being in doubt, might easily be perswaded, whispered daily into her ears, being a Virgin of a most mild disposition, "That She and her Friends were undone, and England overthrown, if She once acknowledged the Pope's Authority in dispensing, or in any other matter whatsoever; That two Popes had pronounced her Mother to have been unlawfully married to Henry the Eighth, and thereupon, by their Sentence already pronounced, the Queen of Scots did lay claim to the Kingdom of England; That the Pope would never revoke his Sentence, neither was any indifferent dealing to be expected from those of Rome, who had been most unjust both towards her Mother and her: moreover, That the French King did now labour tooth and nail at Rome, that Mary Queen of Scots might be pronounced lawfull Queen of England."

Queen Elizabeth being most averse to this Marriage, and most desirous to promote the Protestant Religion, thought nothing more pleasing to God, nothing more effectual to put off her importunate Suitour, than that Religion should forthwith be altered. For Religion being once changed, she doubted not but his mind in suing for Marriage would change also. She commanded therefore the Consultation to be hastened amongst her most inward Counsellours, how the Protestant Religion might be re-established, and the Popish abolished, all Perils being weighed which might grow thereby, and by what means they might be put by. These Perils they foresaw would be either inward, or outward. Outward, either from the Bishop of Rome, who would send forth his fulmination of Excommunication, and expose the Kingdom as a Prey to such as would invade the same; or from the French King, who, taking occasion thereby, would delay the business of Peace begun at Cambray, or rather move War against the English in the Queen of Scots behalf, as against not onely Enemies, but Hereticks also, and would excite Scotland to doe the like, which was now at his devotion; or from the Irish, a people most addicted to the Romish Religion, and most forward to Rebellion; or else from the Spaniard, a Prince most potent in the Netherlands hard by. They resolved, "That for the Pope's Excommunication it was not to be fear'd, but slighted as a senseless lightning: That Peace, if it were offered by the French, was to be embraced, if not, then to be sued for; forasmuch as the same Peace would comprehend Scotland also: nevertheless, that the Protestants of France and Scotland were in nowise to be forsaken: That Berwick, the Marches towards Scotland, as also Ireland, should be manned with stronger Garrisons:

14

That Amity was to be holden with the Spaniard by any means whatsoever, and the ancient League with the House of Burgundy confirmed." The Dangers inward they foresaw would be, from the Noblemen removed from the Queen's Council, from the Bishops and Churchmen that were to be displaced, from the Judges which sate in the Courts of Justice, from the Justicers of Peace in every County, and from such of the Common sort of people as in the Reign of Queen Mary were both in deed and estimation great men, because devoted to the Romish Religion. "These they held were to be thrust out of their places, and restrained by rigour of Law, (as Queen Mary had done against the Protestants:) and That none were to be employed in any place of Government, nor chosen into any Colleges of both the Universities, but Protestants: and withall, That the Popish Presidents, Heads and Masters were to be removed out of the Universities, and the Popish School-masters out of Winchester, Eaton, and other Schools: That those Protestants which then begun to frame a new Ecclesiastical Polity, being transported with a humour of Innovation, should be repressed betimes: and That but one onely Religion was to be tolerated, lest diversity of Religions amongst the English (a stout and warlike Nation) might minister continual fire to Seditions." The care of correcting the Liturgy, which under King Edward the Sixth was set forth in the vulgar Tongue, was committed to Parker, Bill, May, Coxe, Grindall, Whitehead, and Pilkinton, learned and moderate Divines, and to Sir Thomas Smith Knight, a most learned Gentleman; the matter being imparted to no man but the Marquess of Northampton, the Earl of Bedford, John Grey of Pyrgo, and Cecyl.

But some Ministers of the Word, impatient of Delay, whilst they chose rather to fore-run than expect Laws, began to sow abroad the Doctrine of the Gospel more freely, first in private houses, and then in Churches; and the People, greedy of Novelties, began to flock unto them in great number, and to wrangle amongst themselves, and with the Papists, about Questions controverted in Religion: in such sort, that to cut off occasions of Contentions, the Queen set forth a strait Proclamation, that they should not handle any such Questions. But the Epistles, Gospels and Ten Commandments she permitted to be read unto the

people in the English Tongue, howbeit without any Exposition:
also the Lord's Prayer, the Apostles Creed and the Litany she
suffered to be used in the vulgar Tongue. But in all other things
they were to use the Romish Rites and Ceremonies, till a perfect
Form of Religion should be concluded on by the Authority of
Parliament. In the mean time she performed the Obsequies of
her Sister, Queen Mary, with solemn and sumptuous Preparations, in the Church of Westminster; and shortly after of Charles
the Fifth also, who had two years before (a rare example
amongst Emperours, but more glorious than all their Victories)
overcome himself, renounced the Empire, and given over the
World, that he might wholly live to God, and attend upon his
Service onely.

III

The Second Year of Her Reign, Anno Domini 1559

In the beginning of the new Year the Queen anew created William Parr Marquess of Northampton, who in Queen Mary's days was put from his Degree for Treason: Edward Seimour, who by a private Law had, through the malice of his Adversaries, been despoiled of a great part of his Inheritance, and of his Father's Honours, she raised to the Barony of Beauchamp and Earldom of Hertford: Thomas Howard, the second Son of Thomas Duke of Norfolk, she dignified with the Honour of Viscount Howard of Bindon; and Henry Cary of Hunsdon, her Cousin-german by Mary Bolen, and Oliver Saint-John of Bletneshoe, with Title of Barons. All which were averse from the Popish Religion. And now is she brought with Royal Pomp from the Tower of London through the midst of the City to Westminster, with incredible Applause, (which by her sweet Countenance and gratious Speech she increased above measure,) where the next day, after the Rites of her Fore-fathers, she is inaugurated and anointed by Oglethorp Bishop of Carlisle; for that the Archbishop of York and the rest of the Bishops refused to perform that Office, out of a suspicious and jealous fear of the Romish Religion, which both her first Breeding up in the Protestant Religion had stricken them into, and also for that she had very lately forbidden the Bishop in saying Mass to lift up the Host to be adored, and permitted the Litany, with the Epistle and Gospel, to be read in the vulgar Tongue: which they held for most heinous Sins. Yet was she truely Religious, who every day, as soon as she arose, spent some time in Prayers to God, and afterwards also at set hours in her private Chapell: every Sunday and Holy-day she went into her Chapell; neither was there ever any other Prince present at God's Service with greater Devotion. The Sermons in Lent attentively she heard, being all in black, after the manner of old: although she many times said, (as she had read of Henry the Third, her Predecessour,) "that she had rather talk with God devoutly by Prayer, than hear others speak eloquently of God." But concerning the Cross, the Blessed Virgin and the Saints, she had no contemptuous opinion, nor ever spake of them but with reverence, nor suffered others patiently to speak unreverently of them.

Some few days after her Coronation a Parliament was holden, wherein it was first by general voice of all men Enacted, "That the Lady Elizabeth was, and (to use the very words of the Statute) ought by the Law of God, the Common Law of England, and the Statutes of the Realm, to be, the lawfull, undoubted and most certain Queen of England, and was justly and lawfully issued from the Bloud Royal, according to the order of Succession prescribed by the Estates of the Realm in the 35th year of Henry the Eighth." Nevertheless the Statute wherein her Father had excluded her and Queen Mary from the Succession of the Crown was not repealed. Wherein Bacon's wisedom (upon whom, as the Oracle of the Law, the Queen wholly relied in such matters,) in some mens opinion failed him, especially considering that Northumberland had objected it against Queen Mary and her, (and in that respect Queen Mary had repealed it as far as concerned her self) and some Seditious persons afterward took occasion thereby to attempt dangerous matters against her, as being not lawfull Queen; albeit that the English Laws have long since pronounced, That the Crown once worn quite taketh away all Defects whatsoever. But by others this was imputed to Bacon's wisedom, who, in so great a perplexity and inconstancy of Acts and Statutes, whereas those things that made for Queen Elizabeth seemed to be joyned with the Ignominy and disgrace of Queen Mary, would not new gall the Sore which was with age over-skinned; and therefore applied himself unto that Act of the 35th year of Henry the Eighth, which in a manner provided for both their Fames and Dignities alike.

Then in this Parliament, after other matters, an Act was made for restoring the Crown of England to its former Jurisdiction in matters Ecclesiastical: to wit, by renewing the Laws of Henry the Eighth against the See of Rome, and of Edward the Sixth for the Protestants, which Laws were repealed by Queen Mary: and also by Enacting,

> That whatsoever Jurisdictions, Privileges and Spiritual Preeminences, had been heretofore in use by any Ecclesiastical Authority whatsoever, to visit Ecclesiastical men, and correct all manner of Errours, Heresies, Schisms, Abuses and Enormities, should be for ever annexed to the Imperial Crown of England; That the Queen and her Successors might by their Letters Patents substitute certain men to exercise that Authority: howbeit with Proviso, That they should define nothing to be Heresie but those things which were long before defined to be Heresies out of the Sacred Canonical Scriptures, or the four first Oecumenical Councils, or other Councils by the true and proper sense of the Holy Scriptures; or should thereafter be so defined by Authority of the Parliament, with Assent of the Clergy of England assembled in a Synod: That all and every Ecclesiastical persons, Magistrates, Receivers of Pensions out of the Exchequer, such as were to receive Degrees in the Universities, Wards that were to sue their Liveries, and to be invested in their Livings, and such as were to be admitted into the number of the Queen's Servants, &c. should be tied by Oath to acknowledge the Queen's Majesty to be the onely and Supreme Governour of her Kingdoms, (the Title of Supreme Head of the Church of England liked them not,) in all Matters and Causes, as well Spiritual as Temporal, all foreign Princes and Potentates being quite excluded from taking cognizance of Causes within her Dominions.

Against these Statutes nine Bishops in the Higher House, which were present that day, (for now there were no more but fourteen left alive,) stifly repugned; namely,
The Archbishop of York, Heath,
The Bishop of London, Bonner,
The Bishop of Winchester, White,
               Worcester, Pate,
               Llandaff, Antony,
               Coventry, Bayne,

The Bishops of   Excester, Turbervill,
                      Chester, Scot,
                      Carlisle, Oglethorp,
and the Abbat of Westminster, Feckenham.

Of the Temporal Lords not a man opposed them, save onely the Earl of Shrewsbury, and Antony Brown Viscount Montacute: which Viscount the Estates of the Realm in the Reign of Queen Mary sent (as I have said) to Rome, with Thurlbey Bishop of Ely, that England might be reduced into the Unity of the Church of Rome, and Obedience to the See Apostolick. This man, out of a certain burning Zeal to Religion and regard of Honour, sharply urged, "That it were a great Dishonour to England, if it so soon revolted from the Apostolick See, to which it had of late humbly reconciled it self: the greater Peril it would be, if, Excommunication being once thundered forth, it should by this Defection be exposed to the Fury of her neighbouring Enemies. That he, for his part, had, by Authority of the Estates of England, tendered Obedience to the Bishop of Rome, and the same he could not but perform." Most earnestly therefore again and again he besought them, that they would not fall away from the See of Rome, to which they did owe the first receiving and perpetual conservation of the Christian Faith. But when these things were propounded in the Lower House, the far major part with joynt mind gave their Voices and Assent unto them; while the Papists murmured, "That moe of the Protestants were chosen of set purpose, both out of the Countries, and also out of the Cities and Boroughs; and that the Duke of Norfolk and the Earl of Arundell, amongst the Nobility the most potent, had for their own turn or hope, begged voices, as also Cecyl had done by his cunning."

Now, when mens minds differed concerning Religion, it was by one and the same Proclamation commanded, That no man should speak unreverently of the Sacrament of the Altar; and both Kinds were permitted in the Administration. A Conference was also appointed at Westminster between the Papists and the Protestants against the last day of March.

For the Protestants were chosen
Richard Coxe,
    Whitehead,

Edmund Grindall,
Robert Horne,
Edwin Sandes,
Edmund Guest,
John Elmar, and
John Juel:
and of the Papists were chosen,
John White, Bishop of Winchester,
Ralph Bayn, Bishop of Coventry and Lichfield,
Thomas Watson, Bishop of Lincoln,
Dr. Cole, Dean of St. Paul's,
Dr. Langdall, Archdeacon of Lewis,
Dr. Harpsfield, Archdeacon of Canterbury,
Dr. Chadsey, Archdeacon of Middlesex.
The Questions propounded were;

1. Concerning Common Prayer and Administration of the Sacraments in the vulgar Tongue.

2. Concerning the Authority of the Church in constituting and abrogating Ceremonies to Edification.

3. And concerning the Sacrifice of the Mass.

But all came to nothing. For a few words passed to and fro about Writing, for that they could not agree upon the manner of Disputing: the Protestants triumphing as if they had gotten the Victory; and the Papists complaining, "That they were hardly dealt withall, in that they were not forewarned of the Questions above a day or two before; and that Bacon, Lord Keeper of the Great Seal, (a man little versed in matters of Divinity, and a bitter Enemy of the Papists,) sate as Judge, whereas he was onely appointed Moderatour, or Keeper of order." But the very truth is, that they, weighing the matter more seriously, durst not, without consulting the Bishop of Rome, call in question so great matters, and not controverted in the Church of Rome; exclaiming every where, "When shall there be any Certainty touching Faith? Disputations concerning Religion do always bend that way that the Sceptre inclines": and such like. And so hot were the Bishops of Lincoln and Winchester, that they thought meet that the Queen and the Authours of this Falling away from the Church of Rome should be stricken with the Censure of Excommunication: who for this cause were imprisoned. But the wiser sort resolved, that this Censure was rather to be left to the Bishop of Rome, lest they, being Subjects, should seem to shake off their obedience to their Prince, and take up the Banner of Rebellion.

Neither was the Bishop of Rome ignorant of these things, who, being now more stirred, commanded Sir Edward Carne, a Welsh Knight and a Lawyer, (who had been Embassadour at Rome for King Henry the Eighth and Queen Mary, and now for Queen Elizabeth,) to lay down his Office of Embassadour, and (to use the very words themselves) "by vigour of a Commandment given *viva voce* by the Oracle of the most Holy Lord the Pope, in the virtue of his holy Obedience, and under pain of the greater Excommunication, and loss of all his Goods and Lands, not to depart the City, but to take upon him the Government of the English Hospital": (indeed, lest he should give intelligence of the secret Practices of the French against Queen Elizabeth, which he had carefully done before, out of his love to his Country.) Yet is it thought by some, that this crafty old man did voluntarily chuse this Banishment, out of his burning Zeal to the Romish Religion.

In the mean while (to follow the order of time, and omit for a season these Ecclesiastical and Parliamentary matters,) the Commissioners of England and Spain, which treated a Peace at Cambray, contending hard with the French for the Restitution of Calice, could by no means get them to give over the same, though they offered to set off, in regard thereof, above three millions of Crowns due by the French by lawfull Obligation. The Spaniard, because for his sake the English lost it, and because he foresaw that it would be for the benefit of the Netherlands that it should be under the English Jurisdiction, truly and honestly stood for the English, otherwise he would quite draw back from the Peace. On the contrary the French opposed, "That Calice alone was not sufficient to recompence the Damages done to the French by the English, it being by their help that their Towns were taken by the Spaniards, many Villages of Little Britain being burnt and sacked by the English Fleet, their Ships taken, Commerce (the Strength of the Kingdom) interrupted, and an infinite mass of money spent to prohibit the landing of the English. Besides, Calice was the ancient Inheritance of the Crown of France, lost in old time by War, and now by War recovered, and therefore in no wise to be restored: yea and so also the Estates of France had decreed. For to restore it, were nothing else but to put a Sword into the Enemy's hands, and to alienate for ever the hearts of the French from their King. Unjustly therefore and absurdedly did the English demand it again." The English maintained to the contrary, "that most justly and with very great reason they demanded it; to wit, That Calice had for these one or two hundred years been a parcel of the Kingdom of England, and purchased not onely by right of War, but also by Inheritance, and granted by Composition, in lieu of certain other Places which the Kings of England had resigned. That those Damages received were to be imputed to the Spaniards, who had drawn the English against their wills into this War, by which they had received very great Loss, and no Commodity at all. Whatsoever the Estates of France decree, because it is gainfull to them, is not therefore just. Neither could Calice be justly detained, forasmuch as, by Covenant already agreed upon, all places taken in the last War are restored to the other Princes." The French answered, "That this was done in regard of Marriages to be contracted betwixt the other Princes." They propounded therefore, that the eldest Daughter of Mary Queen of Scots by the Dolphin of France should be married to the eldest Son of Queen Elizabeth, which Daughter should have Calice for her Dowry; and withall the Queen of Scots should relinquish her Title which she had in England: or else, that Queen Elizabeth's eldest Daughter should marry with the eldest Son of the Queen of Scots; and withall the English should renounce the Claim they laid to the Crown of France, and all should be remitted which the French did owe to the English, and Calice in the mean time should remain in the Frenchmens hands. These things, as matters uncertain and of another Age, and devised onely to work Delays, the English neglected, and would not harken unto.

Thus far was the matter come, when the Spaniard received intelligence that Queen Elizabeth not onely avoided his offered Marriage, but also altered and changed almost all things in Religion. From this time therefore his care for the Restoring of Calice, which before seemed to be constantly settled, began to faint; and the Spanish Delegates, impatient of delay, when they and the French were in a manner agreed about all other Points, pretended that they would no longer be troubled with a War for Calice, unless the English would supply both money and men for a six years War more largely than before. Thereupon the Cardinal of Lorrain taking courage, boldly affirmed to the Spanish Delegates, "That the Queen of Scots, his Niece, was the true and undoubted Queen of England; the Spaniard therefore, if he loved Justice, ought to labour that Calice might be delivered unto his Niece being most just Queen of England." This sounded not very pleasingly in the Spaniard's ears, to whom the Power of the French was suspect: and they assayed privily to withdraw out of England the Lady Katharine Grey, Grand-daughter to Henry the Eighth's Sister, that they might have one to oppose against the Queen of Scots and the French, if any thing should fall out otherwise than well to Queen Elizabeth, to the end that France might not be augmented with the Addition of England and Ireland. And very stifly they urged, that a Truce might be treated between England and France untill they came to an Agreement; and that Calice in the mean time might be put into the Spaniard's hands, as an indifferent Umpire and Arbitratour. Which the French, and no less the English, refused.

These things had Queen Elizabeth understood before-hand, who having neglected the Marriage with the Spaniard, and altered Religion, could hope for no good at all from the Spaniards. She knew also that the Treaty of Cambray was undertaken on purpose for the rooting out of the Protestant Religion. And certainly in respect of Sex, and want of Treasure, Peace seemed to her more to be desired than the justest War, who was wont to say, "It was more glorious to establish Peace with wisedom, than to make an end of War with Armies in the field." Neither did she think it to stand with her Dignity, or the Honour of the English Nation, to rely upon the Aid of the Spaniard. She thought it therefore best to make her own Peace apart, and to compound with the French about Calice, being thereunto solicited by many Letters of the French King, of Montmorency Constable of France, and Francis of Vendosme, and by Messages from the Duke of Guise sent by the Lord Grey, who, having been taken prisoner at Guines, was set at liberty by him for that cause. For the making of this Agreement, Guido Cavalcanti, a Gentleman of Florence, brought up in England from his Childhood, was imployed; with whom the French King having secret Conference, thought it the safest course that these things should be treated of without the knowledge of the Spaniard, in some obscure Village of England or France, by Delegates sent privily. Contrariwise, Queen Elizabeth, being a Virgin of a manly Courage, professed that she was an absolute free Princess to manage her actions by her self or her Ministers. And though in the Reign of her Sister nothing was done without consulting the Spaniard; yet her will was, that this matter should be treated and agreed upon betwixt her Commissioners and the Commissioners of France, without acquainting the Spaniard, not in an obscure place, but at the Castle of Cambray, which is not far from the City of Cambray. And hereby she incurred no less Displeasure with the Spaniard than before for slighting his Marriage and altering of Religion. Nevertheless the French being wise and wary, to the end to feel how she stood affected towards Marriage and towards the Spaniard, requested first to be resolved of two Scruples. The one, "If he should render up Calice before he knew for certain whom the Queen would take to Husband, Calice might easily fall into the Spaniard's hands, who would buy it at any rate, and Wives would grant any thing to their Husbands whom they loved." The other, "Whether the English were (as the Spaniards gave out) tied by such a League to the Spaniards, that they were to war with them against all people whatsoever." To these two Points it was answered, "That the Queen bare such a Motherly Love to England, that she would not for her Husband's sake forgoe Calice; and though she would never so fain, yet the People of England would in no wise suffer it: That there was no such Confederacy with the Spaniard, but onely an Amity and Friendship: And that she was most free to contract a Confederacy which might be for the benefit of England, with any Prince whatsoever." Hereupon it was thought good, that at the Castle of Cambray Commissioners on both sides should treat about compounding of Controversies, and concluding a Peace. For the Queen of England,

Thurlbey Bishop of Ely;

William Lord Howard of Effingham, Lord Chamberlain to the Queen; and

Nicholas Wotton, Dean of the Metropolitan Churches of Canterbury and York:

and for the French King,

Charles Cardinal of Lorrain, Archbishop and Duke of Rhemes, first Peer of France;

Annas, Duke of Montmorency, Peer, Constable, and Great Master of France;

Jacques Albon, Seigniour of Saint Andrew, Marquess Fransac, and Marshal of France;

J. Morvillier, Bishop of Orleance; and Claud Aubespine, Secretary to the Privy Council.

Betwixt these Commissioners an Agreement was made in these words, or the like in effect.

Neither Prince shall invade other, or assist any which shall invade the other.

If the Subjects shall attempt any thing against this Peace, they shall be punished, and the Peace not broken.

Commerce shall be freely exercised.

The Ships of War, before they put to Sea, shall give security that they shall not rob the other Prince's Subjects.

The Fort of Aymouth in Scotland shall be razed.

The French King shall peaceably enjoy for the term of eight years the Town of Calice with the Appertinences, and sixteen great pieces of Ordnance.

Which term being expired, he shall restore the same with the Town to Queen Elizabeth.

Eight foreign Merchants, not Subjects to the French King, shall pass their words for the payment of 500,000 Crowns, in the name of a pain for not restoring Calice.

Nevertheless Queen Elizabeth's Title to the same Town shall continue good.

Five Hostages shall be delivered till the Merchants bind themselves.

If any thing during the time aforesaid shall be attempted or innovated by Arms, directly or indirectly, by the Queen of England, or her Subjects by her Authority, Commandment or Approbation, against the most Christian King or the Queen of Scots, they shall be freed and absolved from all Promise and Faith given, and the Hostages and Merchants shall be set at liberty.

If any thing in like manner shall be attempted or innovated by the most Christian King, the Queen of Scots, or the Dolphin, against the Queen of England, they shall be bound without all delay to give over the Possession of Calice.

In the same place, at the same time, and by the same Commissioners, a Peace also was concluded betwixt the Queen of England, and Francis and Mary King and Queen of Scots; certain Articles concerning the granting of safe-conducts to Homicides, Thieves, Rankriders upon the Marches, and Fugitives, being referred to English and Scottish Commissioners: Which when they were agreed upon at Upsalington betwixt English Commissioners—

Thomas Earl of Northumberland,
Cuthbert Tunstall, Bishop of Duresme,
William Lord Dacres of Gillesland, and
Sir James a Crofts, Captain of the Town
    and Castle of Berwick—
and Scottish Commissioners—

The Earl of Morton,
The Baron of Humes, and
Saint Clere, Dean of Glascow,

a Peace was proclaimed over all England betwixt the Queen of England, the King of France, the Dolphin, and the Queen of Scots: which was ill taken by the people, as dishonourable to the English for the Loss of Calice, and not restoring thereof; while the Protestants laid the blame upon the Bishops and the Papists, and they again cast it upon the Lord Wentworth the Governour, being one of the Protestants. And he indeed in the Reign of Queen Mary, being absent and unheard, was in that behalf called in question; but now the times being changed, was called again to his Trial, heard, and acquitted by his peers. But Ralph Chamberlain, who was Captain of the Castle of Calice, and John Harleston, who had the charge of the Tower at Risbanck, were afterward condemned of Treason for abandoning their Quarter: but their Punishment was remitted.

When the Assembly of Parliament was now to be dissolved, they all thought good that the Third Estate, or Lower House, should advise the Queen to marry betimes: yet would not the Temporal Lords joyn with them, lest any of them might seem to propound it in hope to prefer himself. Thomas Gargrave therefore, Speaker of the Lower House, with some few selected men, after leave obtained, came unto the Queen, and making his excuse by his Office, the Queen's Courtesie, and the Weightiness of the matter, went forward to this purpose:

There is nothing which with more ardent affection we beg of God in our daily prayers, than that our Happiness hitherto received by your most gratious Government may be perpetuated to the English Nation unto all eternity. Whilst in our mind and cogitation we cast many ways how this may be effected, we can find none at all, unless your Majesty should either reign for ever, (which to hope for is not lawfull;) or else by Marriage bring forth Children, Heirs both of their Mother's Vertue and Empire, (which God Almighty grant.) This is the single, the onely, the all-comprehending Prayer of all English-men. All other men, of what place and degree soever, but especially Princes, must have a care, that though themselves be mortal, yet the Commonwealth may continue immortal. This immortality may your Majesty give to the English, if (as your humane nature, Age, Beauty and Fortune do require,) you will take some man to your Husband, who may be a Comfort and Help unto you, and a Consort in Prosperity and Adversity. For (questionless) more availeth the Help of one onely Husband for the effecting of matters, than the joynt Industry of many men. Nothing can be more contrary to the publick Respects, than that such a Princess, in whose Marriage is comprehended the Safety and Peace of the Commonwealth, should live unmarried, and as it were a Vestal Virgin. A Kingdom received from Ancestours is to be left to Children, who will be both an Ornament and Strength to the Realm. The Kings of England have never been more carefull of any thing, than that the Royal Family might not fail of Issue. Hence it was, that within our fresh memory Henry the Seventh your Grandfather, provided his Sons Arthur and Henry of Marriage even in their tender years. Hence it was that your father sought to procure Mary Queen of Scots to be a Wife for his young Son Prince Edward, then scarce eight years old: and very lately your Sister, Queen Mary, being well in years, married Philip of Spain. If lack of Children use to be inflicted by God as a great Punishment as well upon Royal as private Families; what and how great a Sin may it be, if the Prince voluntarily pluck it upon himself, whereby an infinite heap of Miseries must needs overwhelm the Commonwealth with

28

all Calamities which the mind even dreadeth to remember? Which that it may not come to pass, not onely we few that are here present, but even all England, yea all English-men, do prostrate our selves at your feet, and with humble voice and frequent Sighs do from the bottom of our hearts most submissively pray and beseech you.

These things spake he eloquently and more amply.

She answered briefly:

> In a matter most unpleasing, most pleasing to me is the apparent Good will of you and my People, as proceeding from a very good mind towards me and the Commonwealth. Concerning Marriage, which ye so earnestly move me to, I have been long since perswaded, that I was sent into this world by God to think and doe those things chiefly which may tend to his Glory. Hereupon have I chosen that kind of life which is most free from the troublesome Cares of this world, that I might attend the Service of God alone. From which if either the tendred Marriages of most Potent Princes, or the danger of Death intended against me, could have removed me, I had long agone enjoyed the honour of an Husband. And these things have I thought upon when I was a private person. But now that the publick Care of governing the Kingdom is laid upon me, to draw upon me also the Cares of Marriage may seem a point of inconsiderate Folly. Yea, to satisfie you, I have already joyned my self in Marriage to an Husband, namely, the Kingdom of England. And behold (said she, which I marvell ye have forgotten,) the Pledge of this my Wedlock and Marriage with my Kingdom.

(And therewith she drew the Ring from her Finger, and shewed it, wherewith at her Coronation she had in a set form of words solemnly given her self in Marriage to her Kingdom.) Here having made a pause,

> And do not (saith she) upbraide me with miserable lack of Children: for every one of you, and as many as are English-men, are Children and Kinsmen to me; of whom if God deprive me not, (which God forbid) I cannot without injury be accounted Barren. But I commend you that ye have not appointed me an Husband, for that were most unworthy the Majesty of an absolute Princess, and unbeseeming your Wisedom, which are Subjects born. Nevertheless if it please God that I enter into another course of life, I promise you I will doe nothing which may be

prejudicial to the Commonwealth, but will take such a Husband, as near as may be, as will have as great a Care of the Common-wealth as my self. But if I continue in this kind of life I have begun, I doubt not but God will so direct mine own and your Counsels, that ye shall not need to doubt of a Successour which may be more beneficial to the Commonwealth than he which may be born of me, considering that the Issue of the best Princes many times degenerateth. And to me it shall be a full satisfaction, both for the memorial of my Name, and for my Glory also, if when I shall let my last breath, it be ingraven upon my Marble Tomb, *"Here lieth Elizabeth, which Reigned a Virgin, and died a Virgin."*

In this Assembly of the Estates, besides those matters which I have already related, some things were Enacted and established concerning the not offering of Violence to the Queen's Person; of Tenths and First-fruits to be restored to the Crown; of an uni-form Order of Publick Prayers to be used in all Churches, to wit, the Liturgy and Administration of the Sacraments which was in use under Edward the Sixth, some few things being changed, and a Penalty inflicted upon the Depravers thereof, or such as should use any other whatsoever; of going to Church upon Sundays and Holydays, a Mulct of twelve pence for every day's absence being imposed upon those that should absent them-selves, and the same to be bestowed upon the Poor: also concern-ing seditious Rumours against the Queen, Merchandise, Ship-ping, Cloathing, Iron-works, and of tumultuous and unlawfull Meetings; and, to omit the rest, (by a Law unprinted) concerning the Possessions of Archbishops and Bishops, That they should not give, grant or lease out the Livings of the Church, but for one and twenty years, or three Lives, (as they term it,) to others than to the Queen and her Successours, reserving the old Rents. But that exception, for the Queen, proved gainfull to her Courtiers, that abused her Bounty, and to the Bishops, that sought their own Profit; but to the Church very hurtfull, untill such time as King James in the beginning of his Reign took it away, to the great good of the Church. In this Parliament there was not a man proscribed, a thing usual to be done in the first Parliaments of Kings: there were restored in Bloud Gregory Fines Lord Dacres, and Thomas his Brother, whose Father had been put to death in the Reign of Henry the Eighth; Henry Howard, who was afterwards Earl of Northampton, and his three Sisters, the Children of Henry Howard Earl of Surrey, who was for light causes beheaded by Henry the Eighth a little before he died; John Grey of Pyrgo, Brother to the Marquis of Dorset; Sir James a Crofts, Sir Henry Gates, who were convict of high Treason in the Reign of Queen Mary; and some others.

The Parliament being dissolved, by Authority of the same the Liturgy was forthwith brought into the Churches in the vulgar Tongue; Images were removed without Tumult; the Oath of Supremacy offered to the Popish Bishops, and others of the Ecclesiastical profession, which most of them had sworn unto in the Reign of Henry the Eighth. As many as refused to swear were turned out of their Livings, Dignities, and Bishopricks: and those (as themselves have written) in the whole Realm, which reckoneth more than 9,400 Ecclesiastical Promotions, not above 80 Parsons of Churches, 50 Prebendaries, 15 Presidents of Colleges, 12 Archdeacons, as many Deans, 6 Abbats and Abbesses, and 14 Bishops, being all which sate, saving onely Antony Bishop of Llandaff, the Calamity of his See; namely,

Nicholas Heath, Archbishop of York, who of late had voluntarily given over his Office of Chancellour, and lived securely many years, serving God, and following his Studies, in his Manor of Cobham in Surrey, being in such great grace with the Queen, that she visited him many times with marvellous kindness.

Edmund Bonner, Bishop of London, one that had been employed in Embassies to the Emperour, the Bishop of Rome, and the French King; but with his Authority had joyned such a Sourness of nature, that amongst all men he underwent the note of Cruelty, and was kept in Prison a great part of his life.

Cuthbert Tunstall, Bishop of Duresme, a man passing-well seen in all kind of more polished Literature, having run through many degrees of Honour at home, and worthily performed Embassies abroad, who, being a young man, sharply impugned the Pope's Primacy in a long Epistle to Cardinal Poole; and, being an old man, died at Lambeth in free Custody. Where also

Thomas Thurlbey, Bishop of Ely, led his life, having gotten great commendation of Wisedom by an Embassie to Rome, about tendering Obedience to the See of Rome, and by the Treaty of Cambray:

Gilbert Bourn, Bishop of Bath and Wells, who had deserved well of his See:

John Christopherson, Bishop of Chichester, who, being a very learned Grecian, most faithfully translated much of Eusebius and Philo, for the use of Christendom:

John White, Bishop of Winchester, meanly learned, and a tolerable Poet, as those times afforded:

Thomas Watson, Bishop of Lincoln, learned in deep Divinity, but surly with an austere gravity:

Ralph Bayn, Bishop of Coventry and Lichfield, who was a second Restorer of the Hebrew Tongue, and the King's Professour thereof at Paris, when good Letters reflourished under Francis the First:

Owen Oglethorpe, Bishop of Carlisle:

James Turbervill, Bishop of Excester: and

David Pole, Bishop of Peterborough.

Afterward was displaced

Feckenham, Abbat of the Benedictines at Westminster, a learned and good man, who lived a long time, and, by publickly deserving well of the poor, drew unto him the love of his Adversaries.

These men were first sent to Prison, but most of them were shortly after committed to the custody of their Friends, or of Bishops; save two that were more perverse, namely Lincoln and Winchester, who threatened to excommunicate the Queen. But three, namely, Cuthbert Scot of Chester, Richard Pate of Worcester and Thomas Goldwell of S. Asaph, voluntarily departed the Land, and also certain Nuns, as did likewise afterwards some Noblemen: of whom those of better note were

> Henry Lord Morley,
> Sir Francis Inglefield,   (both of them of Queen Mary's
> Sir Robert Peckham,   Privy Council)
> Sir Thomas Shelley, and
> Sir John Gage.

In the rooms of the dead and fugitive Bishops were substituted the learnedest Protestants that could be found.

Matthew Parker, a religious and learned man, and of most modest manners, who, being Chaplain to King Henry the Eighth, had been Dean of the Collegiate Church of Stoke-Clare: he was solemnly elected to the Archbishoprick of Canterbury, and consecrated at Lambeth, after a Sermon and Invocation of the Holy Ghost, and celebration of the Eucharist, by the laying on of the hands of three quondam Bishops, William Barlow of Bath, John Scory of Chichester, Miles Coverdale of Excester, and John Suffragane of Bedford. He afterward consecrated

Edmund Grindall, an excellent Divine, Bishop of London:

Richard Cox, who had been Schoolmaster to Edward the Sixth, Bishop of Ely:

Edwin Sands, a ready and eloquent Preacher, Bishop of Worcester:

Rowland Merick, Bishop of Bangor:

Thomas Young, a learned Professour of both Laws, Bishop of St. Davids:

Nicholas Bullingham, Doctour also of the Laws, Bishop of Lincoln:

John Juell, a man very well seen in all liberal Learning, Bishop of Salisbury.

Richard Davis, Bishop of St. Asaph:

Edward Guest, Bishop of Rochester:

Gilbert Barkley, Bishop of Bath:

Thomas Bentham, Bishop of Coventry and Lichfield:

William Alley, an eloquent Expounder of the Holy Scriptures, Bishop of Excester:

John Parkhurst, a man very well skilled in humane Learning, Bishop of Norwich:

Robert Horne, a man of flowing and ready Wit, Bishop of Winchester:

Richard Cheiney, one most addicted to Luther, Bishop of Gloucester: and,

Edmund Scambler, Bishop of Peterborough.

William Barlow also, who in the Reign of Henry the Eighth

had been Bishop of St. Davids, and after of Wells, he
confirmed Bishop of Chichester: and

John Scory, a man of learned Judgment, who had before been
Bishop of Chichester, he confirmed Bishop of Hereford.

In like manner in the Province of York, Young, being removed from the Bishoprick of St. Davids to the See of York,
consecrated

James Pilkinton, a man of singular Learning and Honesty,
Bishop of Duresm:

John Best, Bishop of Carlisle: and

William Downham, Bishop of Chester.

What manner of men these were, and what they suffered, being Exiles in Germany in the Reign of Queen Mary, or else
hiding themselves in England, I leave to the Ecclesiastical Historian to relate.

But whereas Learned men were more rare to be found, many
mechanical men out of the Shop, and no less unlearned than
the Popish Priests, attained to Ecclesiastical Dignities, Prebends,
and rich Benefices. Nevertheless most of the Popish Priests
thought it more behovefull for themselves and their Religion, to
swear Obedience to their Prince, renouncing the Pope's Authority, were it for nothing else but that they might shut the
Protestants out of their Churches, and withall be able to relieve
the Wants of those of their own Side which were thrust out.
And this they thought to be pious wisedom, and in a manner
meritorious; and therefore they hoped that the Bishop of Rome
would, according to his Authority, dispense with their Oath.

Thus was Religion in England changed, whilst all Christendom admired that it was wrought as easily, and without Commotion. But indeed it was no sudden Change, (which is never
lightly endured,) but slow and by degrees. For (to repeat summarily what I have said already) the Romish Religion stood a
full month and more after the Death of Queen Mary in the same
state as it was before. The 27th of December it was permitted
that the Epistles, Gospels, Ten Commandments, the Lord's
Prayer, the Creed and the Litany should be used in the vulgar
Tongue. The 22nd of March, when the Estates of the Realm were
assembled, by renewing of a Law of Edward the Sixth, was

34

granted the whole use of the Lord's Supper, to wit, under both Kinds. The 24th of June, by Authority of an Act Concerning the Uniformity of Publick Prayer and Administration of the Sacraments, the Sacrifice of the Mass was abolished, and the Liturgy in the English Tongue established. In the month of July the Oath of Supremacy was ministred to the Bishops and others: and in August Images were removed out of the Churches, broken or burnt. But whereas certain calumnious spirits defamed the Queen, as if she arrogated to her self the Title of Supreme Head of the Church of England, and Authority to celebrate God's Service in the Church, She by a publick Writing declared, that "she arrogated nothing else but what long since belonged to the Crown of England in right, to wit, that she had, next under God, the highest and supreme Government and Power over all Estates of the Realm of England, Ecclesiastical or Temporal; and that no Foreign Power had, or ought to have, any Jurisdiction over them."

By means of this Alteration of Religion, England (as the Politicians have observed) became of all the Kingdoms of Christendom the most free, the Sceptre as it were manumitted from the foreign Servitude of the Bishop of Rome; and more wealthy than in former Ages, an infinite mass of Money being stayed at home, which was wont to be exported daily to Rome (the Commonwealth being incredibly exhausted thereby) for First-fruits, Pardons, Appeals, Dispensations, Palls, and other such like.

The Protestant Religion being now by Authority of Parliament established, Queen Elizabeth's first and chiefest Care was, for the most constant Defence thereof against all the practices of all men, amidst those that were her Enemies in that respect: neither indeed did the ever suffer the least innovation therein. Her second Care was, to hold an even course in her whole life and all her actions: whereupon she took for her Motto, S E M P E R E A D E M, that is, A L W A Y S T H E S A M E. The rest of her Counsels consisted in these points: That she might carefully provide for the Safety of her People; for (as she often had in her mouth) "that the Commonwealth might ever be in Safety, she was never without Care: And that she might purchase herself Love amongst her Subjects," amongst her Enemies Fear, and Glory amongst all Men. For those things she knew to be firm and durable which Wisedom beginneth, and Care conserveth. How by these manly Cares and Counsels she surpassed her Sex, and what she effected by most wisely preventing, diverting, and most stoutly resisting, let present and future Ages judge by those things which with uncorrupt Faithfulness shall be delivered out of the very Commentaries of the Kingdom, as I may so term them.

At this time, whereas the Emperour and the Catholick Princes by many Letters made Intercesion that the displaced Bishops might be mercifully dealt withall, and that Churches might be allowed to the Papists by themselves in Cities, she answered;

> Although those Popish Bishops have insolently and openly repugned against the Laws and Quiet of the Realm, and do now obstinately reject that Doctrine which most part of themselves, under Henry the Eighth and Edward the Sixth, had of their own accord, with heart and hand, publickly in their Sermons and Writings taught unto others, when they themselves were not private men, but publick Magistrates: yet would she, for so great Princes sakes, deal favourably with them, though not without offence to her own Subjects. But grant them Churches to celebrate their Divine Offices in apart by themselves, she cannot with the Safety of the Commonwealth, and without wrong to her own Honour and Conscience. Neither is there any cause why she should grant them, seeing England embraceth no new or strange Doctrine, but the same which Christ hath commanded, the Primitive and Catholick Church hath received, and the ancient Fathers have with one voice and mind approved. And to allow Churches with contrary Rites and Ceremonies, besides that it openly repugneth against the Laws established by the Authority of Parliament, were nothing else but to sow Religion out of Religion, to distract good mens Minds, to cherish factious mens Humours, to disturb Religion and Commonwealth, and mingle Divine and Humane things: which were a thing in deed evil, in example worst of all, to her own good Subjects hurtfull, and to themselves to whom it is granted neither greatly commodious, nor yet at all safe. She was therefore determined, out of her natural Clemency, and especially at their Request, to be willing to heal the private Insolency of a few by some Connivence; yet so, as she might not incourage their obstinate minds by her Indulgence.

36

The Spaniard having now cast off all hope of Marriage with Queen Elizabeth, and being now ready to match with the French King's Daughter, seriously thought notwithstanding of England, which he would by no means should be joyned to the Sceptre of France. To retain therefore the Dignity of so great a Kingdom in his own Family, he perswaded the Emperour Ferdinand, his Uncle, to commend one of his Sons to Queen Elizabeth for an Husband: which he forthwith did by Letters full fraught with Love, and dealt earnestly to that purpose by Gaspar Preinor, free Baron in Stibing, And the Spaniard himself, the better to effect it, most frankly promised to Queen Elizabeth his special and singular Love: and she in like manner as largely offereth unto him, being now ready to pass into Spain by Sea, both her Ships and Havens, and all offices of Kindness, by Sir Thomas Chaloner.

The French King on the other side, in favour of his Son the Dolphin, and of Mary Queen of Scots, (casting his eyes into England) drew not his French Forces out of Scotland, as by Covenant he had promised to doe, but sent more underhand, and more earnestly than before dealt with the Bishop of Rome, that he would pronounce Queen Elizabeth an Heretick and Illegitimate, and Mary of Scotland to be lawfull Queen of England. Which notwithstanding the Spaniard and the Emperour by their Agents at Rome most carefully, but closely, laboured to cross. Nevertheless the Guises had put the French King, being ambitiously credulous, into such a sweet hope of joyning England to the Sceptre of France by the Queen of Scots their Niece, that he openly claimed England for his Son and his Daughter in Law; and commanded, when he could not prevail at Rome, that in all publick Instruments they should use this Title, Francis and Mary by the grace of God King and Queen of Scotland, England and Ireland, and every-where set forth the Arms of the Kingdom of England, quartered with the Arms of Scotland, in their Houshold-stuff, and painted upon the Walls, and wrought into the Heralds Coats of Arms: while the English Embassadour in vain complained, that this was done in exceeding great wrong to Queen Elizabeth, with whom he had very lately contracted Amity, forasmuch as he had not done it while Queen Mary of England lived, who had denounced War against him. He levied also men both Horse and Foot in France and Germany, to be transported into the parts of Scotland bordering upon England. So that Queen Elizabeth could not but misdoubt the French King, who now breathed nothing but bloud and slaughter against the Protestants. But his Attempts were cut off by sudden death, which he caught by running at Tilt at the Nuptial solemnities of his Daughter with the Spaniard, and his Sister with the Savoyard. And certainly in very good time for Queen Elizabeth's good, whom, both as an Heretick, and also Illegitimate, he was minded to assail with all the power he could, on the one side out of Scotland, and on the other side out of France. Yet she (to doe him Honour being dead) solemnized his Funeral as for a King her Friend, with great Pomp, in S. Paul's Church in London. And withall, by him which is now Lord Admiral of England and Ireland, Charles the Son of the Lord Howard of Effingham, she condoled with his Son for his Father's Death, and, congratulating his Succession, put him in mind to observe the Amity lately entred into.

But Francis, and the Queen of Scots his Wife, (by the counsel of the Guises, who now in a manner bare all the Sway in France,) bear themselves openly for King and Queen of England and Ireland, and abstain not from the Arms of England which they had usurped, but more and more shew them abroad every where. And to Sir Nicholas Throckmorton, Embassadour-Legier there, a stout and wise man, when he sharply expostulated these matters, first it was answered, That it was lawfull for the Queen of Scots to bear them with some small Note of Difference, to shew the nearness of her Kindred to the Bloud Royal of England. Throckmorton flatly denied out of the Law of Arms (as they call it) that it was lawfull for any to usurp the Arms of any Family, who is not born of a certain and known Heir of the same House. Afterwards they said, That she arrogated those Arms to no other purpose, but that the Queen of England should abstain from the Arms of France. To this he put them in mind of that which Dr. Wotton had before alledged in the Treaty of Cambray, That Twelve Kings of England had born the Arms of France, and that with so undoubted Right, that in all the Confederacies between the English and the French nothing had been provided to the contrary. At the length he prevaileth, through the Mediation of Montmorency, an Emulatour of the

Guisians, so as they abstained quite from the Title and Arms of England and Ireland. For he thought it to be no Honour to the Kingdom of France, that any other Title or Arms should be assumed or engraven in the King's Seal than those of the King of France; that this one Title was as good as many: and he shewed that the former Kings had used no other Title when they prosecuted their Right to Naples and Millain, &c. But in very deed from this Title and Arms, which, through the perswasion of the Guises, Henry King of France had imposed upon the Queen of Scots being now in her tender age, flowed as from a Fountain all the Calamities wherein she was afterwards wrapped. For hereupon Queen Elizabeth bare both Enmity to the Guises, and secret Grudge against her; which the subtile Malice of men on both sides cherished, Emulation growing betwixt them, and new occasions daily arising, in such sort that it could not be extinguished but by Death. For a Kingdom brooketh no Companion, and Majesty more heavily taketh Injuries to heart.

Some reasonable time after there were sent over no more but three Hostages for Calice, whereas by the Treaty there should have been four; the English Merchants are injuriously handled in France; a Servant of Throckmorton the Embassadour is forcibly taken in the open Streets by Francis, Grand Prior of France, the Duke of Guise, his Brother, and thrust into the Gallies; Pistols are discharged at the Embassadour himself within his own Walls; and, in despight, he is served with no other Vessels to his Table than such wherein the Arm of the Kingdom of England are quartered with those of France: Monsieur de Brossy also is sent into Scotland with a choice Power of men; and from Marseilles and the Mediterranean Sea are Gallies sent for into the British Sea.

Now the Professours of the Protestant Religion in Scotland, who had taken upon them the name of The Congregation, (being perswaded by some importune Ministers, and especially by Knox, a most fervent Impugner of the Queen's Authority, that it was the Duty of the Nobility and Estates, by their own Authority to abolish Idolatry, and by force to reduce Princess within the prescript of the Laws,) had refused to yield Obedience to the Regent, the Queen's Mother, a most modest Matron, changed

Religion, tumultuously firing and sacking Religious places; and had drawn to their party Hamilton Duke of Chastel-herault, (the powerfullest man in the whole Kingdom, one that had been incensed by Injuries of the French,) and many of the chief Nobility, allured with hope of the Revenues of the Church. Insomuch as they seemed to the Lady Regent, and the French Souldiers that served in Scotland, not to aim at Religion, but to attempt a flat Revolt: and James, Prior of Saint Andrews, the Queen's base Brother, (who was afterwards Earl of Murray) the Ring-leader amongst them, was by them accused for affecting the Crown against his Sister. He laboureth to remove the Suspicion, most religiously protesting, that he sought nothing else but God's Glory and the Liberty of his Country, and could not but sorrowfully bewail the oppressing thereof by the Lady Regent and the French.

The Masters of the Congregation began now to complain to Queen Elizabeth by William Maitland of Lidington, Lord Secretary, in a lamentable Oration: to wit, "That from the time the Queen of Scots was married to the Dolphin, the Government of the Kingdom was changed, foreign Souldiers wasted all places, the highest Offices of the Kingdom were bestowed upon French-men, the Castles and strong Holds delivered into their hands, and the purer Money of the Realm embased for their Gain; and that by these and such like cunning practices the French did craftily make themselves way to seize upon the Kingdom of Scotland, if any thing should befall the Queen other than well." Cecyl (whom for his singular Wisedom Queen Elizabeth employed as her chiefest Minister in these and other matters) dealt by Henry Percy, Earl afterwards of Northumberland, that he might understand what was the Scope which those Masters of the Congregation propounded to themselves, by what means they were able to compass that they sought, and (if at any time they were aided) upon what Conditions Amity might grow between the two Kingdoms. They answer with eyes lifted up to Heaven, "That they have no other Aim but to advance the Glory of Jesus Christ, and the sincere preaching of God's Word, to root out Superstitions and Idolatry, to restrain the Fury of their Persecutours, and preserve their ancient Liberty. By what means they may be able to effect this, flatly they know not: but what

God had begun, they hope he will bring to an happy end, with the Confusion of his Adversaries. And that a mutual Amity betwixt the two Kingdoms is the summe of their Prayers; and for confirmation thereof, they vow their Wealth, their Fidelity, their Constancy."

These things are slowly deliberated of in England, because the Scots were unprovided of Arms and Money, and amongst themselves of unstable Constancy: onely they are advised, not rashly to try the chance of War. But as soon as it was once known that the Marquess of Albeuf, the Queen of Scots Uncle, levied Forces by means of the Rhinegrave in Germany for the Scottish War; that Pieces of great Ordnance were conveyed to the Ports; that greater Provisions were made than to suppress a few unarmed Scots, (for this was pretended;) and that the French-men also promised the Danish King, (to the end to draw him to their party) that the Duke of Lorrain should resign his Claim to the Kingdom of Denmark; and that they again more importunately urged the Bishop of Rome's Censure against the Queen, and his Sentence declaratory for the Queen of Scots Title to England: Sir Ralph Sadler, a wise man, was sent to the Borders of Scotland, to be assistent by his Counsel to the Earl of Northumberland, Warden of the Middle March, and to Sir James a Crofts, Governour of Berwick. For to what end these things tended, the Council could not see, unless to invade England and to prosecute that by War which by Titles and Arms they made shew of.

Seriously therefore they consult hereof in England. That a Prince should yield Protection to the Rebellious subjects of another Prince, seemed a matter of very bad example; but to fail the Professours of the same Religion, a point of Impiety. Again, it were a part of preposterous Wisedom, to suffer the French, sworn Enemies to the English Nation, who laid Claim to the Kingdom of England, and enjoyed now a settled Peace on all sides, to remain armed in Scotland, a Country so near neighbouring, and so commodious to invade England in that part of it where the Nobility and the common people were most addicted to the Romish Religion. For this were nothing else but to betray negligently to the Enemies the Safety of every particular, and the Tranquillity of all in general. They must not therefore rest in dull Counsels, but address themselves to Arms. It hath ever been a point of English Providence, to prevent, not to attend, the Enemy: and it hath been always lawfull as well to prevent, as to repell, Dangers, and with the same Policies to defend by which the Enemies do offend. England is never securely safe but when it is armed and powerfull; and the more powerfull will it be when it feareth nothing from Scotland: and that it may not fear, the Professours of the same Religion are to be relieved, and the French driven out of Scotland, against whom not Counsels, but Arms may prevail: which having not long since been grosly neglected, Calice was soft, not without great Damage and Dishonour; and a little before, while the French egregiously dissembled a desire of Peace, Ambleteul and the Forts about Boulogne were surprised at unawares and taken, whereby Boulogne of necessity was rendred. Neither is there any other to be expected of Berwick and the Frontier-Towns, unless Arms be taken out of hand, and no credit given to the French in Scotland, who now pretend a desire of Peace; considering that the French-mens Designs are close, their Ambition infinite, and their Revenues numberless; insomuch as it is long since grown to a Proverb amongst the English, That France can neither be poor, nor abstain from War for three years together. Queen Elizabeth also many times used that saying of Valentinian the Emperour, Have the French thy Friend, but not thy Neighbour. It was therefore thus resolved, That it was just, honest, necessary and profitable, to drive the French forthwith out of Scotland.

Hereupon was William Winter, Master of the Munition for the Navy, sent with a Fleet into Bodotria, (now called Edenborough Frith,) who, to the great terrour of the French, set upon their Ships of war that lay upon the Coast, and upon the French Garrison in the Isle of Inchkeith. Soon after the Duke of Norfolk was made Lieutenant-general in the North parts towards Scotland; William Lord Grey, a most martial man, (who had of late stoutly, but unfortunately, defended Guines against the French,) was made Warden of the Middle and East Marches: and Thomas Earl of Sussex, who had been in the Reign of Queen Mary Lord Deputy of Ireland, was sent back again into Ireland, with Instructions that he should above all things beware lest the Irish being an uncivil People, and therefore the more superstitious, should by the cunning practices of the French be excited to Rebellion under pretext of Religion; that he should fortifie Ophale with Castles and Forts; that he should grant large livings and possessions to those that had served long in the Wars, To hold to them and the Heirs male of their body: that he should admit Surley Boy, a Wild-Irish-man, into those Possessions which he claimed by Inheritance in Ulster, to hold in fee to perform Services; that he should augment the Queen's Revenues moderately, and reduce her Exchequer to the form of the Exchequer in England.

In the mean time Francis Talbot, who was one of the chiefest Counsellours of the Realm, departed this life, being the fifth Earl of Shrewsbury of that Family; leaving for his Successour his onely Son George, by Mary Daughter to Thomas Lord Dacres of Gillesland.

IV

The Third Year of Her Reign,
Anno Domini 1560

No sooner was the Duke of Norfolk come to Berwick, but
presently there resort unto him James the Bastard Prior of S.
Andrews, the Baron of Rethven, and others, who, in the name
of the Duke of Chastel-herault and the Confederates, made a
League with him in the name of the Queen of England, to this
effect:

> Whereas the French go about against all right and reason to sub-
> due Scotland, and unite it to the Sceptre of France, the Queen of
> England shall take the Duke of Chastel-herault, Heir apparent to
> the Crown of Scotland, and the Scottish Nobility and People, into
> her Protection, as long as the French King hath Mary Queen of
> Scots in Marriage, and a year after. She shall send an Army by
> Sea and Land, with all warlike Provision, to expell and exclude
> the French out of Scotland. She shall not enter into Peace with
> the French, but with condition that Scotland may enjoy her an-
> cient Liberty. The Forts and strong Holds recovered by aid of the
> English from the French shall forthwith be razed, or else deliverd
> into the hands of the Duke of Norfolk, at his choice. The English
> shall fortifie no places in Scotland, but by Consent of the Duke of
> Chastel-herault and the Nobility of Scotland. The Confederates
> shall aid the English all they can. They shall hold for Enemies all
> whosoever shall be Enemies to the English. They shall not suffer
> the Kingdom of Scotland to be united to France by any other
> means than as they are now conjoyned by Marriage. If England
> be invaded by the French on this side of the River Tine, the Scots
> shall send 2,000 Horse and 1,000 Foot under the Queen of

44

England's Pay: But if it be invaded beyond the Tine, they shall join with the English to assist them with all the Power they can make, and that at their own Charges, the space of thirty days, as they use to doe for the Defence of Scotland. The Earl of Argile, Justicer-general of Scotland, shall doe his best that the North part of Ireland be reduced into Order, upon certain Conditions on which the Lieutenant of Ireland and he shall agree. Finally, it is prescribed what both of them shall perform, in case Mac-Conel or other Hebridians shall attempt any thing in Scotland or Ireland. For Confirmation of these Articles, before such time as the English Army enter into Scotland, Hostages shall be sent into England, to be changed every sixth or fourth month, at the choice of the Scots, during the Marriage betwixt the French King and the Queen of Scots, and a year after. The Duke of Chastel-herault and the Confederate Earls and Parliamentary Barons shall ratifie these Articles by their Hands and Seals within twenty days: and withal (forasmuch as the Queen of England undertaketh these things in no other respect than in regard of Amity and Neighbourhood, to defend the Scots from the yoke of Servitude,) they shall make declaration, that they will yield Obedience to the Queen of Scots and the King her Husband in all things which shall not make for the taking away of their ancient Liberty.

And now by sundry Messages from foreign Princes, and by Letters intercepted, it came to be known for certain that the French were determined to invade England. And withal Sebastian Martigues, a very noble young Gentleman of the House of Luxemberg, arrived in Scotland with a thousand Foot, all old Souldiers, and one or two Cornets of Horse. D'Oisely, a Frenchman, who was of inward Counsel with the Lady Regent of Scotland, being too confident, propounded to the Nobility of Scotland at Aymouth near Berwick, that they would now with joynt Forces put the King and Queen of Scots in possession of England. But they, well knowing the difficulty of the matter, and lest they might seem to break the Peace lately entred into, refused it. Nevertheless the sound Counsel of the Lady Regent hardly restrained Martigues, who youthfully insulted, and was inflamed with heat to invade England. But that heat was soon cooled, when the Marquess of Albeuf, who set sail toward Scotland with greater Forces, having striven with the violence of a Tempest upon the Coast of Holland, was with the loss of some Ships and many men driven back to Diep, from whence he had put to Sea.

There was come now into England from the Spaniard one Philip Stavely à Glaion, Knight of the Golden Fleece, and Master of the Munition, to lay open the Complaints of the French against the Queen concerning the matters of Scotland, and to persuade a Peace and Concord in the King his Master's name. Nevertheless he secretly warned the Queen to proceed resolutely in her Enterprize in Scotland; although the Spaniard on the contrary openly prohibited the transporting of her Provision for War into England which she made at Antwerp, so as she was fain to make new Provision thereof out of Germany. Neither was it without suspicion which Stavely propounded, that certain Companies of Spaniards might be sent into Scotland, which joyning with the French might repress the Scottish Rebels, and withall hold back the French if they should attempt any thing against England. All this while Michael Seury, the French King's Ordinary Embassadour, sundry times solicited the Queen to call home her Fleet and Army out of Scotland. Neither did she refuse it, so as the French might likewise be called home. But Delays being sought on both sides, the matter was put off from day to day, until J. Monluke, Bishop of Valence, a man not averse from the Protestant Profession, came out of France; who, when he was come hither, answered that he had no Commission for this matter. Nevertheless, being a man of very eloquent speech, he persuaded all he could that the Army and Fleet might be called home out of Scotland; and maintained stifly, that the bearing of the Arms of England was no ways prejudicial to the Queen, but rather an Honour to the Royal Bloud of England. But when he could neither persuade this latter, which seem'd absurd, nor that other, which was thought dangerous, Seury requested Stavely, and the Bishop of Aquila, the Spaniard's Ordinary Embassadour in England, that they would be present as witnesses, what time he should protest against the Queen for Breach of the League of Peace: which they refused, because they had no warrant thereunto. He nevertheless protested in a very long Oration: To whom an Answer was delivered, being published in print, wherein she "protesteth to the whole world, that the breaking of the Leagues, and all the causes of the War, had proceeded altogether from the French; and that nothing could befall her more grievous, nothing more odious than this War."; and other such like matters, which may be easily gathered by that which hath been spoken already, and by another Writing, set forth before, wherein she declared, "That though she had received most unworthy Injuries, the Title and Arms of her Kingdom being usurped, yet could she never be brought to believe that this was done by the Assent of the King or Queen of France, or the Princess of the Bloud, but the bad practices of the Guises, who, abusing the wealth of the King and of the French, were now ready to wound England through the sides of the Scots. But for her part, she could not be careless of her own and her People's Safety." And questionless the Guises, out of their love to the Queen of Scots their Niece, and hatred to Queen Elizabeth for Religion's sake, and Ambition to deserve well of France, by joyning unto it new Kingdoms, bent themselves with might and main to work the Destruction of Queen Elizabeth, relying upon the Promises of some English that were averse from the Protestant Religion. But the Grudges and Heart-burnings which arose in France, about the translating of the publick Government of the State from the Princes of the Bloud to the Guises, diverted them: and she so maturely and circumspectly opposed her self against the hostile Designs of them and others, that from this time she was to her Friends an Admiration, and a Terrour to her Foes.

The same day that Grey entered into Scotland with an Army, Seury and Monluke exceedingly urged to have the Army called home again putting the Queen in hope of the Restitution of Calice, in case she would revoke the same. She answered flatly, that she little esteemed Calice, a poor Fisher-town, in comparison of the Safety and Security of all Britain. And the very same day she sent into Spain Antony Brown, Viscount Montacute, a man of singular wisedom, but most devoted to the Romish Religion, and one that in that respect would be the more welcome to the Spaniard; who, with Sir Thomas Chamberlain, her Embassadour-Legier there, should amongst other things, inform the Spaniard for how just Causes she had sent an Army into Scotland, namely the same which I have delivered already: and should also shew him,

That the Queen of Scots, a sickly young Woman, was married in France to a sickly King, without hope of Issue; That by the practices of the Guises, a Plot was laid to intrap Hamilton Duke of Chastel-herault, (who was by Authority of Parliament declared Heir apparent to the Crown of Scotland) and his Son that was travelling in France; That their Designs tended to the joyning of the Crown of Scotland to the Kingdom of France, and not to preserve it for the Queen; which of how dangerous consequence it might be to his Netherland Provinces and to Spain, he might himself seriously consider. On the other side, That the Confederacy of the Nobility of Scotland was not to be branded with the note of Rebellion, which was made to no other purpose than to preserve the Kingdom (as in duty they ought) to the Queen and her lawfull Successours; which they could not, without Injury to themselves and theirs, suffer to be undermined by the Practices of the Guises, or transferred to the French.

In the beginning of April the English Army, wherein were 1,200 Horse and 6,000 Foot, approached near Leith. This Town is situated upon Edinborough-Frith, the greatest Aestuary or Inlet of the Sea in all Britain, where the River Leith emptieth it self with a wide mouth, and yieldeth a commodious Harbour for Shipping, scarce two miles from Edinborough, the chieftest City of Scotland: and for this commodiousness of the Situation, the French had fortified it for a Refuge and Receptacle to let in their auxiliary Forces. Martigues, drawing forth his Companies of Foot, chargeth the English that first approached, that thereby he might keep them from a Hill where he thought they would intrench themselves: but after they had skirmished about the space of four hours, some being slain on both sides, he was beaten back into the Town. Then a Trench was drawn, and Mounts cast up, from whence, no less than from the Ships, they thundered into the Town every day. The French now and then sallied forth with more Courage than Strength, and gave many proofs of their Valour. Amongst other times, they wone the Trench the 15th of April, cloyed three great Pieces, and took Sir Maurice Barkley prisoner. But Sir James a Crofts and Cuthbert Vaghan soon drove them out, and beat them back into the Town, not without slaughter of their men. At which time Arthur Grey, Son to the Lord Grey, who commanded in the Army in Chief, was shot in the Shoulder. Then the Camp removed near unto the Town, for that the great Shot, by reason of the long distance between, fell many times short. Shortly after, by sudden casualty of Fire, some part of the Town and certain Garners took fire, to the great Terrour of the Townsmen: which Fire the English increased by bending their great Ordnance to that part, and in the mean time, entring the Ditches, they measured the height of the Walls. The 6th of May (as was agreed by common Consent between the English and the Scots) they labour most sharply with their whole Strength to scale and win the Walls: but for that their Ladders were too short, and the Water by stopping of the Sluce very deep, they were beaten back, being over-charged with a multitude of small Shot from above, very many slain, and more hurt. The blame of this Overthrow lighted upon Crofts, for that he, as if misliking the Attempt, (whether out of Judgment, or Favour towards the French, or Malice against Grey, I cannot say,) had stood an idle Spectatour in the Quarter assigned him, and had not relieved them that were distressed. Certainly Norfolk and Grey privily accused him by their Letters to the Queen, not onely in this respect, but also that he had held secret Counsels with the Lady Regent of Scotland, and opposed himself against this Expedition. Whereupon being afterwards called in question in the Council-Chamber, he was removed from his Government to Berwick, and Grey substituted in his place. Nevertheless he lost not the Queen's Favour, who afterwards made him (and that worthily) Controller of her Household. The English and Scottish mens minds being dejected with this first ill Fortune, Norfolk presently confirmed them by sending new Supplies to relieve them. Then they fought by light Skirmishes; untill the French King, being advertised that his men were shut up at Leith in such sort that all passages both by Sea and Land were stopped, and could not well be relieved, by reason of the long distance, and that Seditions at home increased daily, granted authority to the Bishop of Valence, and Charles Rochfoucald Randon, to compound the matter with Queen Elizabeth's Commissioners; who presently sent into Scotland William Cecyl, and Nicholas Wotton Dean of Canterbury and York: For the King and Queen of France and Scotland were pleased to descend beneath their Majesty, to an equal debating of matters with their own Subjects. What time Murray propounded such things as Cecyl judged neither meet to

49

be propounded by Subjects, nor by Princes to be granted. During this Parley died Mary of Lorrain, the Queen's Mother, and Regent of Scotland, a Religious and Prudent Princess, having been spightfully used with unworthy Reproaches by certain hot-spirited Preachers, (as in their own Ecclesiastical History of Scotland, which Queen Elizabeth suppressed at the Press, is to be seen,) and also by the Masters of the Congregation, who, as Native Counsellours of the Realm, had, in the Queen of Scots and her Husband's name, suspended her by their own Authority from all Government, as one that set her self against the Glory of God and the Scottish Liberty.

The Articles agreed upon by the Commissioners the third month after the Siege began are these.

> The Treaty of Peace in the Castle of Cambray, between Queen Elizabeth and Henry the Second of France, shall be renewed and confirmed:
> The Treaty there likewise betwixt England and Scotland shall be ratified:
> Preparations for War on both sides shall cease:
> The Fort at Aymouth in Scotland shall be razed:
> The King of France and Queen Mary shall abstain from the Title and Arms of England and Ireland.
> The Debating of Satisfaction for Wrongs offered Queen Elizabeth, and about Caution for the Fifth Article, is referred to another Meeting to be holden at London; and if then it cannot be agreed, it shall be committed to the Catholick King:
> The King and Queen shall be reconciled with the Noblemen of Scotland their Subjects:
> The Confederates, especially the King Catholick, shall be comprehended.
> This Treaty shall be confirmed within sixty days, and an Oath taken on both sides for Confirmation thereof.

This Peace was published in the Camp and Town to the general rejoycing of all men, forasmuch as they were all weary of the War, the English of wasting the Country round about, the French for lack of Victuals and Provision, and the Scots for want of Pay. And certainly this Peace was holden to be commodious for all Britain, whereby the ancient Liberty of Scotland was retained, the Dignity of England preserved, and its Security obtained, which from that time feared nothing from Scotland: insomuch as the English joyfully acknowledged Queen Elizabeth to be the Foundress of their Security, and the Scottish Protestants as gladly acknowledged her Defendress of their Liberty.

She, out of her singular Love to her Country, was all this while so attentive to the Publick good, that in the mean time she almost quite put out of her mind the Love of potent Princes. For at the same time there sought to her for Marriage Charles Archduke of Austria, a younger Son of the Emperour Ferdinand, by mediation of the Count of Elphenstein: James Earl of Arran, commended by the Protestants of Scotland, with purpose to unite by him the divided Kingdoms of England and Scotland; which purpose was soon rejected, with Commendation of the man: Erric King of Swethland, by means of John his Brother Duke of Finland, whom Gustavus their Father had sent a little before into England for that purpose, having the more hope to speed, for that he was of the same Religion with her; and that with such a credulous Importunity, that he determined to come himself into England, notwithstanding that the Dane in his hostile mind towards him was purposed to intercept him, who thought it stood not with his good, that England and Swethland (between which two Denmark lieth) should be united by this Marriage. His great and singular Love she acknowledged and commended: She answered, "He should be welcome; but she could not yet perswade her self to change her Single life, most pleasing to her, for a Married life. She prayed him therefore to try her Kindness in any other matter, and though he sped not in this Suit, yet he would not think his Love ill bestowed. She advised him also that he would not long defer the chusing of a Wife, and wished he might obtain one most worthy of himself." With such Answers John Duke of Finland returned home the sixth month after, when he had left no means untried to advance the Marriage, wooing the Queen every day, giving liberally to the Courtiers, and alluring the love of the meanest, amongst whom many times he cast Silver money, saying that his Brother, when he came, would distribute Gold amongst the people. His Brother, notwithstanding, being suspicious of him, intreated him hardly at his coming home, as if he had wooed her for himself, and, persevering in his purpose, ceased not to woo her for almost two years together, sending Conditions by Nicholas Guldenstein. And withall (such was his inconsiderate Lightness) he sued for Philip, the Landtgrave of Hesse his Daughter, to Wife; by whom being also rejected, he married with a young Woman of mean condition.

But Charles of Austria hoped and expected that the House of Austria, which had been most fortunate by matching with the greatest Princesses, should be greatned by the Addition of England; and also that by him the old Religion should be, if not restored, yet at the least-wise tolerated. Neither did Queen Elizabeth at the first dash cut off his hope. For she made shew openly, and protested before Elphenstein, and by Letters to the Emperour, "That amongst many most honourable Matches propounded, none was more honourable than this with Charles of Austria. But yet neither the storm of Danger before, nor the fair gail of Honour now, could remove her from her Course of life begun; yet not so far, that she would flatly renounce a wedded life. And she assuredly hoped that God upon whose Bounty she relied wholly, would in these and other matters direct her Counsels to her own and her People's Safety." Adolph also Duke of Holstein, Uncle to Frederick the Second King of Denmark, being excited thereunto by the Dane, to the end to break off the Marriage with the Swede, came into England, being also rapt with the hope of Marriage by occasion of a Letter wherein Queen Elizabeth had wished, that he were joyned to the English in the same nearness as he had been in time past to the Spaniards, and most lovingly promised him Kindness. To whom, after most honourable Welcome, she bountifully gave the Honour of the Garter, and a yearly Pension, and by her singular Kindness bound the Prince unto her; a Prince that had gotten great Glory by the Wars, having of late conquered the Dithmarsians.

And at home also there were not lacking some which (as Lovers use to do) feigned unto themselves vain Dreams of marrying with her: namely, Sir William Pickering Knight, who had some Nobility of Birth, a mean Estate, but some Honour by his Studies of good Arts, Elegancy of life, and Embassies in France and Germany; Henry Earl of Arundell, a man of a very ancient Nobility, great Wealth, but of declining age; and Robert Dudley, the Duke of Northumberland's younger Son, who was restored in bloud by Queen Mary, a man of a flourishing age, and comely Feature of body and lims; whose Father and Grand-father were not so much hated of the people, but he was as much favoured by Queen Elizabeth, through her rare and Royal Clemency, who heaped Honours upon him, saving his life, whose Father would have had Her destroyed. Whether this proceeded from any Vertue of his, whereof he gave some shadowed tokens, or from their common condition of Imprisonment under Queen Mary, or from his Nativity, and the hidden consent of the Stars at the hour of their Birth, and thereby a most strait conjunction of their Minds, a man cannot easily say. (Certainly the Inclination of Princes to some men, and their Disfavour towards others, may seem fatal.) For a beginning of Honour, and first argument of Kindness, having made him Master of the Horse, she chose him, (to the admiration of all men) in the first year of her Reign, into the Order of the Garter, which amongst the English is most honourable, together with the Duke of Norfolk, the Marquess of Northampton, and the Earl of Rutland.

In Spain in the mean time the Lord Viscount Montacute layeth open before the King the necessity of the Scottish War; clearing all he can the Scots from the note of Rebellion: by proofs he coldly shewed, (as one that was a most devout follower of the Romish Religion) that no other Religion was brought into England than that which was consonant to the Holy Scriptures and the four first Oecumenical Councils: and requireth that the League of Burgundy, made of old between the Kings of England and the King of Spain's Forefathers, may be renewed. The Spaniard answereth, "That the renewing of the League was needless:" (Whereas notwithstanding the renewing of Leagues is much in use amongst Princes, which putteth as it were life into the Leagues themselves, and witnesseth their mutual Kindness to the whole world; and he himself and his Father Charles, in the Treaty of Marriage with Queen Mary of England, in the year 1553 had bound themselves to confirm the said League.) "He bewaileth the Change of Religion in England; grieveth at the sending of the Army into Scotland, and the relieving of Rebels; and complaineth that he was not acquainted with these things till it was too late." Nevertheless he ceased not to oppose himself secretly against the Practices of the French, who sought to have Queen Elizabeth Excommunicated, and wrought by his Agents at Rome, that she might not be stricken with the Ecclesiastical Censure without his Consent. He gave secret warning also, for his own Advantage, but too late, that it should be inserted in the Articles with the French, "That it might be lawfull for the English to drive the French out of Scotland, if they should return again; and that Caution should be interposed in plain words for the restoring of Calice." The Viscount notwithstanding discovered that he was offended in mind, and the Queen also perceived it, both by that which I have spoken, and especially by the redelivery of the Ensigns of the Order of Saint George into the Viscount's hands: for hereby he seemed quite to renounce Amity with the English. But he was more offended for a Repulse which he afterwards received, when he made intercession in England by his Embassadour (through the procurement of the Count of Feria, who had married the Daughter of William Dormer by Mary Sidney,) that Jane Dormer, the Daughter of Thomas Newdigate, Widow of Sir Robert Dormer Knight, and Grandmother to the Countess of Feria, Clarentia, a little old Woman, which had been very inward with Queen Mary, and the Distributer of her private Alms to poor women, Richard Shelley, called afterwards the Prior of the Order of Saint John in England, and Thomas Harvey, men most devoted to the Popish Religion, and most dear to the Spaniard, might with good leave remain in the Netherlands and Spain, whither they had withdrawn themselves for Religion's sake without Licence. For by the ancient Laws of England it was provided, under pain of Confiscation of goods and lands, that none but the great Noblemen of the Land and Merchants should without the King's special Licence depart the Realm, nor abide in foreign Countries beyond a time prefixed; and this, either for the recovery of their Health in a hotter Climate, or for the more plentifull adorning of their Wits in the Universities, or else to learn the Discipline of the Wars: and (as she wrote back to the Spaniard) "It was without example, that such a Licence should be granted to Women, of perpetual absence from their Countrey. And though the thing it self, in it self, seemed a matter of no moment; yet seeing they should not receive so much good thereby for their own private benefit and commodity, as others might take courage by the Example to the hurt of the Commonwealth, she thought it a thing not to be granted." The Count of Feria, interpreting this to be done in injury to him, lest he should let it go unrevenged, forcibly drew a Servant of Chamberlain's, the English Ordinary Embassadour in Spain, into the Inquisition, as guilty of Heresie; and being discontented with the Queen and the English, he kindled the Coals of the displeased King's mind, his Wife in vain labouring to the contrary. Yea, it is also reported that he dealt with Pius Quartus, Bishop of Rome new elect, to have her Excommunicate. But he (upon what pretence I know not) sent unto her Vincentio Parpalia, Abbat of Saint Saviour, with secret Instructions and Letters of Flattery, which I will here set down wholly as they are, though to some I may seem to offend against the Laws of an History.

To our most dear Daughter in Christ, Elizabeth
Queen of England

Our most dear Daughter in Christ, Greeting and Apostolical Benediction. How greatly do we desire (according as our Pastoral Office requireth) to take care of your Salvation, and to provide as well for your Honour as the Establishment of your Kingdom, both God the Searcher of our hearts knoweth, and you your self may understand by the Instructions which we have given to this our beloved Son Vincentio Parpalia, Abbat of St. Saviour, a man known unto you, and of us well approved, to be by him imparted unto you. We do therefore (most dear Daughter) exhort and admonish your Highness again and again, that, rejecting bad Counsellours, which love not you but themselves, and serve their own Desires, you would take the fear of God to counsel, and acknowledge the time of your Visitation, obeying our Fatherly Admonitions and wholesome Advices; and promise to your self all things concerning us which you shall desire of us, not onely for the Salvation of your Soul, but also for the establishing and confirming of your Royal Dignity, according to the Authority, Place and Function committed unto us by God; who, if you return into the Bosome of the Church, (as we wish and hope you will) are ready to receive you with the same Love, Honour and Rejoycing, wherewith that Father in the Gospel received his Son that returned unto him. Although our Joy shall be so much the greater than his, in that he rejoyced for the Salvation of one Son onely; but you, drawing with you all the People of England, shall not onely by your own Salvation, but also by the Salvation of the whole Nation, replenish us and all our

55

Brethren in general (whom, God willing, you shall hear shortly to be congregated in an Oecumenical and General Council for abolishing of Heresies,) and the whole Church with Joy and Gladness: yea, you shall also glad Heaven it self, and purchase by so memorable a fact admirable Glory to your name, and a much more renowned Crown than that which you wear. But of this matter the same Vincentio shall treat with you more at large, and shall declare unto you our Fatherly Affection, whom we pray your Highness that you will gratiously receive, diligently hear, and give the same credit to his speech which you would doe to our self. Given at Rome at St. Peters, &c. the 15th day of May 1560, in our first year.

What matters Parpalia propounded I find not, for I do not think his Instructions were put in writing; and to roave at them, with the common sort of Historians, I list not. That Queen Elizabeth still persisted like her self, *Semper Eadem, Always the Same*, and that the matter succeeded not to the Pope's desire, all men know. The report goeth, that the Pope gave his faith, "that he would disannull the Sentence against her Mother's Marriage as unjust, confirm the English Liturgy by his Authority, and grant the Use of the Sacraments to the English under both kinds, so as she would joyn her self to the Romish Church, and acknowledge the Primacy of the Chair of Rome; yea, and that certain thousand Crowns were promised to those that should procure the same."

Now was the time come for Confirmation of the Treaty of Edenborough; which Queen Elizabeth had duly confirmed by solemn Oath, and sent over the same to the King and Queen of France, that they likewise, according to the Covenant, should ratifie it, Throckmorton, the Embassadour-Leiger in France, could by no means persuade them to it: no more could Sir Peter Mewtas Knight, who was afterward sent into France for that purpose; notwithstanding that in the Commission whereby the Bishop of Valence was authorized to make the said Agreement they had promised in express words, that they would confirm the same *bona fide*, and in the word of a King. Why they refused to confirm it, they alledged these Causes. For that the Scots had entred into the Confederacy of Berwick with the English not by the Royal Authority, but by their own, which they ought not to have done: for that it was entred into by Rebels, and signed with the counterfeit Seals and Subscriptions of their faithfull Subjects: and for that they had not performed the Obedience promised in the said Confederacy.

Whilst these things are debated, Francis the Second, King of France, departed this life, before he was full eighteen years of age, in the second year of his Reign, leaving the Queen of Scots a Widow, whether to the greater Grief of the Papists, or Joy of the Protestants, throughout all Britain, I cannot say.

Queen Elizabeth being now more secure, to the end that the Church might both continue uncorrupted, and also be propagated, and that the Commonwealth might the more flourish in Glory and Riches, set forth two wholesome Proclamations By the one she commanded the Anabaptists and such like Hereticks, which had flocked to the Coast-Towns of England from the parts beyond the Seas, under colour of shunning Persecution, and had spread the Poison of their Sects in England, to depart the Realm within twenty days, whether they were natural-born people of the Land or Foreigners, upon pain of Imprisonment and loss of Goods. By the other she restrained a Sacrilegious kind of people, which, under the pretence of abolishing Superstition, began to demolish ancient Tombs, to raze and deface the Epitaphs and Coat-armours of most noble Families, and other Monuments of venerable Antiquity, which had remained after the Fury of prophane men under King Henry the Eighth and Edward the Sixth, to take the Bells out of the Churches, and to pluck off the Lead from the Church-roofs.

The Abby also of Westminster, most renowned for the Inauguration of the Kings of England, their Sepulture, and the keeping of the Regal Ensigns, she converted to a Collegiate Church: and there she instituted, to the Glory of God, and increase of good Literature, a Dean, twelve Prebendaries, a Schoolmaster, an Usher, forty Scholars, (called the Queen's Scholars, whereof six or more are preferred every year to the Universities,) Ministers, Singing-men, twelve Alms-men, &c. and this certainly with happy increase of learned men both for the Church and Commonwealth.

And (which turned to her greater, yea greatest, Glory,) she began by little and little to take away the Brass Money, and restore good Money of clean Silver, for the repairing of the Glory of the Kingdom, and to prevent the Fraud of those which embased Monies both at home and abroad, exchanged the best Commodities of the Land for the base Monies, and exported the current Money into foreign Countries; and also for the abating of the Prices of things vendible which were very much raised, to the great damage of the Commonwealth, and especially of such as received Stipends, Souldiers, Servants and all that took Day-wages for their Labour. And this she happily performed without Commotion, first, by prohibiting any man at any time to melt either good or brazen Money, or to carry it out of the Kingdom; then, by reducing the brass Money to his just Value, the brazen Penny to an Half-penny-farthing, the Coin of Two-pence to Three-half-pence, the Teston of Six-pence to Four-pence, another Teston to Two-pence-farthing, for more Silver there was not in them; and lastly, by buying in the same from the Owners for good Money, (but not without Loss to her self) if it were brought into the Mint within certain days prefixed. So as to Queen Elizabeth it is to be ascribed, that there hath been better and purer Money in England than was seen in two hundred years before, or hath been elsewhere in use throughout all Europe. And within a while after she stamped good Money (which we call Sterling) for the Kingdom of Ireland, of such Value, that the Shilling should be worth Twelve-pence in Ireland, and Nine-pence in England. Certainly this was a great and memorable Act, which neither King Edward the Sixth could, nor Q. Mary durst doe, after that King Henry the Eighth had, first of all the Kings of England, mixed the Money with Brass, to the great Dishonour of the Kingdom, and the Damage of his Successours and People; leaving thereby a notable example of Riot and Prodigality; considering that his Father left him more Wealth than any other King of England ever left to his Successour, very much he gathered by Taxes and Tributes, (and yet we may not believe Cardinal Poole, who hath written that he exacted more than all the Kings since the Norman Conquest,) and infinite Riches he scraped together when by Act of Parliament he seized upon all the Lands in Ireland which the English held being absent, all the First-fruits and Tenths of Ecclesiastical

Benefices in England and Ireland, and upon all the Rents, Livings and Goods of Abbies and Monasteries.

This was the last year of Francis Hastings, Earl of Huntingdon, the second Earl of that Stock, who begat on Katherine Poole, Daughter of Henry Baron Montacute, Brother to Reginald Poole Cardinal, Henry his Successour, and many other Children, in brotherly Love agreeing, but not in Religion.

In Ireland Shan or John O-Neal, a Nobleman of very great Power in Ulster, the true and lawfull Son of Con O-Neal, surnamed Bacco, that is, the lame (whom King Henry the Eighth had created Earl of Tir-Oen,) when he had made away Matthew Baron of Dungannon, his base Brother, (thought falsely to be a legitimate Son,) had despoiled his Father of all Rule, who died soon after for Grief, and by a barbarous kind of Election, throwing up his Shoe over his Head, had taken upon him the Title of O-Neal, fearing now lest the Law would take hold on him, brake forth in open Rebellion. Whereupon five hundred Foot were sent out of England, and certain Troops of Horse levied in Ireland. But after light Skirmishes, when he saw himself too weak for the English, and hated of his own, and Surly Boy, James Mac-Conel and O-Donel up in Arms against him, he layed down Arms, (being perswaded thereunto by the Earl of Kildare, his Kinsman,) and promised to come into England to beg his Pardon: which also he did, as in proper place we will declare.

V

The Tenth Year of Her Reign, Anno Domini 1567

But before such time as the said Commissioners came from the Queen of Scots, and a month or two after the Prince of Scotland's Baptizing, the King her Husband, in the twenty first year of his age, was in the dead time of the night, by bloudy and barbarous hand, to the Detestation of all men, strangled in his Bed, and thrown forth into an Orchard, the House being blown up with Gun-powder. A Rumour was forthwith spread all over Britain, laying the Fact and Fault upon Morton, Murray, and other Confederates: they, insulting over the weak Sex of the Queen, lay it upon her. What George Buchanan hath written hereof both in his History, and also in a little Book intituled *The Detection*, there is no man but knoweth by the Books themselves printed. But forasmuch as he, being transported with partial Affection and with Murray's Bounty, wrote in such sort that his said Books have been condemned of Falshood by the Estates of the Realm of Scotland, to whom more credit is to be attributed; and since he himself, sighing and sorrowing, sundry times blamed himself (as I have heard) before the King, to whom he was School-master for that he had employed his Pen so virulently against that well-deserving Queen, and upon his Death-bed wished that he might live so long, till, by recalling the truth, he might, even with his Bloud, wipe away those Aspersions which he had by his bad Tongue unjustly cast upon her; but that (as he said) it would now be in vain, since he might seem to dote for age: give me leave (that the other side may be heard also) briefly to lay open the whole matter, without all biassing of Love or Hatred, as far as I can be informed, as well out of other mens Writings, which came forth at that time, (but in Favour of Murray and Hatred to the Queen were suppressed in England,) as also out of the Letters of Embassadours and most credible persons.

In the year 1558, at the time of the Marriage of Francis the Daulphin and Mary Queen of Scots, James the Queen's base Brother, commonly called the Prior of St. Andrews, (for he was Head of the Religious in the Metropolitical Church of St. Andrews,) disdaining that Religious name, sued for an higher Title of Honour: which when she, by the Advice of the Guises her Uncles, would not grant him, he returned into Scotland discontented, and under a glorious pretext of Reforming Religion, and maintaining the Liberty of Scotland, began to disturb the Quiet of the Land; and so handled the matter, that, in an Assembly of Confederates, Religion was changed, without acquainting the Queen, and the French-men removed out of Scotland by Aid of the English that were called in. When Francis the French King was dead, he posted into France to his Sister, laboured to purge himself of all whatsoever was done in Scotland, either against her Profit or Reputation, and religiously promised (calling God to witness) all the Offices which a Sister could expect from a Brother. And having also conceived good Hope that she, having been bred up in the Delights of France from her Childhood, would not return into Scotland, he dealt with the Guises, that some man of the Scottish Nobility might be made Regent of Scotland, and pointed as it were to himself as the fittest man. But when he was sent back into Scotland with no other Authority than a Commission, whereby the Queen had given liberty to the Estates of the Realm to assemble and consult about the good of the Commonwealth; he, being frustrate of his Hope, and sore vexed in mind, returning through England, suggested to the English, that if they would have Religion in Scotland maintained, Tranquillity in England preserved, and the Queen's Security assured, they should by all means possible hinder the Queen of Scots Passage into Scotland. Yet she, passing by the English Ships in foggy Weather, arrived safely in Scotland, and using her Brother with all kindness, committed to him in a manner the chief Administration of the Commonwealth. Yet did not all this cut off the' sprouting Twigs of his Ambition, which daily sprung forth more and more both in his Words and Deeds. For he could not contain himself, but now and then he would amongst his Friends lament, that the warlike Nation of the Scots, as well as that of the English, were subjected to the Command of a Woman: And out of Knox his Doctrine, whom he held as a Patriarch, he would many times maintain, "That Kingdoms are due to Vertue, not to Birth; That Women are to be excluded from the Succession of Kingdoms, and that their sovereign Command is monstrous." He dealt also with the Queen by his Friends, that she would substitute four men of the Royal Family of the Stuarts, who, in case she should die without Issue, should succeed one another in the Kingdom, without regard whether they were Legitimate or Illegitimate; hoping that he himself should be one of them, as being the King's Son, though he were unlawfully begotten.

But the Queen, wisely considering that such a Substitution was contrary to the Law of the Land, that it would be prejudicial to the right Heirs, in the Example most pernicious, and dangerous to the Substitutes themselves, also a Bar to herself, that she should not marry again, gently answered, that she would take timely Advice with the Estates of the Realm about a matter of that Weight. And that she might shew herself noble and bountifull to her brother, she honoured him with the Title of Earl of Marre, and afterward of Earl of Murray, (for that the Title of Marre was controverted,) and preferred him to a rich and honourable Marriage; ignorant in the mean time that he affected the Crown, by giving out that he was the lawfull Son of King James the Fifth. Whereunto the better to make his Way, he suppressed, by means of his Favour with the Queen, the most Noble Family of the Gordons, being very powerfull in Vassals and Adherents; of which Family he stood in fear both for himself and the Reformed Religion: Hamilton Duke of Chastel-herault (who was reputed the next Heir to the Crown) he banished the Court; Arran his Son he shut up in Prison; Bothwell he banished into England: and whosoever he thought might oppose him he despoiled of their Dignities. The Queen also herself he held in his power as a Tutour doth his Pupill, being most carefull above all things that she should not so much as once think of Marriage.

And no sooner did he perceive that the Emperour on the one side wooed her for his Brother, and on the other side the King of Spain for his Son, but he strongly disswaded her from them both; alledging that the Liberty of Scotland neither could nor would brook a forein Prince; and that formerly whensoever the Sceptre hath developed upon Women, they have taken no Husbands but of the Scottish Nation. But when he saw that it was the general Desire and Wishes of all the Scots that she should marry, and had some inkling that by the Endeavours of the Countess of Lenox she was inclined to a Marriage with the Lord Darly, he also commended him unto her for an Husband, hoping that he, being a young man of a very mild Disposition, would be at his beck and Direction. Notwithstanding, when he perceived that the Queen entirely loved the Lord Darly, and that his own Favour with her began to grow less, he repented him of his purpose, and admonished Queen Elizabeth that she should by all means possible cross the Marriage.

The Marriage being now consummated, and the Lord Darly declared King, whenas the Queen revoked the Grants made in her Minority to him and others contrary to Law, he took Arms with others against the King and Queen, pretending the cause to be, for that the new King was an Enemy to the Protestant Religion, and had contracted Marriage without the Assent of the Queen of England. But, without once trying the chance of a Battel, he fled (as I said) into England; and there, being frustrate of all hope of Aid, he dealt by Letters with Morton, a man of a deep and subtile Reach, who was his inward Friend, and as it were his Right hand, that seeing the Marriage could not be annulled, yet at leastwise the Love betwixt them as Man and Wife might by close Contrivances be dissolved. And certainly a fit Occasion presented it self, when, domestical Jars arising betwixt them, she, to restrain the young King's swelling Mind, and keep the Prerogatives of Majesty wholly to her self, had begun to set her Husband's Name after her own in the publick Acts, and in stamping of Money to leave it out quite.

Morton, being a man skilled in kindling Discontents, insinuateth himself into the young King's mind by soothing Flatteries, and perswadeth him to put on the Crown of Scotland, even against the Queen's will, and to free himself from the Command of a Woman, seeing it was for Women to obey, and for Men to rule. By this Counsell he hoped not onely to alienate the Queen, but also the Nobility and Commons, quite from the King. And to alienate the Queen, first, he incenseth the King by sundry Slanders to the Murther of David Rizo a Piemontois, lest he, being a subtile Fellow, might prevent their Designs. (This Rizo, being by Profession a Musician, came the year before into Scotland with Morett the Embassadour, and for his Skill and Dexterity was entertained by the Queen into her Family and Favour, and imployed in writing French Letters, and was of her inwardest Counsel in the absence of her Secretary.) Then the more to alienate her, he perswadeth the King to be present himself at the Murther with Reuven and the rest of the Murtherers; who together with him breaking into the Queen's Privy-Chamber at Supper time, while she sate at Board with the Countess of Argile, set upon the man with drawn Swords, as he was feeding at the Cupboard on Meat taken from the Queen's Table, (as the Waiters of the Privy-Chamber use to doe;) and all this before the Queen, being great with Child, and trembling for fear, setting a Pistoll against his Breast; insomuch as she hardly escaped Miscarrying of the Child she went with. Then they haled him forth into a little Chamber or Lobby hard by, and most cruelly murthered him, shutting the Queen into her Privy Chamber, while Morton in the mean time beset all Passages of access.

This Murther was committed the day before Murray was to appear, according to his Summons, to answer his Rebellion in an Assembly of the Estates; who the next day appeared, when no man looked for him, and in so troublesome a time no man appeared against him. So as the Murther of David might seem to have been hastened of purpose for Murray's Safety and Security. Nevertheless the Queen, at her Husband's Request, kindly welcomed him, and rested wholly on his Brotherly Love. But the King now considering the Foulness of the late Fact, and seeing the Queen was very angry, repented him of his rashness, humbly fled with Tears and Lamentations to her Clemency, and craving Pardon for his Fault, freely confessed, that through the Perswasion of Murray and Morton he had undertaken the Fact. And from that time forward he bare such Hatred to Murray, (for Morton, Reuven and the others were fled into England, for the Murther of David, with Murray's Letters of Commendation to the Earl of Bedford,) that he cast in his mind to make him away. But whereas through youthly heat he could neither conceal his Thoughts, nor durst execute them, (such was his Observance towards the Queen his Wife;) he told her, that it would be for the good of the Commonwealth and the Security of the Royal Family, if Murray were made away. She, detesting the matter, terrified him with Threats from such purposes, hoping again to reconcile them. But he, stomaching the Power which the Bastard had with the Queen his Sister, through Impatience communicated the same Design to others. When this came to Murray's ears, he, to prevent the same, under colour of Duty, contriveth more secret Plots against the young King's Life, using Morton's Counsell, though he were absent.

These two above all things thought it best utterly to alienate the Queen's mind from the King, their Love being not yet well renewed; and to draw Bothwell into their Society, who was lately reconciled to Murray, and was in great Grace with the Queen, putting him in hope of Divorce from his Wife, and Marriage with the Queen as soon as she was a Widow. To the performance hereof, and to defend him against all men, they bound themselves under their Hands and Seals; supposing that, if the matter succeeded, they could with one and the same labour make away the King, weaken the Queen's Reputation amongst the Nobility and Commons, tread down Bothwell, and draw unto themselves the whole Managing of the State.

Bothwell, being a wicked-minded man, blinded with Ambition, and thereby desperately bold to attempt, soon laid hold on the Hope propounded, and lewdly committed the Murther; whilst Murray scarce fifteen hours before had withdrawn himself farther off to his own House, lest he should come within Suspicion, and that he might from thence, if need were, relieve the Conspiratours, and the whole Suspicion might light upon the Queen. No sooner was he returned to the Court, but he and the Conspiratours commended Bothwell to the Queen for an Husband, as most worthy of her Love, for the Dignity of his House, for his notable Service against the English, and his singular Fidelity. They suggested unto her, "That she, being a lone and solitary Woman, could not suppress the Tumults that were raised, prevent cunning Practices, and sustain the Burthen of the Kingdom: She should therefore doe well to make him partaker of her Bed, Danger, and Counsell, who both could, would, and durst adventure himself." And to that pass they drove her, that she, being a timorous Woman, frighted with two such tragical Murthers, and mindfull of the Fidelity and Constancy of Bothwell towards her self and her Mother, and having no whither to fly but to the Faith of her Brother, gave her Assent: Howbeit upon these Considerations, that first and foremost the Safety of her young Son should be secured; and then, that Bothwell should be lawfully acquitted, as well of the Murther of the King, as from the Tie of his former Marriage.

What George Earl of Huntley and the Earl of Argile, the chief of the Nobles of Scotland, publickly protested presently after touching this matter, I thought good here to set down, out of a Writing under their own Hands to Queen Elizabeth, which I my self have seen.

> Forasmuch as Murray and others, to cloak their Rebellion against the Queen, whose Authority they arrogate to themselves, do openly calumniate her as guilty of the Murther of her Husband; we do publickly protest and witness these things following. In the month of December 1566, when the Queen lay at Cragmillar, Murray and Lidington acknowledged before us, that Morton, Lindsey and Reuven slew David Rizo to no other intent than to save Murray, who was at that very time to be proscribed. Therefore, that they might not seem unthankfull, they much desired that Morton, and the rest that lived in Exile for the Murther of David, might be brought home again. But this they said could not be, unless the Queen might be divorced from her Husband; which they promised to effect, so as we would give our Assent. Afterwards Murray promised to me Huntley, that my ancient Inheritance should be restored unto me, and that I should be in eternal Favour with the Exiles, if I would favour the Divorce. Then went we to Bothwell, that he might also consent. Lastly we came unto the Queen, and Lidington, in the name of us all, earnestly intreated her that Morton, Lindsey and Reuven might have their Banishment remitted. The King's Errours and Offences

66

against the Queen and the Realm he aggravated with much Sharpness of words, and shewed that it mainly concerned the Queen and State, that there should forthwith be a Divorce; forasmuch as the King and Queen could not live together in Scotland with Security. She answered, that she had rather withdraw her self for a time into France, untill her Husband did acknowledge the Errours of his youth: for she would not that any thing should be done which might be prejudicial to her Son, or dishonourable to her self. Hereto Lidington replied, We which are of your Counsell will look to that. But I command you (said he) that ye doe nothing which may blemish mine Honour, or burthen my Conscience. Let the matter remain as it is, till God remedy it from above. That which ye think will be for my Good, may chance turn to my Hurt. To whom Lidington said, Leave the matter to us, and you shall see nothing shall be done but what is good and approvable by Authority of Parliament. Hereupon, seeing the King was murthered by wicked hand within few days after, we, out of the inward testimony of our Conscience, do hold it most certain that Murray and Lidington were the Authours, Contrivers and Perswaders of this Regicide, whosoever were the Actours.

Thus far they.

Now the Confederates whole Care and labour was, that Bothwell might be acquitted of the Murther of the King. A Parliament therefore is forthwith summoned for no other cause, and Proclamations set forth, that such as were suspected of the Murther should be apprehended. And whereas Lenox, the murthered King's father, accused Bothwell to be the Murtherer of the King, and instantly pressed that he might be brought to his Trial before the Assembly of the Estates began; this also was granted, and Lenox was commanded to appear within twenty days to prosecute the matter against him. Upon which day (he having understood nothing from the Queen of England, and because he could not appear in the City, which was full of his Enemies, without peril of his life,) Bothwell was arraigned, and acquitted by Sentence of the Judges, Morton managing his Cause.

This business being dispatched, the Conspiratours so wrought the matter, that very many of the Nobility assented to the Marriage, setting their Hands to a Writing to that purpose, lest he, being excluded from his promised Marriage, should accuse them as Contrivers of the whole Fact. By means of this Marriage with Bothwell, (who was created Duke of Orkney, or the Orcades,) the Suspicion grew strong amongst all men that the Queen was privy to the Murther of the King: which Suspicion the Conspiratours increased by sending Letters all about; and in secret Meetings at Dunkeld they presently conspired the deposing of the Queen, and the Destruction of Bothwell. Yet Murray, that he might seem to be clear from the whole Conspiracy, craved Leave of the Queen to go into France; and, to take away all Distrust, commended his whole Estate in Scotland to the Queen and Bothwell's Trust. Scarce was he crossed over out of England, when behold, those which had acquitted Bothwell from the guilt of the Murther, and gave him their Consent under their Hands to the Marriage, took Arms against him, as if they would apprehend him; whenas indeed they gave him secret Notice to provide for himself by Flight: and this to no other purpose, but lest he, being apprehended, should reveal the whole Plot; and that they might alledge his Flight as an Argument to accuse the Queen of the Murther of the King. Having next intercepted her, they used her in most disgracefull and unworthy manner, and, cloathing her in a vile Weed, thrust her into Prison at Loch-Levin, under the Custody of Murray's Mother, who having been James the Fifth his Concubine, most malapertly aggravated the Calamity of the imprisoned Queen, boasting that she was the lawfull Wife of James the Fifth, and that her Son Murray was his lawfull Issue.

As soon as Queen Elizabeth was certainly advertised hereof, she, detesting from her heart such unbridled Insolency of Subjects against their Queen, her Sister and Neighbour, (whom she now and then called Perfidious, Rebels, Unthankfull, and Cruel,) sent Sir Nicholas Throckmorton into Scotland, to expostulate with the Confederates concerning this Insolency against the Queen, and to contrive some way how she might be restored to her former Liberty and Authority, how the Murtherers of the King might be punished, and the young Prince might be sent into England, that his Safety might be the better assured, and not into France. From this time whatsoever I shall say touching this matter, while Throckmorton remained in Scotland, take it upon the credit of his Letters, which without all question was most sound and most approved.

Throckmorton found in Scotland many most mortal Enemies to the Queen, who flatly denied both to him, and also to Villeroy and Croc, the French Embassadours, all Access unto her. Yet what should be done with her, the Conspiratours could not agree among themselves. Lidington and some few others thought best she should be restored to her Authority upon these Conditions, That the Murtherers of the King should be punished according to Law; That order should be taken for assuring the Prince his Safety; That Bothwell should be divorced from her, and Religion established. Others thought best she should be confined by perpetual Exile into France or England, so as the French King or the Queen of England would undertake, that she should quit all her Regal Authority to her Son and certain of the Nobility, and abjure the Realm. Others, That she should be arraigned, condemned, and shut up in perpetual Imprisonment, and her Son crowned King. And lastly, others, That she should at once be deprived both of Regal Authority and of Life, and put to Death. And this Knox and some Ministers of the Word thundered out of the Pulpits.

Throckmorton, on the contrary, alledged many things from the Authority of the H. Scriptures concerning Obedience to be yielded to the higher Powers which bear the Sword: and sharply maintained, That the Queen was subject to the Judgment of none but the Heavenly Judge; That she could not be compelled to appear before the Judgment seat of any man upon earth; That there was no Authority of any Magistrate in Scotland which was not substituted by the Queen's Authority, and by her revocable. Against this they opposed a peculiar Privilege of the Scots in their Kingdom, and that in Causes extraordinary extraordinary Decrees must be made, fetching their Reasons from Buchanan, who at that time, by Murray's perswasion, wrote that damned Dialogue, *De Jure Regni apud Scotos*, wherein is maintained, that the People have right to create and depose Kings, contrary to the credit of the Scottish History. Yet ceased not Throckmorton to importune them for the Restoring of the Queen, and his own Access unto her; though Answer was made him now and then by Lidington, "That no Access could be granted unto him, seeing it was denied to the French: That they must not displease the French King, to please the Queen of England, whom they had found not long since to have sought to serve onely her own Turn, when for her own Advantage she removed the French out of Scotland; and very lately, when she shewed but small Favour, and with a sparing hand, to the Scots that lived in Exile for the Death of David Rizo. Moreover, that he should beware lest by reason of this his Importunity the Scots should betake themselves to the Amity of the French, and neglect the English:" And by the French Proverb, *Il perd le jeu qui laisse la partie*, that is, He loseth the Game which leaveth the Side, he gave him secret warning, that the English should not forsake the Scots their Friends.

Then in a long Writing which they delivered to Throck-morton, without any man's Subscription, they protested, that they had not shut up the Queen in Custody to any other purpose, than to separate her from Bothwell (whom she desperately loved to their undoing) untill her immoderate Love towards him, and her womanish Anger against them, were asswaged. And with this Answer they willed him to rest satisfied, till the rest of the Lords were assembled. Nevertheless they shut up the Queen in straiter and straiter Custody, though she with many tears and prayers besought them that she might be more favourably used, if not as a Queen, yet as a King's Daughter, and their Prince's Mother, whom the many times besought them, but all in vain, that she might once see. But (not to prosecute their Injuries against her particularly) at length they assaied by fair words to perswade her that she would voluntarily resign the Kingdom, excusing her self either by Sickness, or the Troubles of swaying the Sceptre, or, (as others more subtilly advised her,) that having resigned, and being kept more carefully, she might the more easily make her Escape. When all this succeeded not, they threatned to bring her to a publick Trial, and find her guilty of an Incontinent life, of Murthering the King, and Tyranny in this respect, that she had violated the Laws and Privileges of the Countrey, namely those which Randan and D'Oiseli had confirmed in the French King's and her name. At length, by putting her in fear of Death, they compelled her, unheard, to set her

Hand to three Writings: by the first whereof she resigned the Kingdom to her Son, who was scarce thirteen months old; by another, she constituted Murray to be Vice-roy or Regent in the Minority of her Son; and by the third, she named, in case Murray should refuse the Charge, these Governours over her Son, James Duke of Chastel-herault, Matthew Earl of Lenox, Gillespik Earl of Argile, John Earl of Athol, James Earl of Morton, Alexander Earl of Glencarn, and John Earl of Marre. And forthwith she signified to the Queen of England by Throckmorton, that she had resigned by Constraint, and had against her will subscribed to the Instrument of her Resignation, by the Advice of Throckmorton, who had perswaded her, that her Resignation extorted in Prison, which is a just Fear, was utterly void. But of these things more in the next year, out of the Accusations and defences of both parties before Commissary-Delegates at York.

The fifth day after her Resignation, James the Queen's young Son was anointed and crowned King, John Knox preaching thereat; Protestation being entred by the Hamiltons, that it should not prejudice the Duke of Chastel-herault in his Title of Succession, against the House of Lenox. But Queen Elizabeth forbad Throckmorton to be present at the Coronation, lest she might be thought by her Embassadour's presence to approve so unjust a Deposing of the Queen.

The twentieth day after the Resignation Murray himself returned into Scotland out of France, and the third day after came with some of the Conspiratours to the Queen, objected against her very many Crimes, and, like a religious Confessour, used many Perswasions unto her, that she would turn to God by true Repentance, and call upon him for Mercy. She bewailed the Sins of her life past: of the things objected, some she acknowledged, some she extenuated, some she excused by humane Frailty, and the most part she flatly denied. She besought him to take upon him the Government for her young Son, and again and again intreated him to spare her Reputation and her Life. He denied it to be in his power to grant this latter, but it must be sued for at the hands of the Estates of the Realm. Yet if she would have her Life and Honour saved, he prescribed her these things to be observed: "That she should not disturb the Quiet of the King and Realm; That she should not withdraw her self out of prison;

That she should not excite the Queen of England or the French King to infest Scotland with foreign or domestick War: and That she should love Bothwell no more, nor think of taking Revenge on Bothwell's Adversaries."

And now being declared Vice-roy or Regent, he bindeth himself by Writing under his hand to doe nothing which may concern War or Peace, the King's Person and Marriage, or the Queen's Liberty, without the Assent of the Conspiratours. By Lidington he warneth Throckmorton, that he make no more Intercession for the Queen; for he and the rest would rather suffer all Extremities, than once endure that she should be at Liberty, and retain Bothwell, bring her Son into Dangers, and her Countrey into Troubles, and proscribe them. "We know (saith he) what ye English-men can doe by War; our Borders ye may waste, and we yours: and we know certainly that the French, according to the ancient League betwixt us and them, will never forsake us." Nevertheless to Lignerol the French Embassadour he denied Access to the Queen, till Bothwell were apprehended, and day by day treated the afflicted Queen more sharply than she deserved at his hands, contrary to that he had promised to the French King. Thus far out of Throckmorton's Letters.

Shortly after Murray put to death John Hepborn, Paris a Frenchman Daglish and other Servants of Bothwell's, which were present at the Murthering of the King. But they (which he full little expected) protested at the Gallows before God and his Angels, that they understood from Bothwell, that Murray and Morton were the Authours of the King's Death. The Queen they cleared from all Suspicion: as Bothwell also himself, being Prisoner in Denmark, many times witnessed, both living and dying, with a religious Asseveration, that the Queen was not privy thereunto. And fourteen years after, when Morton was to suffer death, he confessed that Bothwell had dealt with him to consent to the Killing of the King: which when he utterly refused, unless the Queen commanded him under her Hand; Bothwell answered, that this could not be, but the fact was to be committed even without her Privity.

This rash Deposing of the Queen, and Insolency of the Conspiratours towards the Embassadours, Queen Elizabeth and the

French King took in very ill part, as dishonourable to Regal Majesty, and began to favour the Hamiltons, which stood for the Queen. Pasquier also, Embassadour from the French King, solicited the Queen of England that she might be restored by Force and Arms: But she thought it better that Commerce should be prohibited to the Scots both in France and England till she were set at Liberty, that by this means the People might be divided from the Lords, who seemed to have joyntly conspired against the Queen. But let us for a while pass over these Scottish matters.

When now the eight years were expired, and Calice was according to the Treaty at the Castle of Cambray to be restored to the English, Sir Thomas Smith was sent into France, with Sir William Winter Master of the Munition for the Navy, who, with the sound of Trumpet before the Gate of Calice next to the Sea, with a loud voice in French, demanded Calice with its Territory, and certain warlike Munition, according to the Treaty. And hereof presently an Act was made by a Notary, and certain German Merchants and Low countrey-men, which were there by chance, called to witness. Shortly after he came unto the King at Fossat Castle, where, with Sir Henry Norris the Ordinary Embassadour, he demanded it again. The King referred the matter to his Council: of whom Mich. Hospitall, Chancellour, in a grave and set Speech, argued in this manner.

> By the same Right that the English demand Calice, they may as well demand Paris: for this they wone by War as well as that, and by War they have lost both. The English pretend a new Title to Calice: the Title of the French is as old as the Kingdom it self. Though the English possessed it about two hundred and thirty years, yet the Right was in the Kings of France, and that no less than to the Dukedoms of Guienne and Normandy, which the English detained long time by Arms. Calice, as also those Dukedoms, the French have not purchased, but recoverd by War. The Prescription of time, which they alledge, taketh not place among Princes, but the Right ever prevaileth; and, according to the Twelve Tables, the Authority against an Enemy is perpetual. The English in making Contracts are very advised: and yet in the late Treaty at Troyes, after they had begun a War principally for Calice, they not so much as once mentioned Calice; insomuch as they seemed to acknowledge that they had quite given over

73

their Claim to Calice. The Treaty of Troyes was a renewing of a former Treaty, so as the Treaty was then plainly renewed. Neither is that Clause, concerning the Reservation of Rights, any impediment; forasmuch as it respecteth onely small matters, whereas this of Calice is to be reckoned amongst the greatest. Whatsoever Francis the Second attempted in Scotland cannot prejudice the Right of Charles the Ninth. The things that any private man shall attempt are in some Cases subject to Laws: but in Princes Cases the matter is otherwise. Concerning the Attempts in Scotland, being a Dowry Kingdom, let the English expostulate the matter with the Queen of Scots, who do guess by Conjectures at the purpose of Francis and the Queen; whereas the English entring into New-haven in France, under a goodly shew of keeping it for the King, held it by Arms, fortifying it with a strong Garrison, and great store of Provision and Munition for War, and furnished Condé and the Confederates with Money: and therefore have they through their own fault forfeited their Right to Calice. It hath pleased God, that Calice being recovered by the French, the Wars have ceased between the English and the French Nations, whom he had divided by the interflowing Sea, as the Poet signifieth,

Et penitus toto divisos orbe Britannos,

And Britans that are severed quite from all the world beside. The Queen of England also shall better provide for her own Convenience and good, by embracing Peace with the French, than by recovering Calice. To be short, no man dares be so bold as to perswade the King that Calice should be restored to the English: and if any durst, he were most worthy to be put to death, yea, to be damned to the Pit of Hell.

Hereunto Smith answered

That he little expected that such an outworn Title of the French to Calice should be revived after so long a time. But now at length he pereceiveth, that whatsoever the French either by right or wrong once get into their Possession, that they think to be their own by Right, as if their Right stood onely in Arms, and it made no matter whether they possessed it with a good or bad Conscience. The French think they hold Calice by right of Recovery, having been lost by War long since; whereas they hold it by Convention and Agreement: no later Convention do they admit, and are fully resolved in no wise to keep their Word and Promise for the Restitution of Calice. But these things do weigh down all weight of Reasons whatsoever. The Praise which he attributeth to the English, as men advised in making their Contracts, the French have always arrogated to themselves, and detracted from the English. The renewing of the Contracts is a flat Antistrophe, and may truly be retorted upon the French, to wit, Because the Queen demanded Calice, for that the Franch forfeited their Right by innovating and attempting by Arms in Scotland; contrariwise the French would exclude the English from their Right to Calise, for that afterward the Queen of England made an Attempt by Arms at New-haven. When in these things (saith he) the one would yield nothing to the other, we agreed a Peace at Troyes; which if it induced a Renewing, that Renewing extinguished the Right of the French to Calice, and confirmed the Right of the English, whose day was not yet come, because they could not claim Calice, the eight years term being not then expired. Here rising up, and turning to the Council of France, I appeal (saith he) to your Consciences which were present, whether when we urged to have our Right to Calice reserved in express words, and ye urged to have it omitted, because the time was not yet come, whether (I say) it were not agreed betwixt us, that it should be tacitly reserved under that Clause, viz. All other Claims and Demands shall remain whole and safe; and in like manner the Exceptions and Defences on either side shall be reserved. As for New-haven, the English entred thereinto peaceably, being invited by the Inhabitants and Noblemen of Normandy, with Protestation that they would keep it for the Use of the French King. So they attempted nothing by Arms against the French King, nor innovated to the prejudice of the Treaty: and hold it they did, not by any right of Propriety, but as a Pledge that they might have fair and equal dealing about Calice, which was detained; the Right whereof, as well to the Possession as to the Propriety, was devolved to the Queen by the Attempt of the French in Scotland flatly contrary to the Treaty. And as for the Money, it was lent to Condé and the Confederates, to no other intent than to satisfie the German Souldiers that mutined for their Pay, lest they should spoil the King's Countries and Towns. All which the King also acknowledged by his Edict to have been done *a bon fin, & pour notre Service,* that is, to a good End, and for our Service.

These things and such like Smith alleged.

When Montmorency, Constable, holding up a Sword with a Scabbard set with Flowers de luce, (which is the badge of his Office,) spake much of the great warlike Provision of the English in Newhaven, as if the same had been sufficient to conquer, not one small Town, but all Normandy: "There is no cause (said Smith) why any man should wonder at this, considering that the English being a Nation coasting upon the Sea, know they have not the Winds, which are Masters of the Sea, at command; and therefore they provided timely and fully for the time to come." The French afterward, making a grievous Complaint, that the Protestant Fugitives out of France were not delivered (according to the agreement) to the French Embassadour upon his Demand, prorogued the matter to another time; which by little and little expired as it were in silence, by means of Civil War arising presently upon it in France. And without doubt the French had fully resolved that Calice should never be restored. For as soon as ever it was taken, they threw down the old Forts, began new, and let out the Houses and other Lands for fifty years, and some they gave for ever.

Whilst these things are negotiated in France, Count Stolberg came into England from the Emperour Maximilian, to treat of a Marriage with the Archduke Charles; about which business the Queen had a little before sent the Earl of Sussex to the Emperour, with the Ensigns of the Order of Saint George, who, out of his Love to his Countrey, joyned with Emulation against Leicester, left no Stone unmoved, that the Queen might be joyned in Marriage with some foreign Prince, and Leicester might be put beside his Hope. And Sussex had nothing more frequent in his mouth, than that a foreign Prince was to be preferred before the Noblest Englishman, whether a man respect Honour, Power, or Wealth: insomuch as one, who was of a contrary mind, said merrily in his presence, "Where these three, Honour, Power and Riches, are respected in Marriage, the Devil and the World are the Match-makers and Brokers." Yet Leicester, cherishing his own Hopes, suborned the Lord North, (whom Sussex took with him as a Companion in his Journey,) to listen to what was spoken, and observe what was done, and as much as Sussex advanced the Marriage with the Archduke, he so much to hinder the same privily, by giving secret Hints that the Queen's mind was most averse from Marriage, whatsoever she pretended, and howsoever Sussex made shew to the contrary. Neither did he himself at home cease to discourage the Queen, by whispering in her ears all the Inconveniences of a foreign Marriage.

He laid before her the late Marriage of Queen Mary her Sister with Philip of Spain, whereby she was cast into perpetual Trouble, and England brought into danger of the Spanish Slavery. He discoursed,

> That the Manners, Minds and Dispositions of Outlandish men could not be discovered, which in an Husband, who by an unseparable Tie should be one Flesh with his Wife, are most necessary to be known. To be daily conversant with a strange Language and Manners, was most troublesome, and miserable. That in Children born of foreign Marriage some unwonted and strange thing was imbred. That by the Converse of Strangers strange Manners and new Orders are brought into a Commonwealth. That Princesses by foreign Marriage do for the most part augment, not their own, but another's, Kingdom, subject themselves and theirs to a foreign Command, and discover the Secrets of the Kingdom to Strangers. That a foreign Husband will, out of his imbred Love to his Countrey, prefer his own Countreymen before the English. That England needeth no foreign Aid, which hath Strength enough in her self to defend her self and hers, and repell foreign Force. That by Accession of another Kingdom cometh nothing but greater Expences, Cares and Trouble: and as mens Bodies, so Empires also, do labour with their own Weight. That that saying, That by domestical Marriage somewhat is detracted from the Royal Dignity, is taken up by some in Disgrace of Nobility; whereas even the Royal Majesty, which hath by her Vertue made her way to that Height, fetcheth her beginning from Nobility, and Noblemen are as it were the Roots of the Royal Stock: And thence it is that the Kings of England have always in their Letters to Dukes, Marquesses, Earls and Viscounts, given them the Title of Cousins.

Sussex in the mean time came with a great and goodly Train and Shew by Antwerp, Cologne, Mentz, Wormes, Spires, Ulmes, and Augspurg, into Austria. Where being honourably entertained, he stayed five months at the Emperour's Charge, conferring with him daily of most weighty matters, and of the Marriage of Charles; and, upon a day appointed, invested him at Evening-prayer with the Ensigns of the Order of Saint George, when, out of scruple of Conscience, he refused to be present at the Sacrifice of the Mass. In this Negotiation there arose Difficulties, concerning Religion, the Duke's Maintenance, the Title of King, and the Succession: about all which much arguing there was on both sides. As for the Title, the Archduke Charles should enjoy the Title and Name of the King of England. Touching the Succession, he could not by the Law of the Land succeed, for that would be prejudicial to their Children, of whom notwithstanding it was agreed he should have the Guardianship. And more than this was not granted Philip of Spain when he married Queen Mary. As for his Maintenance, if he would at his own Charge maintain the Train he should bring and keep about him, the Queen would bountifully supply the rest answerable to his Royal Dignity, yea and that also if he should require it. But touching Religion, there stuck the Doubt. The Emperour required, and so did Charles also himself, that a publick Church might be allowed, wherein Divine Service might be celebrated by him and his after the Romish manner. When this would not be harkned unto, the Emperour devised a middle way, that in some private place in the Court he might peaceably use his Service of God, (as was permitted to Popish Princes Embassadours in their Houses,) and that with these Conditions: "That no English-man should be admitted thereto; and neither he nor his Servants should speak against the Religion received in England, or favour those that did speak against it: That if any Offence should arise in respect of his Religion, he should forbear it for a time; and also that he should be present with the Queen at Divine Service to be celebrated after the manner of the Church of England." To be short, this matter being maturely deliberated of in England, the Queen answered, "That if she should grant this, she should offend her Conscience, and openly break the publick Laws of the Realm, not without great peril both of her Dignity and Safety. But if it would please the Archduke Charles to come into England, that she might see him, he should be very well satisfied, and find his Travel worth his pains." So the Emperour dismissed Sussex with great Honour, who turning out of his way to Gratz, took his leave of the Archduke Charles, that in vain hoped for a better Answer from the Queen: for from thenceforth time wore these things out by little and little, which had been 7 years bringing on by honourable Mediatours. Yet did there continue such dearness of Love and mutual Kindness between both Princes, that the Emperour always crossed the Bishop of Rome's Attempts against Queen Elizabeth. The Archduke Charles not long after took to Wife Mary, the Daughter of Albert the Fifth, Duke of Bavaria, who, besides other Children, bare unto him the Queens of Spain and Poland.

About this time came into England Stephen Twerdico and Theodore Pogorella, from that most potent Emperour John Basilides, Emperour of Russia and Moscovia, with rich Furrs of Sables, Luserns, and others, which at that time and in former Ages were in great request amongst the English, both for their Ornament and Wholesomeness. They made large Offers of all Kindness and Assistence to the Queen and the English, which the said Emperour had already abundantly shewed upon these beginnings following.

Whilst certain Merchants of London, whereof the chief were Andrew Judd, George Barns, William Gerard, and Anthony Husey, in the year 1553 fought a way into Cathay by the Frozen or North Sea, under the Conduct of Sir Huge Willoughby, who was frozen to death, Richard Chanceller next after him happily discovered a Passage into Russia, which was before unknown, being brought into the mouth of the River Dwina, under the 64th degree of Latitude of the North Pole, where standeth a little Monastery dedicated to Saint Nicholas. From hence the Emperour sent for them to Mosco by Sleds drawn over the Ice, after the manner of the Countrey: he welcomed them kindly, and dismissed them bountifully, promising large Privileges to the English, if they would traffick in his Empire; heartily rejoycing that Out-landish Merchandizes might be brought into Russia by Sea, which the Russians had before with difficulty received by Narva and the hostile Countries of the Polonian. When Chanceller was returned, and reported these things, and how dear the English Cloaths were sold in those parts, and how cheap Hemp and Flax for Cables, Wax and rich Furrs were sold unto them; those Merchants grew into a Company or Society, by the Assent of Queen Mary, which we call the Moscovia Company, who, having many Privileges granted them by Basilides, from that time had a rich Trade of it, sending every year a Fleet thither. But most gainfull it was to them after that, through Queen Elizabeth's Favour with Basilides, they obtained in the year 1569 that none but the English Merchants of that Company should trade in the North parts of Russia, and that they alone should vend their Merchandizes all over that most spacious Empire, as in proper place we will declare.

With these Russian Embassadours returned into England Anthony Jenkinson, who took a most exact Survey of Russia, described it in a Geographical Map, and was the first Englishman that sailed on the Caspian Sea, and made his way to the Bactrians. To this Jenkinson the Emperour gave certain secret Instructions, which he imparted not to his own people: to wit, "That he should seriously solicite the Queen for a mutual League of Defence and Offence against all men, and to send Ship wrights, Sailers and Munition into Russia: And that the Queen would bind her self by Oath to receive him courteously with his Wife and Children, if he should be thrown out of his Kingdom either by Rebels or Enemies." Thus did a Tyrant, from whom no man can keep any thing safe, seem to himself to be without Safety. And certainly he took it ill that the Queen answered slightly to these Points. And yet he ceased not both by Letters and Embassie to urge these things, as in due place we will shew, now and then requiring that the said Anthony might be sent back, as if he had dealt unfaithfully in Secrets of so great a moment.

In the first month of this year Nicholas Wotton, Doctour of both Laws, Dean of Canterbury and York both at once, a man of noble Birth, but far more noble and famous at home and abroad for his Wisdom, rendered his Soul to God. For being of the Privy Council to King Henry the Eighth, King Edward the Sixth, Queen Mary, and Queen Elizabeth, he was nine times sent Embassadour to the Emperour, the Kings of France and Spain, and other Princes; thrice was he a Commissioner for concluding of Peace between the English, the French and the Scots; and was chosen by King Henry the Eighth one of the sixteen Curators or Overseers of his last Will and Testament.

This year also died Elizabeth Leibourne, the third Wife of Thomas Duke of Norfolk, who being Widow to the Lord Dacres, and married to the Duke about a year, bare him no Children: but to her former Husband she bare George Lord Dacres, who died young by the fall of a Vaulting-horse upon him, as he learned to vault; and three Daughters espoused *de futuro* to three of the Duke's Sons.

I have already shewed in the year 1560 and 1562 how Shan-O-Neal, the lawfull Son of Con O-Neal, by-named Bacco, that is, The lame, the most powerfull Lord of all the North part of Ireland, which is called Ulster, came into England, and humbly craved Pardon for his Rebellion. He, being returned home, manfully defended that part of Ireland against the Invasion of the Scots from Cantire and the Hebrides, killing their Leaders, James Mac-Conel, to whom he was Son-in-law, and Agne his Brother. With which Victory being puffed up, he began to exercise Tyranny over the petty Lords of Ulster. Armagh, the Metropolitan City of Ireland, he defaced with Fire, in Hatred to the Archbishop. O-Donel, who was the next unto him in this Tract, he despoiled of his Goods and Lands, carried him away Prisoner, and ravished his Wife. Mac-Guire he drove out of his ancient Inheritance; making a Prey of Mac-Geniss and others. Whose Protection when the English undertook, he took up the Banner of Rebellion against the Queen; which, by the perswasion of Sir Thomas Cusac Knight, he soon laid down again, and returned to his Obedience, delivering his Son for Hostage. And to keep him in his Duty, the Queen resolved to disannull the Patent of King Henry the Eighth, wherein he declared Matthew (falsly supposed to be the Son of Con) to be Successor of his Father, and to bestow upon this Shan, as his undoubted Son and Heir, the honourable Title of Earl of Tir-Oen, and Baron of Dungannon. But he, being a man of a restless spirit, when he saw that he was able to leavy of his own Followers a thousand horse and four thousand foot, and had already a Guard of seven hundred men, disdained in a barbarous Pride all such honourable Titles, in comparison of the name of O-Neal, and vaunted himself among his own People for King of Ulster, trained the Countrey-people to War, offered the Kingdom of Ireland to the Queen of Scots, and boiled in Hatred against the English in such sort, that he named a Castle which he built in the Lake Eaugh, Feoghnegall, that is, The hatred of the English, and strangled some of his own men for that they fed on English Bread. Yet never spake he of the Queen but with Honour.

Against this Tir-Oen Sir Henry Sidney, Lord Deputy, was commanded to march: and Edward Randolph, a worthy Leader, was sent by Sea to the Coast of Ulster with a Cornet of Horse, and seven hundred Foot, to Dirry, a small Bishop's See near Lough-Foyl, to charge him in the Rere, when the Lord Deputy should set upon him on the other side. Shan, understanding hereof, in a great fury assalted Dundalk, but was beaten off by the Garrison, and received a great Overthrow; and no less at Whites-Castle. Afterwards, as he was about to waste the Countrey of Louth with Fire and sword, he was put to flight by a small Power of English-men, and lost many of his men. Then marched he to Dirry, pillaged the Countrey round about, and provoked the English Garrison to fight; who, marshalling themselves in order of Battel, easily brake through the disordered Multitude, defeated them, and put them to flight. Yet sad was the Victory, by reason of the unhappy death of Randolph the Leader, who, fighting manfully amongst the thickest of the Enemies, was slain. Surely a worthy man in our memory, for never was there any that gained greater Authority together with greater Love amongst Souldiers. In his room succeeded Edward à Sancto Laudo, or Saint-Lo, who grievously punished and endammaged the Rebels in these parts, untill by Victuals and Powder, which blew up many of his men: for then he put his Foot-men aboard the small Vessels he had, and he himself with the Cornet of Horse, whereof George Harvey had the Command, broke through the midst of the insulting Enemies, and by a four days march came to the Lord Deputy, who mourned himself in black at the Funeral of Randolph, for his Vertue.

And now the Lord Deputy marching into Ulster, Shan and his men hid themselves in Woods and Thickets, and once or twice cut off the hindermost Companies near Clogher, and Salmon, a Castle of Turlough Leinigh's, who was then revolted from Shan. But after the Lord Deputy had placed his men in Garrison, and restored O-Donell to his Lands, and was returned to pacifie some Variances betwixt the Earls of Ormond and Desmond, who made mortal Wars one upon another, Shan, taking heart again, harried the Countrey round about, and besieged Dundalk again; which Siege he was fain shortly after to break up again with great Loss and Shame, having many of his men slain. Whereupon being stricken as it were into a fury, he exercised barbarous Cruelty upon his own men; insomuch as many forsook him: and he himself, when he saw his Companies weakned, (for besides those which had forsaken him, there were four thousand slain,) the Passages beset, and all Refuges seized on by the English, was minded to cast himself at the Lord Deputy's feet with an Halter about his Neck, and crave Pardon. But his Secretary disswaded him, advising him first to try the Friendship of the Hebridian Scots, who, during the heat of the War, had returned into Clandeboy (from whence he had driven them out a little before,) under the Conduct of Alexander Oge, that is, The younger, and Mac-Gillespic, whose Brethren, Agne and James Mac-conel, he himself had slain in fight. To these he came with the Wife of O-Donell, whom he had ravished, having, to regain their Favour, sent their Brother Surley Boy, that is, Surley the yellow, before, whom he had kept Prisoner a long time. They, in Revenge of their Brethren and Kinsmen whom he had slain, received him with feigned Courtesie, and soon after taking him into their Tent, amongst their Cups they fell to hot words, for certain opprobrious speeches of Shan against their Mother, drew upon him, and slew him, and most of his Company. This bloudy End had Shan in the middle of June, who had despoiled his Father of his Government, and his base Brother of his Life; a man most polluted with Murthers and Adulteries, a very great Rioter and Glutton, and such a Drunkard, that, to cool his body when it was immoderately inflamed with Wine and Usquebagh, he would many times be buried in the earth, up to the Chin. He left Children by his Wife, Henry and Shan; and more by O-Donel's Wife, and his Concubines. His Goods and Possessions were confiscate by Authority of a Parliament in Ireland, and Turlough Leinigh, the powerfullest man of the House of O-Neal, a man of a quiet spirit, was, with Queen Elizabeth's good will, saluted by the name of O-Neal by popular Election. Nevertheless Hugh, commonly called Baron of Dungannon, Nephew to Shan by Matthew his base Brother, a young man then little set by, who proved afterward the Disturber, yea the Plague, of his Countrey, was received into Grace of Queen Elizabeth, that she might have one to oppose against Turlough, if he should chance to fall away from his Duty.

Thus was Ulster restored to Peace: but in the mean time in Munster there was much Hurliburly, through an unhappy Emulation between two Kinsmen, the Earls of Ormond and Desmond, and upon Contention about their Bounds; insomuch as they fought a Battel near Dromelin, and were sent for into England to plead their Cause at the Council-table. Nevertheless, the matter being somewhat intricate, they were remitted to the Lord Deputy in Ireland, where the Witnesses and Evidence were nigh: but they, being equal in number of warlike Adherents, Spirit, and Friends in Court, resolved to decide the matter by the Sword, despising the Authority of the Laws. The Lord Deputy interposed himself with his Authority and armed Power. But Ormond, who would have his Cause to seem the better, so wrought, that the Lord Deputy was accused as inclining to favour Desmond, and was commanded to surprize Desmond; whom he intercepted at unawares at Kilmalock, with John Desmond his Uncle, and sent them into England, where they were committed to Custody.

VI

The Eleventh Year of Her Reign, Anno Domini 1568

Whilst Thomas Harding, Nichols Sanders and T .P., Divines Fugitives out of England, busily exercised their Episcopal Power received lately from the Bishop of Rome, "of absolving in Court of Conscience all English-men which returned to the Bosome of the Church, and of dispensing also in cases of Irregularity, excepting Causes arising of wilfull Murther, or brought into a contentious or Judicial Court; and also of absolving from Irregularity in respect of Heresie, so as the persons to be absolved do abstain from the Service of the Altar by the space of three years": on the other side, Coleman, Button, Hallingham, Benson, and others, who, with burning Zeal professing a more sincere Religion, allowed nothing but what was drawn from the Fountains of the Holy Scriptures, or out of an affectation of a more pure Discipline, Novelty, or Dissension, openly called in question the received Discipline of the Church of England, the Liturgie, and the Vocation of Bishops, yea condemned them as favouring too much of the Romish Religion, (with which to have any Communion they cried out was impious,) using all the means they could, that all things in the Church of England might be reformed according to the Pattern of the Church of Geneva. These men though the Queen commanded to be committed to Prison, yet incredible it is how much the Followers of this Sect increased every where, through a certain obstinate wilfulness in them, Indiscretion of the Bishops, and secret Favour of certain Noblemen who gaped after the Wealth of the Church: which

Sect began presently to be known by the odious name of Puritans.

Whenas the Frenchmen, who in like manner endeavoured a Reformation of Religion, fearing that the Holy League was made by the Papists against them, had a little before out of just Fear come unto the King armed with their humble Supplication, a Second Civil war broke forth: for the compounding whereof the Queen commanded Norris, her Embassadour, to interpose his Mediation. And certainly a dissembled Peace ensued, full of treacherous Intentions. At what time the Queen-mother of France used the Embassadour and other English-men with flattering and kind Courtesie, and covertly, and as it were glancingly, began to let fall speeches of a Marriage betwixt Queen Elizabeth and her Son Duke of Anjou, who was scarce seventeen years of Age: And this to no other intent (as many thought) than to keep her off from relieving the Protestants of France in the Third Civil war, which she guessed did threatten her.

But Man, the English Embassadour in Spain, was most discourteously dealt withall, who, being accused to have spoken somewhat unreverently of the Bishop of Rome, was excluded from the Court, and afterward thrust out of Madrid into a Countrey village, his Servants compelled to be present at Mass, and the Exercise of his own Religion forbidden; and this whether in more hatred to the Queen or to Religion, I cannot say: whereas she in the mean time shewed all Kindness to Gusman the Spanish Embassadour, allowing him his own Religion. This Usage towards her Embassadour she took in ill part, as done in Disgrace to her; and no less the Injury done at this time by the Spaniards to Sir John Hawkins. This Hawkins had arrived at Saint John de Ullua in the Bay of Mexico, with five Ships for Commerce, laden with Merchandizes and Black-moor Slaves, which were now commonly bought in Africa by the Spaniards, and from their Example by the English, and sold again in America, how honestly I know not. The next day arrived there also the King of Spains Royal Navy; which though he might easily have kept from entring the Haven, yet suffered he them to enter, compounding for Security to him and his and upon certain Conditions, lest he might seem to have broken the League. The Spaniards being let in, who scorned to have Conditions given them within their own Dominions, watched

86

their Opportunity, set upon the English, slew many, took three Ships and pillaged the Goods: yet got they not the Victory without Blood. Hereat the military and sea-faring men all over England fretted, and desired War against the Spaniards, exclaiming that they were League-breakers, inasmuch as it was agreed by the League betwixt the Emperour Charles the Fifth and King Henry the Eighth, that there should be free Commerce between the Subjects of both Princes, in all and singular their Kingdoms, Dominions and Isles, not excepting America, which then belonged to the said Charles. But the Queen shut her Ears against them, being taken off by Scottish matters.

For in Scotland about this time, to wit, the second of May, the captive Queen made an Escape out of Prison in Lough-Levin, to Hamilton Castle, by the Help of George Douglas, to whose Brother's Custody she was committed; where, upon hearing of the Testimonies of Robert Melvin and others, a Sentence declaratory was pronounced by the unanimous Consent of all the Noblemen which were there assembled in good number, That the Resignation extorted from the Queen in Prison through Fear was null from the very first; and that the same was extorted, was confirmed by the Oath of the Queen her self there present. Hereupon within a day or two so great a Multitude flocked unto her from all parts, that she levied an Army of six thousand Warriours, who notwithstanding, when the Battel joyned, were easily defeated by Murray, whilst in fighting they rather used Force than good Advisement. With this sad Success the fearfull Queen being terrified, saved her self by Flight, riding that day sixty miles; and afterwards she came by Night-journeys to the House of Maxwell Baron Heris, and chose rather to commit herself to the mercy of the Sea, and to the Protection of Queen Elizabeth, than to the Fidelity of her own people. Nevertheless she sent John Beton first to her with a Diamond, (which she had before received from her in token of mutual kindness) to let her know that she would come into England, and crave aid of her, in case her Subjects did pursue her any farther in a hostile way. To whom Queen Elizabeth most largely promised all the Love and Kindness of a Sister. But before the Messenger returned, she, quite contrary to the persuasions of her Friends, took Boat with the Lords Heris and Fleming, and a few others, and arrived the 17th of May at Wirkinton in Cumberland, near the Mouth of the River Derwent; and the same day wrote a Letter in French with her own hand to Queen Elizabeth. The chief Heads whereof (forasmuch as they contain an historical narration of things done against her in Scotland more fully than I have related them) I have thought good to set down out of the very Original, which runneth thus.

You are not ignorant (my very good Sister) how some of my Subjects, whom I have raised to the highest top of Honour, have conspired to imprison me and my Husband; and how I also, at your Intercession, received them again to Favour, after they were by force of Arms driven out of my Kingdom. Yet these men brake into my Chamber, cruelly murthered my Servant before my face, when I was great with child, and shut me up in Custody. And when I had pardoned them the second time, behold they pretended a new Crime against me, which they plotted themselves, and signed with their own hands, and were now ready with an Army in the Field to charge me. But I, trusting in mine own Innocency, and to spare the spilling of Bloud, put my self into their Hands. They presently thrust me into Prison, removed all my Servants from me, saving one or two Waiting-maids, my Cook, and my Physician; drove me by Threats and Terrour of Death to resign my Kingdom; and in an Assembly of the Estates convocated by their own Authority, refused to hear me or my Advocates; despoiled me of my Goods, and barred me from all Conference with any man. Afterwards by God's guidance I escaped out of Prison, and being guarded with the Flower of the Nobility, which gladly flocked unto me from all parts, I put my Enemies in mind of their Duty and Allegeance, I offered them Pardon, and propounded that both parties might be heard in an Assembly of the Estates, lest the Commonwealth should be rent any longer with Civil Combustions. Two Messengers I sent about this matter; both of them they cast in Prison: those which aided me they proclaimed Traitours, and commanded them by publick Proclamation that they should presently leave me. I prayed them that the Lord Boyd might upon publick Faith and Assurance treat with them about a Composition: but this also they flatly denied. Yet I hoped that by your Mediation they might have been recalled to their Duty. But when I saw that I must have undergone either Death or a new Imprisonment, I resolved to go to Dunbriton. They in the way opposed themselves against me, slew and put my men to flight in Battel. I betook my self to the Lord Heris, with whom I am come into your Kingdom, trusting assuredly in your singular Kindness, that you will assist me, and excite others by your Example. I do therefore earnestly intreat you that I may be forthwith conducted unto you, who am now in very great Straits, as I shall more fully inform you when it shall please you to take pity on me. God grant unto you a long and safe Life, and to me Patience and Consolation, which I hope and pray that I may obtain of him by your means.

Queen Elizabeth comforted her by Letters sent by Sir Francis Knolles and others, promising her Protection according to the Equity of her Cause: Nevertheless she denied her Access unto her, because she was commonly taxed of many Crimes, and commanded that she should be conveyed to Carlisle by Louder Deputy-warden of the place, and the Gentlemen in those parts, as to a place of more safety, if her Adversaries should attempt any thing against her. Upon receit of this Answer, and Denial of Access, she earnestly besought her again, both by Letters and by Maxwell Baron Heris, "That she might both lay open the Injuries done unto her, and purge her self of the Crimes objected against her: alledging, That it was most reasonable that Queen Elizabeth, being her very near Kinswoman, should hear her, being an Exile, in her own Presence, and restore her to her Kingdom, against those whom she, when they lived in Exile for their Offences against her, had fully restored at Queen Elizabeth's Intercession, and indeed to her own Undoing, unless prevented in time. She besought her therefore that she might either be admitted to speak with her, and be relieved; or else suffered with good Leave to depart out of England forthwith, to crave Aid elsewhere, and might no longer be detained as a Prisoner in Carlisle-Castle; forasmuch as she came of her own accord into England, relying upon her Love so often honourably promised by Letters, Messages and Tokens."

By means of these Letters, and Heris his words, Queen Elizabeth seemed (for who can dive into the secret Meanings of Princes? and wise men do keep their Thoughts locked up within the Closet of their Breasts,) seriously to commiserate the most afflicted Princess her Kinswoman, who having been taken by her own Subjects by Force and arms, thrust into Prison, brought into extreme danger of her Life, condemned without Hearing, and despoiled of her Kingdom, (whereas even against a private man, without Hearing, Sentence is not to be pronounced,) had fled into England to her in assured hope of Aid. And hereunto she was the rather moved, for that the distressed Queen voluntarily offered her Cause to be debated before her, and undertook to prove her Adversaries guilty of all the Crimes whereof they had accused her who was innocent.

But whatsoever Queen Elizabeth's Commiseration were towards her, the Council of England entred into serious Deliberation what should be done with her. If she were detained in England, they feared lest she (who was as it were the very Pith and Marrow of sweet Eloquence) might draw many daily to her part which favoured her Title to the Crown of England, who would kindle the Coals of her Ambition, and leave nothing unassayed whereby they might set the Crown upon her Head: Foreign Embassadours would further her Counsels and Designs; and the Scots then would not fail her, when they should see so rich a Booty offered them. Besides, the Trust of Keepers was doubtfull: and if she should die in England, though by Sickness, it would be wrested to matter of Calumniation, and the Queen would be daily molested with new Troubles. If she were sent over into France, they feared lest the Guises, her Kinsmen, would prosecute her Title again, whereby she had laid claim to England, out of an opinion they had, that she could doe much in England, with some in respect of Religion, with others by the probability of her Title aforesaid, and with the most sort through a mad affectation of Innovation. Moreover the Amity between England and Scotland, which was of special concernment, would be broken, and the ancient League between France and Scotland renewed, which would now be a matter of more dangerous consequence than in times past, when Burgundy was knit in a firm League with England, which at this time had no trusty Friends but the Scots. If she should be sent back into Scotland, the Fear was, lest those of the English party should be put beside their places, and those of the French party advanced to highest Offices, the young Prince exposed to danger, Religion in Scotland changed, the French and other Foreigners let in, Ireland more grievously infested by the Hebridian Scots, and she herself brought into Hazard of her Life by her Adversaries at home. Almost all of them therefore thought it best that she should be detained as taken by right of War, and not be delivered, till she gave Satisfaction for usurping the Title of England, and answered for the Death of the Lord Darly her Husband, who was a native Subject of England. For the Lord Darly's Mother, the Countess of Lenox, had of late with Tears grievously complained to Queen Elizabeth in her own and her Husband's name, and besought her that she might be called to her Trial for the Murther of her Son. But she gratiously comforting her, admonished her, "That she should not charge a Crime upon so great a Princess, her near Kinswoman, which could not be proved by certain Evidence: saying, That the Times were partial and malignant, and Malice blind, which forgeth Crimes against the Innocent; but Justice clear-sighted, which being the Avenger of wicked facts, is to be expected from God."

The Lord Heris on the contrary besought the Queen That she would not hastily believe any thing contrary to the Truth against a Queen unheard; and that a Parliament might not be over-rashly holden in Scotland by Murray, to the Prejudice of the expelled Queen, and the undoing of the good Subjects. Which though Queen Elizabeth earnestly urged, yet Murray the Regent summoned a Parliament in the King's name, proscribed some which stood for the Queen, and seized upon their Lands and Houses. The Queen of England, being highly displeased herewith, gave the Regent to understand by Middlemore, and that in sharp words, that she could not endure that an Example so dangerous to Kings should be given, whereby the Authority of the Sacred Royal Majesty should be had in Contempt amongst Subjects, and troden under foot at the lust of Factious people. But however they forgat the Duty of Subjects, and their Fidelity towards their Queen, yet she could not be unmindfull of any Office either of Kindness or Piety towards the Queen her Sister and Neighbour. He should come himself, or send sufficient Deputies, to answer to the Complaints of the Queen of Scots against him and his confederates, and give just Reasons for the deposing her: otherwise she would forthwith set her at Liberty, and restore her with all the Power she could make to her Kingdom. And withall she warned him not to sell the Queen's Attire and rich Ornaments, though the Estates had permitted it.

Murray obeyed, forasmuch as he had no other means to maintain his Regency than such as depended upon England, and the Lords of the Kingdom which were deputed for this business refused it. He came therefore himself to York, being the City appointed for that purpose, and with him seven of his inwardest Friends, as Deputies for the Infant-King, namely James Earl of Morton, Adam Bishop of Orkney, Robert Commendator of Dunfermelin, Patrick Baron of Lindsey, James Mac-Gilly, Henry Balnaw. And in company of these came Lidington, allured by Murray's Promises, (for at home he durst not leave him,) and George Buchanan, a most sworn man to Murray. And the very same day came thither Thomas Howard Duke of Norfolk, Thomas Ratcliff Earl of Sussex, a little before made President of the North, and Sir Ralph Sadleir Knight, one of the Privy Council, Commissioners appointed to hear and examine the Cause of her Deposing. For the Queen of Scots (who took it very hardly that Queen Elizabeth would not hear her in her own Presence, and yet commanded her Subjects to be heard against her before her Commissioners, considering that she, being an absolute Princess, was not bound but at her own pleasure to answer her Subjects which accused her,) appeared John Lesley Bishop of Rosse, William Baron of Levingston, Robert Baron of Boyd, Gawin Commendator of Kilwinin, John Gordon, and James Cockborn.

After they were come together the 7th of October, and had shewed to one another their Commissions whereby their Authority was granted them, Lidington standing by, turned to the Scots, and with wonderfull freedom of speech admonished them.

That forasmuch as by the Authority granted by Queen Elizabeth to her Commissioners it seemed that she aimed at nothing else, but that the said Scottish Deputies should stain the Reputation of the Queen, the King's Mother, and blemish her Name, that so she, as an indifferent Umpire, might give Sentence there upon; they should therefore advisedly consider how great Hatred and Danger they should draw upon themselves, not onely amongst the Scots which were devoted to the Queen, but also with the other Princes of Christendom, and her Kinsmen in France, by accusing her criminously, and bringing her Reputation in question, in this publick and juridical way, before the English professed Enemies to the Scottish Nation; and what Account they should be able another day to give unto the King of such an insolent Accusation, so prejudicial to the Kingdom of Scotland, when he, arriving at riper years, should construe this to reflect upon the Honour of himself, his Mother, and his Countrey. He therefore thought it the wisest course to forbear this odious Accusation of so Great a Prince, unless the Queen of England would enter into a mutual League with them of Defence and Offence against all men which should be trouble for the same. And of these things (he said) he friendly admonished them in respect of his Office, as being Secretary of Scotland.

They, looking one upon another, held their peace.

The Queen of Scots Deputies, (for to them was the first place of Honour given) before they took their Oath, protested, that although the Q. of Scots thought good that the Causes betwixt her and her disloyal Subjects should be debated before the English; yet did she not thereby acknowledge her self to be under the sovereign Command of any, forasmuch as she was a free Princess, and under the Authority and Vassalage of none. The English Commissioners in like manner protested, that they did in no-wise admit of that Protestation, in prejudice of that Title which the Kings of England have long since challenged, as Superiour Lords of the Kingdom of Scotland.

The next day the Queen of Scots Deputies delivered a Declaration in writing,

> How James Earl of Morton, John Earl of Marre, Alexander Earl of Glencarn, Humes, Lindsey, Rethuen, Sempill, &c. had levied an Army, in the Queen's Name, against the Queen, and having intercepted and most unworthily treated her, had thrust her into Prison at Lough-Levin, broken into the Office of the Mint, taken away the Stamps, the Gold and Silver, coined and uncoined, and crowned her Infant Son King, whose Authority James Earl of Murray had usurped under the Title of Regent or Viceroy, and had seized upon all the Fortresses, Wealth and Revenues of the Kingdom. Then they laid open, How she, as soon as ever she had escaped out of Prison, after eleven months Restraint, had publickly declared upon her Oath, that whatsoever she had done in Prison had been extorted from her against her will by Force,

Threats, and Terrour of Death. Nevertheless, to the end the publick Tranquillity might be established, she had granted Authority to the Earls of Argile, Eglinton, Cassils and Rothsay, to compound the matter with her Adversaries; who notwithstanding when she purposed to cross the Countrey to Dunbriton, set upon her with Armed power, slew very many of her faithfull Subjects, some they carried away Prisoners, others they proscribed, and all this for no other cause but that they had done their Princess faithful Service. Being compelled by the most unworthy Injuries of theirs she had retired her self into England, to crave Aid of Queen Elizabeth, which had been often promised her, that thereby she might be restored to her Countrey and former Dignity.

Some few days after Murray the Regent and the Deputies for the Infant-King (so they termed themselves) answered,

That Henry Lord Darly, the King's Father, being made away, James Hepburn Earl of Bothwell (who was holden to be Authour of the Murther) was gotten in such Grace and Favour with the Queen, that he took her by strong hand, though not against her will, carried her away to Dunbar, and took her to Wife, putting away his Wife he had before: That the Lords of Scotland, being much moved thereat, thought nothing more worthy and befitting them, (forasmuch as that Murther was commonly imputed to a Conspiracy of many Noblemen,) than that Bothwell, the Authour of the Murther, should be punished, the Queen set at Liberty, and loosed from that unjust Marriage, and the Safety of the young King and the Tranquillity of the Realm provided for: That when the matter was now coming on to a Battel, the Queen sent away Bothwell, thundered out Threats against the Lords, and breathed Revenge, insomuch as it was necessary to commit her to Custody until Bothwell were found and punished: That she, being wearied with the Troubles incident to the Crown, had voluntarily resigned her Kingdom, and transferred it to her Son, appointing Murray to be Regent: That hereupon her Son was solemnly anointed and inaugurated King: And that all these things were approved and confirmed by the Estates of the Realm in Parliament, and the Scottish Commonwealth revived by equal and indifferent Administration of Justice; till some men, impatient of the publick Quiet, cunningly got the Queen out of Custody, contrary to what they had sworn, and breaking their Allegeance to the King, took up Arms: over whom though the

King (by God's Blessing) got the Victory, yet they dare still most confidently attempt any thing in their hostile mind against their King and Countrey. Most necessary therefore it is that the King's Authority be maintained inviolate against such Seditious people.

To this the Queen of Scots Deputies, repeating again their former Protestation, opposed their Replication, (as they term it).

Whereas Murray (say they) and the Conspirators affirm, that they took up Arms against the Queen because Bothwell, whom they accuse as Murtherer of the King, was in great Grace and Authority with her; they cannot by that wipe away the note of their perfidiousness, inasmuch as the Queen never knew that he made away the King; yea, on the contrary, she knew that he was acquitted from the Murther by his Peers, and that the same Acquittal was affirmed by the Authority of Parliament, with the consent even of those that now accuse him, and at that time were a means to perswade the Queen to take him to her Husband, as the meetest man of all others to sway the Scepter: and to him they ingaged their Fidelity by a Writing under their Hands, and disapproved not the Marriage so much as by a word, till such time as they had drawn to their Party the Captain of Edenborough Castle, and the Provost of the City. But then in the dead time of the Night they in hostile manner assaulted the Castle of Borthwick, where the Queen lay; and she escaping by favour of the Darkness of the night, they presently levied an Army, under pretence to defend the Queen, and with Banners displayed went to intercept the Queen as she purposed to goe to Edenborough, and, sending Grange before, warned her to dismiss Bothwell, till he should be arraigned: which, to spare the shedding of Bloud, she willingly did. But Grange gave secret Notice to Bothwell to be gone, and gave him his Faith that no man should pursue him; insomuch as he departed by their Consent, whom they might afterwards have easily taken. But, having now taken the Queen, they neglected him, that they might carry on their own ambitious Designs. And whereas they were Subjects, and had vowed their Allegeance to the Queen, and yet had used her more rigorously than stood with her Royal Majesty, no marvel if she spake unto them somewhat roughly. When she willingly referred her Cause to all the Estates of the Realm, and signified the same by Lidington her Secretary, they would not so much as hear him, but carried her secretly by night to Lough-

Levin, and shut her up in Prison. And whereas they say that she, being wearied with the Troubles incident to the Crown, had resigned her Kingdom; it is most untrue: for she was neither spent with Age, nor weakened with Sickness, but was both in Mind and Body able to manage the weightiest Businesses. This is most certain, that the Earl of Athol, Tullibardine and Liding-ton, (who were also of her Council,) advised her to subscribe to the Instrument of Resignation, that so she might escape Death, which was most certainly intended against her; saying moreover, that this could not prejudice her, being a Prisoner, nor her Heirs after her, forasmuch as Imprisonment is a just Fear, and a Prom-ise made by one imprisoned is, by the Judgment of the Learned in the Laws, of no Validity. That Sir Nicholas Throckmorton also persuaded her to the same by a Schedule or Scroll written with his own Hand, whom she also requested to signifie to the Queen of England, that she had unwillingly and constrainedly sub-scribed to the Resignation. Moreover, that Lindsey, when he presented the Instrument of Resignation to her to subscribe, de-nounced unto her the Terrours of Death, and drave her to sub-scribe it weeping, without once reading the same. And the Lord of Lough-Levin Castle refused to set to his Hand as a Witness, for that he saw and certainly knew that she subscribed against her will. Most unreasonable therefore and unjust was the Resig-nation, whereat nothing was assigned her to live upon, nor her Liberty granted her, nor Safety of Life promised her. So that, in the judgment of any indifferent men, such an unjust Resignation cannot seem to have prejudiced her Royal Majesty, which, as soon as she was at Liberty, she renounced (as forced) by a Declaration made before many Lords of the Realm. Neither ought those things to be any Prejudice to the Queen which they boasted they have done by Authority of Parliament: for whereas about a hundred Earls, Bishops and Barons have their Voices in the Parliaments of Scotland; in this tumultuary Parliament there were not above four Earls, one Bishop, one or two Abbats, and six Barons: and of that small number, some there were that entred their Protestation, that nothing should be done in Prej-udice of the Queen or her Successours, because she was a Prisoner. Neither was either the English or French Embassadour admitted to her Presence, that they might understand from her own Mouth whether she voluntarily resigned her Kingdom, though they most earnestly desired it. And the Commonwealth hath been so far from being justly and indifferently governed under the usurping

Regent, that Impiety never raged with more impunity, plucking down Religious Houses, subverting the most noble Families, and afflicting the miserable Commonality. They most earnestly therefore intreated, that the Queen of England would by her Favour, Counsell and Assistence forthwith aid the Queen her Kinswoman, most unworthily abused.

Thus much out of the very original Writings of the Deputies, which I my self have seen.

When the English Commissioners, having heard all this, required Murray to shew the Causes of such Severity against an absolute Queen, and to prove them more substantially, (for what was hitherto produced, was not confirmed by any Witnesses, but by Writings and Letters of suspected credit;) and Lidington had secretly given them to understand, that he had many times counterfeited the Queen's Hand; he refused to accuse his Sister any farther before Strangers, unless the Queen of England would promise on her part the Protection of the Infant-King, and quite to forsake the Queen of Scots. But when they could not by virtue of their Commission promise any such thing, one or two of the Deputies of both sides were called up to London; to whom Queen Elizabeth declared, that she could not yet acquit the Subjects from Blame against their Princess: nevertheless she would intercede with her for them, and hear whether they had any thing farther to alledge in their own Justification. Murray who followed them, flatly refused to accuse his Sister, but upon such Condition as he had insisted on at York.

Now were the English Commissioners recalled, and their Commission determined, to the great Joy of the Duke, who had ever much favoured the Queen of Scots Title to the Succession, and thought that nothing else was now aimed at, but that she might be branded with some note of eternal Infamy, and thereby excluded as unworthy, together with her young Son, from all right of Succession in England; and he thought himself delivered from a double Danger. For he feared lest if he had given Sentence against her, he should both wrong his own Conscience, and undoe her: and if for her, he should incur the implacable Displeasure of the Queen, and the Hatred of all such as were averse from the Queen of Scots in respect of Religion, or for other causes.

97

But whereas Stirs and Commotions were now raised in Scotland by the Friends of the expulsed Queen, and Murray's presence was needfull there, he drew up an Accusation before the Queen, and before Bacon Lord Keeper, the Duke of Norfolk, the Earls of Arundell, Sussex, Leicester, Clinton Lord Admiral, Sir William Cecyl, and Sir Ralph Sadleir, who by a new Patent were made Commissioners to hear and examine the matter: and before them he produced conjectural Articles, the Testimonies of some, and the Decrees made in an Assembly of the Estates, and especially certain Love-Letters and Verses written (as he affirmed) with the Queen's own Hand; and all to prove her guilty of her Husband's Death: and Buchanan's Book, intitled *The Detection*, he delivered to them to reade; which found small credit with the greatest part of the Commissioners, he being a man partial on that side, and of mercenary Credit. And for the Letters and Verses, (forasmuch as they wanted Names, Subscriptions and Dates, and many Falsifiers there every-where are, which can so cunningly resemble and counterfeit other mens Hands, that the true can not be known from the counterfeit,) Queen Elizabeth give little credit to them, though there were between them a womanish Emulation, wherewith that Sex is much transported; and she held it sufficient, that by means of these Accusations some Scandal would stick upon the Queen of Scots.

But when the Queen of Scots Deputies heard that she was so scandalously accused by Murray, they were ready enough to answer: but she had already recalled their Commission, having secretly learned of some English-men skilled in the Laws that she might lawfully doe it, forasmuch as the Queen's former Commission, granted to the Duke and the rest for Cognizance of the Cause was also recalled. And the new Commissioners, whereof she knew one or two to be partial towards her, she flatly refused, unless the French and Spanish Embassadours might be joyned with them, and she might be publickly admitted to defend her Innocency before the Queen and them, and Murray might be stayed, and called to his Trial, who might (she said) be proved to be the Contriver and Plotter of the Lord Darly's Death. All which when Norfolk, Arundell, Sussex, Leicester and Clinton thought to be but reasonable, Queen Elizabeth, being somewhat angry, said openly, That the Queen of Scots would never want an Advocate as long as Norfolk lived. And she held it sufficient, to call together her Privy-Counsellours, as also the Earls of Northumberland, Westmorland, Shrewsbury, Worcester, Huntingdon and Warwick, and to impart unto them the Crimes objected by Murray, yet under an Oath of Secrecy, lest they might prejudice either party. And whereas Murray was called home, and the Lord Boyd (as was commonly bruited abroad) endeavoured privily to convey the Queen of Scots out of Custody, the matter was put off till another time; Queen Elizabeth from her heart (as it seemed) misliking the Insolency of the Scots in Deposing the Queen.

At this time was come out of France Hamilton Duke of Chastel-herault, being privily sent by the Guises, to move a Question against Murray, concerning the Government of the Kingdom of Scotland in the Minority of the King; who stifly maintained before Queen Elizabeth, that, by the Customes and Ordinances of the Countrey, he was to be preferred in the Administration, as next in Bloud unto the King, before Murray, being base born. Murray and the King's Commissioners shewed the contrary, "That the Regency was to be committed, not to the next of Kin, but to the most fit persons to be chosen by the Consent of the Estates: And that it were most unjust, to deliver the young King into his hands, who, ambitiously gaping after the Crown, in regard of his nearness of Bloud, might easily violate his Right out of a desire to reign. And that this was to be feared in the Hamiltons above all others, who had had great Animosities against the King's Fore-fathers the Earls of Lenox, had wickedly murthered the King's Great-grand-father by the Father's side, expelled Matthew the King's poor Grandfather out of Scotland, and this Hamilton himself had by his bitter Hatred much vexed and troubled Henry the King's Father, and delivered his Mother to the French King, that he might the easilier get the possession of the Kingdom himself." Queen Elizabeth, having heard all this, told Hamilton that it was a most unreasonable thing which he demanded: and withall she commanded, that he should not depart out of England, before such time as Murray was returned into Scotland.

Murray, a little before his Departure had cunningly (as I

shall shew anon) propounded to the Duke of Norfolk a Marriage with the Queen of Scots, and also to the Queen her self had secretly given Hopes by Melvin of being restored to her Kingdom: and withall, to alienate Queen Elizabeth from the Queen of Scots, he had spread abroad Rumours, that she had conveyed her Title to England to the Duke of Anjou, and that the same Conveyance was confirmed at Rome. He shewed Letters also (whether true or counterfeit, I will not say,) which the Queen of Scots had written to her Friends, wherein she both taxed Queen Elizabeth, as if she had treated her contrary to what she had promised, and boasted of her Hope of Aid from elsewhere. This indeed troubled Queen Elizabeth, neither could she guess from whence that new Hope should spring: considering that in France the Civil War was broke out so far, that the Bishop of Rhenes was sent to Queen Elizabeth from the King, to request her that she would not intermeddle with the Affairs of France; and the Duke of Alva, who was come the last year into the Netherlands to root out the Protestant Religion, could doe her no good, having his hands full of Troubles.

But (as it came to light afterward, and as Hieronymo Catena, Secretary to Cardinal Alexandrine, hath left in writing,) Robert Ridolph, a Florentine, who had lived long time as a Factor in London, was employed by Pius Quintus Bishop of Rome, (for he durst not send his Nuncio openly,) to excite the Papists in England secretly against Queen Elizabeth; which he most carefully and closely performed. There grew also a Suspicion, (yet a light one,) by means of secret Conferences at York between Lidington, the Bishop of Rosse, and the Duke of Norfolk, whom the other two besought to employ his Counsell and Endeavour for the Safety of the most afflicted Queen, offering him also Marriage with her: which Offer he with a modest Answer refused, as being full of Danger. Nevertheless as far as he could with his Honour, saving his Allegiance to his Prince and Countrey, he promised he would not fail the afflicted Queen. This Suspicion was much increased by the often resorting of Ligon, the Duke of Norfolk's Servant, (a man extremely Popish,) to Bolton, (a Castle of the Lord Scroop's,) where the Queen of Scots was kept under the Custody of Sir Francis Knolles, who pretended onely to see and salute the Lord Scroop's Wife, which was the Duke of Norfolk's Sister. And though by all this there could no certainty be made, yet was the Queen of Scots removed from Bolton, where all the Neighbours round about were Popish, into the more inner parts of the Land, to Tutbury, and committed to the Custody of George Earl of Shrewsbury.

Now Queen Elizabeth took greater Care for the Safety of Religion, the Commonwealth, and her own Person; and the rather, because both the Guises in France, and the Duke of Alva in the Netherlands, had begun to put in Execution their Designs laid at Bayon, for the Extirpation of the Protestant Religion. For in France the Peace propounded in the beginning of this Year was vanished into Smoak, Edicts being published, whereby the Exercise of the Reformed Religion was utterly forbidden, the Professours thereof removed from publick Offices, and the Ministers of the Word commanded to depart the Realm within a time prefixed. And now every-where the Alarm was taken against them, and much Cruelty used toward them, notwithstanding that Queen Elizabeth had with much earnestness solicited by Norris her Embassadour, that a sound and sincere Peace might be made; and had sundry times advised the King, that he would not by unreasonable Remedies incense their minds; and that above all things he would beware of those, who, by rooting out his faithfull Subjects, sought to weaken the Strength of France in that measure, that it might be exposed as a Prey to others. But when he gave no ear to these Intreaties of hers, but gathered Money and Auxiliary forces out of Italy, Germany and Spain; she also, lest she should fail those which were united with her in one common Cause, liberally sent an hundred thousand Angels and Munition for War to the Protestants, (who now religiously protested, that they took not Arms against their King, but for their own Defence,) and entertained with all kind of Courtesie such French people as fled into England; as also Netherlanders, of whom a great multitude had withdrawn themselves into England as to a Sanctuary, while the Duke of Alva breathed nothing but Slaughter and Bloud against them. These by the Queen's Permission seated themselves at Norwich, Colchester, Sandwich, Maidstone, and Hampton, to the great Benefit and Advantage of the English: for they were the first that brought into England the Art of making those slight Stuffs which are called Bays and

Says, and other such like Stuffs of Linen and Woollen weaving.

And here let it not seem from the purpose, if I give a brief touch from what Beginnings the Netherland War brake forth at this time, whereof I must of necessity make often mention, forasmuch as it is joyned and twisted with English matters and Counsels.

When the Spaniard would by no Intreaty be perswaded to moderate his bloudy Edicts concerning matters of Religion in the Netherlands, but exercised much Cruelty over mens Consciences by the Spanish Inquisition, prohibiting the Assembly of the Estates of the Netherland Provinces to be holden, (which was the onely and usual Remedy for compounding of matters,) and governing the Commonwealth by Decrees out of Spain, and not by Advice of the Natives of the Countrey, a few of the Rabble of the people, raising a Tumult, outragiously threw down Images every-where in the Churches, and brake them in pieces. And though this Tumult was soon quieted, yet the Spaniard, following the Advice of those who much desired to lay the Yoke upon a most free Nation, charged the whole People with the publick Crime of Rebellion, taking occasion from this private Rashness of a few; and (as if their Freedom were now quite lost) sent Don Ferdinando Alvares Duke of Alva, a cruel and stern man, to take upon him the Government: who, being no way allied in Bloud to the Prince, was placed in the supreme Command, contrary to the Customs of the Countrey, took away all Authority from the ordinary Provincial Councils, erected new Courts of Audience, condemning the Noblemen by such as were not their Judges, and putting them to death, placing Garrisons of Spaniards in the Cities and Towns, building Citadels to curb them, and forcibly exacting the twentieth penny of Lands, and the tenth of Moveables upon every Alienation; whereby he raised a long and dangerous War.

About this time a great Summe of Money was sent by the Merchants of Genua and other Italian Merchants out of Spain into the Netherlands, in a great Ship of Biscay, and four lesser Vessels which the Spaniards call Zabras, to be employed in Bank. Which Ships being chased by Tury Chastellerie a French-man, and defended by William Winter an English-man, hardly escaped into Plimmouth, Falmouth and South-hampton, Ports of

England. Which as soon as the Queen heard of, she commanded the Officers of those Ports to use the Spaniards with all Kindness, and defend their Ships against the French. And Gerard De-Spesi, Knight of the Order of Calatrava, the King of Spain's Embassadour in England, fearing what the French might doe, solicited the Queen (who upon his Credit thought it to be the King of Spain's Money) that fresh Warrants might be sent for Defence of the Ships against the French, who lay hard by ready to seize on them. Which having obtained, he solicited again, that the Money might be conveyed through England, and so sent safely by Sea to Antwerp. The Queen granted it, and promised Security both by Sea and Land. Mean-while the French men missed narrowly of carrying away one of the Ships, had not the English beaten them off. Therefore to secure the Money, it was thought the wisest course to land it out of the Ships. But before it was all come on shore, De-Spesi, being over hasty to believe the worst, gave the Duke of Alva notice that the Queen had seized the Money. And while he adviseth with the Duke of Alva about the matter, Odet Cardinal of Chastillion, (who had retired himself hither from the French Tumults,) gave notice to Queen Elizabeth, that the Money was none of the King of Spain's, but belonged to certain Merchants of Genua, which the Duke of Alva went about to draw to his own use, for the ruining of the Protestants, against the Merchants wills. Hereupon it was debated amongst the Council of England, whether the money was to be detained, or not. Most of them thought best it should be sent over into the Netherlands, lest the Spaniard, a most potent Prince, being already sufficiently incensed against the English, should be more exasperated. But Queen Elizabeth, being certainly informed by one or two of the Owners of the Money, (who were in great Fear lest the Duke of Alva should seize upon it,) that it belonged wholly to the Merchants, and nothing at all to the King of Spain, who had onely suffered it to be exported out of Spain, resolved to borrow it of the Merchants, giving them Security for the same, as Princes usually doe of Goods found in their Ports, and the Spaniard himself had often done the same of late. And this she protested to the Spanish Embassadour, what time he delivered the Duke of Alva's Letters for sending the Money over, promising religiously to restore it, as soon as it should appear for certain to be the Spaniard's own Money. Upon which very day, to wit, the 29th of December, the Duke of Alva being in a furious Rage seized upon the English-mens Goods everywhere in the Netherlands, and kept the English-men Prisoners with a Guard of Souldiers: so as any man might well perceive by the observation of the time, that the Duke of Alva intended this against the English for a Terrour, howsoever the Queen should make Satisfaction for the Money. But she, nothing terrified, commanded on the contrary the Netherlands and their Wares and Ships in England to be seized on, which were far more than those of the English which the Duke found in the Netherlands: so as he repented him too late of what he had begun, who had unreasonably made the Wound to fester, which in the beginning might easily have been healed.

The last day saving one of this Year was the last day of Roger Ascham's life, (pardon, I pray, this my short Digression in memory of a Good man,) who being born in Yorkshire, and brought up at Cambridge, was one of the first of our Countreymen that polished the Latin and Greek, and the Pureness of the Style, not without commendations for Eloquence. He was a while Schoolmaster to Queen Elizabeth, and her Secretary for the Latin Tongue. Nevertheless, being too-too much given to Dicing and Cock fighting, he lived and died a poor man; leaving behind him two most excellent Books, as Monuments of his Wit, in the English Tongue, whereof he intituled the one *Toxophilus* and the other *Scholarcha*. But return we to the matter in hand.

VII

The Twelfth Year of Her Reign,
Anno Domini 1569

The sixth day of January was set forth at London a Proclamation concerning the English-mens Goods detained by the Duke of Alva, wherein most of the things already spoken of were expressed, and the Blame laid upon De-Spesi. Who published another Writing to the contrary, wherein he signified that the said Proclamation was not set forth by the Queen, but in the Queen's Name by some that bare no Good will to the Spaniard, and favoured the Rebels of the Netherlands. The Queen's former Kindness toward the Spaniards he commended, bewailed the Alienation of her mind without cause, stomached that there was no more Credit given to him being an Embassadour, and to the Duke of Alva's Letters, and marvelled that the said Money was detained, whereas it was more for the Interest of the Queen (he said) to supply the Spaniard with Money against his Rebels, than to take any from him. And finally he taxed her as if she had offered the first Wrong, and excused the Duke of Alva's Fact and himself. And not content herewith, he spred abroad defamatory Libels, wherein he scandalously blurred the Queen's Reputation, under the name of Amadis Oriana. For which he was reprehended, and a Guard set upon him for a day or two: and she at large complained of these and the like things to the Spanish, but all in vain.

Upon the Detaining of this Money certain Lords of England, amongst whom were the Marquess of Winchester, the Duke of Norfolk, the Earls of Arundell, Northumberland, Westmorland,

Pembroke, Leicester, and others, pick'd Quarrels against Cecyl, as they had done once or twice before about the Money sent to the Protestants of France: but indeed the true cause was, for that they thought much of his Power with the Queen, suspected him to favour the House of Suffolk in the Succession of the Crown, and feared lest he would hinder the course of their Designs. They conspired therefore secretly to cast him into the Tower, Throck-morton his Emulatour suggesting to them, that if he were but once imprisoned, means to undoe him would not be far to seek. But the Queen (by whose Discovery I know not) came to the knowledge hereof in good time, and Cecyl, through the mag-nanimous Fortitude of his Princess, (who, coming upon them in the very instant of time, restrained them by her Beck,) easily defeated the Plot that was laid against him. And withall she brake the neck of another more secret Design of theirs, openly to pro-claim the Queen of Scots undoubted Heir of England, if any thing should fall out other than well to Queen Elizabeth; and this in opposition to a Book sent abroad in favour of the Title of Suffolk.

Now came D' Assonville from the Duke of Alva, to demand the Money detained. But because he had no Letters from the Spaniard, the Queen referred him to her Council; to whom at first he refused to apply: yet shortly after he did, had Audience, and after a month's stay returned without effecting what he came about.

And now the English Merchants conveyed their Merchandizes to Hamburgh in Germany, as to a new Mart or Staple, the Duke of Alva prohibited all Commerce with the English, and ap-pointed Searchers, that nothing should be brought in or carried out of the Netherlands by them: amongst which Searchers, John Story, an English Fugitive, Doctour of the Laws, was a busie and active man, who had before consulted with Prestall, a Magical Impostour, against the Queen's Life, and had given Advice to the Duke of Alva about invading his native Countrey. But he being drawn by a Wile into a Ship, which was reported to have brought over English Merchandizes and Heretical Books, they presently set sail with him, and brought him into England, where he was afterwards executed, as we will shew in its proper place.

The Duke of Alva, not yet content with all this, commanded

that none but Ships of War should put to Sea from the Netherlands, and that they should fall upon the English wheresoever they should find them. Which also he procured to be done in Spain, where the English Merchants and Mariners were drawn into the Inquisition, and condemned to the Galleys, and their Goods confiscate. And the King of Spain commanded by his Letters sent to the Count of Mont-Agund, Governor of Andaluzia, that no Oil, Allum, Sugar, Spices, or other such like Commodities, should be transported into England, supposing that if the English were debarred of these things, they would soon break forth into Rebellion: and withall he dealt with the Duke of Norfolk and the Earl of Ormond by secret Messengers, that the one should give the Queen somewhat to doe in Ireland, and the other in England; which they ingenuously revealed, such was their Fidelity to their Princess. As soon as this was known to the Maritime people of England, incredible it is with how great Alacrity they put to Sea, and how readily they exercised Piracy against the Spaniards; insomuch as Proclamations were set forth to restrain them, whereby all men were prohibited to buy any Merchandizes of Sea-robbers.

In these days the Traffick of the English Merchants was no less obstructed in Russia than in the Netherlands, as well by means of the false Dealing of their Factours, and their untoward Dissension amongst themselves, as of the Germans and Russians Hatred against them: whilst the Russians complained of their cunning Dealing, and the raising of the Prices to their Merchandizes: and the English which were not of the Muscovia Company and Germans complained of the Monopoly. To salve those Soars, Thomas Randolph was sent the last year into Russia: who though he were not very welcome to the Emperour, forasmuch, as he seriously solicited onely the matter of Trade, and mentioned nothing at all of the League which I have spoken of before in the year 1567; nevertheless at his Intercession the Emperour, out of his singular Good will to the Queen and the English Nation, granted to the English Company in Russia Freedom from all payment of Custome, and Liberty to carry and vend their Merchandizes wheresoever they would throughout all the Countries of his most spatious Empire, and to transport them into Persia and Media by the Caspian Sea, (whereas the Merchants of other

Nations might not go a mile beyond the City of Moskow;) he gave them also Houses to twist their Ropes and Cables into for Shipping, and a piece of Ground five miles in circuit with Wood to make Iron, and took the English into an *Opprisney*, that is, into a choice Seed of his people.

And now the English began more confidently to survey those Countries, carrying their Merchandizes up the River Dwina in Boats made of one whole Piece or Tree, which they rowed and towed up the Stream with Halsers, as far as Wologda; and from thence by land seven days journey to Yeraslaw; and then, by the Wolga, (which is about a mile over, and runneth through a clayish Soil, beset with Oaks and Birchen-trees,) thirty days and as many nights Journey down the River to Astracan. And from Astracan (where they built Ships) they did (which was a very great and memorable Adventure) many times cross the Caspian Sea, which is very full of Flats and Shelves, and pierced through the vast Desarts of Hyrcania and Bactriana to Teverin and Casbin, Cities of Persia, in hope at length to discover Cathay. But the Wars which shortly after grew hot between the Turks and Persians, and the Robberies of the Barbarians, interrupted this laudable Enterprise of the Londoners. The Emperour sent back Randolph with Presents, and with him Andreas Gregoriwitz Saviena, with a splendid Train, after the manner of that Nation, who was gallantly entertained by the Londoners, and honourably received by the Queen. This Andreas shewed a certain League written in the Russian Tongue, which he required might be ratified by secret Letters in the self-same words in his presence, and be translated with all the Letters into the Russian Tongue, and confirmed by the Queen's Hand, Seal and Oath: as also that the Queen would send an Embassadour of her own into Russia, who in like manner should receive secret Letters of the Emperour's in the same words, confirmed with his Seal and the kissing of the Cross in his presence. The Queen concluded the League with a Clause of Reservation, "So far forth as she lawfully might by the League formerly contracted with other Princes, to yield one another mutual Aid against their common Enemies, so as nothing should be done against Law and Right." And if he should by any Misfortune be constrained, either by domestical or foreign Enemies, to leave his Countrey, she promised most religiously in the word of a Christian Princess, before his Embassadour and her inwardest Counsellours, and confirmed it with her Seal, to receive and entertain him, his Wife and Children, with all Honour worthy so great a Prince, to assign him a convenient place for his Abode, to permit him the free Exercise of his Religion, and Liberty to depart at his pleasure: for these were the things which he had earnestly intreated in those secret Letters. But so far was all this from satisfying that fierce-natur'd man, to whom his own mind and will was a Law, that in a long Letter having reckoned all his Civilities to the English Nation, he twittingly upbraided them therewith, stomached that the Queen sent not an Embassadour with his to receive his Oath, and taxed her as if she neglected him, and were too mindfull of the Merchants Business, (which were matters unbeseeming a Prince;) which Merchants he contemptuously and disgracefully charged as a sordid kind of people, that rather gaped after Wealth than fought their Prince's honour, suspecting that they crossed his Designs, and sharply threatening to recall their Privileges. Which notwithstanding he did not, being pacified by a kind Letter of the Queen's sent by Jenkinson, but most diligently observed her as his Sister as long as he lived, solicited her many times for a more solid Confirmation of the said League, and loved the English passing well above all other nations.

Now Murray, who, by putting the Queen of Scots, the Duke of Norfolk, and others in England, in hopes of the said Queen's Restauration, had procured himself a safe return into Scotland, (for she had restrained the Scots that lay in wait for his Life, and commanded them they should not hinder his Return,) was no sooner come to Edenborough, but he assembled the Noblemen that were addicted to the Queen, pretending to consult about her Restitution. Whither when Hamilton Duke of Chastel herault, (constituted Vice-gerent of the Realm by the Queen,) and Heris, both perswaded by the credulous Queen's Letter, came before the rest, he, fearing some Fraudulent dealing, circumvented them, and, not staying for the coming of the rest, shut them up in Prison, and forthwith heavily prosecuted the Queen's Favourers with all the Injuries of War.

Hereupon Rumours were spred all over Scotland against Murray, to wit, "That he had made an Agreement with Queen Elizabeth, That the young King of Scots should be sent into England to be brought up; That the Castles of Edenborough and Sterling should be manned with English Garrisons; That Dunbriton should be subdued for the use of the English; That Murray should be proclaimed lawfull Successour of the Kingdom of Scotland, in case the King should die without Issue; and That he should hold the Kingdom as Queen Elizabeth's Homager." These things were so commonly bruited abroad, and with a kind of probability did so trouble mens minds all over Britain, that Queen Elizabeth thought it concerned both her and Murray in Reputation, to wipe away these Aspersions. She set forth therefore a publick Writing, wherein she declared "in the word of a Queen, That these things were most untrue, and forged by such as envied the Tranquillity of both Kingdoms: and that there had not (to her knowledge) been any Contract made in word or writing between her or her Ministers and Murray, since he came last into England. But the Earl of Lenox, the young King's Grand-father, requested her, that the King, if he could not be safe in Scotland from the Practices and Attempts of wicked men, might be sent into England." She affirmed moreover, "That she held for false whatsoever was reported of any Contract between Murray and the Earl of Hertford, to wit, that they should mutually aid and assist each other in seizing upon the Crowns of both Kingdoms. In brief, there was no fault (she said) in her, that matters betwixt the Queen of Scots and her young Son were not yet agreed, and she would labour an Accord between them." And labour it she did for certain, although she found some Conflict in her self, on the one side out of Fear grown from an inveterate Emulation, which amongst Princesses never dieth; and on the other side out of Commiseration and Compassion arising from her often calling to mind of humane Frailty.

This Commiseration as the Queen of Scots more moved, so did she diminish her Fear by many Letters most full of Love, wherein she religiously promised, both for her Courtesie she had found, and the very near Kindred betwixt them, that she would attempt nothing against her, nor be beholden to any other Prince for her Restitution. Insomuch as Queen Elizabeth earnestly importuned Murray and other Scots by Wood, which was Murray's Secretary, for the Restoring of her to her former Royal Dignity: and if not so, yet that she might enjoy the Royal Title jointly with her Son: and if this would not be granted, yet that at leastwise she might as a private person spend her days at Home amongst her own People, freely, securely and honourably. But she could never move Murray, who now ruled all the Roast.

At this time a Bruit ran amongst men of better note, that the Duke of Norfolk should marry the Queen of Scots, which according to mens Affections was upon different Reasons desired, while the Papists hoped that hereby their Religion would be advanced, and others that it would make for the good of the Commonwealth. Certainly very many which saw the Queen averse from Marriage, and that foreign Princes, Enemies to England, cast their eyes and minds upon the Queen of Scots as the most undoubted Heir of England, thought it would make more for the setling of things, and the keeping the Queen of Scots within her bounds, "if she were joyned in Marriage to the Duke of Norfolk, the greatest and Noblest man of all the Nobility of England, a man in great Favour with the people, and bred up in the Protestant Religion, than if she were married to a foreign Prince, who might by her endanger both Kingdoms, and come to the Inheritance of both, which they heartily wished might be united in a Prince of the English Bloud, in case any thing other than well should befall the Infant-King of Scots. And him also they propounded to draw into England, that he, the true Heir of England, being brought up amongst the English, might be the more dear to the English, all Scruple concerning the Succession might be taken away, and Queen Elizabeth might be freed from Fear of any thing to be attempted against her by the Duke and the Queen of Scots, when she had him in her own power." Moreover, (to the end that the Duke might not enterprise any thing against him, but love him the better,) they projected "that the Lady Margaret, the Duke's young and onely Daughter, should be espoused unto him *de futuro*." Amongst these Consulters were the Earls of Arundell, Northumberland, Westmorland, Sussex, Pembroke, and South-hampton, with many Barons, yea and Leicester also himself, (whether dissemblingly and cunningly, for the overthrowing of the Duke, is uncertain.) All which notwithstanding were of opinion, that the matter was first to be imparted to the Queen, and left to her Will and Pleasure: and that she should prescribe Laws, whereby her own Person, Religion and the Realm might be most fully secured. But take the matter summarily (if you please) from the very Beginning, out of the written Confession of the Duke himself, which I have seen, and out of the Commentaries and Memorials of the Bishop of Rosse, who had a very great hand in this Business.

When the Commissioners met the last year at York, Lidington and the Bishop of Rosse dealt with the Duke, as they were Hawking, about a Marriage to be contracted betwixt him and the Queen of Scots; as Murray also did himself afterwards at Hampton-Court. This Murray, in private Conference with the Duke, and also with some others, pretended that he desired nothing more, than that matters might be composed in Scotland, and the Queen of Scots, his dearest Sister, restored to her former Authority, so as she would truly and heartily receive her Subjects into former Grace and Favour, all Grudges on both sides being buried in Oblivion. Nevertheless he feared lest if she should take an Husband at her own choice out of France, Spain, or Austria, she would revenge the Wrongs she had received, alter the received Religion in Scotland, and work great Danger to England. To prevent all this, he promised his best Help and Assistence, that she, which had been married, first to a Boy, and afterwards to a Young man improvident and after frantick, (for those were his words,) might now at length be joyned in Marriage with the Duke, a man of ripe Judgment; which would mainly tend to the Tranquillity of both Kingdoms, the Security of both Queens, and the Establishing of Religion; whilst he (out of his great Respect towards the Queen of England) should the more auspiciously keep Scotland in Amity with the English, and the more easily draw the Queen of Scots to the true Religion, which he had imbraced.

The very same things Murray did secretly impart to the Queen of Scots also by Robert Melvin, and officiously offered his Service for the bringing it about. But the Duke answered, that he could resolve nothing touching the said Marriage, before such time as she had cleared her self of the Crimes objected against her. Yet the Bishop of Rosse ceased not to draw him on all he could possibly, who yet seemed something unwilling to it.

Some few days after Sir Nicholas Throckmorton met the Duke

at White-hall, to whom, professing singular Affection in all kind of Duty, he signified, that he understood that the Earl of Leicester would treat with the Duke about a Marriage between him and the Queen of Scots; which Throckmorton said was strange to him, considering that not long before Leicester had sought to procure the same Marriage for himself. But he friendly advised the Duke, that if it fell out so, he should offer the Honour of the Marriage to Leicester, who had sought it before: but if he should instantly press it upon him, that he should refuse it, in regard the Scots accused her of many Crimes. "Yet I (said Throckmorton) do wish with all my heart she were joyned to you in Marriage, both that the true Religion may be preserved, and also that the Queen of Scots may wholly depend upon our Queen and none else. Nevertheless of this I forewarn you, if you doe any thing in this matter, take Leicester's Counsell first; for you will hardly of your self get the Queen's Assent."

Within a day or two after Leicester propounded the matter to the Duke, who answered according as Throckmorton had forewarned him: and when they were come to the Crimes she stood charged with, Leicester extenuated them, and that upon the credit of Richard Candish, whose Service (though suspected) he commended to the Duke. Then Leicester communicateth the matter to Pembroke, and the Duke to Arundell. They together with Throckmorton commend the Duke by Letters to the Queen of Scots for an Husband, as Murray had done before. The Duke also sent her a Letter, testifying his singular Love, and most affectionately offering her all his Service. And ever after this time, what Letters soever he wrote to her, or received from her, he imparted unto them; and often Conferences were had with the Bishop of Rosse about the means of completing the Marriage: and in the month of May 1568 they propounded to the Queen of Scots, by Richard Candish, these Articles written with Leicester's Hand.

> That she should attempt nothing which might be prejudicial to the Queen of England, or to the Children born of her, in the Succession of the Kingdom of England.
> That she should enter into a League of Offence and Defence betwixt the two Kingdoms.
> That she should establish the Protestant Religion in Scotland.

113

That she should receive those Scots which were then her Adversaries into Favour.

That she should revoke her Assignment of the Kingdom of England made to the Duke of Anjou.

That she should take some Nobleman of England to her Husband, and namely the Duke of Norfolk, the Noblest of all the Lords of England.

To these Articles if she would assent, they promised to procure that the Queen of England should also give her Consent thereto; and that she should e'er long be restored to her Kingdom, and confirmed in the Succession of England. These Terms she readily accepted, onely touching the League she could answer nothing without the French King's Knowledge. She protested there was no Assignment made to the Duke of Anjou; nevertheless, if they should require it, she would procure his Renunciation. She wished them first of all to get the Queen's Assent, lest the matter might turn to her own and the Duke's Prejudice, whereof she had had experience before in her Marriage with the Lord Darly contracted without her Assent. Yet they thought good first to try the minds of more of the Nobility, most of whom gave their Assents with this Proviso, so as the Queen were not against it. Neither indeed did the French King or the Spaniard dislike it: onely they misdoubted Murray, lest he, which had been the first Propounder of the matter, and promised his best Assistance, should prove the forwardest to cross it. But notwithstanding they all agreed in this, that Lidington, who was then expected, should first try the Queen's mind. In the mean while the Duke acquainteth the Lord Lumley with all that was done in the matter, and with much adoe obtained of Leicester, that he might advise about it with some other Friends of his: and within a while after he discovered the matter also to Cecyl, with the consent of the Earl of Pembroke.

At which time Leonard Dacres contrived a way how to convey the captive Queen out of the Custody wherein she was kept at Whinfield, in the County of Derby, under the Earl of Shrewsbury. Northumberland, being a Partner in the Plot, discovered the same to the Duke: but the Duke forbad it to be put in execution, fearing lest they would deliver her to the Spaniard to Wife, and hoping e'er long to procure Queen Elizabeth's Assent.

THE TWELFTH YEAR, 1569

Soon after the Rumour of this Marriage came more clearly to Queen Elizabeth's ears, by means of the Women of the Court, who do quickly smell out Love-matters. Which when the Duke understood, he earnestly intreated Leicester, both himself, and also by Pembroke and Throckmorton, that the matter might be forthwith imparted to the Queen. Leicester made Delays, and put it off from day to day, as if it were to wait for a fit Opportunity. But Cecyl, seeing the Duke now perplexed in Mind, advised him to open the matter to the Queen himself, to the end that all Scruple might be the sooner removed out of his own Head and the Queen's. Leicester counselleth him the contrary, promising to break the matter to the Queen in her Progress. But while he with fair words put off the matter from day to day, the Queen took the Duke to her Board at Farnham, and pleasantly gave him warning "to beware upon what Pillow he leaned his Head." At length Leicester fell sick at Tichfield, or at leastwise counterfeited himself so. The Queen coming to visit him, and with comfortable words to chear him, found his Spirits and Bloud to be retired inward through Fear: to whom he now opened the whole matter from the first Beginning, with Sighs and Tears craving her Pardon.

The Queen then called the Duke unto her into a Gallery, and sharply chid him, that he had sought the Queen of Scots in Marriage without acquainting her therewith; and commanded him upon his Allegeance to give over that Enterprise. The Duke willingly and readily promised so to doe, and (as if he quite neglected the Q. of Scots) stuck not to affirm, that his Revenues in England were little less than those of the Kingdom of Scotland, which was now miserably exhausted with Wars; and that when he was in his Tennis-court at Norwich, he thought himself in a manner equal with some kings. But from thenceforth he began to be more cooled in Courage: and when he perceived the Queen, by her Countenance and Voice, to be every day more displeased with him, Leicester in a manner alienated from him, and many of the better sort of the Nobility to withdraw themselves by little and little from his Familiarity, scarcely saluting him, and soon breaking off Discourse with him; he resolved to go to London without taking his Leave, and lodged with the Earl of Pembroke, who bade him to be of good Hope, and cheared him up as well as he could. And the very same day Queen Elizabeth in anger rejected the Scottish Embassadour, who solicited for the Delivery of the captive Queen, and charged she should rest her self contented, lest she saw e'er long those on whom she most depended hop without Heads.

Whenas now the Rumour of the Marriage grew hotter and hotter, and the French Embassadour (rather by Perswasion of some English-men, than by Command of the French King, as shortly after it came to be known,) earnestly urged the Delivery of the Queen of Scots; new Suspicions arose on all sides; and Cecyl, who had always a great Care for the Safety of the Commonwealth and Religion, bent his mind most diligently to sift out the matter. By Letters therefore he dealt with Sussex, Lord President of the North, who was most intimate with the Duke, and most nearly tied to him in Friendship, that if he understood any thing of the Duke's Marriage, he should let the Queen know thereof. What Answer he made I know not. But whereas it had been observed, that the Duke had had now and then secret Conferences at Hampton-Court, with Murray Regent of Scotland, Sir George Cary, the Lord Hunsdon's Son, was privately sent to Murray, to get out of him whether the Duke had imparted any thing to him touching the Marriage.

The Duke in the mean time being terrified with a false Rumour which was spread, that there was a Rebellion raised in the North, and being certified by Leicester that he was to be committed to the Tower, withdrew himself to Norfolk, till such time as his Friends at the Court might divert the Storm that hung over him, (as they had undertaken to doe,) and he himself might by submissive Letters pacifie the Queen's Displeasure. But some there were who were set to observe his Motions and Attempts, yea his very Becks and Gestures. But when he found no Comfort from his Friends, and Heydon, Cornwallis, and others of the chief men of those parts, perswaded him, if in ought he found himself guilty, to fly unto the Queen's Mercy, he wavered in mind being distracted with doubtfull Cares. In the mean time all the whole Court hung in Suspense and Fear lest he should break forth into Rebellion; and it was determined, (as the Report went) if he did so, forthwith to put the Queen of Scots to death.

But the Duke, out of his innate Goodness, and the Conscience of his well meaning, knowing that he came not within any Law of High Treason, (for that Act of Henry the Eighth, that none should marry with the Children of the Sisters or Brethren or Aunts of the King without the King's Privity upon pain of High Treason, King Edward the Sixth had repealed,) and also out of Fear lest the Queen of Scots should upon Suspicion be more hardly dealt withall, wrote Letters to his Friends at the Court, wherein he gave them to understand, that he had withdrawn himself to his Home for Fear of Imprisonment, and that he might in time by absenting himself cure those malignant Rumours, which are always readily entertained at Court: and so most humbly craving Pardon, he forthwith buckled himself to his Journey towards the Court.

At Saint Albans, in his Return, Owen the Earl of Arundele's man, being privily sent from Throckmorton and the Lord Lumley, (who was now in Custody,) wished him to take the Fault wholly upon himself, and not to lay it upon Leicester or others, lest of Friends he made them his Foes. There Edward Fitz-Girald, the Earl of Kildare's Brother, (Lieutenant of the Band of Gentlemen-Pensioners,) met and received him, and conveyed him to Burnham, three miles from Windsor, (where the Queen then lay). The fourth day after, the Abbat of Dunfermelin delivered Letters to the Queen from Murray Regent of Scotland, whereby he signified that the Duke had secretly dealt with him at Hampton-Court to favour his Marriage with the Queen of Scots, and threatened him sore unless he would favour it: That he had promised to favour it, merely to prevent a Plot laid for his Life by one Norton as he was to return; and thereupon the Duke promised him that he should return in Safety, without danger of the said Norton or any others. And that shortly after the Duke did by Letters, written in privy Cyphers, intreat him to give his Assent to the Marriage. Moreover, that the Duke gave him to understand by Boyd, that he would never forsake the Queen of Scots: and farther, That the said Queen's Ministers had in a manner perswaded him the said Regent, that Queen Elizabeth had consented to the Marriage, and had also given her Hope of the Kingdom of England. Queen Elizabeth found also, that she had intimated to some Noblemen of England, to draw them to her Party, that she was in hand with that which would be for the

Security of the Queen, and the most assured Safety of both Kingdoms.

The Duke, who secretly and warily held Correspondence by
Letters (which were sent privily in Ale-bottles) with the Bishop
of Rosse, Leicester and Throckmorton, was about this time examined concerning his Marriage with the Queen of Scots, and
his private Conferences with the Bishop of Rosse; and, confessing many things, was sent to the Tower of London, under the
Custody of Henry Nevill Knight, being sharply reprehended for
that he had departed from the Court without Leave, and accused
as if he sought to trouble the Peace of the Land. Two days after
the Bishop of Rosse was in like manner examined; and Robert
Ridolph, that Gentleman of Florence, with whom Rosse and the
rest had great Familiarity, was committed to Sir Francis Walsingham's Custody. The Earl of Pembroke was commanded to keep
his House, and brought to a private Examination. Nevertheless
in regard of his Nobility and Age, he had the Favour that his
Confession was not set down in writing, for so he requested, in
regard he could not write himself. Certain Noblemen were removed from the Court as accessory to the matter, who craved
Pardon, confessing that they had consented with the Duke to the
Marriage, which Murray had first propounded; yet so, as both the
Duke, the Queen of Scots and they themselves thought good that
the matter should be imparted to the Queen before the Marriage
were contracted. In like manner the Earls of Northumberland
and Westmorland, who had their hands in the Plot, submitted
themselves to the Earl of Sussex, Lord President of the North,
and besought him to make Intercession for them to the Queen.
Divers Books also came forth against this Marriage, against the
Queen of Scots, and against her Title whereby she claimed England as next Heir, written with such a saucy Malapertness, that
the Queen resolved to prohibit them by a strict Proclamation, and
by way of Connivence suffered the Bishop of Rosse to answer
them. Who presently set forth a Book against them, under the
name of Morgan Philips, to maintain the Honour of the Queen
his Mistress, her Title to the Succession, and the Government of
Women, (for this also was wrote against). But his Arguments
for the Title of Succession he afterwards freely confessed, in
his Commentaries, that he had privately borrowed from Anthony

Brown, Lord chief Justice of the Common-pleas, and Carell, two most learned and judicious men in the Laws of England.

In those days came from the Duke of Alva Chapine Vitelli, Marquess of Cetona, with old-dated Letters of the Spaniard, under pretence to compound the Differences about Commerce; but indeed his Errand was to observe the Success of a Rebellion now ready to break forth, and to have the Command of certain Forces which the Duke of Alva had secretly promised out of the Netherlands: who also had sent La-Mott, Governour of Dunkirk, before, (as he himself confessed,) in the habit of a Sailour, to sound the Ports. But when it was found that this Marquess was deputed by the Duke of Alva onely, who likewise himself was no more but a Deputy-Governour, it was doubted whether he should be treated with as an Embassadour. Yet the Queen signified that she would acknowledge him as the Spaniard's Embassadour. But when he produced no other Commission but to demand the Money detained, she, being much desirous of Peace, advised him to procure a more ample Authority for compounding of matters. Which whilst he expected, the Rumour grew rife of a Rebellion ready to break forth in the North parts of the Land.

Touching this Rebellion (to fetch the matter a little higher) there arose a very slight Rumour in the beginning of Autumn; which was at first neglected, because it had no good Ground: but shortly after it increased by reason of the frequent Meetings of the Earls of Northumberland, Westmorland, and others, insomuch as Sussex the Lord President sent for them, and questioned them concerning the said Rumour. Who confessed that they had heard thereof, but that they were guilty thereof they flatly denied, and with many and deep Obstestations vowed to spend their Lives for the Queen against all Rebels whatsoever. Hereupon they were sent home again, and that with Power to inquire after the Authours of such a Rumour. Nevertheless the Rumour increased again in such sort, that the Queen, though she thought nothing was to be rashly credited against such Great Men, yet she commanded them by Sussex to come up forthwith to London, to remove all Suspicion. Sussex notwithstanding (with what intent I know not) commanded them to come unto him, as it were to consult with them about the Affairs of that Province. They at the first made Delays, and soon after flatly denied to come. Hereupon the Queen in all haste by peremptory Letters commanded them, all Excuse set apart, to appear presently before her, to the end she might either quite deterr them from Rebellion, or else they might forthwith break out into Rebellion, before they could gather all their Force together, and the matter grow ripe. For (as was known afterward) certain auxiliary Companies both from the Scottish Confederates, and also from the Duke of Alva, were privily appointed to be landed at Hartlepool in the Bishoprick of Durham.

As soon as Northumberland had read the Letters, being a man of an easie nature, and conscious of his own Guiltiness, greatly addicted to the Romish Religion, and much exasperated with a Wrong done unto him (as he took it) about a rich Vein or Mine of Copper in his Soil, judged from him by virtue of the Queen's Right or Prerogative in Mines Royal, and yet comforted with great Hope of the Queen's Clemency; he wavered in a carefull Doubt, whether he should go unto the Queen, or save himself by Flight, or else break forth into Rebellion. His Friends and Servants being now prepared for Rebellion, seeing him thus wavering and fearfull, called upon him at unawares in the dead of the Night, crying that Oswald Ulstrop and Vaughan, his Enemies, were at hand with an armed Power to carry him away Prisoner. They beseech him not to neglect himself, his Friends, nor the Religion of his Fathers. The Catholicks (say they) are now ready prepared all over England to maintain the Romish Religion, the Bells are tumultuously rung backwards throughout all Towns, to stir up the Multitude. The Earl trembling rose out of his Bed, and withdrew himself to a Lodge in his Park near Topcliff, and the next night to Branspeth, an House of the Earl of Westmorland's, where many who were not ignorant of the matter were assembled already.

For, the better to gather together the silly Multitude, they commanded some to arm and joyn together for the Defence of the Queen; to others they signified, that all the Lords of England had conspired with them for restoring the Romish Religion; to others, that they were forced of necessity to take Arms, lest the ancient Nobility of England should be troden under foot by new Upstarts, and their Countrey delivered for a Prey to Strangers. Hereupon they rush into open Rebellion, and are the first that disturb the publick Peace of the Land, which now had continued unshaken the space of eleven years under Q Elizabeth, Nicholas Morton, a Priest, thrusting them forward, who was sent from the Bishop of Rome to pronounce Queen Elizabeth to be an Heretick, and thereby to have forfeited all Dominion and Power. And immediately they set forth a Writing, wherein they declared, "That they had not taken Arms with any other Intent, than that the Religion of their Forefathers might be restored, corrupt Counsellours removed from the Queen, the Duke and other faithfull Lords, that were put from their Rank and Degree, restored to Liberty and Grace: And that they attempted nothing against the Queen, to whom they vowed themselves now and ever to be most dutifull and obedient Subjects." They sent Letters also to the Papists round about throughout the whole Kingdom, exhorting them to joyn their Forces with theirs. But so far were they from associating themselves with them, that most of them sent the Letters which they received, together with the Bearers, to the Queen, and every one strived who should be forwardest, from all parts of the Land, to offer his person and his Purse against them: and so did even Norfolk himself. Insomuch as she assuredly understood the great and singular Fidelity her Subjects bare her; and in that regard acknowledged with most thankfull Heart the Goodness of God toward her.

The Rebels went first to Durham, an Episcopal See hard by, where they rent and trampled under feet the English Bibles and Books of Common-prayer which they found in the Churches. From thence they went small Journeys, celebrating Mass in all places where they came, trouping together under their Colours, (wherein were painted in some the five Wounds of Christ, in others the Chalice,) Richard Norton, an old Gentleman with a reverend gray Head, bearing a Cross with a Streamer before them, as far as Clifford-moor, not far from Whetherbey, where the twelfth day of their Rebellion they mustered their Army, and found no more but six hundred Horse-men, and four thousand Foot. Here when they certainly understood that the Queen of Scots (for whose Deliverance they had taken Arms) was carried from Tutbury to Coventry, a strong City, under the Custody of the Earls of Shrewsbury and Huntingdon; that Sussex on the side of them had levied a strong Army against them; that Sir George Bowes had a select Party at their Backs, and had fortified Bernard Castle; and that the Lord Scroop, and the Earl of Cumberland had strengthened Carlisle, and were levying a Body of men; they retired, and going back almost the same way they went, came to Raby, the chief House of the Earl of Westmorland. From whence they turned aside, and straitly besieged Bernard-Castle, which for want of Victuals they soon took by Composition; Sir George Bowes with his Brother Robert, and the Garrison-Souldiers, being dismissed by Agreement with their Arms.

Upon which very day, when they were now proclaimed Traitours to their Countrey, Sussex, marched against them with seven thousand men, accompanied with Edward Earl of Rutland, the Lord Hunsdon, the Lord Evers, and the Lord Willoughby of Parham. When Sussex was come to Aukland, the Rebels in fearfull manner fled to Hexham, and shortly after came dispersedly, wandring through Byways, to Naworth Castle: where hearing that the Earl of Warwick and Clinton Lord Admiral pursued them in haste with twelve thousand men from the South parts of England, the two Earls with a small Company, unknown to the rest, presently withdrew themselves into the neighbour Countrey of Scotland. Northumberland lurked privily at Harclaw in poor Cottages among the Grahams, famous Thieves, by whom he was afterwards delivered into Murray's hands. Westmorland found a Lurking-place with Carr of Fernihurst, and Buchluy, and at length escaped with some English-men into the Netherlands, where he led a very poor Life, even to his Old age, living upon a very slender Pension from the Spaniard. The rest, being dispersed, saved themselves, some by Flight, and some by Lurking in close Corners. Threescore and six petty Constables and others were hanged for a Terrour at Durham, amongst whom the man of most note was one Plomtree a Priest. At York were executed Simon Digbey, J. Fulthorp, Thomas Bishop, Robert Peneman; and at London, some few months after, Christopher and Thomas Norton, and some others elsewhere.

Afterwards such of the Rebels as were of best Note were convict of High Treason, and proscribed; namely, Charles Earl of Westmorland, Thomas Earl of Northumberland, Anne Countess of Northumberland, Daughter to Henry Earl of Worcester, Edward Dacres of Morton, John Nevil of Leversege, John Swinborne, Thomas Markenfeld, Egremond Ratcliffe, the Earl of Sussex his Brother, Christopher Nevil, Richard Norton of Norton Coniers, Christopher, Marmaduke and Thomas, of the Family of the Nortons, Robert and Michael Tempest, George Stafford, and about forty moe of Noble Birth. These mens Conviction and Proscription was confirmed in the next Parliament following. The rest, which had no Estates, nor had fled the Land, were pardoned. Thus was the Flame of this Rebellion soon extinct, while Chapine Vitelli (who, as I said, was privy thereunto,) openly before the Queen and the Lords admired, but inwardly fretted, that it was so suddenly and easily extinguished, and that his coming into England was by this means frustrate.

Out of the smothered Fire of this Rebellion there brake forth, as it were out of the Embers, a new Flame at Naworth in Cumberland, near Vallum Severi, called the Picts Wall, kindled by Leonard Dacres, second Son to William Lord Dacres of Gillesland. This Leonard Dacres (when the Lord Dacres, his Nephew by his elder Brother, died, as I said, young,) stomached it much, that so goodly an Inheritance descended by Law to his Nieces, whom the Duke of Norfolk their Father-in-law had betrothed to his Sons, and had commenced a Suit against his Nieces: which when it went not to his Desire, he fell to plotting and practising with the Rebels, and attempted (but in vain) to deliver the Queen of Scots out of Custody. But when they had taken up the Banner of Rebellion sooner than he thought, and were proclaimed Enemies to their Countrey while he was at Court, he, being admitted to salute the Queen, tendered her his best Service against the Rebels, and was thereupon sent home again. By the way (as was found afterwards) he held Correspondence with them, by Messengers that went between him and them, and encouraged them, promising great matters from the Embassadours of foreign Princes, and, amongst other things, that he (having leavied men in the Queen's name) would cut off the Lord Scroope, Warden of the West March, and the Bishop of Carlisle. Which when he could not effect, he sent Letters of Commendation after the Earls that were flying to the Scots, seized upon the Castle of Greystock, and other Houses belonging to the Dacres, fortified the Castle of Naworth as his own Inheritance, and under colour of defending his own, and resisting the Rebels, gathered together three thousand of the Rank-riders of the Borders, and some others which were most devoted to the Name of the Dacres, which in that Tract was a Name of great Reputation.

Against these marcheth the Lord Hunsdon with the old Garrison-Souldiers of Berwick. The Rebels, not trusting to their Strong holds, march forth to encounter him, and with a triangular Battel, flanked on every side with Horse-men, receive him at the little River Gelt. The Fight was maintained on both sides very sharply, and Leonard (though he were crook-backed) omitted nothing that could be desired in a most valiant Leader. But after very many of his men were slain, he left the Victory (though with small Joy) to the Lord Hunsdon, and withdrew himself to the next part of Scotland. From whence shortly after he crossed the Seas into the Low-Countries, and died a poor man at Lovain. So as it seemeth his Father was not much mistaken, who upon his Death-bed prayed God to send him much Sorrow for his Disobedience. The Lord Hunsdon, having taken in the Castles, committed them to the Custody of the Duke of Norfolk's Servants: and the Queen by publick Proclamation pardoned the Multitude, whom he had excited to Rebellion.

The Queen, though she were imbroiled with this Rebellion at home, yet failed not to relieve the Protestants of France, who were now in a distressed and almost desperate Condition. For she exhorted the Princes of the same Profession to take upon them the Defence of the common Cause: she supplied the Queen of Navar with Money, taking Jewels in pawn for the same: and permitted Henry Champernoun (whose Cousin-german Gawin had married the Earl of Montgomery's Daughter) to carry into France a Troup of a hundred voluntier-Gentlemen on horseback, who had in his Colours this Motto, *Finem det mihi Virtus*, that is, Let Virtue give me my End. Amongst these voluntier-Gentlemen were Philip Butshide, Francis Barkley, and Walter Raleigh, a very young man, who now first began to be of any Note. These things were not hid from the French King, who, either to exhaust the Wealth of England, which overflowed to the Relief of the Protestants, or at the least wise to make it run in some other Chanel, determined to raise a new Flame of War in Scotland against England, by Relieving the Scots which held the Castle of Dunbriton for the Queen of Scots. And to this purpose he intended to send thither Sebastian Martigues, a man flourishing in Martial Glory: but he being shot at the Siege of Saint John d'Angeli, this Design quite vanished.

Neither was Ireland at this time free from Rebellions. For Edmund and Peter Boteler, the Earl of Ormond's Brethren, who had wrongfully abused their Neighbours in Munster, refused to obey the Laws, prosecuting the good Subjects with Fire and Sword, and entred into a Confederacy with James Fitz-Moris, of the House of Desmond, Mac-Arti-More, Fitz-Edmund Steward of Imokelly, and others, who, with the Bishop of Rome and the Spaniard, laboured all they could to maintain their Religion, and to out Queen Elizabeth of her Kingdom of Ireland. Whereupon they were proclaimed Traitours, and Sir Peter Carew the elder skirmished with them sundry times with variable Success. Nevertheless, having gathered together certain Companies of people of desperate Fortune, they beseiged Kilkenny, and commanded the Citizens to deliver Warham Saint-Leger's Wife into their hands. But being beaten off by the Garrison-Souldiers, who sallied upon them, they miserably harassed the Countrey round about. To kindle the Flame of this Rebellion there, came privily from the Spaniard Juan Mendoza; and out of England, to quench it, came the Earl of Ormond, who perswaded his Brethren so that they submitted themselves. Yet were they cast into Prison. But the Earl's continual Intercession for them to the Queen obtained that they were not brought to their Trial, as their Offences deserved: for the Earl took it very much to heart, that such a Blot was by their means laid upon that most Noble Family. And one means also to procure this Favour was, the nearness of Bloud between them and the Queen, who now and then with Joy gloried in the untainted Nobility of this Family. But the Lord Deputy sharply pursued the Remainders of this Rebellion by the means of Sir Humphrey Gilbert, and soon dispersed them.

In Ulster also they were up in Rebellion, Turlough Leinigh, through his own Levity, and the restless Fancy of his Ministers, engaging himself sometimes in War, and sometimes embracing Peace. But he was kept within his Duty, not so much by the

English Garrisons, as by the Hebridians, who now and then out of those hungry Islands overflowed his fat Countrey. Against whose Incursions on that side great store of Money was sent ever and anon out of England, to fortifie the Sea-coast: but all in vain, by reason of a certain Unhappiness common as well to England as Ireland, where for the most part such men thrust themselves forward, and are admitted, in such matters, as do sordidly prefer their own private before the publick Good.

VIII

The Four and Twentieth Year of Her Reign, Anno Domini 1581

Hereupon Master Thomas Randolph, chief Postmaster, was sent in the beginning of January into Scotland, with Instructions, that, for Preservation of Religion, and Amity with the English, he should leave no means untried to procure that no violent Course might be taken against Morton, that Lenox might be removed out of Scotland, and that the Noblemen of the English Faction might be encouraged. Randolph playeth the earnest Intercessour for Morton, alledging the man's Deserts with the King, Queen Elizabeth's Honour, (lest she, to whom the King and Realm was so much beholden, should suffer the Repulse in so just a matter,) and the Malice of his Accusers. The King answered, "That he could not but according to his Kingly Office leave the man to his Trial, as being charged with High treason. The Queen's approved Kindness he acknowledged, and would doe nothing (he said) which might any way give her just Offence."

Randolph having afterwards Audience in an Assembly of the Estates, reckoned up Queen Elizabeth's Good offices towards Scotland and towards the King himself. Namely,

> That she had delivered their Kingdom from the French with the expense of the Bloud of Englishmen: That she had defended Religion and the King: That she never had so much as a Thought of conveying him out of the Land, (as was falsely reported,) or of seizing upon so much as an Acre of Land in Scotland; whereas notwithstanding she had not wanted Opportunities to have conquered all Scotland, while the King lay

crying in his Cradle, his Mother was a Prisoner in England, and the Nobility at Variance amongst themselves. But on the contrary she had used all Care to preserve the King and his Kingdom in Safety, he being nearly allied to her in the strictest Bands of Bloud, Neighbourhood, and Religion; of whole Love, as also of the Love of all the Regents, she was most assured, till such time as that Aubigny Duke of Lenox came into Scotland. For from that time he had carried a kind of commanding Hand over the King, averted his Mind from Amity with the English unto the French, (who yet had not to this day acknowledged him for King,) removed the King's faithfullest Subjects, preferred others less faithfull, dealt with Foreigners by his Letters (which Randolph produced) for the Invasion of England, stirred up the King to hate the Ministers of God's Word as turbulent and railing Fellows, and taken no care for due administring of Justice betwixt the Borderers. Which things Queen Elizabeth could not but take very ill, when she saw a Prince of so great Vertue, and so strictly linked to her in Friendship, to be alienated and estranged from her by cunning Practices.

Yet was there nothing then done, either for Morton, or against Lenox, most men suspecting that the Crimes alledged against him were false, and the Letters counterfeit.

Randolph therefore betook himself to other Artifices. Amongst Lenox his Adversaries and Morton's Friends he bewaileth the unhappy Condition of Scotland; layeth before them the Dangers that threaten the King, the Commonwealth, and them; complaineth that the Queen of England's Intercession was ungratefully slighted; and privily adviseth them to attempt by Arms what they could not effect by other means, promising both Men and Money out of England. And indeed he had drawn to his Party Argyle, Montross, Angus, Morton's Brother's Son, Marre, Glencarne, Ruthven, Lindsey, and divers others. But they shortly after disagreeing among themselves, when they saw that the King wholly inclined to favour Lenox, and was not terrified with the English Forces upon the Borders, but had drawn up his own against them, most of them, reverencing the Royal Majesty even in so young a Prince, attempted nothing against Lenox, and thought it enough to pity Morton. Yet Angus and Marre continued their secret Designs with Randolph for Morton, and against Lenox. Whereof when the King was advertised by Wittingham, Angus was commanded to withdraw himself beyond the River Spey, and Marre forthwith to surrender Sterlin Castle into the King's Hands. Randolph, doubting the worst, retired secretly to Berwick, and advised Angus and Marre, matters being now grown desperate, to shift for themselves, either by procuring the King's Favour, or flying to the Protection of the Queen of England. And now were the English Forces called Home from the Borders: and not long after was Morton found accessory to the Murther of the King's Father, and beheaded. For he confessed (as they report) that Bothwell and Archibald Douglass acquainted him with the Plot for making away the King, and that he in so dangerous a time durst not reveal it. Neither could he deny but that, after the Murther committed, he esteemed Douglass, who Murthered the King, amongst his intimate Friends; and that he had given his Faith under his Hand to defend Bothwell, if any man should accuse him of the Murther of the King. Angus and the rest which favoured Morton fled presently into England.

In the Low-countrey Provinces the Confederate Estates sent Colonel Norris with the English and other Forces against the Count of Reneberg, who victoriously carried all before him for the Spaniard, and straitly beleagured Steenwick a Town of Friesland. But Norris gallantly and successfully brought Provisions into the Town twice, put Reneberg's men to Flight, and raised the Siege. But afterwards joyning Battel with Verdugo a Spaniard at Northorn, when the Victory was now as good as in his Hands, the Enemie's Troups being defeated by Sir Roger Williams, the Chance of War suddenly turned, he himself was wounded, and many of his men slain; and amongst them (not to name others) Cotton, Fitz-Williams and Bishop, stout Captains. How Captain Thomas, a Captain of the Epirots, at this time challenged General Norris to a single Combat, and Sir Roger Williams, his Lieutenant, accepted the Challenge, (because, he, being General, might not accept it by the Law of Arms,) I know not whether it be worth the mentioning, considering that after they had tried their Skill a little while in the View of both Armies, and neither of them received a Wound, they drank a hearty Cup together, and so parted Friends. Yet this is not to be omitted, that the English, who of all the Northern

Nations had been till now the moderatest Drinkers, and most commended for their Sobriety, learned in these Netherland Wars first to drown themselves with immoderate Drinking, and by drinking others Healths to impair their own. And ever since the Vice of Drunkenness hath so diffused itself over the whole Nation, that in our days first it was fain to be restrained by severe Laws.

While the Estates and the Spaniard contended in the Netherlands for petty Towns, the Spaniard seized into his Hands the rich Kingdom of Portugal. For Henry King of Portugal dying the last year an old man, many Competitours laid Claim to the Crown, and amongst them Philip King of Spain, King Henry's eldest Sister's Son, who was, if not in Right, yet in Might the strongest. And yet he wanted not some shew of Right: for of all the Competitours he was nearest of Kin to the deceased King, and of the Male sex, and therefore (as he and his Friends thought) to be preferred in the Succession to the Crown before the Females, who were both younger, and in Kindred more remote. The Savoyard was excluded, because he was born of the younger Sister; and Rainutio Farneze, the Prince of Parma's Son, who was born but of the eldest Daughter of Edward King Henry's Brother, and Catharina Dutchess of Braganza, the other Daughter of the said Edward, because they grounded their Title onely upon a Representation, as they call it; which being nothing but a Fiction, the Spaniards maintained that it could not overthrow the true Right. As for Don Antonio, Prior of Crato, the Son of Lewis another Brother of King Henry he was utterly rejected as illegitimate. However the Spaniard offered these things several times to be discussed both by Divines and Lawyers. And when they all with one Consent affirmed his Title to be good, he sent the Duke of Alva, invaded the Kingdom, put Don Antonio to flight, who was elected by the People, and in 70 days subdued all Portugal. But the Title which Katharine de Medicis Queen of France laid to Portugal, which was derived from Alphonsus the Third by the Earls of Bononia above 320 years before, was in a manner exploded both by the Spaniards and Portugueezes, as an outworn Title, drawn as it were from the Mother of Evander, and injurious to so many Kings of Portugal as had since resigned, as if they had unjustly possessed the Crown. Whereat being moved with Anger, and looking with a jealous Eye, upon the growing Power of the Spaniard, which was far and wide extended hereby, and inriched with the Addition of Portugal, East-India, and many Isles, and mis-doubting the Condition of her self and her Posterity, she advised both other Princes and Queen Elizabeth to curb his Ambition betimes, and restrain his too-far-extending Power within some reasonable Limits. And indeed Queen Elizabeth, being carefully provident for herself and her Subjects, willingly hearkned unto her, foreseeing how dangerous the over-swelling Power of her neighbour Princess might be. But for Don Antonio, who was driven out of Portugal into France, and from thence sent over with Recommendations into England, she bountifully relieved him: which she thought she might doe without Offence, in regard she acknowledged him her Kinsman, as descended of the Bloud royal of England, and of the House of Lancaster; neither was there ever such a Proviso but into any League betwixt the Spaniards and the English, that the Portugueezes should not be received into England.

And withall the said Queen of France, and the King her Son, for a Foundation of a stricter Amity with Queen Elizabeth, urged more earnestly than ever before the Marriage with her Son the Duke of Anjou. For the effecting whereof there were sent into England on a very honourable Embassage Francis of Bourbon Prince of Daulphinie, Arthur Cosse Earl of Segondin Marshal of France, Lewis of Lusignan of Saint Gelasie, Seigneur of Lansac, Tanerge Venator of Corconge, Bertrand Salignac a Mota-Fenel-lon, Michael a Chasteau-neuf Seigneur Mauvaisier, Bernard Brisonius a Granela President of the Parliament of Paris, (a man of most excellent Learning,) Claudius Pinarte first Baron of Valois, Pierre Clause Seigneur of Curats and Marcho-mont, and Jaques Vray Secretary of the Duke of Anjou's Treasury. These Honourable persons were as honourably entertained, being nobly banquetted in a large Edifice built at Westminster in all haste for this very purpose, richly and royally furnished, and after entertained with Tiltings performed at a vast Expense by Philip Earl of Arundel, Frederick Lord Windsore, Sir Philip Sidney, and Sir Fulk Grevil, who challenged all Comers: to say nothing of other Courtly Sports and Pastimes, which are not so proper for an Historian to relate.

The Commissioners appointed to confer with them about the

Marriage were William Cecyl Lord Burghley, Lord High Treasurer of England, Edward Clinton Earl of Lincoln, Lord Admiral
of England, Thomas Ratcliffe Earl of Sussex, Francis Russel Earl
of Bedford, Robert Dudley Earl of Leicester, Sir Christopher
Hatton, and Sir Francis Walsingham Secretary. Betwixt these
Commissioners a matrimonial Instrument was agreed upon to
the following purpose.

The Duke of Anjou and the Queen of England shall within
six weeks after the ratifying of these Articles contract Marriage
de præsenti in England. The Duke and his Retainers, provided
they be not native Subjects of England, may freely exercise their
Religion in some certain place to be appointed within his Court
without lett or hinderance. He shall alter nothing in the Religion
now received in England. After the Marriage consummated, he
shall enjoy the Title and Honour of King, but shall leave the
management of Affairs wholly and solely to the Queen. Whereas
he hath demanded, that presently after the Marriage he may be
crowned King, and enjoy that Honour as well while the Marriage
lasteth, as when it shall be dissolved, during his Government of
the Kingdom in the Minority of their Children; the Queen
promiseth to communicate his Demand to the Estates of the
Realm in the first Parliament, which she will call within fifteen
days after the Ratification, and to promote it as far as shall lie in
her power. Letters Patents, &c. shall run in both their Names, as
in the time of Philip and Mary. The Queen shall assign the Duke
a yearly Pension by Authority of Parliament; but how large it
shall be shall be left to her Pleasure; and she shall procure the
Parliament to assign him a considerable Summe of Money yearly,
if he survive the Queen. He shall make the Queen a Dowry to the
yearly Value of forty thousand Crowns of the Sun out of his
Dukedom of Berry, and shall presently put her in Possession
thereof. What shall be concluded concerning their Children in
the Parliament of England, shall be verified and confirmed in the
Parliaments of France, to this effect. The Males or Females shall
succeed their Mother in the Inheritance of England. If there be
two Males, the eldest shall succeed in the Kingdom of France,
and the second in his Mother's Right to England. If there be
but one Male, and he come to enjoy both Crowns, he shall reside
in England eight Months in every two years. And if the Duke
never come to the Title of King of France, their Children shall
succeed in his Appenage. If he out-live the Queen, he shall have

the Guardianship of the Children; provided the Males be not above eighteen years of age, and the Females fifteen. If the Duke die before, their Guardianship shall be left to the Authority and Pleasure of the Parliament. The Duke shall prefer no Foreigner to any Office in England. He shall alter nothing in the Law, but shall maintain all the Customs of the Land. He shall not convey the Queen nor her Children out of the Realm of England, but by her own Consent and the Consent of the Peers of the Realm. If the Queen die without Children, the Duke shall claim no Propriety in the Kingdom of England. He shall not transport the Crown-Jewels out of the Realm. He shall leave all Places in the Kingdom to the Custody of native English-men; neither shall he remove from thence any Warlike Munition. He shall not engage England in any foreign War. He shall maintain the Peace betwixt England and other Kingdoms. The Queen alone shall bear the Superiority, and no Title shall accrue to the Duke as Tenant by the Custome of England. The Duke intendeth not by this Marriage to prejudice his Title in the Succession to the Crown of France. This present Contract shall be read, proclaimed, and recorded in all the Courts of France and England, six months after the day of Marriage; and the Authority of the most Christian King shall be had for the Ratification of these Articles. There shall be a particular Treaty concerning a Confederacy and League betwixt England and France. All these things shall be ratified within two Months on the French King's part upon his Faith and Oath for him and his Heirs, &c. and as soon as may be he shall deliver Writings of Ratification, by which Assurance shall be given that the things here concluded shall be observed *bonâ fide.*

A Reservation also was added apart by itself, signed with the Hands of all the Commissioners, in these words: "But Queen Elizabeth is not bound to consummate the Marriage, untill she and the Duke shall thoroughly satisfie one another in certain Points, and shall thereof certifie the French King in writing within six weeks."

Before such time as those six weeks were expired, John Somers, Clark of the Council, was sent into France about this matter. The King refuseth to hear him, and presseth that the Marriage already contracted may be solemnized out of hand, for that now there remained nothing else behind. Somers sheweth to the contrary by the Writings, that there was first a League defensive and offensive to be entred into. The French King denieth it. Walsingham is dispatched to make up these Differences, who joyntly with Henry Lord Cobham, Embassadour Leiger in France, and Somers, was to inform him of these things following, and others of like nature.

> That although the vulgar sort did hardly censure the delaying of the Marriage, yet did Queen Elizabeth at first incline to Marriage upon no other Account than to satisfie the Desires of her People, who importunately perswaded her to marry, that there might be an established and certain Succession by her Children. And the Duke of Anjou, who sought to her for Marriage, she deservedly preferred before all others in her Love both for his own Vertue, and his Noble and Royal Descent; which Love she still prosesseth to be very great towards him. Nevertheless she as yet forbeareth to give her Assent to the contracting of the Marriage, till she may perceive whether it be a thing pleasing to her People, lest she might seem after to repent too late. That at present many Impediments and Obstructions were in the way: namely, the Civil War in France, and the Duke of Anjou's forlorn Condition, who had undeservedly lost the King's Favour. In England the Minds of the best men were averse from the Marriage, which had been a means of delaying it so long; yet notwithstanding the Queen's Affection was still constant towards him. That the French King pressed the Consummation of the Marriage the Realm might be preserved in Peace and Tran- was engaged in a War against the Spaniard, which he could not give over without a Slur to his Honour, and great Disadvantage to both the Kingdoms of England and France, and the utter Undoing of the Netherlands, whilst the Spaniard's Power daily increased more than was convenient. Moreover, whereas the People of England desired nothing more than that by this Marriage the Realm might be preserved in Peace and Tranquillity, it would be by this means precipitated from a most serene and gladsome Peace into a most dangerous War, considering that the Queen must of necessity be ingaged in her Husband's Quarrel. Wherefore she would have no more treating of the Marriage, till the Duke of Anjou were disingaged from the War he had undertaken, and the League of mutual Defence and Offence were concluded betwixt England and France.

Which verily Queen Elizabeth desired above all things. The French King promised with all his Heart to enter into a League of Defence; but as for a League offensive, he flatly refused to hear any more thereof before the Marriage were solemnized.

Not long after the Duke of Anjou came himself into England, (who was now designed Governour of the Netherlands by the Estates,) after he had by the Help of Queen Elizabeth's Money happily raised the Siege of Cambray. For she had privately supplied him with a great Sum of Money by Henry Seimour, Palavicini, and Bexie a French-man. He had a strong Hope, that if he did not complete the Marriage while he stayed here, yet at least he should gain thus much, that, being supported with Q. Elizabeth's Favour, he should be the more welcome to the Netherlanders, who honoured her as their tutelar Saint. He was received with as great Respect as he could hope for, and no Demonstration could there be given of Honour and Affection which she did not shew him to the full. Insomuch as in the month of November, as soon as she had with great Pomp celebrated her Coronation-day, the Force of modest Love in the midst of amorous Discourse carried her so far, that she drew off a Ring from her Finger, and put it upon the Duke of Anjou's, upon certain Conditions betwixt them two. The Standers-by took it, that the Marriage was now contracted by Promise: amongst whom Aldegond, Governour of the City of Antwerp, dispatched Letters presently away into the Netherlands to signifie as much; and Antwerp testified her publick Joy thereat by Bonefires and Peals of Ordnance. At Home the Courtiers minds were diversly affected; some leaped for Joy, some were seized with Admiration, and others were dejected with Sorrow. Leicester, who had lately plotted and contrived to cross the Marriage, Hatton Vice-chamberlain, and Walsingham, stormed at it, as if the Queen, the Realm and Religion were now quite undone. The Queen's Gentlewomen, with whom she used to be familiar, lamented and bewailed, and did so terrifie and vex her Mind, that she spent the Night in Doubts and Cares without Sleep amongst those weeping and wailing Females. The next day she sent for the Duke of Anjou, and they two, all By-standers being removed, had a long Discourse together. He at length withdrew himself to his Chamber, and throwing the Ring from him, a while after took it again, taxing the Lightness of Women, and the Inconstancy of Islanders, with two or three biting and smart Scoffs.

The Queen pondereth in her troubled Mind what Burghley and Sussex had told her; "That unless she married the Duke of Anjou, no League offensive could be hoped for from the French King: That she of herself alone was too weak to withstand the Greatness and Power of the Spaniard, who, if he should profer his Daughter in Marriage to the King of Scots, would easily draw to the Scottish King's Party all the Papists in England, all the Fugitives, all the Rebels, all that were weary of the present Government, and all of desperate Fortunes, of whom there were every-where great numbers: That the Hopes of all good men, who expected issue from the Queen by this Marriage, would be frustrate, so that now, neglecting her, they would cast their Eyes upon some of the Competitors. Besides, she herself could not but incurr very great Displeasure with the French King and the Duke of Anjou, who, after having spent so long time in so many Consultations, sent such honourable Embassies, and disbursed so much Money, would take it very hardly to be thus deluded, however they might dissemblingly conceal their Displeasure a while for their own Advantage, thereby to procure either Money at present for the Duke of Anjou towards the Low-countrey Wars, or a yearly Pension for the time to come." Neither did less Scruple stick in her Mind, if the Duke of Anjou, being thus neglected, should take a Wife out of Spain, (which some whispered into her ears:) for then she foresaw that Danger would threaten her both from France and Spain too.

In the midst of these perplexed Cogitations concerning Marriage, into which the Consideration of the Times did necessarily ever and anon cast her, some were of opinion that she was fully resolved in her Mind, that she might better provide both for the Commonwealth and her own Glory by an Unmarried life than by Marriage; as foreseeing that if she married a Subject, she should disparage herself by the Inequality of the Match, and give occasion to domestical Heart-burnings, private Grudges and Commotions; if a Stranger, she then should subject both herself and her People to a foreign Yoke, and endanger Religion: having not forgotten how unhappy the Marriage of her Sister Queen Mary with King Philip a Foreigner had been; also how unfortunate that Marriage of her great Grandfather Edward the

Fourth had proved, who was the first of all the Kings of England since the Norman Conquest that ever took one of his Subjects to Wife. Her Glory also, which whilst she continued unmarried she retained intire to herself and uneclipsed, she feared would by Marriage be transferred to her Husband. And besides, the Perils by Conception and Child-bearing, objected by the Physicians and her Gentlewomen for some private Reasons, did many times run in her Mind, and very much deterr her from thoughts of marrying.

She was also much incensed at a Book which was written and published against the Marriage in a smart and stinging Style, (out of a fear lest Religion should be changed) entituled, *The Gulph wherein England will be swallowed by the French Marriage.* In which Book those of the Council who favoured the Marriage are taxed as ungratefull to their Prince and Countrey; the Queen herself (in the midst of several flattering Expressions) is glanced at as unlike herself; the Duke of Anjou slandered with unworthy Reproaches; the French Nation odiously defamed; and the Marriage itself, in regard of the Difference of Religion, (as of the Daughter of God with a Son of Antichrist,) with virulent words condemned, as prophane, dangerous to the Church, and destructive to the Commonwealth, and this proved out of the Holy Scriptures miserably wrested. Neither would the Queen be perswaded that the Authour of the Book had any other Intent but to procure the Hatred of her Subjects against her, (who had always no less Regard of the Love of her People than she had of her own Authority, and (as Princes use to doe) made it her chief Care to preserve her Reputation,) and privily to open a Gap for some prodigious Innovation; considering that the Writer had not so much as mentioned the Security of the Queen and Realm, or Prevention of Dangers to either, and that the Estates of the Realm had before with all earnestness besought her to marry, as the most assured Remedy against the threatening Mischiefs. These things she declared by publick Proclamation, wherein, having condemned the Authour of the Book as a Publisher of Sedition, she highly commended the Duke of Anjou's good Affection towards her and the Protestant Religion, and expressed her Resentment that so great an Injury should be offered to so noble a Prince, and one that had so well deserved, who had desired nothing to be altered either in the Commonwealth or Religion: and withall she commended Simier, the Duke of Anjou's Agent, for his Wisedom and Discretion, whom some had loaden with Calumnies and Slanders. She also advertised the People, that the said Book was nothing else but a Fiction of some Traitours, to raise Envy abroad, and Sedition at home: and commanded it to be burnt before the Magistrate's Face.

From this time forward she began to be a little more incensed against the Puritans, or Innovatours, from whom she easily believed these kind of things proceeded. And indeed within a few days after, John Stubbs of Lincolns-Inn, a fervent hot-headed Professour of Religion, (whose Sister Thomas Cartwright, a Ring-leader amongst the Puritans, had married,) the Authour of this Book, William Page, who dispersed the Copies, and Singleton, the Printer, were apprehended. Against whom Sentence was given, that their Right hands should be cut off, according to an Act of Philip and Mary Against the Authours and Publishers of Seditious Writings. Though some Lawyers muttered that the Sentence was erroneous and void by reason of the false noting of the time wherein the Law was made; and that that Act was onely temporary, and died with Queen Mary. Of this number Dalton, who often bawled it out openly, was committed to the Tower; and Monson, a Judge in the Court of Common-pleas, was so sharply reprehended, that he resigned his Place: forasmuch as Wray, Lord Chief Justice of England, made it appear that there was no Mistake in noting the time; and proved by the Words of the Act, that the Act was made against those who should abuse the King by Seditious Writings, and that the King of England never dieth; yea, that that Act was renewed *anno primo Elizabethæ,* to be in Force during the Life of her and the Heirs of her Body. Hereupon Stubbs and Page had their Right hands cut off with a Cleaver, driven through the Wrist by the force of a Mallet, upon a Scaffold in the Marketplace at Westminster. The Printer was pardoned. I remember (being there present) that when Stubbs, after his Right hand was cut off, put off his Hat with his Left, and said with a loud voice, "God save the Queen"; the Multitude standing about was deeply silent: either out of an Horrour at this new and unwonted kind of Punishment; or else out of Commiseration towards the man, as being of an honest and unblameable Repute; or else out of Hatred of the Marriage, which most men presaged would be the Over-throw of Religion.

These things were done presently after the Duke of Anjou's coming into England. During his Stay here, the Queen, to take away the Fear which had possessed many mens minds, that Reli-gion would be altered, and Popery tolerated, being overcome by importunate Intreaties, permitted that Edmund Campian afore-said, of the Society of Jesus, Ralph Sherwin, Luke Kirby and Alexander Briant, Priests, should be arraigned: who being in-dicted upon the Act for Treason made in the twenty fifth of Edward the Third, and charged to have compassed and imagined the Destruction of the Queen and Realm, to have adhered to the Bishop of Rome, the Queen's Enemy, to have come into England to disturb the Peace and Quiet of the Realm, and to have raised Forces to that end, were condemned to die, and, persisting obstinately to defend the Pope's Authority against the Queen, were executed. For Campian, after he was condemned, being asked, first, whether Queen Elizabeth were a right and lawfull Queen, refused to answer: then, whether he would take part with the Queen, or the Pope if he should send Forces against the Queen, he openly professed and testified under his Hand, that he would stand for the Pope. Afterwards some others also were executed for the same Reasons, whereas in full ten years time after the Rebellion there had been no more than five Papists put to death. But these things I leave to the Writer of the Ecclesiastical History: Yet let me, by his Leave, give a brief Touch here of some few things which are linked with matters that concern the Commonwealth. Such now were the Times, that the Queen, (who never was of opinion that mens Consciences were to be forced) complained many times that she was driven of Necessity to take these Courses, unless she would suffer the Ruine of herself and her Subjects, upon some mens Pretence of Conscience and the Catholick Religion. Yet for the greater part of these silly Priests she did not at all believe them guilty of plotting the Destruction of their Countrey: but the Superiours were they she held to be the instruments of this Villany; for these inferiour Emissaries committed the full and free Disposure of themselves to their Superiours. For when those that were now and afterwards taken were asked, "Whether by Authority of the Bull of Pius Quintus Bishop of Rome, the Subjects were so absolved from their Oath of Allegeance towards the Queen, that they might take up Arms against their Prince; Whether they thought her to be a lawfull Queen; Whether they would subscribe to Sanders's and Bristow's Opinion concerning the Authority of that Bull; Whether if the Bishop of Rome should wage War against the Queen, they would joyn with her or him": they answered some of them so ambiguously, some so resolutely, and some by Prevarication or Silence shifted off the Questions in such a manner, that divers ingenuous Catholicks began to suspect they fostered some treacherous Disloyalty; and J. Bishop, a man otherwise devoted to the Bishop of Rome, wrote against them, and solidly proved, that that Constitution obtruded under the name of the Lateran Council, upon which the whole Authority of absolving Subjects from their Allegeance and Deposing Princes is founded, is no other than a Decree of Pope Innocent the Third, and was never admitted in England; yea, that the said Council was no Council at all, nor was any thing at all there decreed by the Fathers.

Suspicions also were daily increased by the great Number of Priests creeping more and more into England, who privily felt the Minds of men, spread abroad that Princes Excommunicate were to be Deposed, and whispered in Corners, That such Princes as professed not the Romish Religion had forfeited their Regal Title and Authority; That those who had taken holy Orders were, by a certain Ecclesiastical Privilege, exempted from all Jurisdiction of Princes, and not bound by their Laws, nor ought they to reverence or regard their Majesty; That the Bishop of Rome hath supreme Authority and absolute Power over the whole World, yea even in Temporal matters; That the Magistrates of England were no lawfull Magistrates, and therefore not to be accounted for Magistrates; yea, That whatsoever was done by the Queen's Authority since the time that the Bull declaratory of Pius Quintus was published against her, was by the Laws of God and Man altogether void, and to be esteemed as of no Validity. And some of them were not ashamed to own, that they were returned into England with no other Intent, than by reconciling men at Confession, to absolve every one particularly from all his Oaths of Allegeance and Obedience to the Queen, just as the said Bull did absolve them all at once and in general. And this seemed the easier to be effected, because they promised withall Absolution from all mortal Sin; and the safer, because it was performed more closely, and under the Seal of Confession.

IX

The Five and Twentieth Year of Her Reign, Anno Domini 1582

These things and the like extorted from the Estates of the Realm, which were assembled in the month of January at Westminster, new and more severe Laws against the Papists, wherein "they are declared guilty of High Treason, whoever shall disswade the Subjects from their Obedience to their Prince, and from the Religion established in England, or shall reconcile them to the Church of Rome; as also those who shall be so disswaded or reconciled. Those also who shall say Mass are fined in 200 Marks, and Imprisonment for a Year, or longer, till they have payed the Money: they who shall wittingly and willingly be present at Mass are fined in 100 Marks, and Imprisonment likewise for a Year: and they who refuse to frequent Divine Service in their Parish-Churches are fined in 20 Pounds a Month." This the Papists exclaimed was unjustly interpreted of Lunary Months, who had hitherto redeemed their Absence upon Sundays and Holidays for a Shilling to the use of the Poor. But these things let the Ecclesiastical Historians handle more at large.

The Duke of Anjou, having stayed in England full three Months, began his Journey toward the Netherlands in the month of February. The Queen herself, to doe him Honour, accompanied him as far as Canterbury, and commanded the Earl of Leicester, Charles Howard, Hunsdon, Willoughby, Windsor and Sheffield, Barons, Sir Philip Sidney, Sir Francis Russel, Sir George Bourchier, and some other eminent Knights, to wait upon him as far as Antwerp: where he was made Duke of Brabant,

Limburgh, Lorrain, &c. For the Estates of the Confederate Netherlands had before declared the Spaniard to have forfeited his Sovereignty by violating their Laws, broken his Seals in pieces, thrown down his Arms in all places, and absolved the People from their Oath of Allegeance, so that they were at Liberty to chuse themselves another Prince. The Duke granted the Exercise of the Romish Religion to all that would swear Allegeance to him, and abjure the Spaniard. Then he buckled himself to the War, lost Oudenard, and took Alost. Six hundred English, under the leading of Thomas Norris, Barney, Cornish and Gibson, fled from him to the Spaniards, laying the cause thereof upon the imperious Severity of Norris. These men being exposed to all dangerous Brunts, and slightly and contemptuously used, suffered condign Punishment for their Treachery, and too late repented themselves after they had undergone infinite Miseries. However Norris, with 300 Horse and the Remainder of his Companies, gained singular Commendations amongst all men for his Valour and Military Skill. For he courageously received the Prince of Parma, who furiously charged him with great Forces, and made a discreet and sober Retreat to the Walls of Gaunt, while Anjou and the Prince of Orange from the Walls admired his martial Valour. But why do I dwell upon these things? The Duke of Anjou, having now spent in the Netherlands a great Mass of Money which he received out of England, and that without Success, and found that they bestowed upon him nothing but bare and empty Titles, whilst the Government and Management of Affairs remained wholly in the Estates Hands, attempted rashly and unadvisedly to force Antwerp and other Cities, but all in vain, and not without great Loss of his own men; and shortly after left the Netherlands with Dishonour, as having achieved nothing memorable.

Let it suffice to make mention in a word onely of a Comet or Blazing-star seen in the month of May in the 12th Degree of Gemini, near the Star called the little Goat, with a radiant Tail streaming above and beyond the right Shoulder of Erichthonius: as also of an hideous Tempest in Norfolk, with much Lightening, Thunder, violent force of Winds, and a great Storm of Hail, the Stones whereof were three Inches in Thickness, and fashioned like the Rowels of Spurs.

Queen Elizabeth, to strengthen herself abroad against the Spaniard, whom she knew to be exasperated by that Supply of Money sent to the Duke of Anjou, chose Frederick the Second, King of Denmark, whom she had a long time respected as her loving Friend, into the Society of the Order of Saint George; and sent Peregrine Berty, (whom she, as being very sparing in conferring of Honours, with much adoe had admitted to the Title of Baron Willoughby of Eresby before such time as he had given Proof of his Vertue, albeit his Mother were the onely Daughter of the Dutchess of Suffolk, and Heir to the Lord Willoughby,) to invest him with the Ensigns of that Order. The King of Denmark gladly suffered the Chain or Collar of Roses to be put about his Neck, and the Garter to be tied about his Leg: the rest of the Ensigns he received to lay up and keep, but refused to put them on, because they were outlandish; and to take the Oath he absolutely denied, because he had done the same before when he was admitted by the French King into the Order of Saint Michael. Whilst Willoughby remained in Denmark, he represented to the King the Complaints of the English Merchants; who complained heavily, that the Customs were too much raised, whereas in times past they paid in passing the Danish Strait or the Sound for every Ship but a Rose-Noble, that is, the fourth part of an Ounce of Gold, and as much for their Lading or Merchandize, with some small Allowance towards Fires by Night to direct their Course safely, and Barrels or Buoys to shew the Shelves and Rocks. He dealt with him also in behalf of the Merchants to release the Payment of *Last gelt*, whereby was exacted the thirtieth part of all their Merchandize by way of Loan, during the heat of the War betwixt the Kings of Denmark and Swethland, with Promise of Repayment when the War ended. But these things, as being matters of great weight, were put off to another time. For scarce do Princes ever abate of the Customs which they have once imposed, judging that such Royalties (as they call them) do belong as Rights and Privileges to every Kingdom, and are not subject to any foreign Moderation.

Queen Elizabeth also, for her better Security at Home, purposed to compound matters with the Queen of Scots by Sir Walter Mildmay. But finding that the Duke of Guise plotted secretly with certain English Fugitives for her Delivery, and leavied Forces under pretence that they should serve under the Duke of Anjou in the Low Countries, but indeed to be wafted over into England from Auc or Ewe, an obscure Port-town in Normandy belonging to the Duke of Guise; (whereof the French King gave her the first Notice, and out of his Love to Queen Elizabeth crossed it,) the matter was put off to another time, and she was neglected.

But yet to prevent the Duke of Guise his Attempts in Scotland, who was thought to use Lenox his Assistence to avert the King of Scots Affection from the English, William Ruthven, whom the King had very lately created Earl of Goury, raised some Troubles. This William, (not to degenerate from his Father, who bare a deadly Hatred against the King's Mother,) with other Conspiratours, employed all their Wits to remove Lenox and Arran from the King, pretending to provide for the Security of Religion, the King's Safety, and the Amity with England. And thus they went to work. Lenox, who was now made Chamberlain of Scotland, is perswaded to exercise with Rigour the outworn Jurisdiction of Chamberlain; and this to no other intent, but that he might thereby (ignorantly and never dreaming of any such thing) incur the Hatred of the Multitude; which Hatred the Ministers of God's Word should more inflame by declaiming against him publickly out of the Pulpit, as a Papist, a Guisian, and a rigorous Executor of his Authority, and should openly prophesie his Destruction. When Lenox therefore was gone from Perth (where the King then lay) to Edenborough, to exercise the aforesaid Jurisdiction, and Arran was out of the way, Goury, Marr, Lindsey, and others, taking the Opportunity, invited the King to Ruthven Castle, and there detained him against his Will, and terrified him so that he durst not stir abroad. All his faithfullest Servants they removed from him, Arran they carried to Prison, constrained the King to call Home the Earl of Angus from Banishment, (at the Intercession of the Queen of England, who was acquainted with their Plot,) and to send Lenox back again into France: who, being a man of a very mild Spirit, did for the publick Quiet sake surrender up Dunbriton, which he might easily have defended, and refused not to return into France; and this he did at the King's seeming Perswasion, which they had forced him to use with him. And not content with all this, they compelled the King against his will to approve of this their intercepting of him in his Letters to the Queen of England, and to declare an Assembly of the Estates summoned by them to be just and legal. Yet could they not draw Buchanan to approve of this Fact of theirs, either by their Declaration, or by Messengers sent to persuade him; who now with Sorrow repented that he had formerly maintained the Cause of Factious people against their Princes, and soon after died. A man born, as he himself hath written in a Poem, *nec cœlo, nec solo, nec seculo erudito*, that is, neither in a Climate, nor Countrey, nor Age of any Learning; yet happily arriving himself at the Top and Perfection of Poetical Skill, so as he may deservedly be reckoned Prince of the Poets of this Age.

When the French King had certain Intelligence hereof, he dispatched away Mota-Fenellon through England, and Maningville by Sea, into Scotland, with one and the same Instructions, to wit, "That they should take some course or other for procuring the King's Liberty: That they should confirm and encourage the French Faction, draw the King's Mind to embrace Amity with the French, and congratulate him upon this Account, that the Queen his Mother, out of her motherly Piety, granted him the Royal Title, and very willingly admitted him into the Participation of the Kingdom, to wit, that he should be owned for true and lawfull King by the Princes of Christendom and all the people in Scotland, and that all Factions should be for the future taken away." The Queen of Scots in the mean time having her Mind full of Cares and Doubts, being overlay'd with Miseries, and languishing with the Calamity of a long Imprisonment without all Hope of Liberty, deplored her hard Destiny, with the sad Condition of her Son, in a long Letter written in French to Queen Elizabeth, which her Motherly Love and the Anguish of her Mind wrung from her, to this purpose, as I have abbreviated the same out of the very Original.

> Whereas I have been certainly advertised that my Son is surprized by Rebels (as I myself also was some years since,) out of a just Fear lest he should undergoe the same common Condition of Infelicity with myself, I cannot but make my wofull Complaints, and imprint the same (if it may be) in your Conscience,

146

that so my Innocency may appear to Posterity, and their Ignominy by whose unjust Dealings I am most undeservedly brought into these Miseries. But seeing their cunning Practices and Devices (though never so wicked) have hitherto been of more Credit with you than my most Complaints, and your Might may seem to overcome Right, and Force to oppress and bear down Truth amongst men; I will appeal to the ever-living God, in whom onely I acknowledge a Power and Dominion over us that are Princes of equal Jurisdiction, Degree and Authority. And upon him will I call, (with whom there will be no place for Craft nor Fraud,) that in the Last day he will reward us according to our Deserts one towards another, howsoever my Adversaries know in the mean time how to cloak their treacherous Dealings before men (and haply before you). In his Name therefore, and as it were before his Tribunal-seat, I call to your Remembrance, by what cunning Artifices some who were employed in your Name drew the Scots, my Subjects, into Rebellion against me whilst I lived in Scotland, and gave Rise to all those Mischiefs which have hapned there ever since. Which (to omit other Proofs) is certainly known by evident Testimonies to be produced, and by Confession out of Morton's own Mouth, who was in that respect advanced to Honour. Against whom if I had proceeded according to Law and Justice, and you had not aided my Rebels, they could not have stood out long against me and my Friends.

While I was kept in Prison at Lough-Levin, Sir Nicholas Throckmorton was a means to perswade me in your Name to set my Hand to a Writing, and resign the Kingdom; which Writing he affirmed would be invalid, and so the whole World hath taken it to be, until you assisted the Authours of the said Instrument readily with your Favour and Countenance, as also with an armed Power. And tell me *bonâ fide,* would you acknowledge such an Authority and Power of your Subjects over you? Yet thereby was my Regal Authority taken from me, and that by your Advice and Assistence, and my Kingdom translated to my Son, who was then in respect of his Age uncapable thereof. And when I myself was not long since determined to confirm the Kingdom to him lawfully, he was forcibly seized on by certain Traitours, who without question purposed to despoil him (as they had done me) of the Kingdom, if not of his Life also. After I had made an Escape out of Lough-Levin, and was now ready to give the Rebels Battel, I craved your Aid, sending back that Diamond which I had formerly received from you in Pledge of your Love, with large Promises of Assistence against my Rebels time after time renewed, giving me also then your faithfull word, that if I would betake myself to you, you would come to the Borders, and assist me in your own person. I, relying upon this your Promise so often repeated, (though those you employed had many times deceived me with fair words,) resolved to flie unto you in mine Adversity as to a sacred Anchour. And certainly so I had done, had I found as easie Access to you as my Rebels against me have always had. But before I could come to you, I was seized upon, guarded with Keepers, shut up in strong Holds, and have ever since endured Afflictions more bitter than Death itself.

I know you will hit me in the teeth with what passed betwixt me and the Duke of Norfolk: yet I deny that that was any way prejudicial to you or your Kingdom. For it was approved of by the chief Counsellours of the Realm of England, and confirmed by their Subscriptions, which may be produced, who also gave an assured Promise of your Consent. And how (I pray you) could men of that Quality promise your Consent to that which would deprive you of Life, Honour, and your Diadem? yet would you have these things believed by all men.

But when some of my said Rebels repented them when it was too late, and perceived more palpably by the Conference between our Commissioners at York how injuriously I was dealt withall, they were presently beseiged by your Forces in the Castle of Edenborough, and two of the chief of them were miserably bereaved of their Lives, one by Poison, the other by the Gallows. And this after I had at your Request caused them more than once to lay down their Arms, in hopes of Peace, which God knoweth whether my Adversaries ever intended.

From that time forward I determined with myself to try whether I could by my Patience mitigate others Rigour, by bearing quietly all things which should be inflicted upon a captive Queen: yet have I now for this whole Year been quite debarred from all intercourse with my Son either by Letters or Messengers, that so, if it were possible, the Son might be rent and divided from his Mother by a sad and wofull Alienation of Affections.

Conditions of Peace and Concord to be made betwixt us I have often propounded; at Chatesworth eleven years since with your Commissioners, and with yourself by the Embassadours of the most Christian King and mine own, and the last Winter with Beale, have I dealt therein sincerely. But those Conditions have been always rejected, Delays sought and interposed, my Actions and Endeavours misconstrued, and the sincere Affections of my Mind still condemned. And of my long Patience I have reaped no other Fruit, than that by a certain Prescription it grew to a Custome that I was every day more roughly handled than other. These things verily I am no longer able to endure: and howsoever it fall out, if I die, I will make known the Authours of my Death; and if I live, I shall, I hope, cause all wicked Contrivances and Calumnies against me to cease, that I may pass the rest of my life in greater Quiet and Tranquillity.

Wherefore, to take away all Misunderstandings betwixt us, let the Testimonies of the Spaniards that were lately taken Prisoners in Ireland be produced against me, let the Examinations of the Jesuites be brought forth, let very man have liberty to accuse me publickly; so as I in like manner may have liberty allowed me to defend my self, and not be condemned unheard. The basest Malefactours and Prisoners are allowed their Defense, and their Accusers brought before them Face to face. And why am not I so dealt withall, who am an annointed Queen, in Bloud most nearly allied unto you, and next to you the lawfull Heir to the Crown? And this last is that which above all vexeth and troubleth my Adversaries, who labour to set us two at Variance. Alas! there is no reason this should trouble them: I call God and mine own Honour to witness, that I have for this long time thought of no other Kingdom but that of Heaven. Yet are you bound in Conscience, and obliged both in regard of your Duty and Justice, not to prejudice my Son's undoubted Title after my Death, nor to further the secret Contrivances of those who, both in England and Scotland, do labour tooth and nail the Destruction of me and my Son; as is more than too apparent by the Carriage of your Messengers in Scotland, who have behaved themselves seditiously enough, (unknown to you no doubt, though Huntingdon have busily bestirred himself therein.)

Is this Reason, that I who am a Mother should be prohibited not onely to advise my oppressed Son, but so much as to understand in what Condition he is? Had those Messengers been sent for my Son's good, haply, if they had taken my Advice along with them, they might have been more welcome to him for my sake; certainly you had obliged me the more closely to you. Neither was there any Reason why you should so carefully conceal their Sending, or quite take from me at that time all use of my liberty. But, to speak freely, I beseech you to employ no more such Ministers in Scottish Matters. For though Cary (I think) would undertake nothing unbeseeming himself and his Honour; yet can I promise myself no good of Huntingdon, by reason of his bad Behaviour towards me.

Therefore I do earnestly intreat you by the near Kindred that is betwixt us, to have a serious Care of my Son's Safety, to intermeddle no more in Scottish Matters without acquainting me or the French King, and to esteem those for no better that Traitours who detain my Son in Custody, and constrain him against his Will to doe what they list. In brief, I beseech you by the Cross and Passion of Christ our Redeemer, that I may now after so many years Restraint be restored to my Liberty upon reasonable Conditions, and may for the small Remainder of my Life refresh my decayed Body somewhere out of England, after so long Grief and Languishing in Prison. So shall you oblige me and mine, and especially my Son, unto you for ever. And this I will never cease to beg of you with all Earnestness till you grant it me: and that which moveth me so earnestly to crave it is the afflicted state of my Body and Health. Take order therefore that I may hereafter be more courteously used, otherwise in plain terms I shall not be able to endure it: and put me not off to any other Doom or Sentence than your own. Whatsoever hereafter shall befall me, good or evil, I shall take it to come from yourself alone. Vouchsafe me this Favour, that I may understand your Mind from yourself, either by a short Letter, or by the French Embassadour. I cannot rest satisfied with those things which the Earl of Shrewsbury tells me, considering that they are altered every day. When I wrote of late to your Council, you wished me to acquaint yourself onely with my Business. (But there was no reason for you to grant them so large an Authority over me to trouble and afflict me.) Yet I cannot but fear that some of them who are my Adversaries have procured this, lest the rest, when they should have heard my just Complaints, should oppose them, in regard as well of your Honour as of their own Duty towards you. Now it remaineth that I make this special Request unto you, that my Mind being taken up with the Thoughts of another Life, I may have some reverend Catholick Priest allowed me, who may direct me in my Religion for my Soul's Health. This last Office is not to be denied to the silliest Wretches of the meanest Condition. To foreign Princes Embassadours you allow the Exercise of their Religion, and I freely granted it to my Subjects of a different Religion. If this be denied me, (I hope) I shall be excused before God, but my

Adversaries (I fear) will not escape unpunished. Certainly it will be a Precedent for other Princes of Christendom to use the like Severity towards their Subjects of a different Religion, if this Rigour be shewed to me, who am an absolute Princess, and your nearest Kinswoman. For so I am, and so I shall be as long as I live, whether my Adversaries will or no, and though they be never so ill pleased and satisfied at it. To have my Household increased I desire not, but I am necessitated to desire you that I may have two Waiting-women allowed me, whom I shall have need of in this my weak Condition: and let not mine Enemies satisfie their Malice and Cruelty in hindring me of so small a Courtesie. Whereas I am privately accused by the Earl of Shrewsbury, that, contrary to what I promised to Beale, I have dealt with my Son about conveying my Title in Scotland to him without your Privity; I beseech you believe not Beale's Suggestions: I promised nothing but upon certain Conditions, to which I am not at all tied, unless those on your part be performed by you. Since that time I have received no Answer, and a deep Silence hath ensued touching those matters: but the Practices and Contrivances in Scotland to the Destruction of me and my Son have been continued. This so long a Silence I could not construe any thing else but a flat Denial, which I signified to you and your Council by Letters. What the French King and his Mother imparted unto me, I have truly and ingenuously acquainted you withall, and asked your Counsel in it; but I have not heard so much as a Word from you. To submit myself to your Advice touching my Affairs and my Countrey, before I knew what manner of Advice it would be, I never intended: for this might seem a piece of extreme Folly. How my Adversaries in Scotland triumph over me and my Captive Son, is not unknown unto you. For my part I have attempted nothing there which may prejudice you: what I have done hath been for procuring a solid Peace in that Kingdom, whereof, sure, I should have as great a Care as your Council, for I am far more interested therein than they. I desired with all my heart to gratifie my Son by confirming to him the Title of King, and to bury all Discords in Oblivion. Is this to snatch away the Diadem from my Son? But my Adversaries and the Adversaries of my Family would not have it confirmed to him. This they envy him, whilst they carry a Witness against themselves in their own Breast, and by reason of their guilty Conscience mistrust their own Condition.

Let not these and other my Adversaries so far blind your Eyes, as that, while you live and see it, they bring your nearest Kindred to their Graves, and undermine both Crowns: for to that purpose certainly do they carry on their wicked Practices against me, against my Son, and perhaps against yourself too. Can it be any Advantage or Credit to you that by their means I and my Son, and you and I our selves, are so long deprived of one another? Recall your self to your innate Mildness and Lenity, oblige yourself to yourself, and, as you are a Princess, soften your Spirit, and dispose it to lay aside all Displeasure towards me a Princess so nearly related to you in Bloud, and so loving to you; that these matters being compounded betwixt us, I may the more quietly depart this Life, and the Groans and Sighs of my afflicted Soul may not ascend up to God. To whose Majesty I offer up my daily Prayers, beseeching him that these my just Complaints and wofull Lamentations may now at length find Regard with you. At Sheffield the eighth of November, 1582.

Subscribed,

Vostre tres desoleé plus proche parente,
& affectioneé seure, Marie R.

that is,

Your most sorrowfull nearest Kinswoman,
and affectionate Sister, Mary Queen.

X

The Six and Twentieth Year of Her Reign, Anno Domini 1583

With this Letter Queen Elizabeth was variously affected, and (having first permitted Mota-Fenellon the French Embassadour to goe with Davison her own Embassadour into Scotland, watching the time of purpose that he might at unawares meet Lenox as he returned out of Scotland, and having herself after gratiously received the said Lenox, and gently blamed him for the Errours he had committed in Scottish matters,) sent Robert Beale, Clark of the Council, a sharp and sour-natur'd man, to the Queen of Scots, to expostulate with her roundly about these Letters of Complaint, and together with the Earl of Shrewsbury to treat with her about her Liberty, in regard she had very lately by other Letters earnestly requested, that, upon Security given to Queen Elizabeth, she might at length enjoy the same, and be associated with her Son in the Government of Scotland.

Concerning these things a serious Consultation was holden in the Council-Chamber of England, and most of the Council were satisfied that she might be set at Liberty upon these Conditions,

> If she and her Son would promise to attempt nothing which might be prejudicial to Queen Elizabeth, or the Realm of England. If she would acknowledge that whatever was done by her Husband Francis the Second King of France against Queen Elizabeth was done against her Will, and would utterly disclaim the same as unjust; confirm the Treaty of Edenborough, and condemn all other unpleasing Attempts ever since by ingenuously renouncing them. If she would be bound to contrive or act

nothing directly or indirectly against the Government of the Kingdom of England, in either Ecclesiastical or Civil matters, but oppose all such as should any ways attempt the same as publick Enemies. If she would forbear to claim any Right to the Kingdom of England during Queen Elizabeth's life; and afterwards be content to refer the Title of Succession to the Judgment of the Estates of England. If (to the end there might be no place left for Prevarication, and that she might not hereafter alledge, that she condescended to these Conditions being a Prisoner and constrained thereunto,) she would not onely swear to these Conditions herself, but would also procure the Estates of Scotland to confirm them by publick Authority, and the King to ratify them by Oath and Writing and Hostages to be given for the Performance of them.

As for her being joyned with her Son in the Government, it was not thought meet that the Q. of England should be concerned with it: but this they referred to the King of Scots himself and the Estates of Scotland. And if they were so associated together, they should be dealt withall joyntly about the League; if not, severally.

These things were deliberated and consulted of, but without Success, for the Scots of the English Faction utterly rejected the Conditions, crying out that some Scots which were mortal Enemies to the English Nation were by the Advice of the Queen of Scots called Home out of France; and that Holt, an Englishman of the Society of Jesus, was sent privily into Scotland to contrive a way for Invading England.

There was now much striving in Scotland betwixt Mota-Fenellon and Maningville the French Embassadours, and Bowes and Davison Embassadours of England, which of them should by deeper Insinuation allure the King's Mind to the Love of their Nation, and who should draw most men to their Party. Whilst they diligently countermined one the other in their Plots and Designs, the King carried himself evenly and indifferently betwixt them both, and intermedled not in those Factious Stirs, which he laboured rather to compose, well knowing how to temper and mix what was Profitable with what was Just and honest, and in the mean time not to be wanting to Religion or the Commonwealth. But the Ministers of the Word in Scotland were so inflamed with a kind of Zeal against the French, that the same day that Mota-Fenellon was feasted by the Citizens of Edenborough, they appointed a Fast, and all the day long railed upon the French King, the Duke of Guise, and the Embassadours, out of their Pulpits; and a little more they had proceeded to excommunicate all the Guests that dined there. As these Ministers did thus openly, so also some Noblemen of the English Faction, ceased not more closely to persecute and disturb the French Embassadours, untill first Mota-Fenellon, and afterwards Maningville, left the Court and departed, having notwithstanding first cunningly sown the Seeds of Dissension betwixt those who had got the King in their power.

As soon as they were gone, the King profered all Kindness and Respect to the Queen of England by Colonel William Stuart and John Colvill, and asked her Counsel and Advice for composing the present Commotions, and his contracting of Marriage. And now they which had possessed themselves of the King took Heart and Courage when the French Embassadours were removed out of Scotland, and more a while after, when they heard of Lenox his Death. For he, having found but cold Comfort from the French King, who was embroiled with Civil Wars, and now secretly applying himself to work into the Favour of Queen Elizabeth, died at Paris, and at the point of Death openly professed (as he had done before) the Protestant Religion, confuting thereby the Malice of those who had falsly defamed him to be a Papist.

While the Surprizers of the King were triumphing for the Duke's Death, as thinking themselves now sure and certain to keep the King in their power, the King, when they little thought of it, though he were scarce eighteen years of age, disdaining (seeing he was an absolute King) to be under the Tutelage of the three Earls, as he had before wisely yielded to the Time, so now, having got a fit Opportunity, he wrought his own Liberty, and withdrew himself with a few trusty Friends into the Castle of Saint Andrews; taking Occasion from a Rumour spred abroad, that the Noblemen, bearing a deadly Feud and Hatred one against the other, were drawing together Bands of armed men to attend them at the Convention which he had summoned, and therefore he had cause to fear lest his Person should be exposed to Danger amongst their tumultuous Scuffles. And verily he wrote Letters to Queen Elizabeth to that purpose, wherein also he promised that he would constantly maintain Amity with her, and follow her Counsel in settling of his Affairs. But this Accident (he said) happened so unexpectedly, that he could by no means ask her Counsel in it. Afterwards with good Words and a gratious Countenance he advised some of those men by whom he was seized upon to depart the Court for prevention of Disturbances, and promised them Pardon if they would ask it. But of them all Goury onely asked it, and submitted himself, using this Distinction, that he had offended, not in matter, but in form. Then called he Home Arran to the Court, whom he used in his most secret Counsels; and in the next place he seriously set himself to procure a good Agreement betwixt his Nobility, and to clear his Realm and Court from civil Discords.

Whilst he busied himself about these matters, came Sir Francis Walsingham, sent from the Queen of England, out of her great Care lest he should by corrupt Counsels now in his flexible years be alienated from the Amity of the English, to the Damage of both Kingdoms. Walsingham found the King attended with the Flower of his Nobility, and another manner of Face and Appearance of things in Scotland than he expected. At his Audience, he advised him at large the same things which the Queen had before by her Letters put him in mind of out of Isocrates (namely, that "It was the part of a Ruler to be so true and just in his Dealings that more Credit might be given to his Word than to others Oaths,") and that he would have a great care of bad Counsellours and be constant to himself. The King answered wisely and freely, "That if he had written otherwise than he thought, he had done it unwillingly, against his mind, and by Constraint of those that compelled him to it. That he, being a free Prince, was not to be reduced to such Straits that others must impose Counsellours upon him whom he liked not. That he had done nothing but what stood with his Honour and was for his Security. That he had long since vowed the First-fruits of his Friendship to his dearest Sister the Queen of England, and now he offered them gladly and deservedly; and more full Demonstrations of his Friendship he should be able to give, when all his Nobility should be obedient to him, than when he himself was forced to obey one or two of them, and ruled as it were but at their will and pleasure."

Afterwards Walsingham wished him not to impute to Queen Elizabeth those things which had lately fallen out in Scotland: then he shewed him how advantageous to him and to both Kingdoms Amity with England had been heretofore, and might be hereafter, if it were not neglected; and which he said would be firmly established if the Differences betwixt the Nobility of Scotland were by Authority of Parliament buried in Oblivion, if those Noblemen that were removed from the Court might be received again into Favour, Religion maintained inviolate, and a firm League betwixt both Kingdoms established. Neither was Walsingham unprovided of Money to distribute amongst the King's Ministers, that they might bring these things to pass. The King modestly answered, "That he would maintain Amity with England; that he would be wanting in no good Offices towards the Queen, and constantly defend the received Religion." And although he suspected Walsingham to be ill affected both towards him and his Mother, yet he gratiously dismissed him; and being prudently mindfull and carefull of his Affairs beyond what his Age could promise, with great Commendation for his Clemency, he offered a general Pardon to all that had surprized and seized upon him, if they would ask it within a time prescribed. But so far were they from asking it, that they secretly plotted to intercept and surprize him anew. Whereupon they were commanded to depart the Realm within a time prefixed: of whom Marre, Glames, the Commendators of Driborough, Paslet, and some others, betook themselves to Ireland; Boyd, Zester-Wemes, Lochelvine, to the Low-Countries; and Dunfermelin into France. The Earl of Angus was confined within such Bounds in Angus. Onely Goury, hatching new Mischief, stayed beyond the prefixed time, to his own Ruine, as we shall shew anon.

Thus they who had expelled Lenox against his will were themselves, before the year came about, expelled against their wills out of Scotland. The King, as he loved Lenox whilst he lived, so being dead he had him in gratefull Remembrance, and restored his Good name and Repute, which had by his Enemies been blemished and stained, suppressing certain infamous Libels against him. His Children he sent for out of France: his Son Lewis he made Successour in his Father's Honour, and his Daughters he matched some time after to the Earls of Huntley and Marre. And to shew himself a King, and give an early Proof how he could exercise his Kingly Authority, whereas the said Conspiratours had, in a Convention called by their own Authority, decreed their seizing of the King's Person to have been just, and had entred the same in the publick Records; he on the contrary, in a full Assembly of the Estates, declared the same to have been traiterous: although the Ministers, as if they were supreme Judges in the Kingdom, in a Synod convocated by their own Authority, pronounced it to be most just, and thought them to deserve Excommunication who approved not of it.

It is not here to be forgot how in these days, War growing hot betwixt the Moscovite and the Swede in the Northern Climate, John King of Sweden, unable to resist the Power of so great an Emperour, sent Eric of Wisimbrug, his Kinsman, Andreas Riche one of his Council, and Raschy his Secretary, on a noble Embassy to Q. Elizabeth, and by his Letters intreated her to mediate a Peace with the Moscovite by her Embassadour: which she did without Delay, and perswaded the Moscovite to a Peace upon reasonable Conditions. For he dealt now afresh with the Queen about the League before-mentioned, and about his Refuge in England if any Disaster should befall him; and made Suit also for a Wife out of England. Touching these matters Sir Hierome Bowes Knight was sent Embassadour thither, but could hardly satisfie him, for that the Moscovite with much Importunity required an absolute League written in his own words; and would by no means hear that it was not the part of a Christian, nor allowable by the Law of Nations, to exercise Hostility without first denouncing War, or to come to Blows before such time as he that offered the Wrong were required to give Satisfaction, and to abstain from doing farther Injury. The Queen designed him for a Wife the Lady Anne, Sister to the Earl of Huntingdon. But when she certainly understood that he might, by the Laws of his Countrey, put away his Wives at his pleasure; she excused it again by the Lady's Indisposition of Health, and the tender Affection of her Mother, who could not endure the Absence of her Daughter in a Countrey so far distant, and that she had no power to give the Daughters of her Subjects in Marriage without the Consent of their Parents. Nevertheless the Embassadour prevailed with him to confirm the Merchants Privileges: but his Death ensuing the year following, the Trade of the English in Russia, withall decayed by little and little, and the Embassadour was sent back, who returned not without Danger of his Life, and was received by the Queen with Favour and Commendations. He was the first (if an Historian may have leave to mention so trivial a matter) who brought into England the Beast called a *Machlis,* never before seen here: it is like the Beast called an Elk, in Latine *Alce,* but having no Joynts in the Legs, and yet wonderfull swift. He brought also certain Fallow-deer of admirable Swiftness, which being yoked together would draw a man sitting in a Sled with incredible Speed.

Theodore Joannides, the Son of John Basilides, (to joyn Moscovia matters together) succeeded in that vast Empire; a Prince of a duller Spirit, but yet one that would hearken to them that gave him good Counsel. This Theodore granted to all Merchants of what Nation soever free Access into Russia: and being oftentimes solicited by the Queen to confirm the Privileges granted by his Father to the Moscovia Company of English Merchants, to wit, that onely English-men of that Company should come into or trade in the North parts of Russia, and that Custome-free, in regard they were the first that discovered the Passage thither by Sea; he thereupon desired her to give Liberty to all the English to trade into Russia: for to permit some, and deny others, was Injustice. Princes, he said, must carry an indifferent hand betwixt their Subjects, and not convert Trade (which by the Law of Nations ought to be common to all) into a Monopoly to the private Gain of a few. As for his Customs, he promised to exact less by the one half of that Company than of the rest, because they first discovered the Passage thither by Sea. In other matters he confirmed their former Privileges, and added some few more out of his Respect to the Queen, and not for any Desert (as he said) of the Company, many of whom he found had dealt falsly with his People. And other Answer than this could Giles Fletcher, Doctour of Law, who was afterwards sent Embassadour on the same Account, get none. This Fletcher set forth a little Book of the Russian Polity or Tyranny, wherein are very many things worthy of Observation. Which Book notwithstanding was quickly suppressed, lest it might give Offence to a Prince in Amity with England.

Out of Polonia, a Countrey bordering upon Russia, came this Summer into England to see the Queen Albert Alasco, Palatine of Siradia, a Learned man, of a good Feature of body, with a long Beard, and very comely and decent Apparel: who being gratiously welcomed by her, and entertained by the Nobility with great Respect and Feasting, as also by the University of Oxford with learned Divertisements and several Comedies, after four months stay here, withdrew himself secretly, being run far in Debt.

In the County of Dorset there happened this year no less strange a Sight than did in Herefordshire in the year 1571. For a piece of Ground of three Acres in Blackmore removed out of its place, with Trees and Hedges, and passed over other Land, leaving a great Pit, and stopping up an High-way which led to Cerne. Whether this happened through some such boisterous Wind under Ground, where-with Seneca writeth that the Heads of the Gods were turned backward in Jupiter's great Couch; or by reason of much Moisture, the Springs there bubbling up in great abundance, considering that the Ground lay upon a shelving Hill; let others examine.

This was the last year of Thomas Ratcliffe, the third Earl of Sussex of that Family, a man of singular Fidelity to his Countrey, and of a very noble Extraction, his Mother being the Duke of Norfolk's Daughter, and his Grandmother Daughter to Henry Duke of Buckingham, Constable of England. Who, having passed through the highest Honours, (having been sent Embassadour into Germany by Queen Mary to the Emperour Charles the Fifth about the Marriage to be contracted with Prince Philip, and afterwards into Spain to the said Prince Philip about ratifying the Covenants thereof, and to the Emperour Maximilian about Queen Elizabeth's Marriage with Charles of Austria; having also been Lord Lieutenant of Ireland, Lord President of the North parts of England, Lord Chamberlain to the Queen, Chief Forester of England beyond the River of Trent, renowned for his Victories against the Hebridians, and the Scots who infested the Borders,) at length, after striving with a tedious Sickness, died at London without Issue, (though he had had two Wives, Elizabeth Wriothesley, and Frances Sidney,) and left his Brother Henry for his Heir and Successour.

This year also died Henry Wriothesley Earl of Southampton, a man as much devoted to the Romish Religion and the Queen of Scots as any, for which he incurred his Prince's Displeasure, and endured Imprisonment in the Tower. He was Son to Thomas Wriothesley, (whom for his singular Vertue King Henry the Eighth advanced to the Dignity of Baron Wriothesley of Tich-field, to the Order of the Garter, and to the high Honour of Chancellour of England, and made him one of the Overseers of his last Will and Testament; and Edward the Sixth raised to the Honour of Earl of Southampton.) This Henry left by his Wife, the Daughter of Anthony Viscount Montacute, Henry his onely Son and Successour, and a Daughter married to Thomas Lord Arundel of Wardour.

Near the same time was swallowed by the Ocean Sir Humphrey Gilbert Knight, a quick and lively-spirited man, fa-mous for his Knowledge in matters relating both to War and Peace, in his Return from the North part of America, which we call New-found-land, whither he had set sail a little before with five Ships, having sold his Patrimony, in hope to plant a Colony there. But after he had by an Herald or Crier proclaimed that Countrey to belong to the English Jurisdiction, (for Sebas-tian Cabot was the first that discovered it, in the year 1497 be-ing employed therein by Henry the Seventh,) and had assigned Lands to every particular man of his Company; he suffered so much by Shipwrecks and want of necessary Provision, that he was constrained to give over his Enterprise, learning too late him-self, and teaching others, that it is a difficulter thing to carry over Colonies into remote Countries upon private mens Purses, than he and others in an erroneous Credulity had perswaded themselves, to their own Cost and Detriment.

About that time died also Edmund Grindall Archbishop of Canterbury, Primate and Metropolitan of all England, being blind and above 60 years of age; a religious and grave man, who returning from his Banishment under Queen Mary, was made, first, Bishop of London, afterwards Archbishop of York, and lastly Archbishop of Canterbury, and flourished in great Grace with the Queen, untill by the cunning Artifices of his Adversaries he quite lost her Favour, as if he had countenanced the Conventicles of some turbulent and hot-spirited Ministers, and their Prophecies, (as they called them;) but in truth, because he had condemned the unlawful Marriage of Julio an Italian Physician with another man's Wife, while Leicester in vain opposed his Proceedings therein. That little Wealth which he had gathered he bestowed upon the Founding of a School at Saint Bee's in Cumberland, where he was born, and towards the Advancement of Learning in both the Universities. And to his Care (if I may mention so small a matter) are the English-men beholden for Tamarisk, which, having found it by Experience to be exceeding good to ease the hard Distemper of the Spleen, he first of all brought into England.

In his room succeeded John Whitgift, being translated to Canterbury from the See of Worcester; an excellent and very learned man, who gained singular Commendation both by his Justice in the Vice-presidentship of Wales, and by maintaining the Doctrine in the Ecclesiastical Polity of England: which Commendation he farther merited by his Fortitude, Prudence and Patience. Him the Queen (who, as in Civil matters, so also in the Laws Ecclesiastical, was of opinion that no loose Remisness was to be used,) gave in Charge, that he should take special Care to restore the Discipline of the Church of England, and the Uniformity in the Service of God established by Authority of Parliament, which, through the Connivence of the Prelates, the Obstinacy of the Puritans and the Power of some Noblemen, was run out of square; while some of the Ministers closely impugned the Queen's Authority in Ecclesiastical matters, separated the Administration of the Sacraments from the Preaching of the Word, used new Rites and Ceremonies at their pleasure in private Houses, utterly condemned the Liturgy and the Administration of the Sacraments established, as contrary in some things to the Holy Scriptures, as also the Calling of Bishops, and therefore refused to come to Church, and made a flat Schism; while the Papists stood laughing at it, and drew many daily over to their Party, as if there were no Unity in the Church of England.

To take away these Inconveniences, and restore Unity, he propounded these Articles to be subscribed to by the Ministers.

First, That the Queen had the chief and Supreme Power over all persons born within her Dominions of what Condition soever they were; and that no foreign Prince or Prelate had, or ought to have, any Power, Civil or Ecclesiastical, within her Realms or Dominions.

Secondly, That the Book of Common Prayer, and another Book of Ordaining Bishops and Priests, contained nothing in them contrary to God's Word, but might lawfully be used; and that they should use that, and no other Form, either of Prayer, or Administration of the Sacraments.

Thirdly, That they approved the Articles of the Synod at London published by the Queen's Authority in the year 1562 and believed the same to be consonant to God's Word.

By occasion hereof incredible it is what Controversies and Disputations arose, and what Hatred, what Reproachfull speeches he endured at the hands of factious Ministers, and what Troubles, yea and Injuries also, from some Noblemen, who by promoting unfit and undeserving men caused Distraction in the Church, or else gaped after the Revenues and Livings of the Church. Nevertheless through Constancy, Fortitude and Patience, he overcame all Difficulties at last, and restored Peace to the Church: so that not without good Reason he may seem to have chosen that Motto, *Vincit qui patitur,* that is, He overcometh who suffereth with Patience.

And not onely did these men trouble the Church at Home, but also some others, who sprung from these, did the like abroad: namely Robert Brown, a Cambridge-man, a young Student in Divinity, of whom the new Sectaries were called Brownists; and Richard Harrison, a petty Schoolmaster. For these two, presuming by their own private Spirit to judge of matters of Religion, did by Books set forth at this time in Zeland, and dispersed all over England, condemn the Church of England as no Church, and intangled many in the Snares of their new Schism; notwithstanding that their Books were suppressed by the Queen's Command, and solidly confuted by Learned men, and that two or three of the Sectaries were executed at Saint Edmunds-bury.

On the other side, the Writings of certain Papists against the Queen and other excommunicate Princes drew some men, who had the Pope's Power in great Esteem, from their Obedience; and amongst others they so distracted one Somervill a Gentleman, that in all haste he took a Journey privately to the Queen's Court, and, breathing nothing but Bloud against the Protestants, furiously set upon one or two by the way with his drawn Sword. Being apprehended, he confessed that he would have killed the Queen with his own Hands. Whereupon he, and upon his Impeachment Edward Ardern, his Wife's Father, a man of very ancient Gentility in the County of Warwick, Ardern's Wife, their Daughter Somervill, and Hall a Priest, as Accessories, were arraigned and condemned. Three days after Somervill was found strangled in Prison. Ardern was condemned, and the next day after hanged and quartered: the Women and the Priest were spared. This wofull End of this Gentleman, who was drawn in by the Cunning of the Priest, and cast by his Evidence, was generally imputed to Leicester's Malice. Certain it is that he had incurred Leicester's heavy Displeasure; and not without Cause, for he had rashly opposed him in all he could, reproached him as an Adulterer, and defamed him as a new Upstart.

These things at Home. But abroad, the English which lay in Garrison at Alost, a Town in Flanders, being neglected, and having neither Pay nor Victuals, were the last month of this Year driven to those Extremities, that Pigott, who had the Command of them, and the rest of the Captains, breaking their Oath of Fidelity, betrayed the Town for a sum of Money to the Spaniards, and fearing the Disgrace thereof among their own Countreymen, joyned themselves with the Prince of Parma: from whom notwithstanding, when they found he kept not his Word with them, they slunk away by degrees. But the Authours of this Treachery came every one of them to unfortunate Ends. Pigott went into Spain, in hope of Reward: but, being slighted and laugh'd at, he returned again into the Low-Countries, where he was taken by his own Countreymen, and sent into England, and there died miserably in Prison. Dalton, of a Traitour becoming a Pirate, was hanged in England, and Vincent in Brabant. Tailour was stabbed by the Earl of Westmorland; and Walsh, after he had been tossed with a thousand Miseries, was slain in France.

Thus God's Vengeance followeth Traitours at the heels: as Ireland this Year saw by more apparent Examples.

For that infamous Rebel and Traitour to his Countrey, Girald Fitz-Girald, or Giraldides, the eleventh Earl of Desmond of his Family, when his men were spent with Famine and Sword, (who had barbarously vowed to forswear God before they would forsake him,) and when he had scaped the Hands of the victorious English for almost two years by lurking here and there in Corners, was now by a common Souldier found out in a little Cottage, though unknown to him, till having his Arme almost cut off he discovered himself, and was slain by being run through the Body in many places. His Head was sent over into England, and set upon a Pole upon London Bridge.

Such an End had this powerfull man in Ireland, who derived his Pedigree from Maurice Fitz-Girald of Windsor, an Englishman, and of great Renown amongst the first Conquerours of Ireland in the year 1170. He had very fair Lands and Possessions, yea whole Provinces, with Kerry a County-Palatine, many Castles, a number of Vassals and Dependents, and of his own Kindred and Surname he had about five hundred Gentlemen at his Devotion. Of all which, yea and of his Life also, he was bereft within three years, very few of his Family being left, after he had once forfeited his Allegeance to his Prince, through the Perswasion of certain Priests. The principal of whom was Nicholas Sanders, an English-man, who very near at the same instant of time was miserably famished to death, when, forsaken of all, and troubled in Mind for the bad Success of the Rebellion, he wandered up and down amongst Woods, Forests and Mountains, and found no Comfort or Relief. In his Pouch were found several Speeches and Letters made and written to confirm the Rebels, stuffed with large Promises from the Bishop of Rome and the Spaniard. Thus the Divine Justice (if a man may judge) stopped that Mouth with Hunger which had been always open to encourage Rebellions, and to belch forth malitious Lies and Slanders. For (to omit other things) he was the first man that broached that abominable Lie concerning the Birth of Queen Elizabeth's Mother, which no man in those days (though the Hatred and Malice of the Papists was then fresh against her, and might remember it) ever knew, England in full forty years after

never heard of, the Computation of time doth egregiously con-
vince of Falsehood and Vanity, and he, forgetting himself,
(which a Liar should not doe,) doth himself plainly confute.
Yet are there some ill-disposed people who blush not at this day
to beslurr their Writings with this so impudent a Lie.

James Fitz-Eustace, that is, the Son of Eustace, Viscount Bal-
tinglass, a man of great Estimation amongst the Lords of Ireland,
being terrified with the unhappy Fate of these men, fled into
Spain, where he miserably pined away with Sorrow. He had a
little before, out of Zeal to the Romish Religion, taken up Arms
with the Rebels against his Prince, and, writing a short obscure
Letter to the Earl of Ormond his Neighbour, (who deriveth his
Descent from Saint Thomas of Canterbury's Sister,) amongst
other things he with this piece of Wit exhorted him to doe the
like for the Romish Religion, "Had not blessed Thomas of Canterbury died for the Church of Rome, thou hadst never been Earl
of Ormond." For, to expiate the Murther of the said Thomas,
King Henry the Second had in former time given to his Ancestours large Possessions in Ormond.

Sir John Perott Knight, who had born the Office of President
of Munster with Commendation, being this Year made Vice-Roy
or Lord Deputy of Ireland, as soon as he had received the Sword,
summoned the Estates of the Realm to a Parliament, wherein several Laws were enacted, and Desmond, who was lately slain, was
condemned of High Treason, and all his Lands and those of the
other Rebels in Munster confiscate. Which when the Queen was
resolved to lease out at a very easie Rate, thereby to invite Hus-
bandmen thither, that so those fruitfull Fields might not lie un-
tilled, (for the Rebellion had brought a miserable Devastation,)
some of those who were employed to enquire after the Estates of
the Rebels, and others who took their Lands, began to turn the
faithfull and loyal Subjects out of their Possessions with violent
Rudeness, so that the Queen was fain to refrain them by Proclamation, lest the injurious Avarice of some private persons should
kindle a new Fire of Rebellion. Wherein the Lord Deputy did
good Service, though he were now and then blamed by the English, as too favourable to the Irish, and too rigid to the English.
But he, by administring Justice indifferently, and shewing equal
Favour to the Irish and the English, restored the Countrey by lit-

tle and little to a welcome Tranquillity, and by fair and peaceable means reduced the fiercest and rudest of the Inhabitants under the power of the Laws. The Hebridian Scots, who had made an Irruption into Ireland out of the Isles, he sufficiently plagued. Donell Gormi, that is, the Blew, and his Brother Agne Mac-Conell, who had seized upon the small Countrey of Glimes, and Surley Boy, that is, the Tawney, their Uncle, who had invaded Rout, a neighbouring Tract near the Isle of Ricnea, now Rachlin, he drove to those Straits, having by the Valour of Captain Meriman slain many of their Family, that they sware Allegeance to the Queen, and received from her, upon their Intreaty and Petition, certain Lands in that Corner of the Countrey, upon Condition that they should serve the Kings of England onely in their Wars, and none else without their Leave; that they should find so many Horse and Foot in all Expeditions, and pay such a number of Beeves and Hawks every year. These things in Ireland.

XI

The Seven and Twentieth Year of Her Reign, Anno Domini 1584

In the beginning of the Spring certain Scots came privately home out of Ireland, according as they had before laid their Design with Goury, who was now upon new Projects with some others for seizing upon the King's Person again. These men gave out openly, that they aimed at no other thing than the Glory of God, the Sincerity of Religion, the Security of the King and Kingdom, and the maintaining of Amity with the English, against those who by their cunning Artifices and Devices drew the King, whilst he was yet in his tender years, to the Ruine of all. The King hearing hereof, forthwith commanded Colonel Stuart with all possible speed to seize Goury, the Contriver of the Conspiracy, who had already withdrawn himself to the Haven of Dundee, pretending as if he would depart the Realm. Goury, being guilty in his own Conscience, contemned the King's Authority, made an obstinate Resistence, and fought desperately to defend the House he was in; but within an hour or two he was taken and carried to Prison.

The Conspirators in the mean time took Sterlin by a Surprize and forcible Entrance, and the Castle after by Composition; but presently quitted them again, as well because the King had drawn forth his Army into the Field, and was ready in Person to advance against them, as because the Forces which were met were far less than Goury had promised, and they had in vain expected Assistence out of England. And whilst every man for Fear now shifted for himself, Marre, Glames and Angus, (who had joyned with them,) with some others, fled, and coasted the countrey into England, beseeching the Queen to relieve them in their forlorn Condition, and to make Intercession for them to the King, in regard they had lost their Estates and the King's Favour for no other Reason, than because they stood for his Good and the Good of England. The King on the contrary accused them to the Queen of high Misdemeanours, and required to have them delivered into his Hands, according to the League. But there were in the Court those that perswaded the Queen that they were men dutifull and obedient to their King, and highly carefull of his Safety, in regard they attempted nothing against him while they had him in their Hands. And as for that Article for delivering up of Rebels, usually expressed in Leagues, it was long since grown out of use among Princes. These men also went about to perswade the King of Scots to deal favourably with them, being so many in number and so considerable for Quality, lest they should by Despair be driven to worse Undertakings; alledging that Terrour and Violence are but weak and unsuccessful Supports of Power, producing several sad Examples out of the Scottish History; and commending his Mother, and her Husband King Francis, that when the Civil war began in France, they winked at the Miscarriages and Offences of the great ones.

When Walsingham, who extremely favoured the Fugitives, sent his Letters, commanding that, for their Security, they should be received into Lindisfarne, or the Holy Isle; Hunsdon, who was of all men the greatest Friend to the King of Scots, opposed it, judging that that Isle, being a place so strongly fortified, was not to be discovered and made known to the Scots, who might possibly prove Enemies, nor the Secretary to be satisfied herein, unless the Queen expresly commanded it by her own Letters; for that the Jurisdiction of the place did of right belong to him, as Warden of the East March.

Hereupon grew a Dispute, whether the Secretary might not by his own Authority, without the Prince's special Warrant, and without acquainting the Governours of Places, direct and execute the Prince's Business upon all occasions. What was determined herein I find not: but certain it is they were not admitted into the Isle. Yet was it thought good to shew them Favour, that they might be made use of against the contrary Faction in Scotland:

for now the Ministers of the Word spred abroad Rumours in all places, that the King was ready to fall off from Religion; and this upon no other probable Argument, (though they pretended many,) but because his Filial Love and Observance inclined him wholly towards his Mother, and because he received those into his closer Friendship whom he knew to be most devoted unto her.

In the mean time Goury was tried by his Peers at Sterlin. The principal Articles he was charged withall were these. "That whereas the King had raised him to his high Honours, Wealth, and Offices, and had reputed him as his Kinsman, he had notwithstanding entred into a new Conspiracy against his Person, whom he had before kept Prisoner in his House. That he had held nocturnal Consultations with Angus his Servants for the possessing himself of Perth and Sterlin; had by Force and Arms resisted the King's Authority at Dundee; had concealed a Conspiracy on foot for the Destruction of the King and his Mother; and, lastly, had consulted with one Maclen a Witch." He, protesting his Innocency, and his sincere Affection towards the King, acknowledged his Favours, sharply taxed the Earl of Arran as his Adversary and a bloudy-minded man, complained that he was apprehended through his subtile Contrivance, just as he was ready to depart the Land, and fraudulently perswaded, by the Hopes of Life and Pardon offered him, to confess the things objected against him, which therefore in Equity ought not now to be laid to his Charge, seeing they had been deceitfully extorted from him. The reason why he made Resistence (he said) was, because he thought the Warrant for his Apprehension written with Arran's Hand to be of less Force than the Letters of Protection which he had under the King's broad Seal. And whereas he did for a short time conceal the Conspiracy against the King and his Mother, he was not so much to be blamed for that, as to be commended for revealing the same afterward. Lastly, protesting that he hated and detested from his heart all Magicians and Witches, he said openly, that if there were any such, he thought them to be for the most part in Princes Courts. But his Peers, after they had duly sworn that they had been no Instigatours of the King's Advocate to accuse him, pronounced him guilty of High Treason; and the same Evening he was be-

headed. His Head was presently joyned to his Body by his
Friends, which was afterwards buried.

At what time the Scots with such ill Success enterprized these
things against their King for Queen Elizabeth's sake, (as they
pretended,) at the same time some English-men attempted no
less matters, and with no better Success, against their own Queen
for the Queen of Scots sake. Of whom the principal man was
Francis Throckmorton, eldest Son of John Throckmorton, a Justice of Peace in Cheshire, (who not long before had by Leicester's
Policy been turned out of the Commission and fined, for having
(if I be not mistaken in the Lawyers terms) supplied or filled
up some words in a Fine or Judicial Instrument, transcribed out
of an old worm-eaten Original copy, and had not produced it
with all the Defects that were in it at first.) This Francis came
into Suspicion by means of a letter to the Queen of Scots which
was intercepted. No sooner was he committed to Custody, and
had begun tó confess some things, but Thomas Lord Paget, and
Charles Arundel a Courtier, privily fled the Land, and withdrew
themselves into France, where, with others devoted to the Romish
Religion, they heavily bewailed and complained amongst themselves, "That the Queen with without any Fault or Desert of
theirs alienated from them by the subtile Artifices of Leicester
and Walsingham; That they were unworthily disgraced, and
ignominiously used; That strange kind of Tricks and Cheats were
invented, and secret Snares so closely laid, that they must
whether they would or no, and before they were aware, be involved in the Guilt of High Treason; and that there was at
Home no hope at all of any Safety." And verily there were at
this time some subtile ways taken to try how men stood affected.
Counterfeit Letters were privily sent in the Name of the Queen
of Scots and the Fugitives, and left in Papist Houses: Spies were
sent abroad up and down the Countrey to take notice of people's
Discourse, and lay hold of their words: Reporters of vain and
idle Stories were admitted, and credited. Hereupon many were
brought into Suspicion, and amongst the rest Henry Earl of
Northumberland: his Son, Philip Earl of Arundel, was confined to his own House; his Wife committed to Sir Thomas
Sherly's Custody. William Howard, the Earl's Brother, and

Henry Howard, their Uncle, the Duke of Norfolk's Brother, were several times examined about Letters from the Queen of Scots, and from Charles Paget, and about one Mope, then not known who he was, whose Prudence and Innocency could hardly protect them. Neither yet are such ways for Discovery and easie giving Credit to be esteemed altogether vain, where there is a Fear for the Prince's Safety. Certain it is, at this time an horrid piece of Popish Malice against the Queen discovered itself: for they set forth Books wherein they exhorted the Queen's Gentlewomen to act the like against the Queen as Judith had done with Applause and Commendations against Holofernes. The Authour was never discovered, but the Suspicion lighted upon Gregory Martin an Oxford-man, one very learned in the Greek and Latin Tongues. Carter a Book-seller was executed who procured them to be Printed.

And whereas the Papists usually traduced the Queen as rigid and cruel, she (who was always very carefull to leave a good Name and Memorial behind her,) was highly offended with the Inquisitours that were to examine and discover Papists, as inhumanely cruel towards them, and injurious to her Honour. Insomuch as they thought it necessary to excuse themselves by a publick Writing, wherein they protested, "That the Priests were more favourably dealt withall than they deserved: That they were never once questioned for their Religion, but onely for dangerous Contrivances against their Prince and Countrey, and that upon vehement Suspicion, and probable Arguments and Evidence: That Campian was never racked so but that he was presently able to walk, and subscribe his Confession; but Briant, obstinately refusing to speak or write who it was which penned those obscure Papers found about him, was denied Food till such time as he asked it in writing." But these things did not satisfie the Queen, who commanded the Inquisitours to forbear Tortures, and the Judges to refrain from putting to death. And not long after she commanded 70 Priests, some of which were condemned, and others in danger of the Law, to be transported out of England: amongst whom those of chiefest Note were, Gaspar Heywood, Son to that famous Epigrammatist, who was the first of all the Jesuites that came into England; James Bosgrave, of the

Society of Jesus also; John Heart, the most learned of all the rest; and Edward Rishton, that impious ingratefull man to his Prince, to whom though he ought his Life, yet he soon after set forth a Book wherein he vomited out the Poison of his Malice against her.

The Lord Paget and Arundel being come into France, Sir Edward Stafford, the Queen's Embassadour there, diligently observed them, yet could by no means discover what they were contriving. He dealt nevertheless with the French King, that they, Morgan, and other English-men, who were plotting against their Prince and Countrey, might be removed out of France. But he received no other Answer than this: "That if they attempted any thing in France, the King would punish them according to Law; but if they had attempted any thing in England, the King could not take Cognizance thereof, nor proceed against them by Law. That all Kingdoms were free for Fugitives; and that it concerned every King to maintain the Privileges of his own Kingdom: yea, that Queen Elizabeth herself had not long since received and harboured in her Kingdom Montgomery, the Prince of Condé, and others of the French Nation; and that Seguire, the king of Navarr's Embassadour lay in England at this very time, hatching new Troubles against the French King."

In the mean time Don Bernardine de Mendoza, the Spaniard's Embassadour in England, secretly crossed the Sea into France, in a great Rage and Fury, as if he had been thrust out of England, contrary to the Privilege of an Embassadour: whereas indeed, being a man of a violent and turbulent Spirit, and abusing the sacred Privilege of his Embassage by fostering and encouraging of Treason, he was commanded to depart the Land; whereas by the ancient Rigour and Severity in such cases he was to be prosecuted (as many thought) with Fire and Sword. For he had his Hand in these wicked Designs with Throckmorton and others for bringing in of Foreigners into England, and Deposing the Queen. And being gently reprehended for the same, he was so far from clearing himself of the things objected against him by any modest Answer, that he charged the Queen and Council by way of Recrimination with detaining the Genoeses Money, with assisting the Estates of the Low-Countries, the Duke of Anjou, and Don Antonio, and with the Depredations of Drake. But yet, lest the Spaniard should think that Mendoza's Misdemeanours were not hereby punished, but the Privileges of his Embassadour violated, William Waad, Clark of the Council, was sent into Spain, to inform the Spaniard plainly how ill he had performed the Duty of an Embassadour; and withall to let him know, (lest the Queen by thus commanding him away might seem to renounce the ancient Amity that had been betwixt both Kingdoms,) that all Offices of Kindness should by her be still shewed, if he would send any other person who should seem desirous to preserve Friendship, provided the like Kindness might be shewed to her Embassadours in Spain. But the Spaniard not vouchsafing to give Waad Audience, but referring him to his Council; he, taking it in Disdain, boldly declared, that it was a thing usual and customary, even in the Heat of War, for Embassadours to be admitted into the Presence even of an Enemy Prince; and that the Emperour Charles the Fifth, the Spaniard's Father, admitted an Herald to his Presence, who declared War against him from the French King: and therefore he flatly refused to impart the Contents of his Embassie to his Council. And when Idiacio, the Spaniard's Secretary, could not by all the Wit he had learn from him what his Errand was, at length he understood the whole matter from Mendoza, who lay lurking in France. Then, laying aside his publick Quality, he in familiar Discourse told Waad, "That he was sorry there were some that cunningly went about to break off the Amity that was betwixt both Princes, and to beget Misunderstandings. That Injury had been done to the Catholick King himself, rather than to his Embassadours, to Dispesy heretofore, and now to Mendoza: neither was there any Reason why he should accuse Mendoza farther to the King, who had already sufficiently smarted for his Fault, (if he were in any,) by his disgracefull turning out of England; or that he should complain he was not admitted Audience. For the Catholick King had but requited like for like, considering that Mendoza was dismissed by the Queen without Hearing; and as she had remitted Mendoza to her Council, so did the King in like manner refer him to Cardinal Granvell." And though Waad answered, that there was a great Difference betwixt him, who had never done any thing against the Catholick King, and Mendoza, who had notoriously offended the Queen, insolently refusing for a long time to come at her, and having done things unbeseeming an Embassadour; yet could he not be admitted, but returned Home unheard. The greatest part of the Crimes which he would have charged upon Mendoza were taken out of Throckmorton's Confession.

For when Throckmorton was to be apprehended, he had privily sent away a Cabinet of Secrecies to Mendoza. The rest of his Coffers being searched, there were found two Catalogues, in one whereof were written the names of the Ports in England that were convenient to land Forces at; in the other, the names of those Gentlemen all over England that embraced the Romish Religion. As soon as he saw these two Catalogues produced, he cried out that they were counterfeit, never seen by him before, and foisted in purposely for his Ruine: and this he said while he was upon the Rack. But being brought again to the Rack, he refused not to answer his Knowledge to what Questions were demanded of him. And being then asked touching those Catalogues, and to what intent they were written, he devised this Story.

> That going some few years before to the Spaw, he had consulted with Jeney and Sir Francis Inglefield how England might best be attempted by Foreigners, and the form of Government altered: and to that End he had taken those Notes of the Havens, and the Gentlemens Names. That Morgan had given him to understand by Letters out of France, that the Catholick Princes were now resolved that England should be invaded and the Queen of Scots set at Liberty under the Conduct of the Duke of Guise, who now wanted nothing but Money, and an auxiliary Army to be ready in England. That to procure these things Charles Paget was sent privily into Sussex, under the counterfeit Name of Mope, where the Duke of Guise purposed to land. That he had imparted the matter to Mendoza, and shewed him the names of the Havens and of the Gentlemen, who had already been made acquainted with them by the Conspiratours. He denied not but he had promised his Assistence; and withall had told Mendoza what Gentlemen he might safely treat withall about these things, as being a publick Person, which he, being a private man, could not doe without Danger: and that he concluded with him of a

way how certain principal men of the Catholicks might, as soon as the foreign Forces should arrive, raise men, in the Queen's Name, to joyn with the Foreigners.

These things he voluntarily then confessed.

Nevertheless being charged with these matters at the Barr in Guildhall London, he stifly denied every particular, and affirmed that they were vain Fictions of his own, purposely uttered that he might not be put again to the Rack; and openly accused the Queen of Cruelty, and his Examiners of false dealing: imagining he should escape by reason of the distance of time between the Crime committed and his bringing to Trial. For in the 13th Year of Queen Elizabeth several Crimes were reckoned up as High treason, for which yet no man was to be called in question, unless the Delinquent were charged therewith within six months after the Fact committed, and the thing were proved by the Witness and Oath of two men, or by the Party's voluntary Confession without Constraint or Violence. But this time was long since expired, and therefore (he said) he was not to be called in Question. But the Judges shewed, that the matters objected against him were not of that sort there mentioned, but that he was indicted upon an ancient Statute of High treason, made in the Reign of Edward the Third, which admitted of no Circumscription of Time or Proof. And according to this Law was Sentence of death pronounced against him. Being afterwards perswaded, he cast himself upon the Queen's Mercy, and in Writing confessed again at large all those things in a manner which he had done before: which yet (such was his Inconstancy) he again began to deny at the Gallows, but in vain.

William Waad, being returned out of Spain, was sent about this time to the Queen of Scots, about a Treaty to be holden betwixt her and Sir Walter Mildmay, which was propounded two years before, and interrupted, as I have said formerly. To whom she protested with many Asseverations how sincerely she had dealt concerning this Treaty, and withall vowed herself and her whole Ability to the Queen, and promised to depend wholly upon her, if she would vouchsafe to shew her so much Love and Honour. Moreover she religiously promised, if this Treaty did proceed, to mediate, yea to engage, that her Son should receive Angus and the rest of the Scottish Noblemen into Favour;

as also that the Bishops of Rosse and Glascow, her Agents in France, should attempt nothing to the Prejudice of the Queen or the Realm of England, and that they should from thenceforth have nothing to doe with the English Rebels and Fugitives.

These things Queen Elizabeth was glad to hear: and whereas at very near the same time Angus, Marre, J. Hamilton and Glames were fled into England, she, laying hold on the Opportunity, sent Beale to the Queen of Scots, that together with the Earl of Shrewsbury he might let her know, that if she continued in the same Mind which she had expressed to Waad, Mildmay should come shortly to her, and treat with her about her setting at Liberty: and farther, might perswade her in the mean time to mediate with her Son for the Restoring of the Scottish Fugitives, and inform her that they had designed nothing against the King, but onely against certain violent Counsellours, who had seduced him by their evil Counsels: and, lastly, might learn from her as near as might be the Attempts and Designs of the Duke of Guise. She very prudently answered,

> That she much desired the Treaty might proceed, and this she earnestly craved of Queen Elizabeth, as of her elder Sister, to whom she tendered all Respect and Honour. That she had propounded nothing to Waad but what was limited with Conditions; and that he could say no other, whom she took to be an ingenuous honest man. That to the Restoring of the Fugitive Scots her helping Hand would be very necessary, and thereof they should not fail, if she could certainly find that any Advantage would come thereby to her and her Son; provided they would humbly submit themselves to the King, and become obedient to him: otherwise she would not appear for them, but assist her Son to bring them to their Duty. Besides, she denied not but that, when she found herself grow sickly, she committed herself and her Son to the Protection of the Duke of Guise, her dearest Kinsman: That she understood nothing of his Atempts; neither, if she did, would she discover it, unless she had good Assurance given her of her Deliverance: for it were no point of Wisedom, to forsake certain Friends upon uncertain Hopes. She prayed that she might be no more hardly dealt withall, being a free Princess, than Queen Mary dealt in times past with Queen Elizabeth, being then her Subject and Prisoner; or than the French King dealt of late with the King of Navarre, his Subject also,

and up in Arms against him. She prayed also that the Treaty might be completed before any Commissioner were appointed in Scotland touching that matter. And whereas the most Christian King had acknowledged her Ordinary Embassadour, and Seton, who was sent from her Son into France, as Embassadours from Princes of the same Authority, and associate in the Government, she offered the Queen the Honour to publish this Association of her and her Son in Scotland, and besought her that she would no ways prejudice the same.

These things had a Hearing, but were soon laid aside, and the whole Business defeated, by means of certain Fears cast in the way by those who knew how to increase Suspicions between Women that were already displeased with one another; but principally by the Discovery of certain Papers which Chreicton a Scottishman, of the Society of Jesus, passing into Scotland, and being taken by some Netherland Pirates, had torn in pieces: the torn Pieces whereof being thrown over-board were by the Wind blown back again, and fell by Chance into the Ship, not without a Miracle, (as Chreicton himself said.) These being put together by Waad with much Pains and singular Dexterity discovered new Designs of the Pope, the Spaniard, and the Guises, for Invading England.

Hereupon, as also upon occasion of Rumours from all parts that great Dangers were at hand and threatened, to prevent the wicked Designs and treacherous Practices of Seditious people, and to provide for the Queen's Safety, upon which the Welfare both of the Realm and Religion depended, many men of all Degrees and Conditions throughout England by Leicester's means, and out of their own publick Care and Love, whilst they stood not in Fear of her, but were full of Fear for her, bound themselves in an Association by mutual Vows, Subscriptions, and Seals, to prosecute to the death, as far as lay in their power, all those that should attempt any thing against the Queen.

The Queen of Scots, who easily perceived that her Destruction was aimed at by this Association, being weary of her long Misery, and fearing harder Measure, propounded these things following to the Queen and Council by Nawe her Secretary.

That if her Liberty might be granted her, and she might be assured of Queen Elizabeth's sincere Affection and Love towards

178

her, she would enter into a closer Amity with the Queen, officiously love and observe her above all other Princes in Christendom, forget all by-past Displeasures, acknowledge her to be the true and rightfull Queen of England, forbear to pretend or lay Claim to the Crown of England during her Life, attempt nothing against her directly or indirectly, flatly renounce the Title and Arms of England, which she had usurped by the Command of King Francis her Husband, as likewise the Pope's Bull for her Deposing; yea and enter also into the aforesaid Association for the Queen's Security, and into a League defensive, (so far as might stand with the ancient League betwixt France and Scotland,) Provided that nothing should be done during the Queen's Life, or after her Death, which might prejudice her, her Son, and their Heirs, in the Succession, before such time as they were heard in an Assembly of the Estates of England. That for Confirmation hereof, she herself would stay a while in England as an Hostage: and if she were permitted to depart out of England, she would deliver other Hostages. Moreover, that she would alter nothing in Scotland, provided she and her Family might be allowed the Exercise of their Religion. That she would also bury in Oblivion all Injuries done to her in Scotland, (howbeit upon the Condition, that whatsoever had been enacted to her Disgrace and Disparagement might be repealed). That she would recommend such Counsellours to the King as were well affected to Peace with England; and reconcile unto him, as far as lay in her power, such of his Nobility as were fled, if they would submissively acknowledge their Fault, and that Queen Elizabeth would pass her Word and Promise to aid the King against them if at any time they should fly off from their Duty and Obedience. That she would doe nothing about her Son's Marriage without acquainting the Queen: and as she would doe nothing without the Advice of her Son, so she desired that her Son might be included in this Treaty, that so it might be the more strongly and solidly confirmed. She doubteth not but the King of France would be her Surety in the Business, and pass his Word, together with the Princes of the House of Lorrain, for Performance of Covenants.

She prayed that a speedy Answer might be returned hereunto, left any Inconveniences should fall out in the mean time. And lastly, she besought that she might be kept in freer Custody, that thereby the Queen's Love towards her might be more plainly discerned. These things, as savouring of much Respect and Honour, Q.

Elizabeth seemed to take great Pleasure and Contentment in; and it was believed she was then really purposed to set her at Liberty, though there wanted not some in England who, by laying new Fears before her, deterred her from it. But the Business, which was as good as concluded, was quite hindered and dashed by the Scots of the contrary Faction, who cried out, "That there was no Hope of Queen Elizabeth's Safety, if she were set at Liberty; That both Kingdoms were undone, if she were admitted to be Partner with her Son in the Kingdom; that the true Religion in Britain was ruined, if the Exercise of the Romish Religion were allowed her, though it were but within the Court-Walls."

And not content with this, some Ministers in Scotland bitterly inveighed against the Queen, and loaded her with unworthy Calumnies both from the Pulpit and in their ordinary Meetings; and withall notoriously bespattered the King and his Council: for which being commanded to appear before them, they refused with a disdainfull Contempt, as if the Pulpits were exempted from the Authority of Kings, and Church-men were not subject to the Command of the Prince, but to the Presbytery; flatly contrary to the Laws made this year in an Assembly of the Estates, whereby the King's Authority over all his Subjects, as well Ecclesiastical as Lay, was established for ever. By which Laws the King and his Council were made competent Judges in all Causes; and those who declined their Judgment were to be reputed guilty of High Treason: the Assemblies of the Presbyteries, (as also the Conventions of Lay-men) as well general as particular, were prohibited, which had assumed and arrogated to themselves a boundless Authority, both to assemble at their pleasure without the King's Consent, and to prescribe Laws to the King himself and the whole Realm: the popular Equality also of Ministers was taken away, and Bishops restored to their Dignity and Jurisdiction, whose Calling the Presbyteries had condemned as Antichristian: also scandalous and defamatory Writings against the King, the King's Mother, and his Council, and particularly George Buchanan's *History,* and a *Dialogue of the Right and Privilege of the Scottish Kingdom,* were prohibited and suppressed, as containing in them many things to be found fault withall, to be defaced and obliterated.

These things some of the Ministers took so heinously, that they voluntarily departed the Land, and filled all England with their Clamours and Complaints, as if the true Religion of Christ were now quite driven out of Scotland. Queen Elizabeth hearkned not to them, but neglected them as Innovatours and men given to Change, neither suffered she them to preach in England; yet now and then she used their Help, lest Religion in Scotland should receive any Prejudice. And when Arran, who was in high Trust and Favour with the King, officiously offered his Service with all Respect to maintain Amity with the English, she thought it a fit time to make use thereof, that neither the Scottish Fugitives might be prescribed in the Parliament of Scotland now at hand, nor the King's Mind alienated from the Friendship of the English. Whereupon a Conference was appointed between Arran, and Hunsdon Governour of Berwick, upon the Borders of both Kingdoms. But before this Conference came to be holden, the Fugitives and all those that were present at the Attempt upon Sterlin (the Meeting of the Parliament being hastened) were proscribed; and at the Conference, which followed presently upon it, Arran charged them with great and weighty Crimes, and amongst other things, that they had very lately plotted the Destruction of the King. But he promised most religiously that he would be wanting in nothing whereby he might give the Queen Satisfaction; and that he would not doe any thing which might prejudice her, as long as he was in Grace and Credit with the King. Notwithstanding within a month the Scottish Borderers, through the secret Wiles of the Spaniard, (who laboured all he could to divert Q. Elizabeth from the Low-Countrey War,) invaded Rhedesdale, using all manner of Hostility: and not long after the English Borderers sharply revenged the Wrong they had received by Fire and Sword all over Liddesdale.

Now came Embassadour from Scotland Patrick Gray, Heir of that Family, a quaint young Gentleman, and one that thought himself able for the weightiest Business, if not more. The chief Heads of his Embassage were, about Restraining of Incursions on both sides; about Restoring of Goods taken by Piracy; and about either sending back the Scottish Fugitives, according to the League, or removing them farther from the Borders of Scotland, they with others in Scotland daily plotting new Treasons against the King. For the more easie obtaining of these things, and to win the Queen's Affection more fully to the King, he made her believe he would reveal some secret Conspiracies against her. To the first and second Points he received the Answers he desired. As for sending back the Scotts, the Queen answered, "That she was verily perswaded that those Gentlemen had not so much as imagined the least Mischief in their Hearts. That those things which fell out of late in Scotland proceeded not from any Ill will of theirs towards the King, but from mutual Differences arising amongst the Nobility always in the Minority of their Kings, which it concerned the King to make up with all speed, and to bind his Subjects to him in one common Band of Obedience, and suppress all Factions amongst them." Nevertheless, in some part to satisfie the King's just Request, and that she might come to know what were those secret Practices which he spake of, she commanded that the Scottish Fugitives should remove farther from the Borders. What Discovery soever he made, the Queen made shew as if she understood it all before: and many men accused Gray, as if, corrupted with Money, he had blabbed forth somewhat to the Prejudice of the King and his Mother, and had hindered the accepting of those of reasonable Conditions which were propounded by Nawe from the King's Mother.

Whereupon she, whose Patience had now for a long time been abused, began to fall into great Sorrow and Indignation, and, out of a Desire of her Liberty, to open both her Heart and her Ears as well to the treacherous Counsels of her Adversaries, as to the dangerous Advices of her Friends. And the rather, because, as she had before perswaded herself that the late Association was made for her Ruine and Undoing, so now she had heard that she was (through the crafty Contrivance of some) to be removed from the Custody of the Earl of Shrewsbury, (who was a downright honest man, and favoured not their Attempts,) and committed to new Keepers. Which that it might be done the more handsomely, and the Fidelity of the Earl of Shrewsbury, which had been throughly tried and approved, might not seem to be suspected, (for it was not thought good openly to blemish so great a man's Reputation, which notwithstanding they had stained secretly by Calumnies grounded upon the false Accusations of his ill-condition'd Wife,) Suspicions were laid hold on, as if there were a Plot already laid to set her at Liberty; and those raised upon occasion of certain Emblems sent unto her. The Emblems were these: Argus with his many Eyes lull'd asleep by Mercury sweetly piping, with this short Sentence, *Eloquium tot lumina clausit,* that is, So many Eyes hath Eloquence fast clos'd: Mercury cutting off Argus's Head, who was Io's Keeper: A Scien grafted into a Stock, and bound about with Bands, yet budding forth fresh, and thus writing about, *Per Vincula cresco,* that is to say, By Bands I grow: A Palm-Tree pressed down, but rising up again, with this Sentence, *Penderibus innata Virtus resistit,* that is, 'Gainst Weights doth inbred Virtue strive. This Anagram also, *Veritas armata,* that is, Truth armed, according to her Name *Maria Steuarta,* the Letters being transposed, was taken in an ill sense. There were also Letters produced, as if they had been intercepted, wherein the Friends of the Captive Queen complained, that all Hope of delivering her was quite cut off, if she were once committed to the Puritans Keeping. Under pretence hereof she was removed from the Earl of Shrewsbury, who had many times earnestly desired the same, and committed to the Custody of Sir Amias Powlet and Sir Drue Drury, and that purposely, (as some thought) that, being thereby driven to Despair, she might be apt to take rash Counsels and Resolutions, and be the more subject to be insnared. For the Earl of Shrewsbury had kept her for fifteen years with such Wariness and Circumspection, that he had prevented all possible ways of attempting any thing either for her or against her. But now not onely she with Importunity solicited the Bishop of Rome and the Spaniard by Sir Francis Inglefield to hasten what they had in hand with all Speed, whatever should become of her; but also Leicester (who people thought contrived and studied how to prevent her lawfull Succession) privily sent certain cut-throat Murtherers (as some report) to take away her Life. But Drury, being a sincere honest man, and detesting from his heart so foul a Deed, denied them Access to her. Nevertheless there were some employed underhand to her, and several Letters secretly sent her, as well counterfeit as true ones, whereby her weak Sex might be thrust forward to her own Destruction, as we shall shew afterwards.

To alienate Queen Elizabeth wholly from her, it was whispered into her Ears, that Allen for the Catholick Church-men of England, Inglefield for the Laiety, and the Bishop of Rosse for the Queen of Scots, had with unanimous Consent resolved, with the Assent also of the Bishop of Rome and the Spaniard, "That Queen Elizabeth should be deprived of her Crown, the King of Scots disinherited of the Kingdom of England, as being both of them notorious Hereticks, and the Queen of Scots married to some English Catholick Nobleman: That this Noble-man should be elected King of England by the English Cath-olicks, and the Election confirmed by the Bishop of Rome: That his Children by the Queen of Scots should be proclaimed lawfull Successours to the Crown." And all this was taken up on the Credit of Hart a Priest. But who this English-man should be, Walsingham inquired with all imaginable Diligence, but could never find out. But the Suspicion lighted upon Henry Howard, the Duke of Norfolk's Brother, who was a man of noble Bloud, a Bachelour, extremely Popish, and in very great Credit and Repute amongst the Papists.

Within the compass of this Year Charles Nevil, that traitorous Rebel against his Prince and Countrey, the last Earl of Westmor-land of this House, ended his life obscurely in a miserable Exile. From this Family, fruitfull in Nobility, there sprung (besides six Earls of Westmorland) two Earls of Salisbury and Warwick, an Earl of Kent, a Marquess Montacute, a Duke of Bedford, a Baron Ferrers of Ousley, Barons Latimers, Barons Abergaven-ney, one Queen, five Dutchesses; to omit Countesses and Baron-esses, an Archbishop of York, and a great number of inferiour Gentlemen.

In England died this Year no man more worthy to be re-membred than Edmund Plowden, who as he was singularly well learned in the Common Laws of England, whereof he deserved well by his Writings, so for Integrity of Life he was second to no man of his Profession.

But in France died Francis Duke of Anjou, of Sickness which he contracted through Grief and Trouble of Mind. And in Holland died William Prince of Orange, being treacherously shot with three Bullets out of a Gun by Balthazar a Burgundian.

For the sad Loss of these two Queen Elizabeth was very much troubled, and sent B. into France, to let the King understand how heavily she took the Duke of Anjou's Death, whom she had alway found to be a most faithfull and dear Friend to her; and withall to put him in mind what a sad Condition the Netherlanders now were in, the Prince of Orange being slain, and how formidable the growing Power of the Spaniard was: for all the Princes in Italy were at his Beck, the Bishop of Rome was wholly addicted and engaged to him, the Cardinals were as it were his Vassals, all the ablest Persons for matters both of War and Peace were his Pensioners, in Germany the House of Austria, an House extending and branching far and wide, and other Houses allied unto the same by Marriages, did as it were attend upon him and his Service; his Wealth also and Strength as it were so much increased, both by Sea and Land, since the late Addition of Portugal and East-India, that he was far more powerfull and formidable than ever his Father Charles the Fifth was: and if he should once reduce the Netherlanders under his Power, there was nothing to hinder but that the rest of the Princes of Christendom must of necessity stoop to his Greatness, unless it were timely prevented.

XII

The Eight and Twentieth Year of Her Reign, Anno Domini 1585

Queen Elizabeth, that she might bind the French King to her in the firmer Tie of Amity, having the last year chosen him into the Order of the Garter, now sent Henry Earl of Derby with the Robes and Ensigns of that Order into France, solemnly to invest him therewith. The King received them with great Respect and Esteem, being invested at Even-song, (the English refusing to be present at the Mass,) and religiously promised to observe the Laws of the said Order which were not repugnant to the Laws of the Order of the Holy Ghost and Saint Michael, to which he was before formally sworn.

At this time a Parliament was holden, and William Parry, by Nation a Welsh-man, born of obscure Parentage, and of mean Estate, by Title a Doctour of the Law, (though but indifferently learned) a man exceeding proud, neat and spruce, when a Bill was preferred in the Lower House against the Jesuites, was the onely man that stood up to speak for them, pleading that the said Law was "cruel, bloudy, desperate, and of pernicious Consequence to the English Nation." Being willed to shew his Reasons, he obstinately refused, unless it were before the Queen's Council; whereupon he was committed to Custody: but his Reasons being after heard, and Submission made, he was admitted again into the House. Shortly after the same Parry was accused by Edmund Nevill, (who claimed the Inheritance of the Nevills Earls of Westmorland, and the Title of Lord Latimer, as next Heir male,) to have been ingaged in a secret Design for taking away the Queen's Life.

This Parry, (to fetch the matter a little higher,) returning out of Italy above two years since, had, to win Favour and Credit with the Queen, privately revealed what Morgan and other Fugitives had wickedly plotted and agreed on for the taking away of her Life; pretending that he had gone along with them for no other intent, but onely to get out of them the Depth of the Design, that so he might provide for the Queen's Safety. Hereupon she did not lightly give Credit to Nevill's Information; yet commanded Walsingham to ask Parry, whether he had dealt about this matter with any mal-contented and suspected person to feel his Inclination in the Business. He flatly denied that he had; and being otherwise a man quick-sighted enough, yet saw he not the Evasion which the Queen's Lenity had laid before him. For if he had but given the least inkling that he had dealt with Nevill to feel him, whom he had already told the Queen to be a suspected and mal-contented man, he had without doubt avoided the Danger. But a wicked Deed once resolved upon doth many times infatuate the sharpest Wits. But whereas Nevill had no Witness to make good his Accusation, Parry was brought to confront him, when, after some tart biting Words one against another, Parry began to relent a little, and, being sent to the Tower of London, voluntarily confessed these things which I shall briefly relate.

In the year (saith he) 1570 I was sworn one of the Queen's Servants, and continued intirely devoted to her Majesty till the year 1580 at what time I came into Danger of losing my Life with great Disgrace. (For he had broken into Hugh Hare's Chamber, in whose Debt he was, and had wounded him; for which he was by the Law condemned, but had his Life saved by the Queen's gratious Pardon.) From that time I continued troubled in my Mind, and, having procured a Licence, withdrew myself into France; not with any intention to return hither again, for I had devoted myself to the Catholick Religion. At Paris I was reconciled to the Church of Rome. At Venice I had Conference with Benedict Palmio a Jesuit concerning the distressed Catholicks in England; and I gave him some Hint that I had found out a way to relieve them, if the Pope or any learned Divines would justifie it to be lawfull. Palmio extolled this as a pious Design, and me he recommended to the Pope's Nuncio at Venice, whose name was Campeius, and Campeius recommended me to the Pope. I besought by Letters that I might come to Rome with a Safe Conduct. Letters of Safe conduct were sent me from the Cardinal of Como, but not large enough: afterwards others were sent me more large and full: but then I was returned to Paris. There I lighted upon Morgan, who told me, that it was expected by divers that I should doe some notable Service for God and the Catholick Church. I answered, that I was ready to kill the greatest Subject of England. But (said he) why not the Queen herself? And this (said I) might easily be done, if it might appear to be lawfull. For Wattes a Priest (with whom I had Conference about it, concealing Persons names) affirmed flatly it was not lawfull. (And Chreicton also, the Scottish Jesuit, avouched the same; teaching, "That evil was not to be done that Good might come of it: That God was better pleased with Adverbs than with Nouns; and more approved what was done well and lawfully, than what was otherwise Good: and That many Souls were not to be redeemed with the Destruction of any one, without the express Command of God.") Notwithstanding I, having ingaged myself both by Letters and Promises while I was in Italy, thought it an heinous Sin to give over my Enterprise, in case the Pope should approve it by his Letters, and grant me a plenary Pardon, which I begged of him by Letters I sent to him by Ragazonio his Nuncio in France, who highly commended my Design, and sent my Letters to Rome. Being returned into England, I procured Access to the Queen, to whom, after all Bystanders were removed, I discovered the whole Conspiracy, howbeit cloaked with the best Art I could. She heard me without being daunted: I departed not without being terrified; and cannot now forget what she then said, That no Catholicks should be called in question merely for Religion or the Pope's Supremacy, so that they shewed themselves good Subjects. In the mean time, whilst I was a daily Suitour in the Court for the Mastership of Saint Catharine's, I received Letters from the Cardinal of Como, wherein my Enterprise was commended, and myself absolved in the Pope's Name. These Letters I imparted to the Queen. What effect they wrought with her I know not; to me certainly they added Courage, and took away all Scruple. Yet was I not minded to offer her any Violence, if she could by any means be persuaded to deal more favourably with the Catholicks. And therefore, lest I should commit the Murther, I laid away my Dagger still as often as I had Access to her. When I seriously considered her and her truly-royal Vertues, I was distracted with doubtfull Thoughts; for my Vows were recorded in Heaven, my

Letters and Promises amongst Men. These things I often pondered with an unquiet Mind: I was never much beholden to her for anything: my Life indeed she once pardoned me; but to have taken it away upon that Occasion had been cruel and tyrannical. Hereupon I departed from the Court much unsatisfied with my Condition. I lighted upon Doctour Allen's Book against the Justice of Britain, where he taught that Princes excommunicate for Heresie were to be deprived of Kingdom and Life, which Book did strongly encourage me to prosecute my Attempt. This Book I read to Nevil (whom I sometimes invited to my Table) six whole months before he accused me. Afterwards he came to me and said, Let us venture upon somewhat, since we can get nothing from the Queen: and he propounded several things about the Delivery of the Queen of Scots. But I have (said I) a greater Business in my Mind, and of more Advantage for the Catholick Church. The next day he came and swore upon the Bible, that he would conceal and constantly pursue anything that should be for the good of the Catholick Religion: and I sware the like. We then resolved with ten Horsemen to set upon the Queen as she road abroad to take the Air, and to kill her. All which Nevil concealed till now. But having heard that the Earl of Westmorland was dead, whose Estate he had already swallowed in Hopes, he presently brake his Oath, and accused me of these things.

All this he confessed before the Lord Hunsdon, Sir Christopher Hatton, and Sir Francis Walsingham, all three of the Privy Council. He acknowledged also his Fault, and begged Pardon for the same by his Letters to the Queen, to Burghley Lord Treasurer, and to Leicester.

Some few days after he was arraigned at the King's Bench-Bar in Westminster-Hall: where the Articles of his Indictment being read, he confessed himself guilty. And when his Confession was recorded, and Judgment demanded against him, Hatton thought it necessary, for Satisfaction of the Multitude that were present, that his Crime should be clearly and fully represented out of his own Confession, which Parry acknowledged to be voluntary, aud prayed the Judges that he might reade it himself. But the Clark of the Crown read both it, and also the Cardinal of Como's Letters, and Parry's own to the Queen, to Burghley, and to Leicester; which he confessed to be the

very Letters themselves. Yet did he deny that ever he was resolved to kill the Queen. Being now commanded to speak, if he
had any thing to say why Judgment should not be given against
him, he answered perplexedly, as if he were troubled in Conscience for the foul Fact he had undertaken, "I see I must die,
because I have not been constant to my self." Being willed to
declare more plainly what he meant, "My Bloud (said he) be
amongst you." Sentence of Death being pronounced, he in a
Fury cited the Queen to the Judgment-seat of God. The fifth
day after he was laid upon an Hurdle, and drawn through the
midst of the City to Westminster. At the Gallows, when he had
made his Boasts how faithfull a Preserver and Keeper of the
Queen he had been, he said he was never fully resolved in his
Mind to take away the Queen's Life. Thus this vain-glorious
man, not so much as in the least commending himself to God,
suffered the death of a Traitour by the Law in the Court-yard of
the great Palace at Westminster, where was then a full Assembly
of the Estates of the Realm met in Parliament.

In this Parliament some there were who, out of a Desire either
of Innovation or Reformation, struck deeply at the Ecclesiastical
estate, (though the Queen had forbid it,) by bringing in Bills
for restraining the Episcopal Jurisdiction in granting of Faculties,
in conferring of holy Orders, in Ecclesiastical Censures, and in
the Oath *ex officio*; and proposing a new Oath to be taken by the
Bishops in the Chancery and the King's Bench, viz. that they
should act nothing contrary to the Common Law of England:
also requiring Residence of Pastours, that every Pastour should
be resident at his own Cure; and exclaiming as if the Church of
England were destitute of able and learned Pastours, which
without doubt had more learned Pastours at present than any
other Age, or any other Reformed Church, could shew. But the
Queen, who had a high Esteem of moderate Church-men, and
misliked Innovatours, as always changing for the worse, utterly
rejected these Attempts, as tending to overthrow her Prerogative,
and the supreme Authority granted unto her in Ecclesiastical
matters. But the Association which I mentioned before was now
confirmed by the general Consent and Approbation of all. And
it was Enacted, "That 24 or more, of the Privy Council and the
Lords of Parliament, to be deputed by the Queens Commission,

should make Inquisition after all such as should invade the Kingdom, raise Rebellion, or attempt to hurt or destroy the Queen's Person, for or by whomsoever employed that might lay Claim to the Crown of England. And that he for whom or by whom they should attempt the same should be utterly un-capable of the Crown of England, deprived wholly of all Right and Title to it, and prosecuted to Death by all faithfull Subjects, if he should be judged by those four and twenty men to be guilty of such Invasion, Rebellion, or treasonable Attempt, and by publick Proclamation so declared."

Laws also were made for Preservation of the Queen's Person against all Jesuites and Popish Priests who should ground any villanous Plots and Designs upon the Bull of Pius Quintus: to wit,

That they should depart the Realm within forty days. That those who should afterward return into the Kingdom should be guilty of High treason. That he who should wittingly and willingly harbour, relieve and maintain them, should be guilty of Felony. (So they call all capital Crimes under the degree of Treason.) That those who were brought up in Seminaries, if they returned not within 6 months after Notice given, and submitted not them-selves to the Queen before a Bishop or two Justices, should be guilty of High treason. And if any so submitting themselves should within ten years approach the Queen's Court, or come within ten miles thereof, their Submission should be void. That those who should by any means whatsoever send or convey over any Money to Students in such Seminaries should incur the Penalty of a Præmunire, (that is, perpetual Exile, and loss of all their Goods). That if any of the Peers of the Realm, that is, Dukes, Marquesses, Earls, Viscounts, or Barons of Parliament, should offend against these Laws, he should be brought to his Trial by his Peers. That if any should know of any such Jesuites or other Priests abovesaid lurking within the Realm, and should not discover them within 12 days, he should be fined and im-prisoned at the Queen's Pleasure. That if any man should be suspected to be a Jesuite or Priest as aforesaid, and not submit himself to Examination, he should for his Contempt be im-prisoned till he did submit himself. That he who should send his Children or any others to Seminaries and Colleges of the Popish Profession should be fined in a hundred Pounds of English Money. And that those who were so sent thither should

not succeed as Heirs, nor enjoy any Estates which should any way
fall to them: the like for all such as should not return Home
from the said Seminaries within a year, unless they did conform
themselves to the Church of England. That if the Wardens or
Officers of the Ports should permit any others besides Sea-men
and Merchants to cross the Seas without Licence of the Queen or
6 Privy Counsellours, they should be put out of their places, and
the Masters of such Ships as carried them should forfeit their
Ships and Goods, and suffer Imprisonment for a whole Year.

With the Severity of these Laws (which notwithstanding
seemed necessary for the present time) the Papists in England
were very much terrified; and amongst them Philip Howard
Earl of Arundel, the Duke of Norfolk's eldest Son, insomuch
as he purposed to fly the Land, lest he should offend against
them. This Philip had through the Queen's Grace and Favour
been restored in Bloud three years before, and having soon after
lost her Favour through the secret Accusations of some great
Persons, had privily vowed himself to the Popish Religion, living
a very austere Life. Hereupon he was called once or twice before
the Council, and cleared himself of the matters objected against
him; nevertheless he was confined to his own House. After
about 6 months he had his Liberty again, and came to the Parliament: yet he withdrew himself the first day from the Assembly
while the Sermon was Preaching. The Parliament being ended,
he, being now resolved to be gone, wrote a Letter to the Queen,
(which notwithstanding he appointed to be delivered her after
his Departure,) wherein he made a long and sad Complaint
"of the Malice of his potent Adversaries, whereunto he was
necessitated to give place, whilst they triumphed over his Innocency. He recounted the fatal Ends of his Ancestours, namely,
his Great-grandfather, who was condemned without being
heard; his Grandfather, who was beheaded for light and trivial
matters; and his Father, who (as he said) was circumvented by
his Adversaries, and never bare any hostile Mind against his
Prince or Countrey. And added, that he for his part, lest he
should be the Heir of his Forefathers Infelicity, and that he
might the better attend the Service of God, and provide for his
Soul's Good, had quitted his Countrey, but not his Allegance to
his Prince." Before such time as this Letter was delivered he was

gone into Sussex, and being now ready to imbark himself in an obscure Creek, he was apprehended through the Treachery of his own Followers and the Discovery of the Master of the Vessel, and thrown into the Tower of London.

In the same Tower was Henry Percy Earl of Northumberland at this time kept Prisoner, a man of a lively and active Spirit and Courage, (Brother to Thomas, who was beheaded at York,) which Henry was suspected to have plotted secretly with Throckmorton, the Lord Paget and the Guises, for Invading of England, and setting the Queen of Scots at Liberty, whom he always highly favoured. In the month of June he was found dead in his Bed, shot with three Bullets near his left Pap, his Chamber-door being barred on the in-side. The Coroner's Inquest of the Neighbourdwellers being impannelled and sworn according to the Custome, and having viewed the Body, considered the place, found the Pistol with Gun-powder in the Chamber, and examining his man that bought the Pistol, and him that had sold it, gave their Verdict, that the Earl had killed himself. The third day after there was a full Meeting of the Peers of the Realm in the Star-Chamber, where Sir Thomas Bromley Lord Chancellour of England briefly declared, that the Earl had been engaged in traitorous Designs against his Prince and Countrey, which when he found once to be discovered, he had laid violent Hands upon himself, being terrified with the guilty Conscience of his Offence. But to satisfie the Multitude, who are always prone to believe the worst in such cases, he commanded the Queen's Procurator or Attorney, and her learned Counsel in the Law, to shew plainly the Reasons why the Earl had been kept in Prison, and the manner of his Death. Hereupon Popham the Queen's Attorney general, beginning at the Rebellion in the North sixteen years before, shewed out of the publick Records,

That he had been called to his Trial about that Rebellion, and the Design for the delivering the Queen of Scots; and that he had acknowledged his Fault, submitted himself to the Queen's Mercy, and was fined at 5000 Marks. But that the Queen (out of her Clemency) had not exacted one Farthing thereof; and after the Execution of his Brother for the same Crime had confirmed him in the Honour of Earl of Northumberland. That he, notwithstanding all this, had engaged himself in new Designs for

193

Delivering the Queen of Scots, for the Conquering of England, and the Destruction of Religion and the Queen. That Mendoza the Spaniard had given notice to Throckmorton, that Charles Paget, under the counterfeit name of Mope, had secretly conferred with him in Sussex about these matters; and that the Lord Paget had signified the same things in a manner to Throckmorton. That the same also did appear by the Papers of Chreicton a Scottish Jesuite; and that Charles Paget had told the same things to William Shelley, at his Return out of France.

Then Egerton, the second Atturney, (commonly called the Solicitour) argued notably from Circumstances, and from the Earl's extraordinary Care to conceal the Business, that he was guilty thereof: viz.

That the Earl, when no man in England could accuse him of these things but onely the Lord Paget, (with whom Throckmorton was very familiar,) within few days after Throckmorton was taken, provided a Ship by Shelley's means for Paget, wherein he went over into France. That when Throckmorton had begun to confess some things, the Earl removed from London to Petworth, and, sending for Shelley, told him, that he was fallen into Danger of his Life and Estate, and prayed him to conceal all, and to send such out of the way as were privy to the Lord Paget's Departure, and the coming of Charles Paget: which was presently done; and he himself sent his man aside whom he had employed to Charles Paget.

The Solicitour added,

That while he was in Prison he had, by corrupting his Keepers, often dealt with Shelley to understand what he had confessed. That after Shelley had let him know by a Woman which was secretly employed as a Messenger betwixt them, that he could conceal things no longer; that their Conditions were not alike, for himself was to undergoe the Rack, so was not the Earl in respect of his Place and Quality; and had sent him in writing what passages he had confessed; the Earl fetch'd a Sigh, and forthwith said, (as Pantin who waited on him in his Chamber confessed,) that he was now undone by Shelley's Confession.

After all this the manner of his Death was related, from the Evidence of the Inquest, the Testimony of the Lieutenant of the Tower, some of the Warders, and Pantin his Servant: and there-

upon it was concluded that he had with his own Hands murthered himself, out of a Fear lest his Family should be attainted
and utterly ruined. Certainly many good men were much affected
that so great a Person died so miserable and lamentable a Death,
as well because men naturally favour Nobility, as that he had
acquired singular Commendation for his Valour. What Suspicions the Fugitives muttered concerning one Bailife, that was one
of Hatton's Servants, and a little before appointed to be the Earl's
Keeper, I omit, as being a thing altogether unknown unto me,
and I think it not meet to insert any thing upon mere Hear-says
and Reports.

Whence the Seeds of these Mischiefs came which were sown
in England Queen Elizabeth was not ignorant, who had understood that the Guises had now openly entred into a dangerous
Confederacy against the Protestant Religion, the French King,
and herself. She on the other side, to procure a League amongst
the Protestants for Defence of their Religion, sent Sir Thomas
Bodley to the King of Denmark, the Electour Palatine, the Dukes
of Saxony, Wittenberg, Brunswick and Lunenburg, the Marquess
of Brandenburg, and the Landtgrave of Hesse; and amongst
other things gave him Instructions to put the King of Denmark
in mind by the bye, that it principally concerned him to prevent
the Attempts of the Guises, considering that they stuck not to
challenge the Kingdom of Denmark for their Cousin the Duke
of Lorrain, as Grand-son to Christiern the Second King of Denmark by his Daughter. Neither did the Lorrainer himself dissemble or disown the same, when not long since he was a Suitour
to Queen Elizabeth for Marriage.

But into Scotland (lest any Danger should break in upon England from thence as it were by the back Door) she sent Sir Edward Wotton, to let the King know how acceptable his Kindness
towards her was, which he had declared of late by Patrick Gray
and the Justice-Clark; and moreover to draw him to a League of
mutual Offense and Defense, by shewing him the Dangers which
now threatened the Profession of the Gospel; and to offer unto
him, as her Son, as large a yearly Pension as her Father had allowed her; (for the Revenues of the Scottish Crown were much
lessened through the Negligence of the Regents;) and to recommend unto him a Marriage with the King of Denmark's Daugh-

ter; as also earnestly to intercede in the Queen's Name for the Scots that stood exiled in England, who she promised should be presently sent back if she found them guilty of the least Crime against the King. Wotton found the King's Mind inclinable enough to such a League, (notwithstanding that Arran and some of the French Faction laboured to hinder it:) and the Estates of Scotland, that so Religion might be secured, gave their Assent under their Hands to a Treaty concerning such a League; provided the Queen would pass her Royal word, that she would not prejudice the King's Title to the Succession in England as long as he continued firm in Amity with her. But this Business was delayed and hindered by the Murther of Sir Francis Russell, Son to the Earl of Bedford, which Earl died himself also the next day after.

For when Sir John Foster and Thomas Carre of Fernihurst, Wardens of the Middle Marches betwixt the two Kingdoms of England and Scotland, had appointed a Meeting on the 27th of June about certain Goods unjustly taken away, and Security was given on both sides by Oath, according to Custome, and Proclamation made that no man should harm other by word, deed, or look, (as the Borderers speak,) the Scots came to the place of Meeting armed, in Battel-array, with Ensigns displayed, and Drums beating, contrary to Custome and beyond Expectation, being in number about three thousand; whereas the English were not above three hundred. Scarce were the Wardens set to hear the Complaints, when on a sudden, upon an English-man's being taken pilfering, there arose a Tumult, and the Scots discharging a Volley of Shot slew Russell with some others, put the English to Flight, and eagerly pursuing them the space of four miles into England, carried off some Prisoners. Who was the Authour of this Slaughter was not certainly known. The English laid the Fault upon Arran, now Chancellour of Scotland, and upon Fernihurst. The Queen pressed both by her Letters and Commissioners to have the Murtherers delivered into her Hands: inasmuch as Henry the Seventh King of England had formerly delivered up into the Hands of James the Fourth King of Scots William Heron and seven English-men for killing of Robert Carre of Chesford upon such a day of Meeting, and Morton the late Regent sent Carmichael a Scot into England for killing of George

Heron. The King protested his own Innocency in the matter, and promised to send Fernihurst immediately into England, yea and the Chancellour too, if they could be convicted by clear and lawfull Proofs to have premeditately infringed the Security, or procured the Murther. Fenwick an English-man accused Fernihurst of the Fact to his Face: he avoided it by a flat Denial, because the other could produce no Scottish-man for a Witness. For in these Trials on the Borders, according to a certain Privilege and Custome agreed upon amongst the Borderers, none but a Scot is to be admitted for a Witness against a Scot, and none but an English-man against an English-man: insomuch that if all the English-men which were upon the place had seen the Murther committed before their Eyes, yet their Testimony had been of no Value, unless some Scottish-man also did witness the same. Nevertheless Arran was confined to his House, and Fernihurst was committed to Custody at Dundee, where afterwards he died: a stout and able Warriour, ready for any great Attempts and Undertakings, and of an immovable Fidelity to the Queen of Scots and the King her Son; having been once or twice turned out of all his Lands and Fortunes, and banished the Sight of his Countrey and Children, which yet he endured patiently, and, after so many Crosses falling upon him together, persisted unshaken and always like himself.

Whilst the Inquiry after this Murther was protracted from day to day, and it was calmly debated whether the yearly Money offered unto the King under the name of *Aurei* was to be payed according to the English or French Account of Money, the Queen (who took with great Indignation Russell's Death and the Breach of the Security, being perswaded by the Scots who were Arran's Adversaries that he favoured and cherished the Jesuites, and laboured tooth and nail, both in France and Scotland, that the League might not be made with the English,) suffered by way of Connivence the Scottish Fugitives, viz. Angus, and those who by their common Condition of Banishment were reconciled and made Friends with him, namely John and Claudius Hamilton, and Marre, Glames, and the rest that were Exiles in England, to return into Scotland, supplying them with Money to suppress Arran.

The Earl Bothwell, the Lord Humes, Humes of Coldingknoll,

and others in Scotland, had promised them their Assistence beforehand; but especially Maxwell, lately made Earl of Morton, who was in Hope to escape Punishment for a Rebellion which he had raised in Anandale, if Arran were once suppressed. Yea and in the King's Court also Patrick Gray, a sharp and bitter Adversary of Arran's, Belenden the Justice-Clerk, and Maitland Lord Secretary, were drawn by Wotton's Policy to side against Arran.

The Exiles aforesaid upon their entring Scotland set forth a large Proclamation, wherein they commanded all men in the King's Name to lend their helping Hand for Defense of the Truth of the Gospel, for rescuing of the King from corrupt Counsellours, and for maintaining Amity with the English. Fawkirk was the place appointed for Rendezvous, where they mustered 8,000 men.

Arran, (who by the King's Command had kept himself confined at Keneil upon Suspicion of his Murthering Russel,) hearing hereof, posted to the King, and accused Gray as the Authour of this Attempt, who ingeniously cleared himself before the King. While Arran made all possible Preparation for Defense of the Town, the Enemies were at hand ready to scale the Walls. He, knowing that his Head onely was aimed at, and suspecting the Fidelity of his own people, (for he began now to be hated by many,) withdrew himself secretly with but one man over the Bridge. The rest soon after abandoned the Town, and retired into the Castle to the King. The Fugitives presently seize upon the Market-place, and advance their Ensigns against the Castle. The King sent Gray to demand the Reason of their coming. They answer, "To submit themselves, and most humbly to kiss the King's Hand." He offereth them Restitution of all their Lands and Goods if they would depart quietly. They send back word, that they little value their Goods and Lands in comparison of the King's Favour, and beseech him that they may be admitted to his Presence. The King consenteth upon these Conditions: "That they should attempt nothing against his Person, or the Life of such as he should name, nor seek to alter any thing in the Government." They vow to spend their Lives for the King's Safety; and for Alteration of the Government, they protest they never once thought of it. But they pray him that their Adversaries and the Places of strength in the Kingdom may be put into their Hands for their Security. A whole day was spent in Consultation about this matter: yet Necessity compelling, considering there was so great a Multitude in the Castle, and Victuals were scarce, they were at length admitted to the King's Presence. Forthwith the Earls of Montross, Crawford, and Rothes, Colonel Stuart, Downes, Arran's Brother, and others, are delivered into their Hands; Arran, who was fled into the Hebrides, is recalled Home; and themselves are pardoned as good Subjects, and such as had deserved well of the King: Hamilton of Arbroth is made Governour of Dunbriton, Coldingknoll of Edenborough Castle, Angus of the Castle of Tontallon, Marre of Sterlin, and Glames is made Captain of the King's Guard.

Having now by their faithfull Obedience cleared themselves to the King of all those things that were criminously and suspiciously objected against them by their Adversaries, all the Proscriptions of all Persons whosoever, and for what Causes soever, from the King's Inauguration to that very day, were in an Assembly of the Estates decreed to be for ever forgotten, (except those for the Murther of the King's Father, and those that were issued against the Archbishop of Glascow, the Bishop of Rosse, and the Bishop of Dunblane;) and with general consent of all, the King had free Leave and Authority given him to enter into a League with the Queen of England, and to appoint Commissioners for that purpose. Onely Maxwell abused this extraordinary Grace and Clemency of the King, who, having by the Benefit of this general Pardon escaped Punishment for a bloudy Murther and Depredation committed against the Johnstons, was so bold and audacious, that, in Contempt of the Authority of the Laws, he commanded the Sacrifice of the Mass to be celebrated at Dunfreez, which had not been permitted in Scotland for these 19 years past. For which he afterwards suffered Imprisonment the space of three Months.

Neither was the neighbour Countrey of Ireland free in this turbulent time from the Storms of Rebellion. For when the rest of the Provinces of this Isle enjoyed a firm and perfect Peace, there brake forth a grand Rebellion in Connaught, the Western part of Ireland, occasioned by the restless and unquiet Disposition of that Nation, and their Hatred against Sir Richard Bingham their Governour, who was (as they complained) over-sharp and rigid in his Government. He, when he saw the great Lords of Ireland exercise such heavy Tyranny over the silly People, that they durst acknowledge no other Prince but them, left nothing unassayed that he might restrain this Tyrannical Lordliness, and confirm the Queen's Authority amongst them, though he were every foot accused to the Queen and the Lord Deputy, and rendred odious for his Cruelty and Severity. Thomas Roe-Burk, of the noble English Family of Burgh, was the first that opposed him; and being summoned to the Assizes in the County of Mayo, he refused to appear. The Governour dissembled the matter a while: but afterwards he commanded him and one or two turbulent men more of that Family to be seized upon, lest they should break forth into Rebellion. Thomas died in fight before he would be taken: Meilery and Theobald a Burgh were taken and hanged. And the Rebellion had been now supressed in its very first Breaking forth, had not some English-men, who were dissatisfied with the Governour, given secret Notice to the rest of that Family to beware of the Governour, and by no means come near him. They upon this Encouragement perswaded the Joyes and Clandonels, who were men powerfull in Followers and Adherents in that Tract, that the Governour would deal no better with them, but by little and little weaken and take away their Power also. And they so handled the matter by their Friends, that the Lord Deputy commanded the Governour to deal no more so roughly with that noble Family (though degenerated) without his Knowledge and Approbation.

Meanwhile, during the Governour's Absence in Twomond, (where he slew Mahon O-Brean, who was up in Commotion, and took his Castle,) the Sons of Edmund a Burgh of Castle Barry, and Richard the Son of Richard, (who for his wicked Deeds was surnamed by the Irish The Devil's Hook,) gathering together a Multitude of lewd Fellows, seized upon two Castles in Lough Mask, and fortified them: out of which the Governour soon drove them into the Woods and Mountains, and commanded Richard a Burgh, Brother to Thomas, who came in and humbly submitted himself, to be hanged up as a Spy and treacherous person. And when he had so closely pursued the rest, who wandred and straggled up and down the Woods, that scarce any of them appeared, the Lord Deputy commanded him to prosecute them no longer, but take Hostages of them, and receive them into his Protection. Within a short time after, while the Governour lay at Dublin, and Leavies of men were making all over Ireland for the Low-Countrey-War, they took up the Banner of Rebellion again, and many that refused to serve in the Low-Countrey Wars, as namely the Clan-Gibbons, Clandonells and Joyes, joyned themselves with them in great numbers. And being now increased both in Number and Strength, they openly gave out that (according to their ancient Custome) they would have their Mac-William, that is, a principal Lord of that House de Burgh chosen by a popular Election to govern the Countrey; or else they would send for some other Head and Ruler out of Spain: That they would not admit a Sheriff amongst them, nor appear at the Sessions or Assizes. Neither would they return to their Duty, though the Archbishop of Tuam, Birmingham Baron of Athenry, and Dillon, being sent from the Governour, propounded reasonable Conditions to them; but began on a sudden to harass the Countrey-villages in the open Champain-countrey, burning and plundering all before them, and razing the Forts and Strong holds. To the Hebridian Scots they sent John Itcleave and Walter Kittagh a Burgh, to perswade and invite them to enter into Connaught with their auxiliary Forces, whilst there were now but few Garrison-souldiers left in the Countrey, promising them large Possessions if they would drive out the English, and assist the Rebels.

The Lord Deputy hearing hereof at length commanded the Governour to prosecute the Rebels, who, gathering his Forces together, sent the Earl of Clan-Richard, the principal man of the House of a Burgh, and Birmingham, to treat with them about Peace: which when they flatly refused to hear of, he put the Hostages to death, and without Delay, as knowing that nothing was more prejudicial to the English than a lingering War, and nothing more advantageous to the Irish, he and the Earl of Clan-Richard with the Horse protected the Champain-countrey from the Depredations of the Rebels; and John Bingham, the Governour's Brother, entering the Woods with the Foot, hunted them so closely at the Heels from place to place, driving away about 5,000 head of Cattel, (the greatest part whereof was shared amongst the Souldiers man by man, according to the manner of the Countrey,) that after forty days or thereabouts, being grievously famished and spent for want of Food, they crept out of their Lurking-holes, scarce knowing one another by their Faces, and humbly submitted themselves, giving fresh Hostages. Onely the Sons of Edmund a Burgh of Castle Barry (whom they had determined to make their Mac-William) persisted in their Rebellion till their Father was taken and put to death, (having been found guilty by the Law, for exciting his Children to Rebellion,) and his Lands confiscate. And now the Governour had certain Intelligence that 2,000 Hebridian Scots, under the Leading of Kittagh and Itcleave a Burgh, were just ready to break into Connaught. These Scots, with an Army of men hastily gathered and pick'd up, and those Garrison-souldiers he had, he diligently chased and hunted night and day through By-ways and difficult Passages with indefatigable Labour, while they one while lurked in woody Forests near Lough Earne, and another while spent their time in marching forward and backward, winding this way and that way, and he at their Backs, in the Front, and on both Sides, constantly waited on them, watching a fit Opportunity to engage them. At the last he dissembled a Retreat, as if he were too weak for them: when they presently marching on more confidently towards Ardanar upon the River Moin, proclaimed themselves Lords of the Countrey. He being by his Scouts soon advertised of their March found them near Ardanar, where they put themselves in Battel-array, advanced their Banners, and sounded their Bag-pipes. He held them play a while with light Skirmishes, still retreating till he had drawn them from the Bogs into the firm Land, and that all his Forces with great Silence were come together. Then he charged them stoutly, and having slain many, made them give ground. Shortly after his small Shot charged them in the Front, and he himself with his Horsemen set upon them so courageously in the Flank, that he routed their main Battel, and forced them to take the River, where they were all slain and drowned but fourscore, who swam over into Tiraul, and those who went the day before another way to fetch in Booty, but were afterwards almost all slain by John Bingham and the Inhabitants of the County of Slego. There were slain about 3,000 men, and amongst them their principal Leaders, Donell Gormay and Alexander Carrogh, the Sons of James Mac-Conell, who had for a long time infested these Parts, as also those of the House of Burgh which had drawn them to this unhappy Expedition. Of the English few were slain, but many hurt. This was doubtless a notable Victory, and of great Consequence both at present and to future times, the Title of Mac-William in Connaught being hereby quite extinct, and the Insolency of the Island-Scots in Ireland suppressed, which in former times was so intolerable, that to harbour them in Ireland was accounted no less than High Treason, and Perott, to restrain their Depredations, had formerly imposed upon the great Lords of Ulster a certain number of Souldiers to be trained up and exercised for War.

Meanwhile the Estates in the Netherlands, being in great Distress, consulted amongst themselves whether they should fly to the French King or the Queen of England for Succour and Protection: for they were both of them at Enmity with the Spaniard, but jealous one of the other. Neither could the French endure to think that the English, nor the English that the French, their ancient Enemies, should be strengthened and made more powerfull by the Addition of the Netherlands. Pruney, the French Embassadour to the Estates, to divert them from applying to the English, alleged, "That the English were so remote and separated from them by means of the Ocean betwixt them, that they could not assist them upon every Occasion: That their way of Government was harsh and not to be endured, for which cause they were in former times ejected out of France, and were now in danger of losing Ireland: That the Succession there was doubtfull, and whether Mary Queen of Scots or James her Son succeeded, the one as well as the other, to establish and secure their own Affairs, would restore the Netherlands back to the Spaniards. But as for the French, their near Neighbourhood was convenient, their Government mild and gentle, and the Succession certain in the King of Navarre, a Prince of the same Profession with themselves."

They who favoured the English argued the contrary, "That the English were not at such a Distance, but that they might conveniently enough relieve them, and no man hinder them. What the Government of the French was in times past in the Netherlands, may appear by Histories; and what it hath been of late, let

Dixmuyd, Dunkerk and Dendermond speak, which were treacherously surprized, as likewise Bruges, Alost, Newport and Antwerp, which were furiously and treacherously attempted by them: and what their Fidelity hath been, which hath been so often obliged by Edicts, but still violated and broken, let their barbarous Massacres committed in their Cities witness. That the Succession in England was sure and certain in King James, a Prince very well affected to the true Religion. Besides, the English were of the same Religion, and exact Observers of the ancient League with Burgundy; that their Traffick had brought infinite Wealth into the Netherlands, and their Havens were very convenient for the Netherlands." Nevertheless the Estates by an honourable Embassie craved Aid and Protection of the French King, by whom they were received with a kind of timorous Silence, and, as well out of Jealousie towards the English, as Hatred against the Spaniard, a long time put off with Delays; so as at length they returned Home without speeding: and the Estates having some Hope upon account of the former Kindness of the Queen of England towards them, resolved to fly unto her Protection.

Hereupon a Consultation was holden in England, whether they were to be received into Protection. Some were of opinion that they were forthwith to be received, and assisted, lest the Spaniard, having subdued them, should from thence endanger England. There were also some who thought they were to be esteemed as Rebels, and unworthy of Help, as having shaken off their Allegiance to their Prince.

> That the Spaniard had broken none of the Articles of his Joyfull Entrance, which was the Pretence they had used for their Rebellion and casting off their Prince. But if he had broken them, yet was he not liable therefore to lose his Principality. And though some think that Obedience is to be denied him for a time, till he have reformed what hath been done amiss; yet others think that by the Law of God, to which the Law of Man must give place, Princes are to be obeyed merely for Conscience sake, as Powers ordained by God. That God hath given them the Authority of Commanding, and left to Subjects the Commendation of Obeying. That good Princes are to be wished for; but whatsoever they are, they are to be born withall. That those Provinces were dedevolved to the Spaniard, not by popular Election, but by Right of

Inheritance from his Ancestours, and the Donation of Emperours. Moreover, that the Netherlanders themselves had received all the Privileges which they enjoy from Princes; and had forfeited the same again by their Treason, in formerly taking up Arms against their present Prince. That they who now intended to crave Protection were not the Estates of the Netherlands, but most of them of the vulgar sort of men, under the Pretence and name of the Estates. These therefore held it the wisest course, for the Queen to intermeddle no farther in the Netherlandish Affairs, but to strengthen and fortifie her own Kingdom, to engage all her good Subjects daily more strictly to her by her Bounty and Clemency, to restrain the bad, gather Money, furnish her Navy with all sort of Provision, provide the Borders toward Scotland with strong Garrisons, and maintain the ancient military Discipline of England, (as if the same were of late corrupted and adulterated by the Low Countrey War). So would England become impregnable, and she on every side be secure at Home, and a Terrour to her Enemies. That this was the best way for those who had too powerfull Neighbours to avoid and prevent War. For no man would willingly provoke those whom he saw to be provided of Money and Strength, backed by the Love of their Subjects, and ready and prepared to take Revenge. Great Indiscretion therefore it were, to spend Money and Souldiers, which are as it were the vital Spirits of War, in a Foreign Quarrel in behalf of other Princes, or indigent States, (and those Subjects to another,) who will always be expecting fresh Relief; or else out of Necessity or Ingratitude will at length provide for their own State and Security, and neglect their first Helpers. Whereof the English had heretofore had Experience in France to their Cost in the Quarrel of the Burgundian, and not long since also in the Defence of the Protestants there.

But they who were of this Opinion incurred great Displeasure and Ill will among the Military sort of men, as persons inclining to the Spaniard's Party, degenerate, and faint-hearted Cowards.

The Estates Deputies, as soon as they had Access to the Queen, earnestly besought her that she would accept of the Government of the Confederate Provinces of the Netherlands, and receive the People thereof, who were most unjustly and unworthily oppressed, into her Protection and perpetual Vassalage. The Queen heard them gratiously, but refused both their Government and Protection. Nevertheless, for the raising of the Siege of Antwerp, which was then closely pressed by the Prince of Parma, she agreed to send them forthwith 4,000 men, for which Sluis with the Ordnance and Ammunition in it should be delivered into her hands as Caution. But whilst this was doing, Antwerp was yielded up on Composition, the River of Scheld having been barred up with such admirable Works that no Relief could be brought into the City.

After the Queen had seriously and carefully for some time considered of things, and had thoroughly weighed the barbarous Cruelty of the Spaniards towards her Neighbours the Netherlanders, and their Hatred against England and the Religion which she embraced; (for the Spaniard was certainly perswaded that the Netherlands could never be reduced to his Obedience, unless England were first conquered;) lest the War should be brought home to her own Doors, (Scotland yet wavering,) and the Spaniard's Power should too far extend and increase in Countries so near adjoyning unto her, and for Situation so convenient both for translating the War into England, and for the Trade of Merchants, as well by Sea as up and down the River Rhyne, as also for prohibiting the carrying of all Provision for Shipping to the Enemy; Countries provided of a strong Fleet and stout and able Sea-men, insomuch that if they were joyned with the English Fleet, she might easily become Mistress of the Sea, and withall so rich and strong, that they had for a long time curbed their insulting Enemies, without foreign Assistence; as also lest they should put themselves under the Protection of the French: she resolved, that it was both Christian Piety to relieve the afflicted Netherlanders, Embracers of the same Religion which she professed; and good Wisedom also to provide for the Safety of the People committed to her Charge, by preventing the pernicious Designs of her Enemies; and that not out of any desire of Glory, but out of mere Necessity for Preservation of her own and her People's Security. Hereupon she openly undertook the Protection of the Netherlanders, whilst all the Princes of Christendom admired at such manly Fortitude in a Woman, which durst, as it were, declare War against so puissant a Monarch: insomuch as the King of Sweden said, "That Queen Elizabeth had now taken the Diadem from her Head, and adventured it upon the doubtfull Chance of War."

Betwixt her and the Confederate Estates these Conditions were agreed upon.

> The Queen shall send the Confederate Provinces an auxiliary Force of 5,000 Foot and 1,000 Horse, under a Governor-General, an honourable Person, and shall find them Pay during the War, which the Estates shall repay when a Peace shall be concluded; namely, in the first Year of the Peace, the Expences disbursed in the first Year of the War, and the rest in the four Years next following. In the mean time Flushing and the Castle of Rammekins in Walcheren, and the Isle of Briell, with the City and two Forts, shall be delivered into the Queen's Hands for Caution. The Governours of these Places shall exercise no Authority over the Inhabitants, but onely over the Garrison-souldiers, who shall pay Excise and Impositions as well as the Inhabitants. The said Places, after the Money is repayed, shall be restored again to the Estates, and not delivered to the Spaniard, or to any other Enemy whatsoever. The Governour-General, and two English-men whom the Queen shall name, shall be admitted into the Council of the Estates. The Estates shall make no League with any without the Advice and Consent of the Queen; neither shall the Queen without the Advice of the Estates. Ships for the common Defence shall be rigged and set forth in equal number by both Parties, and at the common Charges, to be commanded by the Admiral of England. The Havens and Ports shall be open and free to both sides.

With other Articles which are to be had in print.

In Memory hereof the Zelanders, transported with Joy, coined Money with the Arms of Zeland on one side, namely, a Lion rising out of the Waves, and this Inscription, *Luctor & emergo*, that is, I struggle and get above water; and on the other side with the Arms of the several Cities in Zeland, and this Motto, *Authore Deo, Favente Reginâ*, that is, God being the Authour, a Queen our Favourer. The Queen also hereupon set forth a Book, wherein she shewed, that Leagues and Associations had been made in former times between the Kings of England and the Princes of the Netherlands, and the Cities thereof apart, for yielding one another mutual Protection and Assistence. Then she related the barbarous Cruelty of the Spaniards towards the miserable Netherlanders, and their wicked Contrivances against her, who had studied so much to make Peace betwixt them, and had been the principal means to hinder those People from an absolute and total Revolt. Neither had she any other Intention now in sending Forces to their Aid, but onely that the Netherlanders might peaceably injoy their ancient Freedom, she and her Subjects their Security, and both Nations a free Trade and Commerce.

And withall, that she might not stay to expect the War at her own Doors, but give the Spaniard somewhat to doe abroad, she sent Sir Francis Drake as Admiral, and Christopher Carlile as General of the Land-Forces, to the West-Indies with a Fleet of 21 Ships, whereon were embarked 2,300 volunteer souldiers, besides Sea-men; who unexpectedly and on the sudden surprized the Town of S. Jago in the Isle of S. Jago near Cape Verd, the Town giving Name to the Island, and being situate in a low Valley: here with Peals of Ordnance they celebrated the day of the Queen's Inauguration, to wit, the seventeenth day of November. Having sacked the Town, they found not the least Gold in it; but of Meal, Wine and Oil great quantities. The fourteenth day after they departed from that Coast, and many of them who had layn aboard in the open Air were taken with a violent Disease called a Calenture, and died thereof; which Disease is ordinary in that unwholesome Air to Strangers that come thither and lie abroad in the Evening. On the first of January they arrived at Hispaniola, and about ten miles from the City of Santo Domingo the Souldiers were landed in a safe place, which was discovered to them by a Spaniard whom they had taken; and there setting themselves in Battel-array, they marched towards the City; and having beaten back 150 Spanish Horse which made head against them, and put certain Musquetiers to Flight which lay in Ambush, they entred pell-mell with them into the City at two Gates which look Westward, and at the same time the Townsmen in great Fear ran all out of the City at the North-Gate. The English marched up in a Body to the Market-place near the great Church; and not being enough to defend so large a City, they fortified that part of it with Bulwarks, and afterwards possessed themselves of other convenient Posts in it: and being now absolute Masters of the City, they stayed there a full month. And because the Townsmen offered but a small summe of Money to redeem the Town, they began first to burn the Suburbs, and then to fire and demolish the fairest Buildings within the City itself, till such time as the Citizens redeemed their Houses with 25,000 Ducats, which they could hardly make up amongst them. The Booty was not great, except of Ordnance, Meal, and Sugar. For onely brass Money, Glasses, and Earthen Dishes from the East Indies, were in use and fashion there. In the Town-hall were to be seen, amongst other things, the King of Spain's Arms, and under them a Globe of the World, out of which issued an Horse with his Fore-feet springing forward, with this Inscription, *Non sufficit Orbis*, that is, The World sufficeth not. Which was laughed at, and looked upon as an Argument of the boundless Avarice and Ambition of the Spaniards, as if nothing could suffice them.

From hence they sailed to the Continent of America, and landed five miles from Cartagena: and while Drake with his Pinnaces and Boats well manned in vain attempted the Haven of the City, which was defended by a Fort and chained up, Carlile putting his men in Battel-array, led them in the dead of Night all along the Shoar. A Troop of Horse shewed themselves onely, and presently retreated: whom Carlile pursued till he came to a narrow Neck of Land between the inner Road of the Haven and the Ocean, fenced from side to side with a Stone-wall, through which there was but one Passage, and that scarce broad enough for a Cart to pass, and defended with Barricadoes and five great Pieces of Ordnance, which were several times discharged against the very Front of the Army, but in vain. Carlile knowing well how to avoid that Danger, by the Help of the dark Night, and taking Advantage of the ebbing Water, led his men somewhat lower over the Sand to the very Entrance of the Passage, which the English manfully brake through, notwithstanding that two Gallies constantly plaied upon the Flank of them with eleven great Pieces and three hundred Musquetiers from the said inner Road. Then they soon mastered the Palisadoes, which the enemy had providently set up at the Entrance of every Street, putting the Spaniards and the Indians, who shot poisoned and envenomed Arrows at them, to Flight, and so became Masters of the Town; where they staied six weeks, compounding at last to spare the Town for 110,000 Ducats, which were presently paid down, and shared equally amongst the Sea-men and Souldiers which had most need. Besides this they got but small Booty. For the

Citizens, having Notice aforehand from Hispaniola, had conveyed away all their richest Treasure before their coming, to places more remote. The Calenture still raging amongst them, and daily lessening their Numbers, their Design for the taking of Nombre de Dios was laid aside, and they set Sail homewards by that Cape of the Isle of Cuba which hath its Name from Saint Antonio, where they took in fresh Rain-water out of the Ponds and Pits which they found.

Then coasting along the Shoar of Florida they seized upon two Towns, Saint Antonie's and Saint Helen's, both of them quitted and forsaken by the Spanish Garrisons, and burnt them. Afterwards holding on their Course along a wasted Coast, they lighted upon certain English-men, who had seated themselves in Virginia, so named in Honour of Queen Elizabeth a Virgin, whom Sir Walter Raleigh, who was in great Favour with Queen Elizabeth, had of late sent thither for a Colony; a man never sufficiently to be commended for the great Pains he took to discover remote Countries, and to advance the Glory of the English Navigation. To Ralph Lane, their Captain, Drake offered all Kindness and Assistence, and a Ship or two with Provision of Victuals, also some men, if he thought good to stay there, and prosecute his Enterprize; if not, he proferred to bring him back into England. But whilst they were shifting the Victuals into those Ships, an extraordinary Storm carried them away, and so dispersed the whole Fleet, that they met not again till they came into England. Hereupon Lane and those who were planted there, being in great Penury and want, and out of all Hope of Provisions out of England, their Number also much diminished, with one voice besought Drake that he would carry them back again into their own Countrey, which he readily and willingly did.

And these men who were thus brought back were the first that I know of that brought into England that Indian Plant which they call Tabacca and Nicotia, or Tobacco, which they used against Crudities being taught it by the Indians. Certainly from that time forward it began to grow into great Request, and to be sold at an high Rate, whilst in a short time many men every-where, some for Wantonness, some for Health sake, with insatiable Desire and Greediness sucked in the stinking smoak thereof through an earthen Pipe, which presently they blew out again at their Nostrils: insomuch as Tobacco-Shops are now as ordinary in most Towns as Tap-houses and Taverns. So that the English-mens Bodies, (as one said wittily,) which are so delighted with this Plant, seem as it were to be degenerated into the nature of Barbarians, since they are delighted, and think they may be cured, with the same things which the Barbarians use. In the Voiage were lost 700 men, and all of them almost of the Calenture. The Booty was valued at 60,000 Pounds of English Money. Two hundred and fourty Brass and Iron great Pieces were gotten from the Enemy and brought home.

Whilst these things were doing in America under the Torrid Zone, John Davis with two Ships, set forth at the Charge of William Sanderson (one that hath well deserved of Geographical Learning by setting forth Globes) and other Londoners, searched for a Passage under the Frozen Zone, by the upper part of America, to the East-Indies. He held his Course Northward, and at 500 Leagues from the Southern Cape of Ireland called Missen-head got Sight first of the Coast of Groenland and its high Mountains covered with Snow; the Island being compassed about as it were with an icy Bulwark for the breadth of two Leagues from the Land, so that there was no Access to it. Following therefore the Tract hereof, which winded first towards the West, and then towards the North, to the 64th Degree of Latitude, and having passed the Ice, he fell upon certain flourishing green Islands, and found there People of an indifferent Stature, with small Eyes, no Beards, and of a civiler Disposition than most of the Northern People were. From hence he sailed Northwestward, in a Sea without Ice, at the 66th Degree of Latitude, and discovered a Land which by little and little extended itself to the West, with a Strait all the way of an equal Breadth; into which he entred, and sailed about forty Leagues: but towards the end of August he set Sail homeward, full of Hope to perfect the Discovery. The next year after he entred again into the same Strait, sailed 80 Leagues in it, and found that Sea every way full of scattering Islands, and in his Return discovered it to be very full of Fish. Hereupon this Voiage was undertaken the third time with two Ships to Fish, and another to discover the Passage; wherewith having passed to the 83d Degree in the same Strait, which he observed to be 40 Leagues wide, he returned Home.

In the mean time a Proclamation was set forth to restrain the Covetousness of some private men in England, who converted arable Lands and the richest Pasture-grounds to the sowing of the Herb *Isatis*, commonly called Woad, for the use of Dyers, with great Prejudice to Cloathiers, and the Countrey-men which fed on White-meats made of Milk. Whereupon they were forbidden to sow that Herb within 8 miles of any of the Queen's Houses, and within four miles of Cities, Market-towns, and all other Towns where Cloathing was used.

And for the more advantageous and gainfull vending of English Cloaths, Licence was granted to Ambrose Earl of Warwick, and his Brother the Earl of Leicester, Thomas Starkey, Gerard Gore, and divers other Merchants of London, for the term of 2 years, to trade with the Moors in the Eastern parts of Barbary, to make good and repair the Losses they had before sustained in Africa; and all others were prohibited to trade upon those Coasts. These Merchants Muley Hamlet the Xeriff took into his Protection.

In the beginning of this Year died Edward Clinton, Lord Admiral of the Sea, who was created Earl of Lincoln by Queen Elizabeth in the year 1572 and lieth buried at Windsor, being falsely surnamed Fiennes in the Inscription of his Tomb. (Which I note, not to tax others, but lest I be taxed myself.) Henry his Son succeeded him in the Earldom; in the Admiralship of the Sea, Charles Lord Effingham, Lord Chamberlain to the Queen. And in his Place of Lord Chamberlain succeeded the Lord Hunsdon, Governour of Berwick, substituted in that Government some few years since in the room of Francis Russell Earl of Bedford. Which Francis (who was the Second Earl of Bedford of this Family, and a true Lover of Religion and Vertue,) having survived three of his Sons, Edward, John and Francis, so that there remained but onely one Son, William Lord Russell of Thornhaugh, and three Daughters, married to the three Earls of Warwick, Bath and Cumberland, died of a Gangrene the next day after his Son Francis was slain (as I said before) upon the Borders of Scotland, and lieth entombed with his Father at Cheiney in the County of Buckingham. After him succeeded Edward, his Grand-son by his third Son Francis, being under Age.

Amongst these, though he were of less Note, we must not pass

Richard Caldwell over in Silence, who died this Year, being of Brazen-Nose College in Oxford, and a Doctor of Physick. This man merited well of the Commonwealth, by giving a Chirugery-Lecture to the College of Physicians in London, (which College was first founded by Thomas Linacre) and endowing it with a handsome Allowance: the Lord Lumley being admitted into a share of the Honour. He was buried at Saint Benet's Church not far from the place, and his Tomb adorned with the Sculpture of several Implements used by Chirurgeons.

At the latter end of this Year, the Earl of Leicester, tickled with an ambitious Desire of Command and Glory, and being easily perswaded by those who sought their own Security and Power at Court more than his Honour, crossed the Seas into Holland, with the Title of General of the Queen of England's auxiliary Forces, and with some kind of Command over the Admiral of England and the Queen's whole Fleet. He set out with great Preparation and a splendid Retinue, being accompanied by the Earl of Essex, the Lords Audley and North, Sir William Russell, Sir Thomas Shirley, Sir Arthur Basset, Sir Walter Waller, Sir Gervase Clifton, and other Knights, and a select Troup of 500 Gentlemen. At his Departure the Queen gave him in Charge amongst other things, that he should not so much as think of any thing which would not stand with her Honour, and the Quality of the place he bare; and that he should diligently inform himself what Garrisons the Estates maintained, and by what means they did it, what way they went in raising and falling the Rates of Money, (for herein they surpass and are skilled above all other men,) that so the Souldiers might not receive their Pay at one Rate, and spend it at another. She charged him to cut off and hinder all Supplies of Provision from the Enemy, to restrain and curb the Pirats of Dunkerk; and most passionately and heartily she recommended to his Care the Noblemen of those Parts, more especially the Prince of Orange his Children.

XIII

The Nine and Twentieth Year of Her Reign, Anno Domini 1586

The Earl of Leicester arriving at Flushing was entertained by his Nephew, Sir Philip Sidney, Governour of the Place, and afterwards by the Cities of Zeland and Holland, with all manner of Honour, hearty Acclamations, triumphal Arches, votive Tables, Feastings, and the like. Being come to the Hague in Holland, in the month of January, the chief Government and absolute Authority over the Confederate Provinces was given him by a Grant in writing from the Estates General, (as they call them) with the Title of Governour and Captain General of Holland, Zeland, the United and Confederate Provinces. And now being attended with a noble Guard, saluted of all men by the Title of Your Excellency, and soothed up with Flatteries, as seated in the highest and most illustrious degree of Honour, he began to take upon him as if he were a perfect King. But the Queen, taking it very ill that the Estates had conferred so large Honour on him, and that he had accepted it, nipped the man at unawares in his swelling Pride by this one short Letter.

> How contemptuously you have carried yourself towards us, you shall understand by this Messenger, whom we send to you for that purpose. We little thought, that one whom we had raised out of the Dust, and prosecuted with such singular Favour above all others, would with so great Contempt have slighted and broken our Commands in a matter of so great Consequence, and so highly concerning us and our Honour. Whereof though you have but small Regard, contrary to what you ought by your

Allegiance, yet think not that we are so careless of repairing thereof, that we can bury so great an Injury in Silence or Oblivion. We therefore command you that, all Excuse set apart, you do forthwith, upon your Allegiance which you owe unto us, doe whatsoever Henage our Vice-chamberlain shall make known to you in our Name, upon pain of farther Peril.

In another Letter to the Estates General she thus expostulated with them. "That they had to her Disgrace, and without her Knowledge, conferred the absolute Government of the Confederate Provinces upon Leicester, her Subject; whenas she had absolutely refused it herself, and by a publick Manifesto had declared to the whole World, that she intended onely to relieve and succour her Neighbors in their Distress, and no ways to take upon her the Sovereignty over them." She admonisheth them therefore "to turn Leicester out of that absolute Authority, whose Commission she had limited; not that she thought their Cause unworthy to be favoured and assisted, but to provide for and secure her own Honour, which she esteemed more dear to her than her Life itself." The Estates wrote back to her. "That they were sorry they had incurred her Displeasure by granting absolute Authority to Leicester without her Knowledge. They intreat her to be pacified, considering the Necessity thereof; forasmuch as such an Authority was necessarily to be granted to one or other, to avoid Troubles and Dissensions. Neither indeed was the Authority so great as the word Absolute might seem to import, considering that the Principality itself, and the Supreme Rule and Dignity of Dominion, remained wholly in the Peoples hands. And to revoke the Authority already granted, were nothing else but to plunge the State of the Netherlands into extreme Dangers." By these Letters of the Estates, and the sorrowfull Lines of Leicester, who knew well enough how with Tears, and a pretended Trouble for what had past, to reconcile the favour of his mild Princess to himself, her Displeasure by little and little vanished away and was forgotten.

Leicester in the mean time receiveth all the Contributions of the Provinces, maketh military Laws, and while he goeth about to impose new Payments upon all Traffick and Merchandize, procureth himself great Hatred among the People. Now had the Prince of Parma, Governour of the Netherlands under the

Spaniard, besieged Grave (a Town of Brabant upon the River Maes) for several months by Charles Count Mansfield, who had raised Works round about it. To relieve this Town the Earl of Leicester sent Grave Hohenlo or Hollack, a German, and Sir John Norris General of the English Foot: but as soon as they had begun to build a Fort as near the Town as they could, that from thence they might victual and relieve the Town, the Spaniards fell upon them, and beat them from their Work: but the English Companies coming presently in, they were themselves beaten back with great Slaughter of their men, seven of their Officers being slain; and of the English, Norris lightly hurt. Grave Hollack shortly after cutting through the Bank, and letting out the Waters, relieved the Town with Victuals and a fresh Supply of men by Boats. As soon as the Prince of Parma himself was come, and had thundered a while into the Town with his great Ordnance, Van Hemart, Governour of the Town, a young man raw and unversed in military matters, not so much as expecting an Assault, compounded for his own and the Townsmens Lives, and yielded up the Place: whilst in the mean time Leicester drove the Spaniards out of the Betuwe, (which is properly called Batavia,) an Island made by two Rivers, the Rhyne and the Wael, and near the Tol-huys erected a strong Sconce. For the delivering up of Grave Hemart afterward suffered Death, for an Example and Terrour to others.

The Prince of Parma marched next into Gelderland, and encamped before Venlo; where Skenk a Frieslander and Sir Roger Williams a Welshman, two venturous men, undertook a desperate Exploit, to break through the Enemie's Camp at Midnight, and enter into the City: and indeed, after the Slaughter of some of their Enemies, they made their way as far as the Prince of Parma's own Tent. But being there repelled, they retreated frustrate of their Hope, yet not without Commendations amongst martial men of their bold Attempt: and Venlo was shortly after yielded up.

In the mean time the Lord Willoughby, Governour of Bergen-op-Zoom, intercepted the Enemie's Provision of Corn: whilst in other parts Sir Philip Sidney, and Grave Maurice the Prince of Orange his Son, surprized Axele, a Town of Flanders. Encouraged with this Success, Sidney made an Attempt by night

upon Gravelin, being fed with Hopes and drilled on by some
of the Garrison, but found himself deluded: and having lost
some few of his men, slain by La Motte Governour of the
Town, who had contrived the Plot, he escaped himself in Safety
with the rest. Sir William Pelham, General of the English Horse,
the whilst ranged all over Brabant. From Venlo the Prince
of Parma took his March to Berck, garrison'd by 1,200 English
under the Command of Colonel Morgan, and laid Siege to it.
To raise this Siege Leicester made haste thither: but when he
saw himself to be too weak in men, ill provided of Victuals, no
place of Retreat near, and the Enemie's Camp very strongly
intrenched and fortified to draw the Enemy from the Siege of it,
he besieged Duisburg; and after he had with his Ordnance
made a Breach in the Walls, and was ready to give an Assault,
they came to a Parley, and the City was yielded into his Hands
before the Prince of Parma could be drawn from Berck to relieve
it.

But the Prince of Parma misdoubting Zutphen, a Town hard
by, commanded a supply of Victuals to be conveyed thither.
A second Convoy being dispatched thither in foggy Weather,
the English in the Fog lighted upon the Spaniards that had
convoyed it. Whereupon they fell to Skirmishing. The English
being charged with 2 or 3 Volleys of Shot one after another
from a strong place of Advantage, yet stood their Ground, overthrew a Troop of Horse under the leading of George Cressiac
an Albanois, and took him Prisoner after he had been unhorsed
by the Lord Willoughby, Hannibal Gonzaga with many others
being slain. Of the English few were missing: but Sidney, one
as good as many, having his Horse killed under him, was shot
into the Thigh as he was mounting again, and died the 25th
day after, leaving behind him a great Miss of him amongst
good men. He died in the very Flower of his Age, having out-
lived his Father scarce four months: for whom Leicester his
Uncle, at his Return into England, made a splendid Funeral
after the military Fashion in Saint Paul's Church at London.
James King of Scots honoured him with an Epitaph; both the
Universities consecrated their Tears, and New College in Oxford set forth a most elegant Description of his noble Acts.
These things, and far more than these, his great Vertue, ex-

cellent Wit, most exquisite Learning, and sweet Conditions, deservedly merited.

Leicester, though full of Sorrow and Heaviness hereat, vigorously assaulted the Sconces near Zutphen: and the better to force the Town, he took the Island in the River, and in it the principal Fort. Then setting upon the lesser Fort, he took it through the Valour of Edward Stanley, who, catching hold of a Spaniard's Pike wherewith he charged him, held it so fast, that by the same he was drawn up into the Sconce: whereat the Spaniards were terrified, and in great Haste and Fear quitted it. Leicester knighted Stanley for his Valour, gave him forty Pounds of English Money in hand, and a yearly Pension of an hundred Marks during his Life. The Night following the Spaniards abandoned the great Sconce with all the Munition, and retired into Zutphen. Leicester thought it not good formally to besiege the same, which (it being now the depth of Winter) he thought sufficiently blocked up by the Garrisons in the Towns round about it. For at Deventer, within six English miles Northward, lay Sir William Stanley with 1,200 Foot, English and Irish; in the Sconces of Zutphen next Deventer lay Rowland York with 800 Foot and 100 Horse; at Doesburg, within 6 miles Southward, lay Sir John Boroughs with 800 Foot and 200 Horse; and to the Eastward were Garrisons put into Lochem, Sherenberg, and Dotecum.

Leicester, after he had drawn the rest of his men into Towns, and the Prince of Parma was departed farther off, returned to the Hague, where he was received by the Estates with these expostulatory Complaints: "That the Money was ill managed; That he listned to corrupt and destructive Counsels; That the English Companies were not full; That foreign Souldiers had been leavied without Consent of the Estates; That military Discipline was neglected, Wagons and Pioniers were taken up by force, the Privileges of the Provinces disregarded and slighted, and new kinds of Contributions invented." These things they pray him that he will prudently remedy in time. He, being now minded to goe over into England, putteth them in Hopes of Redress, and giveth them fair Words. But when the day came that he was to depart, he intrusted the Governments of the Provinces to the Council of State; and the same day privately made another Act of Restriction, reserving to himself all the Authority over the Governours of Provinces, Cities and Forts; also he took from the Council of State and the Presidents of Provinces their wonted Jurisdictions; and so sailed over into England the third day of December. Thus went the English Affairs in the Netherlands all this Year.

But in England, Philip Earl of Arundel, who had now been Prisoner in the Tower a full year, was accused in the Star-Chamber, "That he had relieved several Priests, contrary to the Laws; That he held Correspondence by Letters with Allen, and Parsons the Jesuite, the Queen's Enemies; That he had publickly in Writing questioned the Justice of the Kingdom; and That he had Intentions of departing the Realm without Licence." The Earl protesting his Obedience to the Queen, and his Love to his Countrey, modestly excused himself by his Affection to the Catholick Religion, and his Ignorance of the Laws, and, confessing his Fault, submitted himself to the Censure of the Bench; who fined him in ten thousand Pounds, and Imprisonment during the Queen's Pleasure. But of these things I am to speak more fully in the Year 1589.

At this time came over into England from Frederick the Second King of Denmark Henry Ramely, Chancellour for German Affairs, in a military Equipage, and attended with a Guard of Musquetiers; who made a large Declaration of the King's good Affection towards the Queen and the Peace of Christendom. For the procuring whereof with the Spaniard he promised his best Assistence; "lest (as he said) the Enemy of Mankind should any longer water the Seed of War, which he had sown in the Netherlands, with the Bloud of men." The Queen heard him very gratiously, had often Conference with him, entertaining the man with singular Courtesie, and highly commended the King of Denmark's pious Affection. But she made him Anwer by the Lord Burghley Lord Treasurer, Charles Howard Lord Admiral, Henry Lord Hunsdon Lord Chamberlain, and Sir Francis Walsingham Secretary, "That she desired nothing more than to embrace a Peace with her Neighbour-Princes, provided there was no Fraud in it: but well understanding the Attempts of the Spaniard against her, she could not but provide for her own Safety, the Defence of the true Religion of Christ, and the preserving of the Privileges of her Confederate Neighbours inviolate." Much after the same rate also was Answer given to Bodellan, whom the Prince of Parma had privily sent into England to try if he could procure a Peace.

In the mean time she largely supplied the King of Navarre with Money by Sir Horatio Pallavicini, through whose Sides the Guisians struck at the Reformed Religion in France. But there was nothing she was more carefull and intent about, than to establish a firm and lasting Amity betwixt England and Scotland, and to joyn them in a League of mutual Defence and Offense, thereby to cut off all hopes, not onely from her foreign Enemies, but also from the Queen of Scots herself, of any Assistence out of Scotland. For she suspected that the said Queen, being vexed in her Mind, did harbour dangerous Projects and Designs in her Breast since the time that those Conditions which she had offered were rejected, the Association entred into, and she herself committed (as I said before) to the Custody of Sir Amias Powlet and Sir Drue Drury. And certain it is, as evidently appeareth by the Adversaries own Writings, that the Jesuites on the one side, and the Fugitive Noblemen on the other side, with different Affections and Purposes, suggested to her very dangerous Advice and Counsel. For the Jesuites, when they saw no hope remaining of Restoring the Romish Religion either by her or her Son, betook themselves to new Strategems, and began to forge a new and pretended Title to the Succession of the Kingdom of England for the Spaniard (whose Grandeur alone they laboured to increase). To this end they sent into England (as Pasquier saith) one Samier, (if the name be not counterfeit,) a man of their Society, to draw Noblemen and Gentlemen to the Spaniard's Party, and thrust her forward to her own Danger, by telling her, that if she were troublesome, neither she nor her Son should reign; and by exciting the Guises, her Kinsmen, to new Attempts against the King of Navarre and the Prince of Condé, that being ingaged therein they might not be at leisure to help her.

But to conclude the League which was begun by Wotton (but interrupted by Russell's Death, and now endeavoured to be hindred by Desneval, Embassadour from France, and Corcellie, a man of a turbulent and unquiet Spirit, who had of late been disgracefully turned out of England,) Mr. Thomas Randolph was sent into Scotland, whose Dexterity in Scottish matters was looked upon as prudent and fortunate, though to the King he were not very acceptable, in regard of those Tumults which he had of late been the Authour of in Scotland. Randolph propounded to the King the same Conditions of a League which Wotton had propounded before. The King would have to be added to them, and set down in the Draught of the League, the Articles touching the annual Pension assigned him, and about the not prejudicing him in his Title to the Crown of England. The Embassadour, according to his Instructions, promised that those two Points should be provided for in a particular Article by themselves, provided he would continue constant in maintaining Amity with England. The King also (out of his great Love to his subjects) propounded farther, that the Scots might enjoy the same Privileges and Immunities in England which the English themselves did. But when the Embassadour had shewed him that that could not be granted but by Act of Parliament, and that the Estates of England would not easily yield to it; he deliberately and particularly gave his Assent to the Articles propounded, and commanded the same to be imparted to the Nobility of his Realm, that they might be confirmed by their Subscriptions also, although the French Embassadour endeavoured to make him believe at first, that the Queen sought this League, not out of any Love or Respect to the King, but out of a just Fear lest e'er long her Enemies which conspired against her should be too hard for her; and afterwards went about to terrifie him with Threats, that the old Amity with the French, which had been so highly beneficial to the Scots, would be by this means dissolved; and, lastly, besought him that nothing might be done herein without the Advice of the French King.

But he could work nothing upon the King, who knew these to be nothing but vain Scar-crows, either to hinder or delay the matter. For he knew that by the late Confederacy with the Netherlanders the English were very much strengthened. He gave therefore this serious Answer, "That he had put his Confidence in the Goodness of God, and not in the Amity and Friendship of those who were Enemies to God's Glory: and That it was as lawfull for him to make a League with the Queen without acquainting the French King, as for the French King to have made a League with the Queen of late without acquainting him." And though the Queen, being somewhat sparing, sent him less Money than he expected, lest she might be thought to buy the League, and gave him no express Assurance concerning the Succession: yet he, out of his Zeal to religion, and his singular Affection and Inclination towards both her and the publick Peace, commanded both the League to be concluded, and (to satisfie her) the Carrs also, who were suspected of Russell's death to be sent into England. But they fled away and escaped the day before they were to be sent.

Shortly after, in the beginning of June, there met at Berwick Edward Earl of Rutland, William Lord Evers, and Master Thomas Randolph, Commissioners sent by the Queen of England; and Francis Earl of Bothwell, Robert Lord Boyde, and James Humes of Coldingknoll, Commissioners appointed by the King of Scots: who concluded a League of Stricter Amity, (as they termed it, the word offensive not so well pleasing the Scots,) which followeth in these words.

> Whereas the Reign and Government of these Princes hath fallen into such uncertain and dangerous Times, wherein the Neighbour-Princes, who will needs be called Catholicks, acknowledging the Pope's Authority, do enter into mutual Leagues and Confederacies for the rooting up and extirpating the true, pure and Evangelical Religion, not onely out of their own Territories and Dominions, but also out of the Kingdoms of other Princes, and thereunto do bind themselves by faithful Vows and Promises: Lest those who profess the Evangelical Religion should seem to be less carefull for the Defence and Protection thereof, than they who profess the Romish Religion are seriously labouring the Subversion of the same; the said Princes, for the greater Security of their own Persons, upon whose Safety dependeth the Safety of all their People, and for the Preservation of the true, ancient and Christian Religion, which they now profess, have thought meet that a stricter Alliance and mutual Confederacy be sincerely entered into than ever hitherto hath been between their Majesties Progenitours.
>
> First therefore, to the end that this so pious and necessary a Purpose and Intention of both Princes in this troublesome State of Affairs may be brought to its wished Effect for the publick

Good and the Propagation of the Evangelical Truth, it is covenanted, agreed and concluded, That the said Princes shall by
this social and Sacred League provide for and endeavour the
Defence and Preservation of the true, pure and Evangelical
Religion, which they now profess, against all others whosoever
who shall enterprise, attempt or doe any thing against either of
them in order to subverting the said Religion; and that they
shall use their utmost Endeavour and Diligence that the rest of
the Princes who embrace the same true Religion may be brought
to associate with them in this so holy a purpose and confederacy,
and with joynt Forces maintain the true Worship of God in their
Countries and Dominions, and defend and govern their People
under the said Ancient and Apostolical Religion.

Item, It is covenanted, accorded and concluded, That this
social League for maintaining and upholding the Christian and
Catholick Religion, which at this times is embraced by both
Princes, and by God's Blessing received and countenanced
through their Kingdoms and Dominions, shall be a League both
of Defence and Offence against all men whatever, who shall hinder, or any ways go about to hinder the free Exercise thereof in
their Kingdoms and Dominions; all Treaties, Alliances and Confederacies whatsoever formerly entred into betwixt either of
them and the Disturbers or Adversaries of the said Religion, be
they who they will, to the contrary notwithstanding.

And if at any time it shall happen that any Prince or State
whatsoever, of what Condition soever they be, shall invade or
infest the Kingdoms, Dominions or Territories of either of the
said Princes, or any part thereof, or shall any way hurt or injure
their Majesties Persons or their Subjects, or attempt the said
things, or any of them; it is covenanted, accorded and concluded,
That neither of these Princes, being certified from the Prince
invaded, or suffering such Injury or Hurt, shall at any time,
openly or secretly, directly or indirectly, give or afford any Aid,
Counsel or Favour to the said Invaders or Infestors, any Tie of
Consanguinity or Affinity, Alliance of Amities or Confederacies
formerly entred into, or hereafter to be entred into, notwithstanding: and this in what kind of Invasion soever it be, and by
whomsoever it shall be made or attempted.

It is agreed, accorded and concluded, That the aforesaid Princes
shall assist one another in manner as followeth: that is to say,
the King of Scots, in case the Realm of England be invaded or
infested by a foreign Power in those Parts thereof that are

remote from the Kingdom of Scotland, shall, after Demand made
by the Queen of England, without Delay send 2,000 Horse and
5,000 Foot, or any lesser number of men, at the Choice and
Demand of the said Queen; and shall cause the same to march,
at the Queen's Charges, from the Borders of Scotland lying next
unto England into any other Part of England whatsoever.

Item, That the Queen of England, in case the Realm of
Scotland be invaded or infested by a foreign Power in those parts
thereof that are remote from the Kingdom of England, shall,
after Demand made of the said Queen by the King of Scots,
without delay send 3,000 Horse and 6,000 Foot, or any lesser
number of men, at the Pleasure and Choice of the said King;
and shall cause the same to march, at the Charges of the said
King, from the Borders of England next adjoyning to Scotland
into any other Part of Scotland whatsoever.

Item, It is covenanted, accorded and concluded, That if the
Kingdom of England be invaded by any man whatsoever in the
Northern Parts, within 60 miles of the Borders of Scotland,
then the most Illustrious King of Scots, being requested and
called upon by the most Serene Queen of England, shall cause to
be gathered, and shall without delay effectually gather, all the
Power and Strength he can make, and shall joyn the same with
the English Forces, and in hostile manner pursue and prosecute
the Invaders of the Realm of England, and all their Abettors and
Favourers whosoever, for the Space of 30 Days together, and
those Days being expired, if Occasion or Necessity require, of
more, even for as long time as the Subjects of Scotland have
anciently been accustomed, and at this day in right are bound,
to give their Service and Help for the Defence of the Kingdom
of Scotland.

Item, That when the King of Scots shall be certified by the
Queen of England of any Invasion or other Disturbance whatso-
ever in her Kingdom of Ireland, he shall not onely forbid the
Inhabitants of the County of Argyle, and the Isles and Places to
the same adjoyning, and of all other Parts of the Kingdom of
Scotland whatsoever, to enter into the Kingdom of Ireland, and
effectually hinder them from entring; but also, whensoever it
shall hereafter happen that the Inhabitants of any Part of the
Kingdom of Scotland shall enter, contrary to the Meaning and
Intent of this Treaty, with any extraordinary or unusual number
of men, in a hostile manner, into any Part of the Kingdom of
Ireland, the said King, being certified by the Queen of such their

Entrance, shall by publick Proclamation declare such Infestors and Disturbers, who shall in an hostile manner harrass that Kingdom, to be Rebels, Disturbers of the publick Peace, and Traitours, and shall accordingly prosecute them as such.

Item, That neither Prince shall for the time to come aid, favour, succour or relieve any Traitour, Rebel, or him that shall openly revolt from his Prince, or suffer them any way to be aided, succoured and relieved by others, or permit them openly or secretly to make their Abode in his or her Dominions; but shall each of them, from the time of Notice or first Demand made by the Prince from whom they have revolted, without Delay or Procrastination, deliver up, or cause to be delivered, the said Traitours or Rebels, according to the Agreements expressed in former Treaties betwixt us and our Predecessours, or at leastwise shall compell them to retire from the Frontiers and Borders of their Dominions: and moreover, as long as the said Rebels or Traitours shall make their Abode in their said Dominions, shall make just and due Satisfaction for all Injuries and Mischiefs which may be done by the said Rebels.

Item, That for compounding and adjusting of all and every the Injuries and Controversies which have happened and arisen on the Borders, upon account of the Borders, or amongst the Borderers, from the time that the most Illustrious King of Scots first took the Government of the Realm into his own Hands, and for the Space of four years going next before the Said term, the two Princes respectively shall within 6 months after the concluding of this League send able and fit Commissioners, well affected to the Peace, furnished and impowered with Instructions meet and sufficient for that Purpose, to some convenient place on the Confines of both Kingdoms, who shall compound and determine all such Causes and Controversies by an honourable and friendly Treaty and Agreement.

Item, That neither of the said Princes shall contract Amity, or enter into any League or Confederacy with any other Prince, State or Society of men, to the prejudice of this present League and Union, without the express consent of the other Confederate Prince, by Letters of the said Prince, subscribed with his own Hand or sealed with his Privy Seal, first had and obtained.

Item, That both Princes, when either of them shall be duly required by the Embassadours or Commissioners of the other Prince so to doe, shall both by their Oath and under their Great Seal, approve, confirm and ratifie this Sacred League and Alliance; and moreover for the better Strengthening thereof, shall, within a certain time to be appointed by the mutual Consent of both Princes, deliver, or cause to be delivered, their Royal Instruments or Letters Patent to the same purpose.

Item, That all former Treaties of Amities, Contracts and Agreements, made betwixt the Predecessours of the aforesaid Princes, and their Kingdoms and Dominions, though they may seem to be antiquated and out of Date, shall still continue in their Strength, Force and Vigour. As likewise that this present Treaty of mutual Confederacy and stricter Amity and Alliance shall in no sort derogate from former Treaties and Confederacies entred into by the said Princes with other their Confederates, or in any respect weaken or lessen the Force and Authority thereof, (the Defence of the purer Religion, which the said Princes do now maintain and embrace in their Kingdoms, onely excepted;) in which sense and latitude we understand and intend that this present League of Defence and Offence shall remain in its full Strength, firm and inviolate.

Item, That the King of Scots shall, when he arrives at the full age of 25 years, as soon as conveniently may be, approve and confirm the present Treaty, and cause it to be approved and confirmed, by a publick Assembly of the Estates of his Realm. And the same also shall the Queen's Majesty doe and perform, and cause to be done and performed, in Parliament, by the Nobility and other States of her Kingdoms of England and Ireland.

The same month that this League was ratified a dangerous Conspiracy was discovered against Queen Elizabeth; the Original and Progress whereof I will lay down as briefly as I can out of the voluntary Confessions of the Conspiratours themselves. In the English Seminary at Rheims some there were who, with a certain Astonishment admiring and reverencing the Omnipotency of the Bishop of Rome, did believe that the Bull of Pius Quintus against Queen Elizabeth was dictated by the Holy Ghost: these men persuaded themselves, and others that eagerly desired and itched after the Glory of Martyrdom, that it was a meritorious Act to kill such Princes as were excommunicate, yea that they were Martyrs who lost their Lives upon that account. These things Gifford, a Doctour of Divinity, Gilbert Gifford and Hodgeson Priests, impressed so deeply upon one John Savage, (a Bastard by report,) a man ready for any Undertaking, that he

226

willingly and readily vowed to kill Queen Elizabeth. At the same time they wrote a Book, (and that onely on purpose to lull the Queen and Council fairly asleep in Security, while they privily made way for their wicked Designs) wherein they admonished the Papists in England not to attempt any thing against their Princess, but to fight against their Adversaries onely with the Weapons of Christians, *viz.* with Tears, spiritual Reasonings, daily Prayers, Watchings and Fastings: And withall they spread a false Rumour abroad by their Tale-bearers, that George Gifford, one of the Band of the Queen's Gentlemen-pensioners, had sworn the Queen's Death, and in that respect had drawn a considerable Sum of Money from the Duke of Guise.

About Easter John Ballard, a Priest of the Seminary at Rheims, who had been visiting many of the Papists in England and Scotland, and feeling their Pulses, returned into France in company with one Maud, Walsingham's Spy, (a notable crafty Dissembler, who had egregiously deceived the unwary Priest) and tampered with Don Bernardine de Mendoza, the Spaniard's Ordinary Embassadour then in France; and with Charles Paget, a man thoroughly devoted to the Queen of Scots, about Invading of England; judging it to be now a very fit time, whilst the martial-spirited men were absent in the Netherlands: neither could they ever hope for a fairer Opportunity, forasmuch as the Bishop of Rome, the Spaniard, the Duke of Guise, and the Prince of Parma, were all resolved to set upon England, thereby to divert the War from the Netherlands. And though Paget demonstrated clearly, that it was in vain to invade England as long as Queen Elizabeth lived; yet was Ballard sent back again into England, having first been ingaged by Oath to procure Assistence with all Speed to joyn with the Invaders, and to effect the Queen of Scots Liberty.

At Whitsontide arrived in England that silken Priest in Souldier's Habit, called commonly by the borrowed Name of Captain Foscu. At London he brake the Business to Anthony Babington of Dethick in Derbyshire, a young Gentleman of good Birth, rich, ripe-witted, and learned above most of his years: who, being addicted to the Romish Religion, had a little before gone over into France, unknown, without Licence, and grew familiarly acquainted with Thomas Morgan, one that retained to the Queen of Scots, and with the Bishop of Glascow her Embassadour. These two, by their continual extolling the heroical Vertues of so great a Queen unto him, had put him into an assured Hope of acquiring great Honours by her Service: which the ambitious young Gentlemen soon laid hold on. They recommended him also, when he little thought of it, by Letters to the Queen of Scots. For when he was returned into England, she wrote several kind and loving Letters to him. And from that time Morgan made use of his Help in conveying Letters to her, till such time as she was committed to Sir Amias Powlet's Keeping: for then the young Gentleman, perceiving the Danger, gave over. To this Babington (I say) Ballard brake the Business aforesaid. He was flatly of Opinion, that the Invasion of England would signifie nothing so long as Queen Elizabeth lived. But when Ballard had told him that she would not live long, for Savage was now come into England, who had vowed to kill her; Babington was not satisfied that so weighty a Business should be entrusted to Savage alone, lest he should fail of the Enterprise, but rather to six stout Gentlemen, of which number he would have Savage to be one, that so he might not break his Vow. Babington therefore contriveth a new Project for Invading the Realm by Foreigners, concerning the Havens where they should land, the Aid that should joyn with them, the Delivering of the Queen of Scots, and the Tragical Execution of the Queen, as he termed it.

Whilst his Mind was wholly intent upon his Business, he received Letters by an unknown Boy in a Cypher familiar betwixt the Queen of Scots and him, wherein she gently blamed him for his long Silence, and desired him to send her with all speed a Pacquet of Letters come from Morgan, and delivered by the French Embassadour's Secretary. Which he did, and withall by the same Messenger sent a Letter of his own unto her, wherein "he excuseth his Silence, in regard he wanted Opportunities of sending any thing to her ever since she was committed to the Custody of Sir Amias Powlet a Puritan, a mere Leicestrian, and a most bitter Enemy of the Catholick Faith," (for so he called him.) "He relateth what Conference he had had with Ballard; informeth her that six Gentlemen were made choice of to commit the Tragical Execution; and that he himself with an hundred more would at the same time set her at Liberty. He prayed her that the heroical Actours in this Business" (for so he termed them) "might have Rewards assigned them, or else their Posterity, if they happened to perish in the Attempt." To this Letter answer was made the 27th of July: "Babington's most entire affection to the Catholick Religion and to her is commended and applauded: but he is advised to go circumspectly and wisely to work. *viz.* That the Association amongst them should be entred into upon pretence that they stood in fear of the Puritans. That there should be no Rising before such time as they were assured of foreign Assistence. That some Disturbance should be raised in Ireland while the Stroke was giving on this side. That Arundel and his Brothers and the Earl of Northumberland should be wrought over to her Party: and That Westmorland, Paget, and others, should be privily called home." The Way also for her delivery was thus laid; *viz.* "either by Overthrowing a Cart in the Gate, or setting Fire on the Stables, or by Intercepting her as she rode abroad for her Recreation in the Fields betwixt Chartley and Stafford. Lastly, Babington is commanded to pass his Word to the Six Gentlemen and the rest concerning their Reward for their Service."

He had now associated to himself several Gentlemen who were very zealous for the Romish Religion: amongst whom those of most eminent Note were, Edward Windsore, Brother to the Lord Windsore, a young man of a softly Disposition; Thomas Salisbury, of a Knightly Family in Denbighshire; Charles Tilney, a Gentleman of an ancient House, the onely Hope of the Family, and one of the Band of Gentlemen-pensioners to the Queen, whom Ballard had lately reconciled to the Romish Church; both of them young Gentlemen of comely Personage: Chidiock Tichburne, of the County of Southampton; Edward Abington, whose Father had been Under-treasurer, or (as they commonly call him) Cofferer of the Queen's Household; Robert Gage, of Surrey; John Travers and John Charnock, of Lancashire; John Jones, whose Father was Yeoman or Keeper of the Wardrobe to Queen Mary; Savage, whom I have spoken of already; Barnwell, of a noble Family in Ireland; and Henry Dun, Clark in the Office of First-fruits and Tenths. One Pollie also insinuated himself into their Company, a man who perfectly understood the

Affairs of the Queen of Scots, a cunning Counterfeit and Dissembler, who is thought to have revealed all their Consultations from day to day to Walsingham, and to have egged on the young Gentlemen in this desperate Undertaking who were prone enough of themselves to what was bad; though Nawe, the Queen of Scots Secretary, had given them secret Warning to beware of him.

To these men Babington breaketh the Design, but not all parts of it to every one of them. To Ballard, Tichburne and Dun he sheweth his own Letters and the Scottish Queen's. Tilney and Tichburne he perswadeth to be Executors of the Murther. They at first refuse to imbrue their Hands in the Bloud of their Princess. Ballard and Babington labour to prove to them, that it is lawfull to kill Princes Excommunicate; and if ever Equity and Justice be to be violated, it is to be done for the Promotion of the Catholick Religion. Being hereupon with much ado perswaded, they gave a kind of Consent. Abington, Barnwell, Charnock and Savage take the Oath readily and chearfully to commit the Murther. Salisbury could by no means be perswaded to have his Hand in Killing the Queen, but voluntarily promised his Help for setting the Queen of Scots at Liberty. Over and above those before named, Babington pitcheth upon one Tichenor to make up the Crew, of whose Fidelity and Boldness he was well satisfied; but he was at present absent a great way off. Babington chargeth them not to acquaint any man with the Business, but upon an Oath of Secrecy first taken. The Conspiratours met ever anon to confer about these matters, either in Saint Giles's Fields, or Saint Paul's Church, or in Taverns, where they every day banquetted and feasted, being puffed up with Hope of great Honours; now and then commending the Valour of those Scottish Gentlemen who had not long before surprized the King at Sterlin; and of Gerard the Burgundian, who murthered the Prince of Orange. And to such a height of foolish Vanity they proceeded, that they would needs have those men that were appointed to be the Assassinates pictured to the life, and Babington in the midst of them, with this Verse.

Hi mihi sunt Comites, quos ipsa Pericula ducunt.

These men are my Companions, whom very Dangers draw. But forasmuch as this Verse pleased them not, as being too open and plain, they put in stead of it, *Quorsum hæc aliò properanti-bus?* that is, To what end are these things to men that hasten to another Purpose? These Pictures (they say) were begun, and privately shewed to the Queen, who knew none of them by their Favour save onely Barnwell, who had often come to her about Business of the Earl of Kildare's, to whom he retained: but being by other Tokens put in mind of him, she remembred the man very well. Sure it is, that when upon a time she walked abroad, and saw Barnwell, she beheld him undauntedly, and turning herself to Hatton, Captain of the Guard, and others, she said, "Am not I fairly guarded, that have not a man in my Company that wears a Sword?" For so Barnwell himself related to the rest of the Conspiratours, and shewed them how easily she might have been made away at that time, if the Conspiratours had been there in readiness. Savage also affirmed the same.

Nothing now more perplexed Babington, than lest the Promise made of foreign Aid should not be performed. Therefore to make sure thereof, he resolved himself to go over into France, and to that purpose to send Ballard privately before, for whom by his Money, under a counterfeit Name, he had procured a Licence to travel. And that there might not be the least Suspicion of himself, he insinuated into Walsingham by means of Pollie, whom I spoke of before, and earnestly besought him to procure him a Licence from the Queen to travel into France, promising to doe her extraordinary good Service in pumping out and dis-covering the secret Designs of the Fugitives in behalf of the Queen of Scots. Walsingham commended the young Gentle-man's Purpose, and promised him not onely a Licence to travel, but also many and great matters if he performed what he under-took. Yet did he linger and delay him, sifting out in the mean time, by his own and other mens Cunning and Diligence, the whole Plot, when they thought that the very Sun was a Stranger to it: but this he did principally through the Discovery of Gilbert Gifford a Priest.

This Gifford was born of a good Family at Chellington in the County of Stafford, not far from Chartley, where the Queen of Scots was Prisoner; and was sent about this time into En-gland by the Fugitives, under the counterfeit Name of Luson, to put Savage in mind of his Vow, and privately to lurk here as a Messenger to convey Letters betwixt them and the Queen of Scots: for so dangerous was that Service, that they could draw neither the Countess of Arundel, nor the Lord Lumley, nor the Lord Henry Howard, nor yet George Shirley, to undertake it.

The Fugitives, to make Trial whether Gifford would be faithfull in the safe conveying of their Letters, sent at first several empty Papers (which we call Blanks,) made up like Letters, which when they found, by the Answers they received, to have been delivered, they grew then more confident of him, and sent frequently other Letters written in Cyphers concerning their Business. But Gifford, whether pricked in Conscience, or formerly corrupted with Money, or terrified with Fear, had before this come to Walsingham privately, informed him what he was, and to what purpose sent into England, offered him his best Service in Love to his Prince and Countrey, and promised to impart unto him all the Letters he should receive either from the Fugitives, or from the Queen of Scots. Walsingham, laying hold on the opportunity offered, entertained the man kindly, sent him into Staffordshire, and wrote to Powlet, that he should connive at the corrupting of one of his men by Gifford. Powlet, unwilling that any of his own Servants should (as he said) became a Traitour by such dissembling, denied it; yet permitted he him to corrupt a Brewer or some such man who dwelt hard by. Gifford with a few Pieces of Gold soon corrupted the Brewer, who privately put in the Letters, and received Answers of them, through an Hole in the Wall, which was stopped with a loose Stone; which Letters forthwith came to Walsingham's Hands by Messengers ready on purpose to carry them. Walsingham opened them, wrote them out, found out the Cyphers by the singular Art and Skill of Thomas Phelipps, and by the Direction of Arthur Gregory sealed them up again so cunningly, that no man could ever judge they had been opened, and so sent them to those to whom they were directed by the Superscriptions. Thus were intercepted those foremention'd Letters of the Queen of Scots to Babington, and his in Answer to her, and another of hers to him, (wherein was cunningly added (after the opening) a Postscript in the same Characters, desiring him to set down the Names of the six Gentlemen and it's likely other things too;) also the Letters which were written the same day and Date to Mendoza the Spanish Embassadour, to Charles Paget, the Lord Paget, the Archbishop of Glascow, and Sir Francis Inglefield: all which were first copied out, and then sent over Sea.

Queen Elizabeth, as soon as she understood by these Letters that so dreadfull a Storm hung over her head, on the one side from her own Subjects at Home, and on the other side from Strangers abroad, gave Command, for the timely Suppressing of the Conspiracy, that Ballard should forthwith be apprehended. Him therefore they seized on before he was aware in Babington's House at the very moment when he was ready to set forward on his Journey for France. Hereupon Babington grew very much troubled and pensive, tossed with a thousand Uncertainties of an unresolved Mind: and while his Thoughts ran now this way now that way, at length he betook himself to Tichburne, and advised with him what was best to be done. Tichburne's Counsel was, that the Conspiratours should forthwith disperse themselves and fly. But Babington thought it the best Course, to send Savage and Charnock presently to execute the murther: but first, that they might get the better Access, he thought good to provide Savage of more handsome and courtly Apparel, and hereof he discoursed with them the same day in St. Paul's Church. But presently his Mind altered, and, concealing the inward Anguish of his troubled Breast, he pressed Walsingham (then absent at Court) by Letters and earnest Intreaties, that he might now at length have his Licence granted to travel into France; and withall solicited him for the Delivery of Ballard, who would be of special Use and Service to him in the Business he had undertaken. Walsingham feedeth him with fair Promises from day to day. That Ballard was apprehended, he layeth the Blame upon Young, that subtile Discoverer of Papists, and upon the Pursuivants; and, as it were out of Love and Friendship, warneth Babington to beware of that kind of men: and now he easily perswadeth the young Gentleman to lodge in his House at London till the Queen had signed his Licence, and till himself could return to London, that they might have the more secret and secure Conference about matters of such Moment and Consequence, and that there might no Suspicion arise of him amongst the Fugitives when he should come into France upon account of his frequent Repair to his House. In the mean time Scudamore, Walsingham's man, was commanded to have a diligent and watchfull Eye upon him, and to keep him company in all places, under Pretence of securing him from Pursuivants.

Thus far had Walsingham spun this Thred alone, without acquainting the rest of the Queen's Council: and longer he would have drawn it, but the Queen would not suffer it, "Lest (as she said herself) by not heeding and preventing the Danger while she might, she should seem rather to tempt God, than to trust in God." A Note was therefore sent from the Court from Walsingham to his Man, that he should more strictly observe Babington. This Note being unsealed, was delivered so to him that Babington, sitting at the Board next him, read it along with him. Hereupon his Conscience accusing him, and suspecting that all was come to light, the next Night, when he and Scudamore and one or two more of Walsingham's men had supped plentifully in a Tavern, he arose from the Board as if he intended to pay the Reckoning, and, leaving his Cloak and Sword behind him, made all the Haste he could in the dark to Westminster, where Gage changed Cloaths with him, who presently stripped himself again in Charnock's Chamber, and put on Charnock's Cloaths; and immediately they withdrew themselves into Saint John's Wood near the City, whither also Barnwell and Dun made their Retreat. In the mean time they were publickly proclaimed Traitours all over England. They were now fain to lurk in Woods and blind Corners; and having in vain tried to borrow Money of the French Embassadour, and Horses of Tichburne, cut off Babington's Hair, disguised and sullied the natural Beauty of his Face with the Rind of green Walnuts, and being hardly put to it by Hunger, they went to an House of the Bellamies near Harrow on the Hill, which Bellamies were strongly addicted to the Romish Religion. There were they hid in Barns, there were they fed, and cloathed in rude Countrey Habit. But the tenth day after they were discovered and brought up to London, the City testifying their publick Joy by ringing of Bells, making of Bone-fires, and singing of Psalms: insomuch as the Citizens were highly commended and thanked by the Queen of these Testimonies of their good Affection.

The rest of the Conspiratours were taken soon after, most of them in places near the City; Salisbury in Cheshire, having his Horse run through by those that pursued him, and with him Travers, after they had swam over the River Wever. Jones was taken to Wales, who, being privy to the designed Invasion, had concealed them in his House after he knew them to be proclaimed Traitours; and had horsed Salisbury in his Flight, and changed Cloaks with his man, which was a Priest. Onely Windsore was not to be found. Many days were spent in Examining of them, who cut one anothers Throats by their Confessions, and discovered the whole Truth of the Business.

All this while was the Queen of Scots and her Servants kept by Powlet with so strict a Watch and so closely observed, that she was utterly ignorant of all these Occurrences, though they were commonly known and talked of all over England. But as soon as these Conspiratours were apprehended, Sir Thomas Gorges was sent to give her a brief Account thereof: which News he surprized her with, and that of set purpose, just as she had taken Horse to ride a-Hunting. Neither was she permitted to return to the place of her Custody, but was led about (under a Shew of doing her Honour) from one Gentleman's House to another's dwelling thereabouts. In the mean time Sir John Maners, Sir Edward Aston, Sir Richard Bagot, and Master William Waad, (who was lately sent into those parts, and wholly ignorant of the matter,) by Authority granted them under the Queen's Warrant and Letters, committed Nawe and Curle, her two Secretaries, to several Keepers, that they might have no Conference either with one another, or with the Queen. And then breaking open the Doors of her private Closet, they sent all her Cabinets wherein her Papers were kept, sealed up with their own Seals, to the Court. Then Powlet (as he was commanded) seized upon all her Money, lest she should corrupt any body with Bribes, and passed his word for the true restoring the same. Her Cabinets being searched before Queen Elizabeth, there were found many Letters from persons beyond Sea, as also Copies of Letters written to several, Breviaries, and about 60 Indexes or Tables of private Cyphers and Characters; Letters also from some English Noblemen to her, full of expressions of Love and Respect. Which notwithstanding Queen Elizabeth dissembled and concealed in Silence, according to that Motto which she used, *Video & taceo,* that is, I see, but say nothing. But they having got some Inkling thereof, began from that time to shew themselves deadly Adversaries to the Queen of Scots, lest they might seem to have favoured her before.

Now Gifford, having acted his Part thus far in this Scene, was sent away back into France as if he had been banished hence; but first he left behind him with the French Embassadour in England an indented Paper, with Direction that he should deliver the Letters he received from the Queen of Scots, or from the Fugitives, to no other person but him that should shew the Counterpane thereof; which Counterpane was privily sent by him to Walsingham. This Gifford, being returned into France, was after some months cast into Prison for incontinent and dishonest living; and being withall suspected there of these things, he died miserably, freely confessing most of the Passages already mentioned, which were also found penned down in some Papers he had by him in his Coffers.

On the 13th of September seven of the Conspiratours were arraigned, confessed themselves guilty, and were condemned of High Treason. The next day but one after seven others were in like manner arraigned, pleaded Not Guilty, and submitted themselves to be tried by God and the countrey, as the manner is; who were all found guilty out of their own Confessions, and condemned. Pollie onely of the number, though he were privy to all the Business, yet because he affirmed that he had revealed several things to Walsingham, was not arraigned. On the 20th of the same month (a Gallows and a Scaffold being set up for that purpose in Saint Giles's Fields, where they were wont to meet,) the first seven were hanged, cut down, their Privities cut off, their Bowels taken out before their Faces while they were alive, and their Bodies quartered, not without some note and touch of Cruelty.

Ballard, the Arch-plotter and Contriver of this Treason, craved Pardon of God, and of the Queen if so he had sinned against her. Babington (who beheld Ballard's Execution without being the least daunted, while the rest turned away their Faces, and fell to Prayers upon their Knees,) ingenuously acknowledged his Offence. Being taken down from the Gallows, and now ready to be cut up, he cried aloud several times in Latin, *Parce mihi,*

Domine Jesu, that is, Spare or Forgive me, O Lord Jesus. Savage brake the Rope, and fell down from the Gallows, and was presently seized on by the Executioner, his Privities cut off, and his Bowels taken out alive. Barnwell extenuated his Crime upon the account of Religion and Conscience. Tichburne humbly acknowledged his Fault, and moved the Multitude to Pity and Commiseration of his Case. As in like manner did Tilney, a man of a modest Disposition and comely Personage. Abington, a man of a turbulent Spirit, sought to terrifie them with Menaces and Threats of Bloud which should, he said, be spilt e'er long in England.

The next day the other seven were drawn to the same place, and suffered the same kind of death; but somewhat more favourably, by the Queen's express Command, who detested the former Cruelty: for they all hung till they were quite dead before they were cut down and bowelled.

Salisbury was the first, who died very penitent, admonishing the Catholicks not to attempt to restore Religion by Force and Arms. In like manner did Dun, who next followed him. Jones protested that he disswaded Salisbury from the Attempt, and utterly condemned Babington's proud and rash Headiness, and the Design for Invasion. Charnock and Travers having their Minds wholly fixed on Prayer, recommended themselves to God and the Saints. Gage extolled the Queen's great Grace and Bounty to his Father, and detested his own perfidious Ingratitude towards his Princess, to whom he was so deeply engaged. Hierom Bellamy, who had concealed Babington after he was openly proclaimed Traitour, (whose Brother was guilty of the same Crime, and strangled himself in Prison) with Confusion and deep Silence brought up the Rere.

These being thus executed, Nawe a French-man and Curle a Scot, who were the Queen of Scots Secretaries, being examined about the Letters, Copies of Letters, Notes and Cyphers found in the Queen's private Closet, voluntarily acknowledged, and subscribed to it, that the Letters were of their Hand-writing, as they were dictated from the Queen's own Mouth in French to Nawe, and translated into English by Curle, and so wrote in Cyphers. Neither did they deny but she had received Letters from Babington, and that by her Command they had written back to him to

237

the same purpose as I have before related. Whether these Secretaries were bribed to confess this I cannot say: Yet this appears out of some Letters, that when Curle about this time claimed Promise of Walsingham, Walsingham taxed him as unmindfull of the extraordinary Favour he had done him, and told him he had confessed nothing but what he could not deny, because Nawe his Fellow justified it to his Face.

Shortly after was Sir Edward Wotton sent into France, to inform the King of the whole Management of the Conspiracy, and to shew him the Copies of the Letters of the Queen of Scots and others, attested by the Depositions of certain Noblemen of England, to justify the Truth thereof; that so the French King might see into what great Dangers the Queen of England had been brought by the Practices of Morgan, Charles Paget, and others in France.

And now what should be done with the Queen of Scots the Council were of several Minds and Opinions. Some thought that no new rigorous Course was to be taken with her, but onely that she was to be committed to closer Custody, both because she was not the Authour of the Mischief, but onely Accessory to it; as also because she was sickly, and not like to live long. Others were of opinion that, for the Security and Preservation of Religion, she was forthwith to be put to death, and that by Law. Leicester thought rather by Poison, and sent a Divine privately to Walsingham to satisfie him that it was lawfull. But Walsingham protested he was so far from consenting that any Violence should be done unto her, that he had of late crossed Morton's Counsel, who advised that she should be sent back into Scotland, and put to death in the very Frontiers and Borders of both Kingdoms. Then they differed in opinion by what Law she should be proceeded against, whether by the Statute of the 25th year of Edward the Third, (whereby "he is made guilty of Treason who shall compass or imagine the Destruction of the King or Queen, raise War in his or her Kingdom, or adhere to his or her Enemies,") or by the late Act in the 27th of Queen Elizabeth, whereof I have made mention before. At length it was carried by those who thought she was rather to be tried by this last Act, as being made for this very Purpose and Occasion, and therefore to be put in Execution. To the end therefore that

Process might be made and Sentence pronounced according to this Act, made the last Year against all such as should raise Rebellion, invade the Realm, or attempt any Violence towards the Queen, several of the Privy Council and other Noblemen of England were made Commissioners by the Queen's Patent for her Trial. Whose Names (because it may concern Posterity to know the Rank and Titles of the Noblemen of England) I have thought good to set down out of the very Original, which runneth thus in the ordinary Form of the Court.

Elizabeth by Grace of God, of England, France and Ireland Queen, Defender of the Faith, &c. To the most Reverend Father in Christ, John Archbishop of Canterbury, Primate and Metropolitan of all England, and one of our Privy Council; and to our trusty and well-beloved Sir Thomas Bromely Knight, Chancellour of England, and one of our Privy Council; and also to our trusty and well-beloved William Lord Burghley, Lord Treasurer of England, another of our Privy Council; and also to our most dear Cousin William Lord Marquess of Winchester, one of the Lords of the Parliament; To our most dear Cousin Edward Earl of Oxford, great Chamberlain of England, another of the Lords of the Parliament; and also to our most dear Cousin George Earl of Shrewsbury, Earl-Marshal of England, another of our Privy Council; and to our most dear Cousin Henry Earl of Kent, another of the Lords of the Parliament; and also to our most dear Cousin Henry Earl of Derby, another of our Privy Council; and to our most dear Cousin William Earl of Worcester, another of the Lords of the Parliament; and also to our most dear Cousin Edward Earl of Rutland, another of the Lords of the Parliament; and to our most dear Cousin Ambrose Earl of Warwick, Master of our Ordnances, another of our Privy Council; and to our most dear Cousin Henry Earl of Pembroke, another of the Lords of Parliament; and also to our most dear Cousin Robert Earl of Leicester, Master of our Horse, another of our Privy Council; and to our most dear Cousin Henry Earl of Lincoln, another of the Lords of the Parliament; and also to our most dear Cousin Antony Viscount of Montague, another of the Lords of the Parliament; And to our trusty and well-beloved Charles Lord Howard, our high Admiral of England, another of our Privy Council; and to our trusty and well-beloved Henry Lord of Hunsdon, our Lord Chamberlain, another of our Privy Council; and also to our trusty and well-beloved Henry Lord Abergavenny, another of the Lords of the Parliament; and to our trusty and well-beloved Edward Lord Zouch, another of the Lords of the Parliament, and also to our trusty and well beloved Edward Lord Morley, another of the Lords of the Parliament; and to our trusty and well-beloved William Lord Cobham, Lord Warden of our Cinque-ports, another of our Privy Council; and also to our trusty and well-beloved Edward Lord Stafford, another of the Lords of the Parliament; and also to our trusty and well-beloved Arthur Lord Grey of Wilton, another of the Lords of the Parliament; and also to our trusty and well-beloved John Lord Lumley, another of the Lords of the Parliament; and also to our trusty and well-beloved John Lord Stourton, another of the Lords of the Parliament; and to our trusty and well-beloved William Lord Sandes, another of the Lords of the Parliament; and also to our trusty and well-beloved Henry Lord Wentworth, another of the Lords of the Parliament; to our truly and well-beloved Lewis Lord Mordant, another of the Lords of the Parliament; and to our trusty and well-beloved John Lord Saint-John of Bletnesho, another of the Lords of the Parliament; and also to our trusty and well-beloved Thomas Lord Buckhurst, another of our Privy Council; and to our trusty and well-beloved Henry Lord Compton, another of the Lords of the Parliament; and also to our trusty and well-beloved Henry Lord Cheyney, another of the Lords of the Parliament: To our trusty and beloved Sir Francis Knolles Knight, Treasurer of our Houshold, another of our Privy Council; and also to our trusty and beloved Sir James Croftes Knight, Controller of our said Houshold, another of our Privy Council; and to our trusty and beloved Sir Christopher Hatton Knight, our Vice-chamberlain, another of our Privy Council; and also to our trusty and beloved Sir Francis Walsingham Knight, one of our principal Secretaries, another of our Privy Council; and also to our trusty and beloved William Davison Esquire, another of our principal Secretaries, and of our Privy Council; and to our trusty and beloved Sir Ralph Sadleir Knight, Chancellour of our Dutchy of Lancaster, another of our Privy Council; and also to our trusty and beloved Sir Walter Mildmay Knight, Chancellour of our Exchequer, another of our Privy Council; and to our trusty and beloved Sir Amias Powlet Knight, Captain of our Isle of Jersey, another of our Privy Council; and to our trusty and beloved John Wolley Esquire, our Secretary for the Latin Tongue, another of our Privy Council: And also to our trusty and beloved Sir Christopher Wray, Knight, Chief Justice assigned for the Pleas to be holden before us; and to our truly and beloved Sir Edmond Anderson Knight, our Chief Justicer of the Bench; Sir Roger Manwood Knight, our Chief Baron of our Exchequer; Sir Thomas Gawdy Knight, one of our Justicers assigned for the Pleas to be holden before us; and William Periam, one of our Justicers of the Bench, Greeting, &c.

Then, (not to write it all down *verbatim*) after the Recital of the Law or Act (as our Lawyers term it) made the last Year, thus it followeth:

Whereas since the end of the Session of Parliament, *viz.* since the first day of June in the 27th Year of our Reign, diverse things have been compassed and imagined tending to the Hurt of our Royal Person, as well by Mary Daughter and Heir of James the Fifth King of Scots, and commonly called Queen of Scots, and Dowager of France, pretending a Title to the Crown of this Realm of England, as by divers other persons, *cum scientia* (in English, with the Privity) of the said Mary, as we are given to understand; And whereas we do intend and resolve, that the aforesaid Act shall be in all and every part thereof duly and effectually put in Execution according to the Tenour of the same, and that all Offences abovesaid, in the Act abovesaid mentioned, as afore is said, and the Circumstances of the same, shall be examined, and Sentence or Judgment thereupon given, according to the Tenour and Effect of the said Act: To you, and the greater part of you, we do give full and absolute Power, License and Authority, according to the Tenour of the said Act, to examine all and singular matters compassed and imagined tending to the Hurt of our Royal Person, as well by the aforesaid Mary, as by any other person or persons whatsoever *cum scientia* (in English, with the Privity) of the said Mary, and all Circumstances of the same, and all other Offences whatsoever abovesaid, in the Act abovesaid (as afore is said) mentioned, and all Circumstances of the same, and of every of them; And thereupon, according to the Tenour of the Act aforesaid, to give Sentence or Judgment, as upon good Proof the Matter shall appear unto you. And therefore we command you, that you do at such certain days and places, which you or the greater part of you shall for that purpose set and agree upon, diligently proceed upon the Premisses in form aforesaid, &c.

The greatest part of these Commissioners met on the 11th of October at Fotheringhay Castle in the County of Northampton, seated upon the Bank of the River Nen, where the Queen of Scots was then in Custody. The next day the Commissioners sent unto her Sir Walter Mildmay, Powlet and Edward Barker publick Notary, who delivered into her Hands Queen Elizabeth's Letters: which when she had read, with a Countenance composed to Royal Dignity, and with a quiet and untroubled Mind, she thus delivered herself:

> It grieveth me much that the Queen, my most dear Sister, is misinformed of me; and that I, after so many years strait durance in Prison, and my being grown lame in my Limbs, have lain wholly neglected, though I have offered so many reasonable Conditions for my Liberty. Though I have given her full and faithfull Notice of several Dangers that threatned, yet hath no Credit been given to me, but I have been still contemned and slighted, though I be so nearly allied unto her in Bloud. When the Association was entred into, and the Act of Parliament made thereupon, I foresaw that whatsoever danger should happen, either from foreign Princes abroad, or from ill disposed people at home, or for Religion's sake, I must bear the whole blame, having so many mortal Enemies in the Court. Certainly I might take it very ill, and that not without just reason, that a League hath been lately made with my Son without my knowledge or privity: but such matters I omit. As for this Letter, it seemeth strange to me, that the Queen should command me as a Subject, to submit my self to a Trial. I am an absolute Queen, and will doe nothing which may be prejudicial either to Royal Majesty, or to other Princes of my place and rank, or my Son. My Mind is not yet so far dejected, neither will I faint or sink under this my Calamity. I refer my self to what I have formerly protested before Bromley, now Chancellour, and the Lord La-ware. The Laws and Statutes of England are to me altogether unknown, I am destitute of Counsellours, and who shall be my Peers I cannot tell. My Papers and Notes are taken from me, and no man dareth appear to be my Advocate. I am clear from being guilty of any thing against the Queen, I have stirred up no man against her, and am not to be charged but upon mine own Words or Writings, which I am sure cannot be produced against me. Yet can I not deny but I have recommended my self and my condition unto foreign Princes.

The next day Powlet and Barker returned to her from the Commissioners, to let her know that this Answer of hers was put in Writing, and ask her whether she would own it and stand to it. When she had heard it distinctly read, she acknowledged it to be rightly and truly taken, and said she would stand to it. "But this (said she) I have quite forgotten, which I would now have to be added. Whereas the Queen writes that I am subject to the Laws of England, and to be tried and judged by them, because I have lived under the Protection of them; I answer, that I came into England to crave her aid and assistence, and have been ever since detained in Prison, so that I could not enjoy the protection or benefit of the Laws of England; nay, I could never yet understand from any man what manner of Laws those were."

In the Afternoon came to her some that were chosen and deputed from amongst the rest of the Commissioners, together with men learned in the Civil and Canon Law. The Lord Chancellour and the Lord Treasurer justified their Patent and Commission, and shewed, that neither her Imprisonment nor her Prerogative of Royal Majesty could exempt her from Answering in this Kingdom, with fair words advising her to hear what should be objected against her: otherwise they threatned, that by Authority of the Law they could and would proceed against her, though she were absent. She answered, "That she was no Subject, and rather would she die a thousand Deaths than acknowledge herself a Subject, considering that by such an Acknowledgment she should both wrong the Sublimity of Regal Majesty, and withall confess herself to be bound by all the Laws of England, even in matter of Religion. Nevertheless she was ready to answer all things in a free and full Parliament: as for this Meeting and Assembly, it was (for ought she knew) devised against her (being already condemned and forejudged to die) purposely to give some shew and colour of a just and legal Proceeding. She warned them therefore to look to their Consciences, and to remember that the Theatre of the whole World is much wider than the Kingdom of England." Then she began to complain of the Injuries done her. But the Lord Treasurer, interrupting her, began to reckon up Queen Elizabeth's Kindnesses towards her: namely, That she had punished divers who had opposed and denied her Title to the Crown of England; and had been a means to keep her from being condemned by the Estates of the Realm for endeavouring marriage with the Duke of Norfolk, for the Rebellion in the North, and several other matters. All which when she seemed to make little esteem and account of, they returned back to the rest of their Fellows.

Within a few hours after they sent her by Powlet and the Solicitour the Contents of their Commission, and the Names of the Commissioners, that she might see they were to proceed according to Equity and Reason, and not upon any cunning niceties of Law, or take any extraordinary course. She took no Exceptions against the Commissioners, but objected strongly against the late-made Law, upon which the Authority of their Commission solely depended, as that it was unjust, devised of purpose against her, that it was without Example, and such whereunto she would never subject herself. She asked by what law they intended to proceed. "If by the Civil or Canon Law, then (said she) you must send for Interpreters of it from Pavia or Poictiers, or some other foreign University, for in England are none to be found fit for it." She added also, that it was manifest by the plain words of the Queen's Letters, that she was already fore-judged to be guilty of the Crime, before she was heard; and therefore there was no reason why she should appear before them. She farther required to be satisfied touching some Scruples she had concerning several things in those Letters, which she had for her own Satisfaction confusedly and in haste taken Notice of, but would not deliver them in writing: "for it stood not (she said) with her Royal Dignity to play the Scrivener."

Touching this matter the formerly-deputed Commissioners were sent unto her again: whom she told, that she did not well understand what those words meant. "Seeing she is under the Queen's Protection." The Lord Chancellour answered, "That this was plain to every one that understood any thing; yet was it not for Subjects to interpret what the Queen's meaning was, neither were they made Commissioners for that intent and purpose." Then she required to have her Protestation which she had formerly made, shewed and allowed. It was answered, "That it never had been, nor now could be, allowed, because it was prejudicial to the Crown of England." She asked what Authority they would proceed. It was answered, "By Authority of their Commission, and by the Common Law of England." "But (said she) ye make Laws at your Pleasure, whereunto I have no reason to submit my self, considering that the English in times past refused to submit themselves to the Salick Law in France. And if they would proceed by the Common Law of England, they should produce Precedents and like Cases, forasmuch as that Law consisteth much of Cases and Custome. And if by the Canon Law, none else ought to interpret the same but the Makers thereof." It was answered, "That they would proceed neither by the Civil nor Canon Law, but by the Common Law of England: That it might nevertheless be proved both by the Civil and Canon Law, that she ought to appear before them, if she would not refuse to hear it." And indeed she refused not to hear it, provided (as she said) it were by way of Interlocution and Discourse, not judicially.

After that she fell into other Speeches: "That she never had any thoughts tending to the destruction of the Queen; That she had been provoked and incensed with several Injuries and Indignities; That she should be a stone of Offence to others, if she were so unworthily handled; That by Nawe she had offered her best Assistence for revoking the Bishop of Rome's Bull; That she would have justified her Innocency by Letters, but she was not allowed to doe it; and finally, That all the Offices of Kindness and Good-will which she had tendered these 20 years had been rejected and slighted." While she thus wandred from the Business by these Digressions, they recalled her back, and prayed her to speak plainly, whether she would answer before the Commissioners or not. She replied, "That the Authority of their Commission was founded upon a late Law made to intrap her; That she could by no means away with the Queen's Laws, which she had good reason to suspect; That she had still a good Heart full of Courage, and would not derogate from her Progenitours the King's of Scotland, by owning herself a Subject to the Crown of England; for this were nothing else but openly to confess them to have been Rebels and Traitours. Yet she refused not to answer, provided she were not reduced to the Rank of a Subject. But she had rather utterly perish than to answer as a criminal person."

To this Hatton, Vice-chamberlain to Queen Elizabeth, answered: "You are accused (but not condemned) to have conspired the Destruction of our Lady and Queen anointed. You say you are a Queen; be it so: however in such a Crime as this the

Royal Dignity it self is not exempted from answering, neither by the Civil or Canon Law, nor by the Law of Nations, nor of Nature. For if such kind of Offences might be committed without punishment, all Justice would stagger, yea fall to the ground. If you be innocent, you wrong your Reputation in avoiding Trial. You protest yourself to be innocent, but Queen Elizabeth thinketh otherwise, and that not without ground, and is heartily sorry for the same. To examine therefore your Innocency, she hath appointed Commissioners, honourable persons, prudent and upright men, who are ready to hear you according to Equity with Favour, and will rejoice with all their hearts if you shall clear yourself of what you are charged with. Believe me, the Queen herself will be transported with joy, who affirmed unto me at my coming from her, that never any thing befell her that troubled her more, than that you should be charged with such Misdemeanours. Wherefore laying aside the bootless claim of Privilege from your Royal Dignity, which now can be of no use unto you, appear to your Trial, and shew your Innocency; lest by avoiding Trial you draw upon yourself a Suspicion, and stain your Reputation with an eternal Blot of Aspersion."

"I refuse not (said she) to answer in a full Parliament before the Estates of the Realm lawfully assembled, provided I may be declared the next in Succession; yea before the Queen and her Council, so that my Protestation may be admitted, and I may be acknowledged the next of Kin to the Queen. To the Judgment of mine Adversaries, with whom I know all defence of mine Innocency will signifie nothing, I will by no means submit my self." The Lord Chancellour asked her whether she would answer if her Protestation were admitted. "I will never (said she) submit my self to the late Law mentioned in the Commission." Hereupon the Lord Treasurer concluded, "We notwithstanding will proceed in the Cause to morrow, although you be absent and continue refractary." "Examine your Consciences, (said she) be tender of your Honour; God reward you and yours according to your Judgment upon me."

On the morrow, which was the 14th of the month, she sent for certain of the Commissioners, and prayed them that her Protestation might be admitted and allowed. The Lord Treasurer asked her whether she would appear to her Trial, if her Protestation were onely received and entred in writing, without Allowance. She yielded at last, but with much adoe and an ill will, lest she should seem (as she said) to derogate from her Predecessours or Successours; but was very desirous to clear herself of the Crimes objected against her, being persuaded by Hatton's Reasons, which she had seriously weighed and considered.

Soon after those Commissioners that were there assembled themselves in the Presence-chamber. At the upper end of the Chamber was placed a Chair of State for the Queen of England under a Canopy of State. Over against it, below and at some distance, near the Transome or Beam that ran cross the Room, stood a Chair for the Queen of Scots. By the Walls on both sides were placed Benches, upon which sate, on the one side the Lord Chancellour of England, the Lord Treasurer of England, the Earls of Oxford, Kent, Derby, Worcester, Rutland, Cumberland, Warwick, Pembroke, Lincoln, and the Lord Viscount Montacute; on the other side, the Barons Abergavenny, Zouch, Morley, Stafford, Grey, Lumley, Stourton, Sandes, Wentworth, Mordant, Saint-John of Bletneshoe, Compton and Cheiney. Nigh unto these sate the Knights that were of the Privy Council, Sir James à Croftes, Sir Christopher Hatton, Sir Francis Walsingham, Sir Ralph Sadleir, Sir Walter Mildmay, and Sir Amias Powlet. Right before the Earls sate the two chief Justicers, and the chief Baron of the Exchequer; and on the other side two Barons, the other Justicers, Dale and Ford, Doctours of the Civil Law: and at a little Table in the midst sate Popham the Queen's Attorney, Egerton the Queen's Solicitour, Gawdy the Queen's Serjeant at Law, the Clerk of the Crown, and two Notaries.

When she was come in, and had placed herself in her Seat, after Silence commanded, Bromley Lord Chancellour, turning towards her, spake briefly to this effect: "The most Serene Queen Elizabeth, being informed (not without great Grief and Trouble to her Mind) that you have conspired the Destruction of her Person and the Realm of England, and the Subversion of Religion, hath according to her Place of Duty, lest she might seem to neglect God, herself, and her People, and out of no Malice of Heart at all, appointed these Commissioners to hear the matters which shall be objected against you, and how you can clear yourself of them, and make your Innocency appear to the World."

She then rose up and said, "That she came into England to crave the Aid which had been promised her, and yet had she been ever since detained in Prison." She protested "That she was no Subject of the Queen's, but had been and was a free and absolute Queen, not to be constrained to appear before Commissioners, or any other Judge whatsoever, for any Cause whatsoever, but before God alone, the highest Judge; lest she should derogate from her own Royal Majesty, the King of Scots her Son, her Successours, and other absolute Princes. Yet that she now appeared personally, to refute and wipe off the Crimes objected against her." And hereof she prayed her own Attendants to bear Witness.

The Lord Chancellour, not acknowledging that any Aid had been promised her, answered, "That this Protestation was in vain, for whosoever (of what Place, Quality and Degree soever he be) should offend against the Laws of England in England, he was subject to the said Laws, and was to be examined and tried by the late Act. The said Protestation therefore, being made in Derogation of the Laws and Queen of England, was not to be admitted." The Commissioners nevertheless commanded that as well her Protestation, as the Lord Chancellour's Answer, should be recorded.

After the Commission was openly read, which was grounded upon the Act so often already mentioned, she boldly and resolutely offered her Protestation against the said Act, as made directly and purposely against herself; and herein she appealed to their own Consciences.

When Answer was made by the Lord Treasurer, "That every person in the Kingdom was bound by the Laws though never so lately made, and that she ought not to speak against the Laws; and that the Commissioners were resolved to proceed according to that Law, what Protestations or Appeals soever she interposed": she said at length, "that she was ready to hear and answer touching any Fact whatsoever committed against the Queen of England."

Gawdy now opened the Statute from Point to Point, affirming that she had offended against the same; and hereupon he made an historical Discourse of Babington's Conspiracy, and concluded, "That she knew of it, approved it, assented unto it, promised her Assistence, and shewed the way and means for effecting it."

She answered with a stout Courage, "That she knew not Babington; that she never received any Letters from him, nor wrote any to him: That she never plotted the Destruction of the Queen; and that to prove any such thing, her Subscription under her own Hand was to be produced: That for her part she never so much as heard a word thereof: That she knew not Ballard, nor ever received him: but understanding by some that the Catholicks in England took many things very hardly, she had advertised the Queen by Letters of it, and besought her to take Pity on them: That divers who were utterly unknown to her had offered her their Help and Assistence, yet had she excited or encouraged no man to any unlawfull Attempt; and being shut up in Prison, she could neither know nor hinder what they went about."

Hereupon it was urged out of Babington's Confession, that there had been Intercourse of Letters betwixt her and Babington. She confessed that there had passed Letters betwixt her and many men, yet could it not be thence gathered that she was privy to all their wicked Designs. She required that her Subscription under her own Hand might be produced; and asked what hurt it were for her to demand the Letters again which had been kept from her almost a whole Year. Then were read the Copies of Babington's Letters to her wherein the whole Conspiracy was contained.

"As for these Letters (said she) it may be that Babington wrote them, but let it be proved that I received them. If Babington or any other affirm it, I say plainly, They lie. Other mens Faults are not to be thrown upon me. A Packet of Letters which had been kept from me almost a whole year came to my Hands about that time, but by whom it was sent I know not."

To prove that she had received Babington's Letters, there were read out of Babington's Confession the chief Heads of certain Letters which he had voluntarily confessed that she wrote back to him. Wherein when mention was made of the Earl of Arundel and his Brothers and the Earl of Northumberland, the Tears burst forth, and she said, "Alas! what hath that noble House of the Howards endured for my sake?" And presently, having wiped away the Tears, she answered, "That Babington might confess what he list, but it was a flat Lie that she had contrived any such means to escape: That her Adversaries might easily get the Cyphers which she had made use of to others, and with the same write many things forgedly and falsely: That it was not likely she should make use of Arundel's Help, whom she knew to be shut up in Prison; or Northumberland's, who was so very young, and to her altogether unknown."

There were read also several things picked out of Savage's and Ballard's Confessions, who had confessed that Babington communicated to them several Letters which he had received from the Queen of Scots.

She affirmed, "That Babington received none from her; nay, that she was very angry and offended with some who had secretly given her Advice concerning the Invading of England, and had charged them to beware what they did."

Next was produced a Letter wherein Babington's Plot was commended and approved. Hereof she required a Copy, and affirmed,

> That it came not from her, but haply might be written by her Alpahabet of Cyphers in France. That she had used her best Endeavours for the Recovery of her Liberty, as very Nature itself alloweth and dictateth, and had solicited her Friends to get her Deliverance: yet to some, whom she listed not to name, when they offered her their Help for her Delivery, she gave not the least Answer. Nevertheless she had a great desire to divert the Storm of Persecution from the Catholicks, and for this she had been an earnest Suitour to the Queen. For her part, she would not purchase the Kingdom with the Death of the meanest ordinary man, much less of the Queen. That there were many which attempted dangerous Designs without her Knowledge; and by a Letter which she had very lately received, she was asked Pardon by some, if they should enterprise any thing without her Privity. That it was an easie matter to counterfeit the Cyphers and Characters of others; as a Young man did very lately in France, who gave himself out to her Son's base Brother. That she was also afraid this was done by Walsingham, to bring her to her End, who (as she heard) had practised both against her Life and her Son's. She protested that she never so much as thought of the Destruction of the Queen: That she would gladly and freely rather loose her own Life, than that the Catholicks should be so afflicted and prosecuted in Hatred of her, and undergoe so heavy Punishments for her sake.

And here the Tears gushed forth abundantly.

"But (said the Lord Treasurer) no man that hath showed himself a good Subject was ever yet put to Death for his Religion; some indeed have been for Treason, while they maintained and avouched the Pope's Bull and Authority against the Queen." "Yet I (said she) have heard otherwise, and read it also in Books set forth in print." "The Authours (replied he) of such Books as those write also that the Queen hath forfeited her Royal Dignity."

Walsingham, who found himself just before so openly taxed by her, took his Opportunity, and, rising up, protested that his Heart was free from all Malice. "I call God (said he) to Witness, that as a private person I have done nothing unbeseeming an Honest man, neither in my publick Condition and Quality have I done any thing unworthy of my Place. I confess that, out of my great Care for the Safety of the Queen and Realm, I have curiously endeavoured to search and sift out all Plots and Designs against the same. If Ballard had offered me his Assistence, I should not have refused it, yea I would have rewarded him for his Pains and Service. If I have tampered any thing with him, why did he not discover it, to save his Life?"

With this Answer she said she was satisfied. She prayed him "not to be angry that she had spoken so freely what she had heard reported; and that he would give no more Credit to those that slandered her, than she did to such as accused him. Spies (she said) were men of doubtfull and little Credit, who make shew on one thing, and speak another: and desired him that he would not in the least believe that ever she had consented to the Queen's Destruction." And now again she burst forth into Tears; "I would never (said she) make Shipwreck of my Soul by conspiring the Destruction of my dearest Sister." It was answered by the Lawyers, that this should soon be proved by Witnesses. Thus far in the Forenoon.

In the Afternoon, to prove this, was openly produced the Copy of a Letter which Charles Paget had written, and Curle one of her Secretaries testified she had received, concerning a Conference betwixt Mendoza and Ballard about the Design for Invading of England, and setting her at Liberty. "This (she said) was nothing to the purpose, and proved not that she had consented to the Destruction of the Queen."

The Lawyers proceeded to prove farther, that she was both privy to the Conspiracy, and also actually conspired the Destruction of the Queen; and that by Babington's Confession, and by Letters that had passed betwixt her and him, wherein he had called her his most dread and Sovereign Lady and Queen. And by the way they took notice of a Plot that was laid for conveying the Kingdom of England to the Spaniard. She confessed that a Priest came to her, and said, that "if she would not concern herself in the Business, she and her Son both should be excluded from the Inheritance." But the Priest's name she would not tell. She added, "that the Spaniard did lay Claim to the Kingdom of England, and would give place to no Title but hers."

Then they pressed her with the Testimonies of her Secretaries, Nawe and Curle, out of Babington's Confession, and the Letters and Answers betwixt her and Babington; the intire Credit of which Proofs rested upon their sole Testimony, yet were they never brought face to face before her. Curle she acknowledged to be an Honest man, but not a competent Witness against her. "As for Nawe, he had been for some time a Secretary (she said) to the Cardinal of Lorrain, and recommended to her by the French King, and might easily be drawn, either by Reward, or Hope, or Fear, to give a false Testimony, for he had several times taken rash Oaths; and Curle was so pliable to him, that at his Beck he would write whatsoever he bad him. It might be (she said) that these two might insert some things into her Letters which she never dictated to them: It might also be that such Letters came to their Hands, which notwithstanding she might never see." And then she brake forth into such Expressions as these: "As well the Majesty as the Safety of all Princes must fall to the Ground, if they depend upon the Writings and Testimonies of Secretaries. I dictated nothing to them but what nature prompted me to, that I might at last recover my Liberty. And I am not to be convicted but by mine own Words or Hand-writing. If they have written any thing prejudicial to the Queen my Sister, they have written it altogether without my Knowledge, and let them bear the Punishment of their inconsiderate Boldness. Sure I am, if they were here present, they would clear me of all Blame in this case. And, if my Notes were in my Hands, I could answer particularly to these things."

Whilst she was thus speaking, the Lord Treasurer charged her, that she had Intentions to send her Son into Spain, and to convey her Title and Claim in the Kingdom of England to the Spaniard. To this she answered, "That she had no Kingdom to dispose of or convey; yet was it lawfull for her to give those things which were hers at her Pleasure, and not to be accountable to any for what she did."

When her Alphabets of Cyphers, which were sent over to Babington, the Lord Lodowick and Fernihurst, were objected to her out of Curle's Testimony; she denied not "but she had written out many, and amongst others that for the Lord Lodowick, when she recommended him and another to the Dignity of Cardinal, and that (she trusted) without Offence: since it was as lawfull for her to hold Correspondence by Letters and to negotiate her Concernments with men of her Religion, as for the Queen to doe it with the Professours of another Religion."

Then they again urged her closer with the Testimonies of Nawe and Curle, which agreed together. And she returned her former Answers, or else repelled their Testimonies by a flat Denial; protesting again that she neither knew Babington nor Ballard.

The Lord Treasurer here saying that she knew Morgan well enough, who had sent Parry over privately to murther the Queen, and that she had assigned him a yearly Pension; she replied, "That she knew not whether Morgan had so done, but she knew that Morgan had lost all for her sake, and therefore it concerned her in Honour to relieve him; and she was not bound to revenge an Injury done to the Queen by a Friend that had deserved so well at her hands: however she had endeavoured to deterr him from any such wicked Attempts. On the other side, (said she) I am sure Pensions have been allowed in England to Patrick Gray and other Scots my Adversaries, as also to my Son." The Lord Treasurer answered, "When the Revenues of the Kingdoms of Scotland were by the Negligence of the Regents much diminished and impaired, the Queen conferred somewhat out of her noble bounty upon your Son the King, her near Kinsman."

Afterwards were produced the principal Heads of several Letters sent to Inglefield, to the Lord Paget, and to Bernardine de Mendoza, about foreign Assistence. But when she had answered,

"That these things tended not to the Destruction of the Queen; and if Foreigners endeavoured to set her at Liberty, it was not to be laid to her Charge; and that she had several times plainly let the Queen know that she would seek to procure her own Release-ment:" the matter was put off till the next day following.

The next day she insisted upon her former Protestation, and required to have it recorded, and a Copy thereof delivered to her; lamenting "that those so reasonable Conditions which she had many times propounded to the Queen were still rejected, even then when she promised to deliver her Son and the Duke of Guise's Son for Hostages, that the Queen or Kingdom of England should receive no Prejudice nor Detriment by her; by which she then saw herself quite out of all Hope of obtaining her Liberty. But now she was most unworthily dealt withall, whilst her Honour and Reputation was called in Question before ordinary lawyers, who by wrested Conclusions drew every Circumstance into a Consequence; whereas Princes anointed and consecrated are not subject to the same Laws that Private men are. Moreover, whereas the Power granted to the Commissioners was, to examine matters tending to the Hurt of the Queen's Person; the Cause was now so handled, and Letters so wrested, that the Religion which she professed, the Immunity and Majesty of foreign Princes, and the private Intercourse betwixt Princes, were called in Question, and she herself made to stoup and descend beneath her Royal Dignity, and to appear as a Criminal before a Tribunal seat; and all this to no other purpose, but that she might be quite excluded from the Queen's Favour, and her own Right to the Succession: whereas she onely made a voluntary Appearance, to clear herself of the Matters objected against her, lest she might seem to neglect the Justification of her own Honour and Innocency." She called also to their minds, "how Queen Elizabeth herself was formerly brought in Question about Wiat's Conspiracy, whereof notwithstanding she was perfectly innocent:" religiously affirming, "that though she wished with all her Heart the Safety of the Catholicks might be provided for, yet she desired not that it should be brought to pass by the Death and Bloud though but of one man. For her part, she had rather act the Part of Hester than of Judith; make Intercession to God for the People, than deprive the meanest of the People of his Life."

She expostulated that her Enemies had divulged abroad that she was irreligious. "But time was (said she) when I would have been instructed in the Protestant Religion, but some would not suffer me to be so, as if they cared not what became of my Soul." And now concluding, "When ye have done all ye can (said she) against me, and have excluded me from my Right, ye may chance fail of your Hope and Expectation." And withall making her Appeal to God, and to the Princes who were her Kinsmen, and again renewing her Protestation, she prayed that there might be another Meeting about this matter, and that an Advocate might be allowed her to plead her Cause, and that, seeing she was a Princess, she might be believed upon the word of a Princess. "For it were extreme folly (she said) to stand to their Judgment whom she saw so evidently and notoriously to be armed with Prejudice against her."

To this the Lord Treasurer answered: "Whereas I bear a double Person and Quality, one of a Commissioner, the other of a Counsellour, hear me first a few words as I am a Commissioner. Your Protestation is recorded, and a Copy thereof shall be delivered you. Our Authority is granted us under the Queen's Hand and the Great Seal of England, from which there lies no Appeal: neither do we come with Prejudice, but to judge according to the exact Rule of Justice. The Queen's learned Counsel do aim at nothing else but that the Truth may come to light how far you have offended against the Queen's Person. Full Power is given us to hear and examine the matter, although you were absent: yet were we desirous you should be present, lest we might seem to have derogated from your Honour. We purposed not to charge you with any thing else but what you were privy to, or have yourself attempted, against the Queen's Person. The Letters which have been read were read to no other Purpose, but to make out your Offence against the Queen's Person, and the things relating to it, which are so interlaced with other matters, that they cannot be severed. The whole and intire Letters therefore, and not Parcels picked out here and there, have been openly read, because the Circumstances do make appear what things you dealt with Babington about."

Here she interrupted him and said, "The Circumstances might be proved, but never the Fact. That her Integrity depended not upon the Credit and Memory of her Secretaries, though she knew them to be honest and sincere men. Yet if they had confessed any thing out of Fear of Torments, or Hope of Reward and Impunity, it was not to be admitted, and that for just Reasons, which she would shew elsewhere. Mens minds (she said) are variously moved and led with Affections: and those men would never have confessed such things against her but for their own Advantage or Hopes. Letters may be directed to others than those to whom they are written, and many things have been often inserted which she never dictated. If her Papers had not been taken away, and she had her Secretary with her, she could the easier confute the things objected against her."

"But nothing (said the Lord Treasurer) shall be objected but since the nineteenth day of June: neither would your Papers doe you any good, seeing your Secretaries, and Babington himself, without putting to the Rack, have affirmed that you sent those Letters to Babington: which though you deny, yet whether more Credit be to be given to an Affirmation than to a Negation, let the Commissioners judge. But to return to the matter. This which followeth I speak to you as a Counsellour. Many things you have propounded time after time concerning your Liberty. That they have failed of Success, it is long of you, or of the Scots, and not of the Queen. For the Lords of Scotland flatly refused to deliver the King in Hostage. And when the last Treaty was holden concerning your Liberty, Parry was sent privily by Morgan, a Dependent of yours, to murther the Queen." "Ah! (said she) you are my Adversary." "Yea, (said he) I am Adversary to all Queen Elizabeth's Adversaries. But enough of these things: let us proceed to Proofs." Which when she refused to hear; "Yet we (said he) will hear them." "And I also (said she) will hear them in another place, and defend myself."

Now were her Letters to Charles Paget read again, wherein she shewed him that there was no other way for the Spaniard to reduce the Netherlands to Obedience, but by setting up such a Prince in England as might be usefull and serviceable to him: also her Letters to the Lord Paget, to hasten his auxiliary Forces for the Invasion of England; and Cardinal Allen's Letter, wherein he called her his most dread Sovereign Lady, and told her that the Business was recommended to the Prince of Parma's Care.

As these Letters were reading, she interposed the following Expressions. "That Babington and her Secretaries had accused her to excuse themselves. That she never heard of the Six Murtherers; and that all the rest was nothing to the Purpose. As for Allen, she held him for a reverend Prelate; and she acknowledged no other Head of the Church but the Bishop of Rome. In what Rank and Quality she was had and reputed by him and foreign Princes she well knew; neither could she hinder it, if in their Letters they called her Queen of England. As for her Secretaries, seeing they had done contrary to their Duty and Allegeance sworn unto her, they deserved no Credit. They who have once forsworn themselves, though they swear the next time with never so serious Oaths and Protestations, are not to be credited. Neither did these men think themselves bound by any Oath whatsoever in Court of Conscience, inasmuch as they had sworn Fidelity and Secrecy to her before, and were no Subjects of England. That Nawe had many times written otherwise than she had dictated to him, and Curle wrote whatsoever Nawe bade him. But, for her part, she was willing to bear the Blame of their Miscarriage in all things but what might lay a Blot and Stain upon her Honour. And haply also they confessed these things to save themselves, supposing that they could doe her no Hurt by confessing, who they thought would be more favourably dealt withall, as being a Queen. As for Ballard, she never heard of any such man, but of one Hallard, who had offered her his Service; which notwithstanding she refused, because she had heard that he had also engaged his Service to Walsingham."

Afterwards, when some short Passages out of her Letters to Mendoza (which Curle had confessed himself to have written in Cyphers) were read, and from thence she was charged as if she had purposed to convey her Right in the Kingdom to the Spaniard, and that Allen and Parsons lay now at Rome for that Purpose; she still complaining that her Secretaries had broken their Allegeance whereto they were bound by Oath, answereth as followeth: "I being a close Prisoner, oppressed and languishing with Cares and pensive Thoughts, and without all Hope of Liberty, no Probability appearing of effecting those things which many people expected by my means, who declined daily through Age and indisposition of Body; it seemed good to some, that the Succession to the Crown of England should be established on the

Spaniard, or else some English Catholick. And a Book was sent me to justify the Spaniard's Title; which not being approved of by me, I incurred Displeasure with some men. But now, all my Hopes in England being desperate, I am fully resolved not to reject foreign Help."

The Solicitour put the Commissioners in mind what would become of them, their Honours, Estates and Posterities, if the Kingdom were so conveyed. But the Lord Treasurer shewed that the Kingdom of England could not at all be conveyed, but was to descend by Right of Succession according to the Laws; and asked her, if she had any more to say.

She required to be heard in a full Parliament, or that she might in person speak with the Queen (who would, she hoped, have regard of a Queen,) and the Council. And now rising up with great Presence of Countenance, she had some Conference with the Lord Treasurer, Hatton, Walsingham, and the Earl of Warwick, apart by themselves.

These things being done, the Court was adjourned till the 25th of October to the Star-Chamber at Westminster. Thus far touching this Matter out of the Commentaries and Memorials of Edward Barker, principal Register to the Queen's Majesty, Thomas Wheeler, publick Notary, Register of the Audience of Canterbury, and other persons of Credit which were there present.

On the said 25th day of October all the Commissioners met, except the Earls of Shrewsbury and Warwick, which were both of them sick at that time. And after Nawe and Curle had upon Oath, *vivâ voce*, voluntarily, without hope of Reward, avowed, affirmed and justified all and every the Letters and Copies of Letters before produced to be true and real, Sentence was pronounced against the Queen of Scots, and confirmed by the Seals and Subscriptions of the Commissioners, and recorded in these words. "By their unanimous Assents and Consents they do pronounce and deliver this their Sentence and Judgment, at the Day and Place last above recited, and say, That since the Conclusion of the aforesaid Session of Parliament in the Commission aforesaid specified, namely, since the aforesaid first day of June in the 27th year aforesaid, and before the Date of the said Commission, divers Matters have been compassed and imagined within this

Realm of England, by Anthony Babington and others, *cum scientia,* in English, with the privity———of the said Mary, pretending a Title to the Crown of this Realm of England, tending to the Hurt, Death and Destruction of the Royal Person of our said Lady the Queen. And also, that since the aforesaid first day of June in the 27th year aforesaid, and before the Date of the Commission aforesaid, the aforesaid Mary, pretending a Title to the Crown of this Realm of England, hath compassed and imagined within this Realm of England divers Matters tending to the Hurt, Death and Destruction of the Royal Person of our Sovereign Lady the Queen, contrary to the Form of the Statute in the Commission aforesaid specified."

This sentence (which depended wholly upon the Credit of the Secretaries, and they not brought face to face, according to the first Act of the 13th Year of Queen Elizabeth) begot much Talk and various Discourse amongst People, while some thought them persons to be believed, and some unworthy of any Credit. I have seen Nawe's Apology to King James, written in the year 1605 wherein with a solemn Protestation he excuseth himself, that he was neither the Authour, nor Perswader, nor the first Revealer of the Design that was undertaken; neither failed he of his Duty through Negligence or want of Discretion: yea, that he did that day stoutly oppose the principal Articles of Accusation against his Lady and Mistress. Which notwithstanding appeareth not by the Records. The same day a Declaration was published by the Commissioners and the Judges of the Land, "That the said Sentence did nothing derogate from James King of Scots in his Title or Honour, but that he was in the same Place, Degree and Right, as if the said Sentence had never been pronounced."

Some few days after a Parliament was holden at Westminster, begun by a deputative Commission granted by the Queen to the Archbishop of Canterbury, the Lord Treasurer, and the Earl of Derby, and that not without former Precedents. In which Parliament the Proscription of the Lord Paget, Charles Paget, Sir Francis Inglefield, Francis Throckmorton, Anthony Babington, Thomas Salisbury, Edward Jones, Chidiock Tichburne, Charles Tilney, and the rest of the Conspiratours, was confirmed, and their Goods and Possessions confiscate. The Estates also of the Realm, having by their Votes approved and confirmed the Sen-

tence given against the Queen of Scots, did with unanimous As-
sent present their Petition to the Queen by the Hands of the Lord
Chancellour, wherein they instantly besought her, that for the
Preservation of Christ's true Religion, the Quiet and Security of
the Realm, the Preservation of the Queen's Person, and the Safety
of themselves and their Posterity, the Sentence given against
Mary Queen of Scots according to the Law might be published.
Their Reasons were drawn from the Dangers that threatened
Religion, the Queen's Person and the Realm, by means of her,
who having been bred up in the Popish Religion, and sworn a
Confederate in the Holy League for the Extirpation of the Protestant Religion, had now for a long time arrogated unto her self
the Kingdom while the Queen lived, whom, as being Excommunicate, she held it lawfull to doe Mischief to as far as lay in her
Power, and to take away her Life a thing meritorious; one who
had overthrown and ruined sundry flourishing Families in the
Kingdom, and cherished all the treasonable Designs and Rebellions in England. To spare her therefore were nothing else but
to spill the People, who would take all Impunity in this case very
much to Heart, and would not think themselves discharged of
their Oath of Association, unless she were punished according to
her Deserts. Lastly, they called to her Remembrance, how fearfull the Examples of God's Vengeance were upon King Saul for
sparing Agag, and upon King Ahab for sparing the Life of
Benhadad. These things the Estates of the Parliament urged to
her.

The Queen with great Majesty both of Countenance and
Speech answered to this purpose.

> So many and so great are the unmeasurable Graces and Benefits
> bestowed upon me by the Almighty, that I must not onely most
> humbly acknowledge them as Benefits, but admire them as Mir-
> acles, being in no sort able to express them. And though none
> alive can more justly acknowledge himself bound to God than I,
> whose Life he hath miraculously preserved from so many Dan-
> gers: yet am I not more deeply bound to give him Thanks for
> any one thing, than for this which I will now tell you, and which
> I account as a Miracle, namely, That as I came to the Crown with
> the hearty Good will of all my Subjects, so now after 28 Years
> Reign, I perceive in them the same, if not greater, Affection

towards me; which if I should once lose, I might perhaps find my
self to breathe, but never could I think that I were alive. And now
though my Life hath been dangerously shot at, yet I protest there
is nothing hath more grieved me, than that one who differs not
from me in Sex, one of like Quality and Degree, of the same
Race and Stock, and so nearly related to me in Bloud, should fall
into so great a Misdemeanour. And so far have I been from
bearing her any Ill will, that upon the Discovery of some treasonable Practices against me, I wrote privately to her, that if she
would confess and acknowledge them by a Letter betwixt her
and me, they should be wrapped up in Silence. Neither did I
write this with a Purpose to intrap her, For I knew already as
much as she could confess. And even yet though the matter be
come thus far, if she would truly repent, and no man would
undertake her Cause against me, and if my Life alone depended
hereupon, and not the Safety and Welfare of all my People, I
would (I protest unfeignedly) willingly and readily pardon her.
Nay, if England might by my Death obtain a more flourishing
Condition and a better Prince, I would most gladly lay down my
Life. For for your sakes it is and for my People's that I desire to
live. As for me, I see no such great Reason (according as I have
led my Life) why I should either be fond to live, or fear to die. I
have had good Experience of this World; I have known what it
is to be a Subject, and I now know what it is to be a Sovereign.
Good Neighbours I have had, and I have met with bad; and in
Trust I have found Treason. I have bestowed Benefits upon Ill-
deservers; and where I have done well, I have been Ill requited
and spoken of. While I call to mind these things past, behold
things present, and look forward toward things to come, I count
them happiest that go hence soonest. Nevertheless against such
Evils and Mischiefs as these I am armed with a better Courage
than is common in my Sex; so as whatsoever befalls me, Death
shall never find me unprepared.

And as touching these Treasonable Attempts, I will not so far
wrong my self or the Laws of my Kingdom, as not to think but
that she, having been the Contriver of the said Treasons, was
bound and liable to the ancient and former Laws, though the late
Act had never been made; which notwithstanding was in no sort
made to prejudice her, as divers who are inclined to favour her
have imagined. So far was it from being made to intrap her, that
it was rather intended to forewarn and deter her from attempting
any thing against it. But seeing it had now the force of a Law, I

thought good to proceed against her according to the same. But you Lawyers are so curious in scanning the nice Points of the Law, and proceeding according to Forms, rather than Expounding and Interpreting the Laws themselves, that if your way were observed, she must have been indicted in Staffordshire, and have holden up her Hand at the Bar, and have been tried by a Jury of Twelve men. A proper way, forsooth, of Trying a Princess. To avoid therefore such Absurdities, I thought it better to refer the Examination of so weighty a Cause to a select number of the noblest Personages of the Land and the Judges of the Realm: and all little enough. For we Princes are set as it were upon Stages in the Sight and view of all the World: the least Spot is soon spied in our Garments, the smallest Blemish presently observed in us at a great Distance. It behoveth us therefore to be carefull that our Proceedings be just and honourable. But I must tell you one thing, that by this last Act of Parliament you have reduced me to such Straits and Perplexities, that I must resolve upon the Punishment of her who is a Princess so nearly allied to me in Bloud, and whose Practices against me have so deeply affected me with Grief and Sorrow, that I have willingly chosen to absent my self from this Parliament, lest I should increase my Trouble by hearing the Matter mentioned; and not out of Fear of any Danger or treacherous Attempts against me, as some think. But I will now tell you a farther Secret, (though it be not usual with me to blab forth in other cases what I know). It is not long since these Eyes of mine saw and read an Oath wherein some bound themselves to kill me within a Month. Hereby I see your Danger in my Person which I will be very carefull to prevent and keep off.

The Association you entred into for my Safety I have not forgotten, a thing I never so much as thought of, till a great number of Hands and Seals to it were shewed me. This hath laid a perpetual Tie and Obligation upon me to bear you a singular Good will and Love, who have no greater Comfort than in your and the Commonwealth's Respect and Affection towards me. But forasmuch as the matter now in hand is very rarely exampled and of greatest Consequence, I hope you do not look for any present Resolution from me: for my manner is, in matters of less Moment than this, to deliberate long upon that which is but once to be resolved. In the mean time I beseech Almighty God so to illuminate and direct my Heart, that I may see clearly what may be best for the Good of his Church, the Prosperity of the Commonwealth, and your Safety. And that Delay may not breed Danger we will signifie our Resolution to you with all Conveniency. And whatever the best of Subjects may expect at the Hands of the best Princess, that expect from me to be performed to the full.

On the 12th day after, when she had thoroughly weighed the matter in her Mind, being distracted with doubtfull Cares and Thoughts, and as it were in some Conflict with her self what to doe in so important a Business, she sent the Lord Chancellour to the Higher House, and Puckering to the rest in the Lower House, advising them to enter anew into the serious Consideration of so weighty an Affair, and to find out a more pleasing Expedient, whereby both the Queen of Scots Life might be spared, and her own Security provided for.

After long and serious Deliberation, judging that both the Welfare and Detriment of the Prince concerned all the Subjects, they unanimously concurred again in their former Opinion; and that for these Reasons. "The Queen's Safety (they said) could no way be secured as long as the Queen of Scots lived, unless she should either seriously repent and acknowledge her Offence; or were kept with a closer and stricter Guard, and sufficient Security given by Bond and Oath for her good Demeanour; or delivered Hostages; or else departed the Realm. As for her Repentance, they were out of all Hopes of it, considering that she had so ill requited the Queen who had saved her Life, and would not yet acknowledge her Fault. As for a surer Guard, stricter Custody, Bonds, Oath, and Hostages, they esteemed them all as nothing worth, because if the Queen's Life were once taken away, all these would presently vanish. And if she should depart the Realm, they feared lest she should presently take up Arms and invade the same."

These Reasons the Lord Chancellour, and Puckering Speaker of the Lower House, explained and opened more at large, pressing hard that the Sentence might be put in Execution: "because, as it were Injustice to deny Execution of the Law to any one of her Subjects that should demand it; so much more to the whole Body of her People of England unanimously and with one voice humbly and instantly suing for the same." The Queen answered as followeth.

Very unpleasing is that Way, where the setting out, Progress and Journey's End yield nothing but Trouble and Vexation. I have this day been in greater Conflict with my self than ever I was in all my Life, whether I should speak, or hold my peace. If I should speak, and not complain, I shall dissemble: if I should be silent, all your Labour and Pains taken were in vain: and if I should complain it might seem a strange and unusual thing. Yet I confess that my hearty Desire was, that some other means might have been devised to provide for your Security and my own Safety, than this which in now propounded. So that I cannot but complain, though not of you, yet to you, since I perceive by your Petition that my Safety dependeth wholly upon the Ruine of another. If there be any that think I have spun out the time of purpose to get Commendation by a seeming Shew of Clemency, they doe me Wrong undeservedly, as he knoweth who is the Searcher of the most secret Thoughts of the Heart. Or if there be any that are persuaded the Commissioners durst pronounce no other Sentence for Fear they should thereby displease me, or seem to fail of their Care for my Preservation, they do but burthen and wrong me with such injurious Conceits. For either those whom I put in Trust have failed of their Duties: or else they acquainted the Commissioners in my Name, that my Will and Pleasure was, that every one should act freely according to his Conscience; and what they thought not fit to be made publick, that they should communicate to me in private. It was of my favourable inclination towards her, that I desired some other way might be found out to prevent this Mischief. But since it is now resolved, that my Security is desperate without her Death, I find a great Reluctancy and Trouble within me, that I, who have in my time pardoned so many Rebels, winked at so many Treasons, or neglected them by Silence, should now seem to shew my self cruel towards so great a Princess.

I have, since I came to the Government of this Realm, seen many defamatory Libels and Pamplets against me, taxing me to be a Tyrant. Well fare the Writers hearts; I believe their meaning was to tell me News. And News indeed it was to me to be branded with the note of Tyranny. I would it were as great News to hear of their Wickedness and Impiety. But what is it which they will not venture to write now, when they shall hear that I have given my Consent that the Executioner's Hands should be imbrued in the Bloud of my nearest Kinswoman? But so far am I from Cruelty, that, though it were to save mine own Life, I would not offer the least Violence: neither have I been so carefull how to prolong mine own Life, as how to preserve hers and mine: which that it is now impossible to doe I am heartily troubled. I

am not so void of Sense and Judgment, as not to see mine own
Danger before mine Eyes; nor so indiscreet, as to sharpen a Sword
to cut mine own Throat; nor so egregiously careless, as not to
provide for the safety of mine own Life. This I consider with my
self, that many a man would hazzard his own Life to save the
Life of a Princess: but I am not of their Opinion. These things
have I many times thought upon seriously with my self.

But since so many have both written and spoken against me,
give me leave, I pray you, to say somewhat in mine own Defense
that ye may see what manner of Woman I am, for whose Safety
and Preservation you have taken such extraordinary Care.
Wherein as I do with a most thankfull heart discern and reade
your great Vigilancy; so am I sure I shall never requite it, had I
as many Lives as all you together.

When first I took the Sceptre into my Hand, I was not unmindfull of God the Giver, and therefore I began my Reign with Securing his Service, and the Religion I had been both born in, bred
in, and I trust shall die in. And though I was not ignorant how
many Dangers I should meet withall at Home for my altering
Religion, and how many great Princes abroad of a contrary Profession would in that Respect bear an Hostile mind towards me:
yet was I no whit dismayed thereat, knowing that God, whom
alone I eyed and respected, would defend both me and my Cause.
Hence it is that so many Treacheries and Conspiracies have been
attempted against me, that I might well admire to find my self
alive at this present day, were it not that God's holy Hand hath
still protected me beyond all Expectation. Next, to the end I
might make better Progress in the Art of Ruling well, I had long
and serious Cogitations with my self what things were most
worthy and becoming Kings to doe: and I found it absolutely
necessary that they should be completely furnished with those
prime capital Vertues, Justice, Temperance, Prudence and Magnanimity. Of the two latter I will not boast my self, my Sex doth
not permit it, they are proper to Men. But for the two former
and less rough, I dare say, (and that without Ostentation) I never
made a Difference of Persons, but high and low had equally
Right done them: I never preferred any for Favour whom I
thought not fit and worthy: I never was forward to believe Stories
at the first telling; nor was I so rash as to suffer my Judgment to
be forestalled with Prejudice before I had heard the Cause. I will
not say but many Reports might haply be brought me too much in
Favour of the one side or the other: For a good and a wary Prince

may sometimes be bought and sold, whilst we cannot hear all our selves. Yet this I dare say boldly, My Judgment (as far as I could understand the Case) ever went with the Truth. And as Alcibiades advised his Friend, not to give any Answer till he had run over the Letters of the whole Alphabet; so have I never used rash and sudden Resolutions in any thing.

And therefore as touching your Counsells and Consultations, I acknowledge them to have been with such Care and Providence, and so advantageous for the Preservation of my Life, and to proceed from Hearts so sincere and devoted to me, that I shall endeavour what lies in my Power, to give you cause to think your Pains not ill bestowed, and strive to shew myself worthy of such Subjects.

And now for your Petition, I desire you for the present to content yourselves with an Answer without Answer. Your Judgment I condemn not, neither do I mistake your Reasons: but I must desire you to excuse those thoughtfull Doubts and Cares which as yet perplex my Mind; and to rest satisfied with the Profession of my thankfull Esteem of your Affections, and the Answer I have given, if you take it for any Answer at all. If I should say I will not doe what you request, I might say perhaps more than I intend: and if I should say I will do it, I might plunge my self into as bad Inconveniences as you endeavour to preserve me from: which I am confident your Wisedoms and Discretions would not that I should, if ye consider the Circumstances of Place, Time, and the Manners and Conditions of men.

After this Assembly of the Estates was prorogued.

About this time were the Lord Buckhurst and Beale sent to the Queen of Scots, to let her know that Sentence was pronounced against her; and that the same was approved and confirmed by Authority of Parliament as just and lawfull, and the Execution therefore instantly desired by the Estates, out of a due Regard of Justice, Security and Necessity: and therefore to persuade her to acknowledge her Offences against God and the Queen, and to expiate them before her Death by Repentance; letting her understand, that as long as she lived, the Religion received in England could not be secure. Hereat she seemed to triumph with a more than wonted Alacrity, giving God Thanks, and rejoicing in her Heart, that she was taken to be an Instrument for the re-establishing of Religion in this Island. And earnestly she besought that she might have a Catholick Priest allowed her to direct her Conscience, and administer the Sacraments unto her. A Bishop and a Dean whom they commended to her for this purpose she utterly rejected, and sharply taxed the English Nation, saying, "That the English had many times put their own Kings to Death; no Marvell therefore if they now also shew their Cruelty upon me, who am issued from the Bloud of their Kings."

The Publication of the Sentence was stayed for some time by the Intercession of L' Aubespine the French Embassadour: but in the month of December, through the earnest instance of some Courtiers, it was publickly proclaimed all over the City of London, the Lord Mayor the Aldermen and principal Officers and Citizens being present, and afterward throughout the whole Realm. In this Proclamation the Queen seriously protested, that this Publication was extorted from her, to the exceeding Grief of her Mind, by a kind of Necessity, and at the earnest Prayers and Intreaties of the Estates of the Realm: though there were some that thought this to proceed from the Art and Guise of Women, who, though they desire a thing never so much, yet will always seem rather to be constrained and forced to it.

The Publication of this Sentence of Death being made known to the Queen of Scots, so far was she from being dismayed thereat, that with a settled and steadfast Countenance, lifting up her Eyes and Hands towards Heaven, she gave Thanks to God for it. And though she were by Powlet her Keeper devested of all the Badges of Dignity and Royalty, and made no more account of than the poorest Woman of the meanest Condition; yet she endured it with great Patience of Mind. And having with much adoe obtained Leave of him to write, she by a Letter sent to Queen Elizabeth the 19th of December endeavoured to clear herself

from all Hostile Malice against her; and thanked God for the Sentence of her Condemnation, who was now pleased to put a Period to her wofull and lamentable Pilgrimage in this Life. She prayed her that for the Kindnesses and Favours following she might be beholden to herself, and to none else (for from those zealous Puritans who now bare the chief sway in England she could expect no good). First, that when her Adversaries were glutted and satiated with her innocent Bloud, her Body might be conveyed by her Servants into some Holy Catholick Land to be buried; she would willingly into France, where her Mother's Soul rested in Peace. For in Scotland the Sepulchres of her Ancestours were violated, and the Churches either demolished or prophaned: and in England, among the ancient Kings, the common Progenitours of them both, she could have no Hope to be interred with Catholick Rites and Ceremonies. So might her Body at length rest in Peace, which as long as it was joyned with the Soul could never find any Rest or Quiet. Secondly, (in regard she feared the secret Tyranny of some,) That she might not be put to Death in private without Queen Elizabeth's Knowledge, but in the Sight of her Servants and others, who might give a true Testimony of her Faith in Christ, her Obedience toward the Church, and her Christian Departure, to prevent those false Reports which her Adversaries might otherwise throw out and asperse her with. And, thirdly, That her Servants might freely and peaceably depart whither they pleased, and enjoy those Legacies which she had bequeathed them by her Will and Testament. These things with most earnest Prayers she intreated of her in the Name of Jesus Christ, by their near Kindred, by the Soul and Memory of Henry the Seventh the common Progenitour of them both, and by the Royal Dignity which she had born. Then she complained, That all her Regal Ornaments were taken from her by Command of some of the Council, by which she suspected that their Malice might break forth to greater matters. She added, That if they had shewed her Letters and Papers which were taken from her, fairly and without any Fraud, it might have plainly appeared by them, that there was no other cause of her Ruine but the over-carefulness and Solicitude of some for Queen Elizabeth's Safety. Lastly, she earnestly besought her, that she would write back a few words to her touching these matters with her own Hand.

Whether this Letter ever came to Queen Elizabeth's Hands, I can not say. But divers Discourses were raised about this Affair, according to the several Affections and Dispositions of men; to say nothing of the Declamations and Exclamations of the Ecclesiastical sort of people on both sides, who for the most part are very fiery and vehement.

Some indifferent Censurers there were who thought she was too sharply dealt withall, and had hard Measure, in regard she was a free and absolute Princess, and had no Superiour but God alone: they said, she was Queen Elizabeth's very near Kinswoman, who had also by Henry Midlemore made her a large Promise, on the Word of a Prince, of all Courtesie and kind Hospitality, as soon as she was arrived in England, being thrown out of her Kingdom by her Rebels; and yet on the contrary had kept her still in Prison, and violated the sacred Rights of Hospitality: that she could not be otherways reputed than as a Prisoner taken in War; and it was always lawfull for such as were taken Prisoners in War, to use what means they could to work their own Safety and Liberty: that she could not commit Treason, because she was no Subject, and *Par in parem non habet potestatem,* that is, Princes of equal Degree have no Power or Sovereignty one over another; and thereupon the Sentence of the Emperour against Robert King of Sicily was disannulled, because he was no Subject of the Empire: that Embassadours, who are Princes Servants, if they conspire against the Kings to whom they are sent in Embassie, are not to be charged as guilty of Treason, much less Princes themselves: and, that the Purpose or Intention is not to be punished, unless the Effect follow. Moreover, that it was a thing never heard of, that a Prince should be subjected to the Stroke of an Executioner. Also, that she was condemned contrary to the Law of God, the Civil Law of the Romans, and the Common Law of England; yea, contrary also to the first Act of Parliament made in the 13th Year of Queen Elizabeth, by which it is enacted, That no man is to be arraigned for intending the Destruction of his Prince's Life, but by the Testimony and Oath of two lawfull Witnesses to be produced Face to Face before him; whereas in this Trial no Witness was produced, but she was overborn with the Testimony of her Secretaries, who notwithstanding were absent from the Trial.

Much arguing also there was about the Credit and Validity of the Testimony of Servants, Prisoners and Domesticks: and that Saying of the Emperour Hadrian was commended, Witnesses, not Witnessings, are to be believed.

These men muttered and complained,

That Spies and Emissaries were employed, by crafty Dissimulation, counterfeit Letters, and other cunning Devices, to circumvent her, (being a Woman easily to be wrong'd and abused, and very desirous of her Liberty,) to fish out her secret Counsels, and to encourage and put her on to dangerous Designs, which never would have entred into her Thoughts, if she had been kept with that Care as was requisite, and such cunning Fellows had not been privily sent to her of set Purpose to intrap her. That in all Ages it hath still been ordinary with great Courtiers, to thrust forward those whom they hate, even against their Wills and Inclinations, to such Attempts as shall bring them within the compass of Treason, and treacherously to plunge the suspectless Innocent, if once imprisoned, into inextricable Dangers.

Others there were who took her

not to be a free and absolute Queen, but a Titular Queen onely, because she had resigned her Kingdom, and when she first came into England had put herself under the Protection of the Queen of England; after which, as by Carrying herself well she enjoyed the Benefit of the Laws, so by Misdemeanour she was subject to the Equity and Justice thereof, according to that Rule of the Lawyers, He deserveth not the Benefit of the Law who offendeth against the Law. Otherwise, better were the Condition of a foreign Prince, if he might doe what he listed in another Prince's Kingdom, than his that reigneth never so well. They reputed her also to be a Subject, though not originally, yet *pro tempore,* because two absolute Princes with Regal Authority cannot be in the same Kingdom at one time. That it was a received Opinion of the Learned in the Laws, A King out of his own Dominions (except it be upon a warlike Expedition) is but a private Person, and therefore can neither confer Honours, nor exercise any Royalty. Moreover, That she by her Misdemeanours had lost *merum Imperium,* her absolute and just Power and Sovereignty; and that such as are Subjects by their Abode onely and place of Habitation might commit Treason. As for her Kindred, That no Kindred is nearer nor dearer than our Countrey: Our Countrey is to us as another God, and our first and greatest Parent. And as touching the promised Offices of Civility and Hospitality, That they could not privilege her to offer Wrongs and Mischiefs afterwards with Impunity: that those Promises were to be understood, things continuing in the same state, and not altered. He which shall afterwards commit a Crime deserves not to enjoy the Security which was before promised him. Sacred indeed are the Laws of Hospitality, but more sacred are the Laws of our Countrey. That Princes, as well as the Pope, do never bind their own Hands. And all men are more strongly tied and engaged to the Commonwealth than to their own Promises. And for her being dealt withall as a Prisoner taken in the Wars, they alledged, out of I know not what Authour, That onely such Prisoners of War are to be spared, from whom we need to fear no Disturbance of the Peace; others not: and, That a Prince hath Power and Jurisdiction over another Prince that is his Equal, whenever that other Prince makes himself subject to the Judgment of his Equal, either by Express Words, or private Contract, or by trespassing within the Jurisdiction of his Equal. That the Pope repealed the Emperour's Sentence against Robert King of Sicily, because the Fact was not committed within the Emperour's, but within the Pope's, Territories. That Embassadours are by the Law of Nations privileged in respect of the Necessity of their Embassy to be free from Violence; but so are not Kings that shall attempt Mischief and Disturbance in another King's Dominions. Again, That in case of Treason the Purpose and Intention is to be punished, though it never be brought to Effect: and that to attempt the Death of the Prince, yea to know of such an Attempt and conceal it, comes within the compass and Guilt of Treason. That many Kings have been condemned and put to Death; namely, Rhescuporis King of Thrace by Tiberius, Licinius and Maximianus by Constantine the Great, Bernard of Italy, and Conradine of Sicily, &c. And, to conclude, (which is as much as all the rest,) That the Safety of the People is the highest Law; and no Law is more sacred than the Safety of the Commonwealth. That God himself hath given and ordained this Law, That all things which are good and profitable for the Commonwealth should be accounted just and lawfull. Yea, that the very Bishops of Rome, not so much for the publick as their own Security, have put to death several Ecclesiastical Princes: as Boniface the Eighth caused Celestine the Fifth, after his Deposing from the Popedom, to be put to death, fearing lest for his singular Piety he should be called again to the Papacy; and Urban the Sixth caused five Cardinals to be sowed up in Sacks and thrown into the Sea, others he beheaded, and the Bodies of two he commanded to be dried in an Oven and carried about upon Mules, for a Terrour to others. Farthermore, that her Secretaries were not to be accounted of as Servants; and that domestick Evidences were to be admitted concerning those things that were done privately and secretly at Home. That it was a mere Nicety to make Question whether those Accusers that were voluntarily sworn, and themselves accessory to the Crime, were to be brought Face to Face to maintain their Accusation in criminal Cases. To be short, that there was no great and notable Example extant which did not carry with it some Colour and Appearance of Injustice.

These things and like to these we then heard familiarly bandied to and fro.

In the mean time the King of Scots (such was his singular Piety towards his Mother) laboured all that possibly he could by William Keith to save her Life, and omitted nothing that became a most dutifull and pious Son, and a prudent King. But without any Success at all; for the Scots were rent into Factions amongst themselves, and more there were that favoured Queen Elizabeth than the captive Queen: insomuch as some of them secretly solicited Queen Elizabeth by Letters to hasten her Execution: and the Scottish Ministers, being commanded by the King to recommend his Mother's Preservation to God in their Prayers at Church, peremptorily refused to doe it; such was their Hatred to the Religion which she professed. Nevertheless the King, as he had before by frequent Messages and as frequent Letters made Intercession for her to the Queen, so now by repeated and more importunate Letters and Messages he again solicited for her. Wherein he complained, "That it was great injustice and Indignity, that the Nobility, Council and Subjects of England should give Sentence against a Queen of Scots, that was also descended of the Bloud Royal of England: and no less Injustice to think that the Estates of England can by Authority of Parliament exclude the true and undoubted Heirs from their Right of Succession and lawfull Inheritance;" (as some for a Terrour now and then threatened).

He sent also Patrick Gray and Robert Melvin, to let the Queen know, "That out of his singular Love and Friendship he could not believe but she, who had by her Vertues, and specially by her Clemency, purchased herself all over the World so renowned a Name, free from all Blot and Imputation of Cruelty, would still preserve the same, and not by any means stain it now with the Bloud of his dear Mother, who was of the same Regal State and

Condition, of the same Bloud, the same Sex with herself, and whom (forasmuch as he was bound in Conscience to have a pious and religious Care of his Mother's Life) he could not forsake, or leave to the Cruelty of those who had now for a long time gaped after his Destruction as well as his Mother's. In other Letters to her, after he had at large declared with what thoughtfull Care and Anguish of Heart he was perplexed about so weighty a Business, which nearly concerned and touched him in regard both of Nature and Honour, and into what Straits and Hazzard of his Reputation amongst his own People he should be plunged, if any Violence be offered to his Mother; out of an inward sense of Sorrow and his filial Affection he propounded to Queen Elizabeth these things following to be seriously weighed and considered by her. "How much it concerned him in Honour, who was both a King and a Son, if his dearest Mother, and she an absolute Princess, should be put to an infamous Death by her who was so nearly allied and engaged to her both in Bloud and League of Amity. Whether by the Law of God there could be any just proceeding by Law against those whom God hath appointed to be his supreme Ministers of Justice, whom he hath called Gods on earth, whom he hath anointed, and once anointed hath forbidden to be touched, and will not suffer them to go unpunished that shall doe them Violence. How strange and monstrous a thing it would be, to subject an absolute Prince to the Judgment of Subjects. How prodigious, if an absolute Prince should be made so dangerous a Precedent for the prophaning and vilifying her own and other Princes Diadems. And moreover, what should drive her to this Rigour and Severity? Honour, or Profit? If Honour, she would purchase more Honour by sparing her: for so would she, with eternal Commendations of her Clemency, oblige unto her by this Favour both himself, and all the Princes of Christendom, whose Affections otherwise she could not but alienate from her, with the loss of her Fame, and incur the Brand of Cruelty. And if Profit were the thing that moved her to it, it was to be considered, whether any thing were profitable which was neither just nor honest. He concluded with this Request, That his Embassadours might bring him back such an Answer as might beseem a most Religious Queen to give, and not be unfit for a King and a loving Kinsman to receive." But his Embassadours unsea-

273

sonably mingling Threatenings with Intreatings, they were not very welcome, and indeed after a few days were dismissed with small Hope of speeding in what they came about.

Monsieur Pompon de Bellievre, who was sent from the French King upon this Occasion, having got Access to the Queen in Company with L' Aubespine a Chasteau-neuf the Ordinary Embassadour, and briefly signified with what contrary Affections the French King was distracted, on the one side out of his singular Respects towards her, and on the other side by reason of the strait Alliance betwixt him and the Queen of Scots, propounded these and the like Considerations in writing several times to the Queen in her behalf.

> That it very much concerned the most Christian King of France, and all other Kings, that a Queen, a free and absolute Princess, should not be put to Death.

> That the Queen's Safety would be more endangered by the Death of Queen Mary, than it would be by her Life: That if she were delivered out of Prison, she could probably attempt nothing against the Queen, being now in a sickly Condition, and having but a short time to live.

> That although she had laid Claim to the Crown of England, she was not to be blamed for it, but it was wholly to be imputed to her young and tender years and to bad Counsellours.

> That she came at first a Supplicant into England, and therefore having been unjustly detained, she was now at length to be either ransomed, or mercifully dealt withall. Moreover, that an absolute Prince was not to be called in Question; which made Tully say, "So unusual a thing is it for a King to be put to Death for any Crime; that before this time it was never so much as heard of."

> That if she were innocent, she was not to be punished; if guilty, she was to be spared. For this would turn to far greater Honour and Advantage, and would be recorded eternally as an Example of the English Clemency: That the Story of Porsenna in this Case was to be remembered, who snatched the Right hand of Mutius Scævola out of the Fire, and set him at Liberty, though he had conspired his Death.

> That it was a prime Rule and Precept for well Governing, To be sparing of Bloud: That Bloud crieth for Bloud: That to use the Extremity of Rigour towards her could not but seem a cruel and bloudy part.

That the French King would doe his best to repell and frustrate the Attempts of all men whatsoever who should offer Violence to the Queen: and That the Guises, the Queen of Scots near Kinsmen, would engage themselves to doe the like by Oath and Covenant under their Hands; who, in case she should be put to Death, would take it very hardly, and haply not leave her unrevenged.

Lastly, they required that she might not be proceeded against according to so rigorous and extraordinary a Sentence: Otherwise, the French King could not but take a very great Displeasure thereat, howsoever other Princes should hap to resent it.

To these Reasons Answer was made from Point to Point in the Margin as followeth.

That the Queen of England trusted, the most Christian King of France would have no less a Regard and Respect for her than he had for the Queen of Scots, who had practiced the Destruction of an innocent Princess, her near Kinswoman, and a Confederate with the French King. That it was expedient and necessary for Kings and Commonwealths, that wicked Attempts (especially against Princes) should not go unpunished.

That the English, which acknowledge the Sovereign Authority of Queen Elizabeth onely in England, could not acknowledge two supreme, free and absolute Princes in England at one time; or account any other whomsoever equal to her in England as long as she lived. Neither indeed did they see, how the Queen of Scots, and her Son who at present reigneth, can be reputed both at one time for supreme and absolute Princes.

Whether the Queen's Safety would be exposed to greater Danger upon her being executed, depended upon future Accidents and Contingencies: the Estates of England, upon serious Deliberation of the matter, thought otherwise. There would never be Occasions wanting for bad Attempts, especially when the matter was now come to that pass, that the one had no Hope of Safety unless the other were ruined: and this Saying they might call to mind, *Aut ego illam, aut illa me*, Either I must take away her Life, or she will take away mine. The shorter the time to come of her Life was, the sooner and more eagerly would the Conspiratours hasten the Queen's Danger.

That the Title which she claimed to the Crown of England she would not yet renounce, and therefore she was with good Reason detained in Prison, and so to be detained (though she came a

Supplicant into England) till she had renounced the same. And the Crimes which she had committed since she was a Prisoner she ought to suffer for, whatever were the Cause of her first casting into Prison.

That the Queen had formerly most gratiously spared her Life, when by unanimous Consent of the Estates she was condemned for a Rebellion raised about an intended Marriage between her and the Duke of Norfolk: and to spare her again were but unadvised and cruel pity. That no man was ignorant of that Saying of the Lawyers, A man offending in another's Territory, and there found, is punished in the place of his Offence, without regard of his Dignity, Honour, or Privilege. And that this was both justifiable by the Laws of England, and by the Examples of Licinius, Robert King of Sicily, Bernard King of Italy, Conradine, Elizabeth Queen of Hungary, Joan Queen of Naples, and Dejotarus; for whom Tully pleading, said, It was no unjust thing that a King should be found guilty and put to Death, though it were not usual. For thus the words run, "Which I speak first touching a King's Forfeiture of Life and Estate. Which thing though it be not unjust, especially when thy Life is in Danger from him, yet it is so unusual, &c."

That she ought to be punished, having been found Guilty upon a just and legal Trial; considering that what is just, the same is honest, and what is honest, is also profitable and expedient.

That the Story of Porsenna suited not with the present Case; unless a man should imagine a numerous Combination of men to have laid Wait for the Queen's Life, and should thereupon perswade her to set the Queen of Scots at Liberty without any Hurt, out of a Fear of them, and with some Regard to her own Honour, but none to her Safety, as Porsenna discharged Mutius after he had affirmed that 300 like himself had conspired and vowed this Death. Moreover, Mutius attempted this against Porsenna in a just and declared War; and when Mutius was let go, Porsenna verily perswaded himself that all the Danger was over: but the Case here is quite otherwise.

That Bloud indeed is to be spared, but it must be innocent Bloud: This God hath commanded. True it is indeed, that the Voice of innocent Bloud crieth for Bloud: And this can France, both before and since the Massacre at Paris, well witness and testifie.

That Death that is justly inflicted cannot seem bloudy; as

neither is Physick, prepared duly and as it ought to be, esteemed violent.

That howsoever the Guises, the Queen of Scots Kinsmen, might take the matter, yet it is highly concerned the Queen to regard rather the Safety of herself, the Nobility and People of England, (upon whose Love and Affection she wholly depended,) than the Displeasure of any whosoever. That the matter was come to that pass, that what was said of old concerning to Princes, Conradine of Sicily and Charles of Anjou, might now be spoken of two Queens, it might now be truly said, The Death of Mary is the Life of Elizabeth, and the Life of Mary is the Death of Elizabeth.

That the French King's or the Guises Promises could not secure the Queen and Realm, much less make Satisfaction for her Life if she should be made away.

That the French King could neither discover or hinder secret Plots against himself at Home; much less was he like to hinder those against the Queen of England: For Treason is plotted in secret, and therefore hard to be prevented. If the Fact were once committed, what would it avail to claim their Promises? How should an incomparable Prince's Death be made Amends for? And in so sad and wofull a Confusion of all things, what Remedy could be found for the languishing Commonwealth?

That the Obligations and Oaths of the Guises were of small Value, who judged it meritorious to kill the Bishop of Rome's Adversaries, and could very easily procure Dispensations for their Oaths. And what English-man, if Queen Elizabeth were slain, and the Queen of Scots of the House of Guise advanced to the Crown, durst accuse them of the Murther? And if any should accuse them, could they thereby make her alive again?

And the Embassadours in calling this a rigorous and extra-ordinary Sentence have spoken rashly and unadvisedly, (forasmuch as they have seen neither Process nor Proofs) and have more sharply than is fitting taxed the Estates of the Realm of England, choice men for their Nobility, Vertue, Prudence and Piety: yea, they have inconsiderately uttered such words in the French King's Name, as if they meant by Threats to terrifie the Queen and the Estates of the Land. The English-men use not to be terrified by the French-mens Threats from taking Courses to secure their own Tranquillity, when they in the mean time could direct them no proper way to avoid the instant and threatning Dangers.

XIV

The Thirtieth Year of Her Reign, Anno Domini 1587

While these things, either out of Hatred or Affection, were curiously and copiously argued according to mens Apprehensions of things, L' Aubespine, the French Embassadour Leiger in England, a man wholly devoted to the Guisian Faction, supposing it the best way to provide for the captive Queen's Safety and Preservation, not by Arguments, but by underhand Practices and Artifices, tampered about taking away Queen Elizabeth's Life (at first more closely) with William Stafford a young Gentleman, and ready to catch at new Hopes of Advancement, whose Mother was one of the Queen's honourable Bed-chamber, and his Brother at that time Embassadour Leiger in France; and afterwards more plainly and openly, by Trappy his Secretary, who promised him, if he would effect it, not onely infinite Glory and a vast deal of Money, but also special Favour with the Bishop of Rome, the Duke of Guise, and generally with all the Catholicks. Stafford, as detesting the Fact, refused to doe it; yet recommended one Moody, a notable Hackster; one ready for any Mischief, as a man who for Money would without doubt resolutely doe the Business. This Moody lying then in the common Gaol of London, Stafford gave him to understand that the French Embassadour would very gladly speak with him. He answered, he was very ready so to doe, in case he were once out of Prison: in the mean time he desired that Cordalion, the Embassadour's other Secretary, with whom he was well acquainted, might be sent unto him. The next day Trappy was sent, accompanied by Stafford. Trappy, after Stafford was removed a little aside, conferreth with Moody about the best way of Killing the Queen. Moody propoundeth either to doe it by Poison, or by a Bag of Gunpowder of twenty pound weight to be put under the Queen's Bed, and secretly fired. These two ways pleased not Trappy, who wished that such another resolute Fellow could be found as that Burgundian who murthered the Prince of Orange.

These things were soon after revealed to the Queen's Council by Stafford. Whereupon Trappy, intending suddenly to go for France, was seized upon, and being questioned touching these matters, confessed what I have said. Upon this the Embassadour himself was sent for the 12th of January to Cecyl House, whither he came in the Evening, where were present by the Queen's Appointment Cecyl Lord Burghley, Lord Treasurer of England, the Earl of Leicester, Sir Christopher Hatton Vice-chamberlain to the Queen, and Davison one of her Secretaries. They let him know, that they had sent for him to inform him for what Reason they had apprehended Trappy his Secretary as he was going for France: and they acquainted him with all things particularly which Stafford, Moody, and Trappy himself, had confessed, and commanded them to be called in to witness the same to his Face. The Embassadour, having heard all the Story with great Impatience and a frowning Countenance, now rose up and said, "That he, being the King's Embassadour, would not hear any Accusation to the Prejudice of the King his Master, and against the Privileges of Embassadours." When it was answered, "That they were not produced as Accusers, but that he might see these things not to be feigned and pretended, and that he himself might have liberty to charge Stafford with Falshood," he was satisfied. As soon as Stafford was brought in, and began to speak, he interrupted him, railing upon him, and affirming that Stafford was the first man that propounded the matter; and that he had threatned him, unless he would desist, to send him bound Hand and Foot to the Queen; but yet had spared him out of his singular Love to Stafford's Mother, Brother and Sister. Stafford, falling upon his Knees, deeply protested upon his Salvation, that the Embassadour first propounded the matter to him. The Embassadour being now more vehemently moved, Stafford was commanded to withdraw, and Moody was not brought in.

And when Burghley had gently reproved the Embassadour, as

conscious or accessory to the plotting of so foul a Fact, both by his own words and Trappy's Confession; he answered, "Although he had been accessory to it, yet seeing he was an Embassadour, he ought not to discover the same to any but the King his Master onely." When Burghley replyed, "That if it be not for an Embassadour to make any such Discovery when a Prince's Life is by wicked Contrivances brought into Danger, (which notwithstanding is a thing controverted,) yet it is the Duty of a Christian to repell and hinder such Injuries, and that where the Safety not onely of a Prince, but also of any private Christian, is concerned." This he strongly denied, and withall told him how a French Embassadour not long since in Spain, having Knowledge of a Design against the King of Spain's Life, discovered it, not to the King of Spain, but to the King his Master, and was therefore commended by the King and his Council. But Burghley gravely advised him to beware how he committed Treason any more, or forgat the Duty of an Embassadour, and the Queen's Clemency, who should not by punishing a bad Embassadour prejudice the good: and that he was not acquitted from the Guilt of the Offence, though he escaped the punishment.

By means of this Attempt such as bare a mortal Hatred against the Queen of Scots took occasion to hasten her Death. And to strike the greater Terrour into the Queen, (knowing that where a man's own Safety lies at the Stake, there Fear excludeth all Pity,) they caused false Rumours and terrifying Reports daily to be spread all over England: viz. "That the Spanish Fleet was already arrived at Milford Haven; That the Scots were broken into England; That the Duke of Guise was landed in Sussex with a strong Army; That the Queen of Scots was escaped out of Prison, and had raised an Army; That the Northern parts were up in Rebellion; That there was a new Conspiracy on foot to kill the Queen, and set the City of London on Fire; yea, That the Queen was dead;" with other such like Stories, which men either crafty for their own Ends or really fearfull are wont to feign to themselves, and to make worse out of a natural Propensity they have to cherish and increase Rumours, and Princes lightly credulous do easily entertain.

With such Scar-crows and affrighting Arguments as these

they drew the Queen's wavering and perplexed Mind to that Pass, that she signed a Warrant for putting the Sentence of Death in Execution. And one of the principal Perswaders to it (as the Scots report) was Patrick Gray a Scot, sent purposely by the King of Scots to disswade the Queen from putting his Mother to Death; who many times buzzed into the Queen's ear that Saying, *Mortua non-mordet,* that is, A dead Woman biteth not.

Yet she, being a Woman naturally slow in her Resolutions, began to consider in her Mind, whether it were better to put her to Death, or to spare her. As for putting her to Death these things were against it: "Her own innate Clemency, lest she should seem to shew herself cruel to a Woman, and that a Princess, and her Kinswoman; Fear of Infamy with Posterity in after Histories; and imminent and certain Dangers as well from the King of Scots, who would now be advanced to a Step higher in his Hopes of England, as from the Catholick Princes and desperate men, who would now adventure upon any thing." And if she should spare her, she foresaw that no less Danger threatened her. "The Noblemen that had given Sentence against the Queen of Scots would endeavour underhand to get into Favour with her and her Son, not without manifest Hazzard to herself; The rest of her Subjects, who had been so carefull for her Safety, seeing she had frustrated their Pains and Care, would take it very ill, and for time to come neglect her Preservation; Many would turn Papists, and entertain greater Hopes, when they should see her preserved as it were by Fate to a Probability of enjoying the Crown; The Jesuites and Seminaries, whose Eyes are upon her onely, seeing her sickly, and fearing that she would not live long, would leave no means untried to hasten Queen Elizabeth's Death, that so their Religion might be restored."

The Courtiers also continually suggested unto her these things following, and the like:

> Why should you spare her, when she is guilty and justly con-
> demned, who, though she subscribed to the Association for your
> Safety, yet presently after resolved unmercifully to ruine you
> who were altogether innocent, and by destroying you to destroy
> Religion, the Nobility, and People? Clemency and Mercy is a

Royal Vertue, but not to be extended to the merciless. Let the vain shew of Mercy give place to wholsome Severity. Have a care that your unseasonable Mercy and Favour involve you not in the greatest Misery. It is Commendation enough of your Clemency, to have spared her once: to spare her again were nothing else but to pronounce her guiltless, condemn the Estates of the Realm of Injustice, encourage your Favourers to hasten their wicked Designs, and discourage your faithfull Subjects from Caring for the Commonwealth. Religion, the Commonwealth, your own Safety, the Love of your Countrey, the Oath of Association, and the Care of Posterity, do all with their joynt Prayers beseech you, that she which endangereth the Subversion of all these may forthwith be put to Death: and except they may prevail, Safety itself will never be able to save this Commonwealth; and Historians will leave it recorded to succeeding Ages, that the bright Sunshining and glorious Days of England under Queen Elizabeth ended in a foul, cloudy and dark Evening, yea in an eternal Night. Posterity will blame us for lack of Wisedom, that could foresee these Mischiefs, (which adds to the Misery thereof,) and yet could not prevent them; and will impute the Mass and Heap of future Calamities not so much to the Adversaries Malice, as to the gross Carelessness of these Times. The Life of one Scottish and Titular Queen ought not to weigh down the Safety of all England. In so important a matter there ought to be no Delay; for Delay bringeth Danger: nor any space of time allowed to Plotters of Mischief, who will now have their last Refuge and Recourse to bold Attempts, since besides Impunity they will be in Hope of Reward for their Labour. He that doeth not what lies in his power to avoid Dangers, doth rather tempt God, than trust in God. The Mischiefs which threaten from Foreigners, the Cause being once taken away, will be all taken away with it: neither can they doe England any Harm but by her. Whatsoever Mind or Power the Bishop of Rome hath to hurt us will all fall to the ground with her. The Spaniard can have no just Cause to be offended, who for his own Security put to Death his onely Son Charles, and now for ambitious Ends layeth wait for the Life of Don Antonio of Portugal. The French King most religiously maintaineth Amity with England, and him it highly concerneth that by the timely Death of the Queen of Scots the Hopes of the Guisians should be quashed, who, presuming upon the expected future Power of their Kinswoman, do at present insolently insult over their King. The King of Scots indeed may by the very force of natural Affection, and out of a Respect to his Honour, be deeply troubled for his Mother: But his Wisedom will carry him rather to expect the coming forward of things themselves leisurely and with Security, than to be over-hasty in compassing them with Danger. And the nearer he is to the Height of his Hope, the farther will foreign princes be from assisting him; it being a thing usual with them by any means to hinder the growing Power of another.

They produced also Examples at Home in our own Countrey, (for whatever is done by Example is done more excusably,) "how the Kings of England for their own Security have carried themselves toward their Kinsmen and Competitours: namely, Henry the First toward Robert his eldest Brother; Edward the Third, or rather his Mother, toward Edward the Second; Henry the Fourth toward Richard the Second; Edward the Fourth toward Henry the Sixth and his Son the Prince of Wales, and toward his own Brother George Duke of Clarence; Henry the Seventh toward Warwick, the Duke of Clarence his young Son; and Henry the Eighth toward De la Poole Earl of Suffolk, Margaret Countess of Salisbury, and Courtney Marquess of Excester: All which were for light Causes (if their Faults be compared with hers) made away." And not onely did the Courtiers use these Perswasions with the Queen, but some Preachers also more tartly than was fit, and some of the Vulgar sort (either out of Hope or Fear) more sawcily than became them, exercised their Wits at their pleasure upon this Subject.

In the midst of these doubtfull and perplexed Thoughts, which so troubled and staggered the Queen's mind, that she gave herself wholly over to Solitariness, sate many times melancholick and mute, and frequently sighing muttered this to herself, *Aut fer, aut feri,* that is, Either bear with her, or smite her, and, out of I know not what Emblem, *Nè feriare, feri,* that is, Strike, lest thou be stricken; she delivered a Writing to Davison, one of the Secretaries, signed with her own Hand, commanding a Warrant under the Great Seal of England to be drawn up for the Execution, which should lie in readiness if any Danger chanced to break forth in that time of Jealousie and Fear; and commanded him to acquaint no man therewith. But the next day, while Fear seemed to be afraid of her own

Counsels and Designs, her Mind changed, and she commanded Davison by William Killegrew that the Warrant should not be drawn. Davison came presently to the Queen, and told her that it was drawn and under Seal already. She was somewhat moved at it, and blamed him for making such Haste. He notwithstanding acquainted the Council both with the Warrant and the whole matter, and easily perswaded them, who were apt to believe what they desired, that the Queen had commanded it should be executed. Hereupon without any Delay Beale (who in respect of Religion was of all others the Queen of Scots most bitter Adversary) was sent down, with one or two Executioners, and a Warrant, wherein Authority was given to the Earls of Shrewsbury, Kent, Derby, Cumberland, and others, to see her executed according to the Law; and this without any Knowledge of the Queen at all. And though she at that very time told Davison that she would take another Course with the Queen of Scots, yet did not he for all that call Beale back.

As soon as the Earls were come to Fotheringhay, they, together with Sir Amias Powlet and Sir Drue Drury, to whose Custody she was committed, came unto her, told her the Cause of their coming, reading the Warrant, and in few words admonished her to prepare her self for Death, for she was to die the next day. She undauntedly and with a composed Spirit made this Answer: "I did not think the Queen my Sister would have consented to my Death, who am not subject to your Law and Jurisdiction: but seeing her Pleasure is so, Death shall be to me most welcome: neither is that Soul worthy of the high and everlasting Joys above, whose Body cannot endure one Stroak of the Executioner." She prayed them that she might have Conference with her Almoner, her Confessour, and Melvin the Master of her Houshold. For her Confessour, it was flatly denied that he should come at her: and the Earls recommended to her the Bishop or the Dean of Peterborough to comfort her: whom she refusing, the Earl of Kent, in an hot burning Zeal to Religion, turning towards her, brake forth into these words amongst other Speeches; "Your Life will be the Death of our Religion, as contrariwise your Death will be the Life thereof." Mention being made of Babington, she constantly denied his Conspiracy to have been at all known to her, and the Revenge of her Wrong she left to God. Then enquiring what was become of Nawe and Curle, she asked whether ever it were heard of before, that Servants were suborned and accepted for Witnesses against their Master's Life. When the Earls were departed from her, she commanded Supper to be hastened, that she might the better dispose of her Concernments. She supped temperately and sparingly, as her manner usually was. Being at Supper, and spying her Servants, both men and women, weeping and lamenting, she comforted them with great Courage and Magnanimity, bade them leave Mourning, and rather rejoyce that she was now to depart out of a world of Miseries. Turning to Burgoin her Physician, she asked him whether he did not now find the Force of Truth to be great. "They say (quoth she) that I must die because I have plotted against the Queen's Life; yet the Earl of Kent tells me that there is no other Cause of my Death, but that they are afraid for their Religion because of me. Neither hath my Offence against the Queen, but their Fear because of me, drawn this End upon me, while some under the Colour of Religion and the Publick good aim at their own private Respects and Advantages." Towards the end of Supper she drank to all her Servants, who pledged her in order upon their Knees, mingling Tears with their Wine, and begging Pardon for their Neglect of their Duty; as she also in like manner did of them. After Supper she perused her Will, read over the Inventory of her Goods and Jewels, and wrote down the names of those to whom she bequeathed every Particular. To some she distributed Money with her own Hand. To her Confessour she wrote a Letter that he would make Intercession for her to God in his Prayers. She wrote also Letters of Recommendations for her Servants to the French King and the Duke of Guise. At her wonted time she went to Bed, slept some Hours; and then awaking, spent the rest of the Night in Prayer.

The fatal day now being come, which was the 8th of February, she dressed herself as gorgeously and curiously as she was wont to doe upon Festival-days, and, calling her Servants together, commanded her Will to be read, prayed them to take their Legacies in good part, for her Ability would not extend to giving them any greater matters. Then fixing her mind wholly upon God in her Oratory or ordinary place of Prayer, with

Sighs, Groans and Prayers she begged his Divine Grace and Favour, till such time as Thomas Andrews, Sheriff of the County, acquainted her that she must now come forth. And forth she came with State, Countenance and Presence majestically composed, a chearfull Look, and a matron-like and modest Habit; her Head covered with a linen Veil, and that hanging down to the Ground; her Prayer-beads hanging at her Girdle, and carrying a Crucifix of Ivory in her Hands. In the Porch she was received by the Earls and other Noblemen, where Melvin her Servant, falling upon his Knees, and pouring forth Tears, bewailed his hard Hap, that he was to carry into Scotland the wofull Tidings of the unhappy Fate of his Lady and Mistress. She thus comforted him, "Lament not, but rather rejoyce; thou shalt by and by see Mary Stuart freed from all her Cares. Tell them that I die constant in my Religion, and firm in my Fidelity and affection towards Scotland and France. God forgive them who have thirsted after my Bloud as Harts do after the Fountain. Thou O God, who art Truth itself, and perfectly and truly understandeth the inward Thoughts of my Heart, knowest how greatly I have desired that the Kingdoms of England and Scotland might be united into one. Commend me to my Son, and assure him that I have done nothing which may be prejudicial to the Kingdom of Scotland; admonish him to hold in Amity and Friendship with the Queen of England; and see thou doe him faithfull Service."

And now the Tears trickling down, she bade Melvin several times Farewell, who wept as fast as she. Then turning to the Earls, she prayed them "That her servants might be civily dealt withall; That they might enjoy the Legacies she had bequeathed them by Will and Testament: That they might stand by her at her death; and might be sent back into their own Countrey with Letters of safe Conduct." The former Requests they granted: but that they should stand by her at her Death, the Earl of Kent shewed himself somewhat unwilling, fearing some Superstition. "Fear it not, (said she) these harmless Souls desire onely to take their last Farewell of me. I know my Sister Elizabeth would not have denied me so small a matter, that my Women should be then present, were it but for the Honour of the Female Sex. I am her near Kinswoman, descended from Henry the

Seventh, Queen Dowager of France, and anointed Queen of Scots."

When she had said thus much, and turned herself aside, it was at last granted that such of her Servants as she should name should be then present. She named Melvin, Burgoin her Physician, her Apothecary, her Chirurgoen, two Waiting-Women, and others; of whom Melvin bare up her Train. So the Gentlemen, two Earls and the Sheriff of the Shire going before her, she came to the Scaffold, which was built at the upper end of the Hall; on which was placed a Chair, a Cushion, and a Block, all covered with black Cloath. As soon as she was set down, and Silence commanded, Beale read the Warrant: she heard it attentively, yet as if her Thoughts were taken up with somewhat else. Then Fletcher Dean of Peterborough began a long Speech to her touching the Condition of her Life past, present, and to come. She interrupted him once or twice as he was speaking, prayed "him not to trouble himself, protesting that she was firmly fixed and resolved in the ancient Catholick Roman Religion, and for it was ready to shed her last Bloud." When he earnestly perswaded her to true Repentance, and to put her whole Trust in Christ by an assured Faith; she answered, that "in that Religion she was both born, bred, and now ready to die." The Earls said they would pray for her: to whom she said, "That she would give them hearty Thanks if they would pray with her; but to joyn (said she) in Prayer with you who are of another Profession, would be in me a heinous Sin." Then they appointed the Dean to pray: with whom while the Multitude that stood round about were praying, she fell down upon her Knees, and, holding the Crucifix before her in her Hands prayed in Latin with her Servants out of the Office of the Blessed Virgin Mary.

After the Dean had made an end of Praying, she in English words recommended the Church, her Son, and Queen Elizabeth, to God, beseeching him to turn away his Wrath from this Island; and professing that she reposed her Hope of Salvation in the Bloud of Christ, (lifting up the Crucifix,) she called upon the celestial Quire of Saints to make Intercession to him for her: she forgave all her Enemies, and kissing the Crucifix, and signing herself with the Cross, she said, "As thy Arms, O Christ, were spread out upon the Cross, so receive me with the stretched-out Arms of thy Mercy, and forgive my Sins." Then the Executioners asked her forgiveness, which she granted them. And when her Women-servants had taken off her upper Garments, (which she was eager and hasty to have done) wailing and lamenting the while, she kissed them, and signing them with the Cross, with a chearfull Countenance bade them forbear their Womanish Lamentations; "For now she should rest from all her Sorrows." In like manner turning to her Men-servants, who also wept, she signed them likewise with the Cross, and smiling bade them Farewell. And now having covered her Face with a linen Hand-kerchief, and laying herself down to the Block, she recited that Psalm, "In thee, O Lord, do I trust, let me never be confounded." Then stretching forth her Body, and repeating many times, "Into thy Hands, O Lord, I commend my Spirit," her Head was stricken off at two Stroaks: the Dean crying out, "So let Queen Elizabeth's Enemies perish;" the Earl of Kent answering, "Amen," and the Multitude sighing and sorrowing. Her Body was embalmed, and ordered with due and usual Rites; and afterwards interred with a Royal Funeral in the Cathedral-Church of Peterborough. A pompous Obsequies was also performed for her at Paris by Procurement of her Guises, who, to their great Commendations, performed all the highest Offices of Kindness to their Kinswoman both alive and dead.

This lamentable End had Mary Queen of Scots, Daughter to James the Fifth King of Scots, great-grand-daughter to Henry the Seventh King of England by his eldest Daughter, in the six and fortieth year of her Age, and the eighteenth of her Imprisonment. A Lady fixed and constant in her Religion, of singular Piety towards God, invincible Magnanimity of Mind, Wisedom above her Sex, and admirable Beauty; a Lady to be reckoned in the List of those Princesses which have changed their Felicity for Misery and Calamity. While yet an Infant, she was earnestly desired by Henry the Eighth King of England for his Son Prince Edward, and by Henry the Second King of France for Francis the Daulphin; both of them striving who should have her to his Daughter-in-law. At five years old she was conveyed into France, and at fifteen married to the Daulphin. She was Queen of France a Year and four Months. After the

Death of her Husband she returned into Scotland, was married again to Henry Stuart Lord Darly and bare James, the First Monarch of Great Britain. By Murray her base Brother, and other her ungratefull and ambitious Subjects, she was much tossed and disquieted, deposed from her Throne, and driven into England. By some English-men who were carefull for preserving their Religion, and providing for the Queen's Safety, she was (as indifferent Censurers have thought) circumvented; and by others, that were desirous to restore the Romish Religion, thrust forward to dangerous Undertakings; and overborn by the Testimonies of her Secretaries, who seemed to be bribed and corrupted with Money. Near her Tomb this Epitaph following was set up, but soon after taken away.

An Epitaph

Mary Queen of Scots, a King's Daughter, the King of France his Widow, the Queen of England's Kinswoman and next Heir, a Princess accomplished with Royal Vertues and a Royal Soul, having many times (but in vain) demanded her Royal Privilege, is by barbarous and tyrannical Cruelty extinct, who was the Ornament of our Age, and a Light truly Royal; and by one and the same wicked Sentence is both Mary Queen of Scots doomed to a natural Death, and all surviving Kings, being made as Common people, are subjected to a civil Death. A new and unexampled kind of Tomb is here extant, wherein the Living are inclosed with the Dead: for know, that with the Sacred Ashes of Saint Mary here lieth violate and prostrate the Majesty of all Kings and Princes. And because (Reader that travellest this way) the unrevealable Secret of Kings doth most sufficiently admonish Kings of their Duty, I say no more.

By this so lamentable a Fate of this great Princess appeared most conspicuously (as some understanding persons have observed,) the wise Disposition and Ordering of the Divine Providence. For those things which both the Queens, Elizabeth and Mary, most of all desired, and in all their Councils propounded to themselves, were hereby attained. Queen Mary (as she said just before her Death) desired nothing more ardently, than that the divided Kingdoms of England and Scotland might be united in the Person of her dear Son: and there was nothing which

Queen Elizabeth wished for more earnestly, than that the true Religion might be preserved in England together with the Safety and Security of the People. And that the high and great God granted them both their Prayers England now seeth with unexpected Felicity, and most joyfully acknowledgeth the same.

As soon as the Report was brought to Queen Elizabeth's Ears, who little thought of such a thing, that the Queen of Scots was put to Death, she heard it with great Indignation, her Countenance altered, her Speech faultered her, and through excessive Sorrow she stood in a manner astonished; insomuch as she gave herself over to passionate Grief, putting herself into mourning Habit, and shedding abundance of Tears: her Council she sharply rebuked, and commanded them out of her Sight, causing them to be examined: Davison she commanded to appear and be tried in the Star-chamber. And as soon as Grief would give her leave, she wrote this following Letter in haste with her own Hand to the King of Scots, and sent it by Robert Cary.

My dearest Brother, I would to God thou knewest (but not that thou feltest) the incomparable Grief my Mind is perplexed with upon this lamentable Accident, which is happened contrary to my Meaning and intention, which, since my pen trembleth to mention it, you shall fully understand by this my Kinsman. I request you, that as God and many others can witness my Innocency in this matter, so you will also believe, that if I had commanded it, I would never deny it. I am not so faint-hearted, that for Terrour I should fear to doe the thing which is just; or to own it when it is once done: no, I am not so base nor ignobly minded. But as it is no Princely part, with feigned Words to conceal and disguise the real Meaning of the Heart; so will I never dissemble my Actions, but make them appear in their true and proper Colours. Persuade yourself this for Truth, that as I know this is happened deservedly on her part, so if I had intended it, I would not have laid it upon others: but I will never charge myself with that which I had not so much as thought of. Other matters you shall understand by the Bearer of this Letter. As for me, I would have you believe, there is not any which loveth you more dearly, or taketh more Care for the Good of you and your Affairs. If any man would persuade you the contrary, you may conclude he favoureth others more than you. God preserve you long in Health and Safety.

Whilst Cary was upon his way with this Letter, Davison was brought into the Star-chamber before certain Commissioners chosen for that purpose: namely Sir Christopher Wray Knight, Chief Justicer in the King's Bench, who for that Occasion was made Lord Privy-Seal; the two Archbishops, of Canterbury and York; the Earls of Worcester, Cumberland and Lincoln; the Barons Grey and Lumley; Sir James Croftes, Controller of the Queen's Household; Sir Walter Mildmay, Chancellour of the Exchequer; Sir Gilbert Gerard, Master of the Rolls; Sir Edmund Anderson, Chief Justicer at the Common Pleas; and Sir Roger Manwood, Chief Baron of the Exchequer. Before these Commissioners Popham the Queen's Attorney charged Davison with Contempt toward the Queen's Majesty, Breach of his Allegeance, and Neglect of his Duty, in that, "whereas the Queen (according to her innate Clemency) never intended that the Queen of Scots, though condemned, should have been put to Death, for Causes best known to herself alone, and not to be searched into by others, nor could by any means be persuaded to consent thereto, either by the Estates of the Realm, or by the repeated Instances and Reasons of the Council, notwithstanding that she had, for preventing of Dangers, commanded a Warrant for her Execution to be drawn up, and committed it to Davison's Trust and Secrecy: He nevertheless, being her sworn Secretary, forgetting his Allegeance and Duty, and in Contempt of her Majesty, contrary to what the Queen had commanded him, had acquainted the Council therewith, and put the Warrant in Execution, without her knowing any thing at all of it."

Davison, according to his singular discretion, answered with a somber kind of Confidence, "That he was very sorry that in so just a Cause concerning the Queen of Scots, and the Sentence given against her, a Sentence of all others the most weighty and serious, he should now again trouble the Commissioners, and that, if not with the Loss, yet at least with the Impairing, of his Credit, which to him was as dear as all things else. But most heavily of all he took it, that he was charged to have offended contemptuously against her Majesty, who by how much she had been the more gratious and bountifull unto him, and he the more engaged unto her for her singular Favours, so much the more heinous might his Offence seem. If he should confess

291

himself guilty of the Crimes, objected against him, he should wrong his own Reputation, which was more pretious to him than his Life. And if he should contest with the Queen in his own Defence, he should doe that which was unbefitting the Obedience of a Subject, the dutifull Behaviour of a Servant, and the Faith and Place of a Secretary." He protested before God and the Commissioners, "That he had done nothing in this matter wittingly and willingly, but what he had persuaded himself was the Queen's Will and Pleasure, wherein if he had wronged himself either through Ignorance or Negligence, he could not but be exceedingly troubled at it, and be ready patiently to undergoe the Commissioner's Censure."

As to Particulars, he affirmed, "That when the Queen blamed him for making such haste to get the Warrant under the Great Seal, she gave some Signification, but no express Command, that he should keep it in his own hands. Neither doth he believe himself to have offended against his Trust of Secrecy, seeing he never spoke a word of the Business to any but the Council. Whereas he recalled not the Warrant after the Queen had told him that she had changed her Resolution, he affirmed, That it was agreed by all the Council that it should be presently sent away, and Execution done, lest the Commonwealth or the Queen should receive any Hurt."

Hereupon Egerton the Queen's Solicitour began to press Davison with his own Confession, reading a Piece thereof. But Davison prayed him "to reade the whole, and not Parcels picked out here and there: but he had rather (he said) it should not be read at all, because there were contained in it some Secrecies not fit to be divulged abroad; saying withall, That as he would not contest with the Queen, so could he not endure that his Modesty should prejudice the Truth and his own Integrity."

Gaudy and Puckering Serjeants at Law now charged him home and sharply, that he had craftily abused the Wisedom of the Queen's Council, and that by the Confession of Burghley Lord Treasurer, who doubting whether the Queen had absolutely resolved to have Execution done, Davison confidently affirmed it; as he likewise did to the rest that subscribed the Letters for the manner of the Execution. Davison here prayed the Queen's learned Council, with Tears running down his Cheeks, that they "would not urge the matter any further, but remember that he would not contest with the Queen, to whose Conscience and the Commissioners Censure he wholly submitted himself."

Manwood, in the first place, made an historical Relation touching the Queen of Scots, beginning from her Usurping the Arms of England in her tender Age, quite down to Babington's Conspiracy; commended and approved the Sentence given against her according to the Law; extolled the Queen's Clemency, which because Davison had inconsiderately prevented, he censured him to be fined in ten thousand Pounds, and imprisoned during the Queen's Pleasure.

Then Anderson argued, that he had done the thing which was just, though he had not done it after a due and just manner: otherwise he thought him to be no bad man.

Of the same Opinion was Gerard.

Mildmay (having first declared with what mature Deliberation and serious Gravity the Trial against the Queen of Scots was managed, and by how earnest Intreaties and Obtestations of the People Queen Elizabeth was persuaded to publish the Sentence) made use of that place of Scripture against Davison, "The heart of the King is in the Hand of the Lord;" and therefore no man, much less an Officer and a Servant, ought underhand and deceitfully to prevent Princes of their Purpose; without whose Knowledge and Consent nothing was to be done, especially in matters of so great Importance as is the Death of a Princess. He cleared him of Malice, but taxed him with Unskilfulness in Princes Affairs, and condemned him of Rashness and too much Haste in preventing the Queen's Intention. And that men of his Place and Rank might not for the future dare to commit the like Offence, he agreed in Opinion with the rest concerning his Fine and Imprisonment.

Croftes blamed him for his unadvisedness in revealing things which ought to have been concealed; considering that Princes, what they impart to one of their Council, that many times they do not let the rest know of.

The Lord Lumley was of Opinion with the Judges, that the Sentence was justly pronounced against the Queen of Scots. But he affirmed withall, "That never in any Age was there such a Contempt against a Prince heard or read of, that the Queen's

Council, in the Queen's Palace, in the Council-Chamber near the Queen, who was as it were President of the Council, should resolve upon a matter of such Consequence without her Advice or Knowledge, when both they and Davison might have had so easie Access unto her. Protesting that if he had but one onely Son, and he were in the same Fault, he would censure him to be severely punished. But being persuaded of the man's ingenuous and honest Intention, he would inflict no heavier Punishment upon him than the rest had done before."

After him followed the Lord Grey, who in a set and tart Speech, as being inflamed with a religious Zeal, thus roundly delivered himself:

Davison (said he) is charged to have demeaned himself contemptuously towards the Queen, and that Contempt is aggravated with these Circumstances; That he hath caused the Queen of Scots to be put to Death, hath divulged certain Secrets, and concealed from the Queen the sending away of the Warrant. But what Queen was it whom he caused to be put to death? Even she from whom, as long as she lived, Dangers daily threatned our Religion, our Queen, our Commonwealth, and every particular man of us; and by means of whom, though she be now executed, we are at this day put to this Trouble. So that he which hath delivered England from so great Dangers may seem worthy rather to be honoured and esteemed. I do not take him to have revealed Secrets, who imparted the Business to no other than the Council and Managers of the weightiest Affairs, whom it specially concerned to know such Matters; and the Queen herself had already acquainted one or two of them with the thing. If Davison have offended, he is most to be blamed for this, that when the Queen was entring upon a new Resolution, he did not let her know that the Warrant was already sent away. But he, without Question, was divided in doubtfull and perplexed thoughts, whether he were best venture the Queen's Favour by sending away the Warrant without her Knowledge, or by recalling it endanger the Queen's Safety anew. Who remembreth not how turbulent a Time it was, and what frighting Rumours were spread abroad in all places? If any Violence had then been offered to Religion or the Queen, or her Life had been taken away while the Warrant was in his Hands, should not he have born the Blame of it? Should not we ourselves, our Wives and Children, have fallen violently upon him? Should we not have imbrued our

Hands in his Bloud? should we not have cursed his Indiscretion to the Pit of Hell? and should we not, to his eternal Infamy, have erected a Monument of his Inconsiderateness ingraven with Letters of Bloud? Whatsoever either Punishment or Fine ye lay upon him shall not displease me; but to be sure he shall never with me lose the esteem of a good and honest man.

These things we heard Gray reason copiously, eloquently and boldly.

The three Earls concurred with the rest touching Davison's Penalty; but concerning his Reputation, with Grey.

The Archbishop of York reasoned theologically concerning his Disobedience proceeding from the Blindness of his Understanding, and Corruption of his Mind.

The Archbishop of Canterbury approved the Fact, commended the Man; but the Manner and Way of doing it he utterly condemned.

Wray Lord Privy-Seal, having summarily repeated the Opinions of the Commissioners, confirmed the Penalty indicted: and withall signified, that albeit the Queen had been offended (and that not without just Cause) with her Council, and had thereupon left them to Examination; yet now she forgave them, and withall acknowledged, that they had been very carefull and diligent in their Actions and Counsels for the Preservation of Religion and the Commonwealth, and for preventing of all Dangers.

Davison prayed the Commissioners to be a means to the Queen, "not for the honourable Office of Secretary which he formerly held, nor for his Liberty, nor the Abatement of his Fine, but that he might be restored to her Favour." Which notwithstanding he never recovered, though she sometimes relieved his Wants.

Thus was Davison, a man of good Ingenuity, but not well skilled in Court Arts, brought upon the Court-Stage of purpose (as most men thought) to act for a time this Part in the Tragedy; and soon after, the Part being acted, and his Stage-attire laid aside, as if he had failed in the last Act, he was thrust down from the Stage, and, not without the Pity of many, shut up a long time in Prison.

What was done publickly against Davison I have said already: but how he excused himself in private, take here a compendious

Account upon his own Credit, and out of an Apologetical Discourse of his to Walsingham.

The Queen, (saith he) after the Departure of the French and Scottish Embassadours, of her own Motion commanded me to deliver her the Warrant for Executing the Sentence against the Queen of Scots: when I had delivered it, she signed it readily with her own Hand: when she had so done, she commanded it to be sealed with the Great Seal of England; and in jesting manner said, 'Go tell all this to Walsingham who is now sick; although I fear me he will die for Sorrow when he hears it.' She added also the Reasons of her deferring it so long; namely, lest she might seem to have been violently or malitiously drawn thereto, whereas in the mean time she was not ignorant how necessary it was. Moreover she blamed Powlet and Drury, that they had not eased her of this Care; and wished that Walsingham would feel their Pulses touching this matter. The next day after it was under the Great Seal, she commanded me by Killegrew that it should not be done: and when I had informed her that it was done already, she found fault with such great haste; telling me that, in the judgment of some wise men, another Course might be taken. I answered, that that Course was always best and safest which was most just. But fearing lest she would lay the Fault upon me, (as she had laid the putting of the Duke of Norfolk to death upon the Lord Burghley,) I acquainted Hatton with the whole matter, protesting that I would not plunge my self any deeper in so great a Business. He presently imparted it to the Lord Burghley, and the Lord Burghley to the rest of the Council; who all consented to have the Execution hastened, and every one of them vowed to bear an equal share in the Blame, and sent Beale away with the Warrant and Letters. The third day after, when, by a Dream which she told of the Queen of Scots death, I perceived that she wavered in her Resolution, I asked her whether she had changed her Mind. She answered, 'No; but another course (said she) might have been devised:' and withall she asked me whether I had received any Answer from Powlet. Whose Letter when I had shewed her, wherein he flatly refused to undertake that which stood not with Honour and Justice; she, waxing angry, accused him and others (who had bound themselves by the Association) of Perjury and Breach of their Vow, as those that had promised great matters for their Prince's Safety, but would perform nothing. Yet there are (said she) who will doe it for my sake. But I shewed her how dishonourable and unjust a thing this would be; and withall into how great Danger she would bring Powlet and Drury by it. For if she approved the Fact, she would draw upon herself both Danger and Dishonour, not without the Note of Injustice: and if she disallowed it, she would utterly undoe men of great Desert and their whole Posterity. And afterwards she gave me a light Check the same day that the Queen of Scots was executed because she was not yet put to death.

How high a Displeasure soever against Davison and how great Grief Queen Elizabeth either conceived or pretended for the Death of the Queen of Scots, certain it is that the King of Scots, her onely Son, who respected his Mother with the greatest Piety that could be imagined or found in a Son, took exceeding great and hearty Grief mixt with deep Displeasure at the same, and very much lamented and mourned for her. For he did not think that Queen Elizabeth, in regard of the mutual Love betwixt them, and the League of stricter Amity but lately contracted, would have neglected all the Intercessions and Mediations of Princes, and brought his Mother, a Princess of equal Majesty with herself, and so nearly allied unto her in Royal Bloud, under the Hand of a base Executioner. Robert Cary, the Lord Hunsdon's Son, who was sent out of England to excuse the Queen, and lay all the Fault upon her Council and Davison, he suffered not to enter into Scotland, scarce would give him the hearing by another, and with much adoe received the Letters which he brought. He nulled the Commission of his Embassadour in England, and breathed nothing but Revenge. For there wanted not some that went about to persuade him, that the Princes of Christendom would never suffer so great an Affront done to the Royal Majesty and to the Name of Kings to escape unrevenged.

The Estates of Scotland, who were now assembled in good number, professed that they were ready to spend their Lives and Estates in Revenge of his Mother's Death, and the Defence of his Title to the Crown of England, and that they could by no means brook this Injury, done not so much to the King, as to the whole Nation of the Scots. There were some who persuaded the King to desire an Assistence of Shipping from the King of Denmark, whose Daughter he now sought in Marriage, against the Crown of England. Others, addicted to the Popish Religion, advised him that he should rather joyn with the Spaniard, the

French King, and the Bishop of Rome; by which means he might easily possess himself of England. Above all things, that he should give no credit nor to rely upon the Protestants of England; for they now ruled all, and secretly plotted his Destruction; using that Saying against them, "He will not spare the Son who hath destroyed the Mother." Others there were who privately advised him to declare himself openly for neither Party, but to hold both Papists and Protestants in Suspense. For if he stood openly for the Protestants, all the Papists of Europe would level their Designs against him as their Mark to shoot at, and would erect another Prop and Buttress for themselves in England, which would prove dangerous and prejudicial to him. There were also some who persuaded him to maintain a strict and religious Amity with England, not to hazzard his certain Hopes upon the uncertain Chance of War, and to be firm and constant to himself in the Received Religion, wherein if he once wavered, he should neither get himself Friends, nor rid himself of Foes. These things men persuaded him, every man as his private Advantage led him. The King, being a wise Prince, and apprehensive above his Years, considered all things seriously with good and long Deliberation by himself alone, and advised also with some few others, using no haste in the Business, which is always blind, but a mature and due Consideration.

But Queen Elizabeth throwing all the Blame upon Davison, and the unadvised Credulity of her Council, sought to asswage his Grief by little and little, lest unseasonable and sudden Consolations might more irritate him; and waited till his Sorrow were lessened by longer Time, and would suffer itself to be easilier dealt withall. And when she perceived that the French eagerly excited the young King to avenge his Wrongs, fearing lest by their cunning Wiles and his own boiling Heat to take Revenge, he might be drawn away from the Protestant Religion and the Amity of the English, she bent herself withall her Art and Skill to pacifie his exculcerated and already alienated Mind by all possible means not unbeseeming a Princess.

By her Favourers therefore in Scotland, and shortly after by the Lord Hunsdon Governour of Berwick, she propounded these things following to be well considered by him.

First, of how dangerous Consequence it would be for him to break out into a War against England for this Reason, when all the Estates of England had judged the late Proceeding most necessary for the Safety of the whole Island, and also in it self just. Secondly, whether he were able to undertake such a War, since England was never better provided of Martial men, Forces and Wealth; and Scotland never weaker, as having been exhausted by Civil Wars. If he relied upon foreign Aid, how hardly and too late he might obtain it, his Mother's Condition might teach him, who so often craved it in vain. And if he should obtain any, what success could he hope for, seeing England, joyning with the Fleets of Holland and Zeland, feared not the Attempts of the most potent Kings of Europe? In the French King or the Spaniard what confidence could he put; since his own Power being once increased by the Addition of England would oppose all their Designs; and his Religion is directly contrary to their Profession, that they cannot aid him without Damage to themselves? Neither would the French King be well contented to see the King of Scots made stronger by the Addition of England, lest he should then prosecute anew the ancient Title of the English in France, or assist the Guises his Kinsmen, who now gape after the Kingdom of France. As for the Spaniard, he will, without Question, serve his own Ambition, considering that he boasteth himself to be the first Catholick Prince of the Bloud Royal of England, and of the House of Lancaster, though falsly. In which respect certain Jesuits and others went about even in the Queen of Scots life-time to advance him to the Crown of England by Election, as the meetest man to restore the Romish Authority in England, preferring him before his Mother and himself. Yea, they began also to persuade the World that she intended to bequeath the Kingdom of England by her last Will and Testament to the Spaniard, in case her Son should continue to adhere to the Protestant Religion.

What these things tend to, and what Assistence may be hoped for from the Spaniard, let the King consider. And withall, if he revolt from the Religion he hath been bred up in, with how great Ignominy he shall plunge his own Soul into eternal Perdition, and all Britain into Ruin and Destruction. Besides, he must consider with himself, if he purpose Revenge, whether the Estates of England, which gave the Sentence against his Mother, would not quite exclude him also by a new Sentence from his Title of

Succession: whose Love he may easily purchase by yielding to necessity, and bridling the Passions of his Mind, (seeing that which is done cannot be undone;) and may in due time peaceably enjoy the most flourishing Kingdom of England; and in the mean time may live in Security, and be thought by all indifferent men to have sufficiently discharged his Honour, considering that while time was he omitted no Duty of a most pious Son toward his Mother. And let him really persuade himself this, that the Queen of England will most lovingly and kindly esteem of him as her Son, and bear a Motherly Affection towards him.

These things she caused to be inculcated into the King of Scots ears: and to put him out of Doubt that his Mother was put to Death without her Privity and Intention, she determined to send him the Sentence against Davison, testified by the Subscriptions of all the Commissioners, yea and by the Great Seal of England; and another Instrument likewise, (the more to pacifie him,) under the Hands of the Judges of England, affirming that the said Sentence against his Mother would not in the least hurt or prejudice his Title to the Succession.

With these and such like Reasons while she gently soothed the King, she sent Drake (to prevent the War which she saw threatned her from the Spaniard) with four of her Royal Ships and some others to the Coast of Spain, to surprize and destroy his Shipping in the Havens, and intercept his Provision. Drake, entring into the Port of Cades, chased six Gallies (which made head against him) under the Forts; and sunk, took or fired about an hundred Vessels wherein was great Store of Munition and Victuals, and amongst them a great Gallion of the Marquess of Sancta Cruce, and another of Raguse laden with Merchandize. From thence returning to the Sacred Promontory, called Cabo Saint Vincent, he assaulted three Forts, and took them by Composition; and firing the Fishermens Boats and Nets all along the Coast, came to Cascaies at the Mouth of the River Tayo, where he challenged the Marquess Sancta Cruce to fight, who not once so much moved against him, but suffered him freely to spoil the Coast, and take their Shipping, without Impeachment or Molestation. From thence setting Sail towards the Isles of Azores, he lighted by chance upon a very great Merchant Ship, called a Carack, richly laden, and named the *Saint Philip,* returning from the East-Indies, and easily mastered it. Which Accident the Sea-men on both sides, in regard of the name of Philip, interpreted to presage some Disaster to Philip of Spain. Sure it is that from this short Expedition great Advantages redounded to the English. For the Spaniards, having sustained so great a Loss of Provision and Munition for War, were constrained to give over their Design for Invading of England this Year; and the English ever after that time more courageously adventured upon those huge Castle-like Ships, which before they were afraid of: also they so fully understood by the Merchants Papers the rich value of the Indian Merchandizes, and the Manner of Trading in that Eastern World, that they afterwards set up a gainfull Trade and Traffick thither, establishing a Company of East-India Merchants.

At the same time in another part of the World, Thomas Cavendish of Suffolk, (who two years before set sail from England with three Ships) passing the Straits of Magellan, fired many petty Towns of the Spaniards upon the Coasts of Chili, Peru and New Spain, took and pillaged nineteen Merchant Ships, and amongst them a very rich Ship of the King's near Callifornia, and returned home this Year by the Philippines, the Moluccaes, the Cape of Good hope, and Saint Helen's Isle, with a rich Booty and great Glory, as being the second after Magellan who sailed round about the World. The Particulars of this Voyage if any man desire, let him repair to the English Voyages exactly described in three Volumes by Richard Hackluit.

As Drake and Cavendish at this time purchased themselves great Fame and Commendations; so two other English-men, William Stanley and Rowland York, procured themselves the disgracefull and infamous Note of Traitours. This York was a Londoner, a man of a loose and dissolute Behaviour, and desperately audacious, famous in his time amongst the common Hacksters and Swaggerers, as being the first that, to the great Admiration of many at his Boldness, first brought into England that bold and dangerous way of Foining with the Rapier in Duelling; whereas the English till that time used to fight with long Swords and Bucklers, striking with the Edge, and thought it no part of a Man either to foin or strike beneath the Girdle. This York, having received I know not what Injury at Leicester's

Hands, fled, and served a while under the Spaniard in the Netherlands; but at length was reconciled, and made Governour of a Fort near Zutphen. But scorning at his Heart to put up the former Disgrace, he soon contrived to be revenged; for, being bribed with Money, he not onely betrayed the Place to the Enemy, but also drew Stanley, who had served with singular Fidelity and Valour in the Irish War, to be Partner with him in his Treachery, affirming with several Oaths and Protestations, that by the Confessions of the Conspiratours he was charged to be guilty of Babington's Plot, and was forthwith to be sent into England to be hanged; and persuaded him to betray Deventer, a strong and wealthy City, to the Spaniards, contrary to his Oath taken to Leicester and the Estates. But considering at last the Notoriousness of his Offence, he satisfied himself in his Conscience against the Imputation of Treason, in that he had restored the Place to the true Lord and Owner, which had been kept from him by Rebels; and, being a rank Papist, he soon after sent for Priests to instruct his Regiment, consisting of thirteen hundred English and Irish, in the Popish Religion, giving out that this should be a Seminary Regiment of Souldiers, to defend the Romish Religion by their Swords, as the Seminary-Priests did by their Writings. And indeed for this purpose Allen, who was not long after made Cardinal, not onely dispatched Priests to him with all expedition, but set forth a Book also, wherein, according to Pius Quintus his Bull against Queen Elizabeth, he both commended the Treason, and excited others to the like Perfidiousness, as if they were neither bound to serve nor obey an Excommunicate Queen. But mark with what Success.

The Spaniards set York and Stanley together by the Ears. York they poisoned, and rifled his Goods. His Body was three years after digged up by the Estates, and hanged upon a Gibbet, where it rotted. Stanley and his Regiment were removed out of Deventer, and posted from place to place, exposed to Dangers, and so far neglected, that some of them perished miserably for lack of Food, and some ran away one after another. Stanley himself, in hope of Reward for his Service, went into Spain, and offered his farther Service for Invading of Ireland: but he was neither received with that Honour he expected, nor was any Credit given unto him: for the Spaniards (they say) have this

Proverb, "A Traitour may have some Honour done him, but never any Credit given him." And now he found too late that he had in the first place betrayed himself.

These Treasons procured Leicester great Ill will amongst the Confederate Netherlanders, because the Traitours were still very intimate with him; and also to the whole English Nation, whom therefore those who were more free and lavish of their Tongues reproached and scandalized, till it was forbidden by Proclamation. But the Estates in a long Letter to the Queen accused Leicester of ill Governing the Commonwealth in matters of Money, War and Trade; and to his Restriction and easie Credulousness they imputed all the Damages received by such kind of Traitours. The Queen for the Examining and Compounding of the matter, and to sound their Inclinations touching a Peace with the Spaniard, sent Thomas Sackvill Lord Buckhurst, (lately made one of the Privy Council in Leicester's Absence,) Norris and Bartholomew Clerk, who faithfully managed these matters. But whereas Buckhurst's officious Diligence seemed to tend to the intrapping of Leicester, Leicester's Displeasure against him and settled Favour with the Queen prevailed so far, that Buckhurst at his Return was confined to his House for several months.

Sluys being afterward besieged by the Prince of Parma, Leicester was sent for out of England by the Estates to relieve it. This Town being furiously battered with 17,000 great Shot, and a large Breach made, was defended a while by Sir Roger Williams, Sir Francis Vere, and Captain Nicholas Baskerville, with a Garrison of Wallons and English, with great Commendations for their Valour; but at length they were forced to surrender it, when Leicester, who was drawn near to succour them, being too weak for the Enemy, was fain to retire. And sure it is the Estates would not allow him a sufficient Army, who reserved to themselves in reality that great Power which they had conferred upon him in Name and Words onely. And he himself disdained to be subject to private men of meaner Quality under the Notion of Estates, who pretended to carry the same Authority over him their Governour, which Charles the Fifth held over his Governours of the Netherlands. Hereupon brake forth first Grudges, then open Enmities, on both sides; and far greater, after he once begun to mention a Peace with the Spaniard: For they could not endure to hear of the Name of Peace, as a thing contrary and pernicious to their Designs. But when he perceived his Authority daily to be slighted and contemned among them, he betook himself to more subtile and crafty Counsels, and attempted to bring Leiden and other Cities under his Power. But being with the Loss of some men frustrate of his Hope, and having caused great Discontent, he was called Home again into England by the Queen, resigned his Government, and left the free Administration of the Provinces to the Estates, being derided by those that envied him, and the Title of His Excellency, which of all English-men he was the first that ever used, exploded and hissed off the Stage.

At his Departure he privately distributed amongst some whom he had drawn to his Faction certain Medals or Tokens made in Gold, on the one side whereof was his own Picture; and on the other side a Flock of Sheep, some Sheep straying, and a Dog ready to goe away looking back behind him. Near the Dog was, *Invitus desero,* that is, Unwillingly I forsake, and near the Sheep, *non gregem, sed ingratos,* that is, not the Flock, but the Unthankfull. And no doubt but he had it in his Head to usurp the Government. But these People have by their Policy and Wisedom not onely retained their ancient Freedom, against both the Power of the Spaniards, who have the Knack also to fight with Gold and other Arts, and the wily Subtilties of the French and English, and the crafty fox-like Fetches of the Prince of Orange; but also have incredibly increased the same, by means of the Favourable Inclination of their Neighbours towards them: and (which is more strange) whereas other Nations are impoverished by War, they are the onely men that thrive and are enriched thereby. Grave Maurice of Nassau, Son to the Prince of Orange by Ann of Saxony, Daughter to Maurice that heroical Electour, being 20 years of Age, was by the Estates made Governour, in Leicester's room, over the United and Confederate Provinces; and Peregrine Lord Willoughby was made General of the English Forces in the Low-Countries by the Queen. Both which the Leicestrian Faction put to much Trouble. For the Garrisons of Gertruydenberg, Naerden, Worcom, Heusden, and especially Medemblike, being addicted to the English, as if they had sworn Allegeance to the Queen, raised Tumults and Seditions. And Sir William Russell, Governour of Flushing, having drawn to his Party those of Armuyden and Campvere was suspected by the Estates, who were very full of Jealousie and Mistrust, as if he had a Design to reduce the Isle of Walcheren under the Power of the English. And this Suspicion was increased by the Coming of the Admiral of England; who though he laboured to make up the matter, yet they, misdoubting themselves, bewrayed their Suspicion and Jealousie, both publickly, by coining Money with two Earthen Pots swimming in the Sea, (according to the old Fable,) and wittily inscribing, *Si collidimur, frangimur*, that is, If we knock together, we are broken in pieces; and also privately by Letters to the Queen. Who being very carefull of them, and not neglecting herself, as foreseeing the Dangers by means of the Spanish Fleet now threatning her, commanded the Lord Willoughby to reduce the Seditious people under their Obedience to the Estates: which he together with Grave Maurice happily effected.

Leicester being returned, and smelling that there was an Accusation framed against him by Buckhurst and others for ill managing of Affairs in Holland, and that he was to be summoned before the Council, cast himself down privately at the Queen's Feet, and with Tears craved her Protection; beseeching her, "That whom she had sent forth with Honour at his first Departure, she would not now receive with Disgrace at his Return; and whom she had raised up from the Ground, she would not now bring alive to his Grave." And with such flattering Speeches he so mollified the Queen's offended Mind, that her noble Displeasure abated, and she received him into former Grace and Favour. Insomuch as when he was expected the next day to come to his Answer, he took his Place in the Council, and did not kneel at the upper end of the Table, as the manner is; and when the Secretary began to reade the Heads of his Accusation, he interrupted him, complaining that he was injuriously dealt withall in his Absence, for that his publick Commission was restrained by private Instructions: and so appealing to the Queen, he avoided the whole Weight of the Accusation, not without the secret Chafing and Indignation of his Adversaries.

This Year, in the month of February, departed this Life

Henry Nevil Baron of Abergavenney, great Grand-son to Edward Nevil, who in the Reign of Henry the Sixth obtained this Title in Right of his Wife, the onely Daughter and Heir of Richard Beauchamp, or *De bello campo,* Earl of Worcester and Baron of Abergavenney. By which Title when the onely Daughter of this Henry, the Wife of Sir Thomas Fane Knight, claimed the Title of Baroness of Abergavenney, there grew a remarkable Suit for the Title betwixt her and the next Heir male, to whom the Castle of Abergavenney was bequeathed by Will and Testament, and the same Testament confirmed by Act of Parliament.

There died also at this time, and all in the Month of April, four other Persons of honourable Note amongst us: *viz.* Ann Stanhope, Dutchess of Somerset, being 90 years of Age, formerly Wife of Edward Seimour Duke of Somerset, and Protectour of England; who by her womanish Contending with Catharine Parr, Queen Dowager of King Henry the Eighth, for Precedence of Worth and Dignity, was the cause of great Bustles in the Family of the Seimours, while she was persuaded by Dudley Earl of Warwick, (who plotted the Ruin of this noble and potent House,) that she, being the Protectour's Wife, ought not to bear up the Train of the Queen Dowager, who was married to the Protectour's Brother, or to give her Place: Sir Ralph Sadleir, Chancellour of the Dutchy of Lancaster, a man famous for his many and great Employments for the State, and the last Knight Banneret of England, to which Dignity he was raised at Mussel-borough Field: Thomas Bromley, Cancellour of England, under 60 years of Age, a famous Lawyer: And the 6th day after, Edward Earl of Rutland, whom the Queen had designed to be his Successour, being the third Earl of the House of Manours, a profound Lawyer, and a man accomplished with all polite Learning, leaving behind him one onely Daughter, Elizabeth, Wife to William Cecyl Grand-son to the Lord Treasurer Burghley. Sir Christopher Hatton, a man in great Favour with the Queen, of a Courtier was made Lord Chancellour; which the great Lawyers of England took very great Distaste at. For, ever since the Ecclesiastical men were put beside this Preferment, they had with singular Commendations for their Equity and Wisedom born this highest place of Gowned Dignity, which was bestowed in old time for the most part upon Church-men and Noble-men.

But Hatton was advanced to it by the cunning Court-arts of some, that by his Absence from Court, and the troublesome Discharge of so great a Place, which they thought him not to be able to undergo, his Favour with the Queen might slag and grow less. Yet executed he the Place with the greatest state and splendour of any that ever we saw; and what he wanted in Knowledge of the Law, he laboured to make good by Equity and Justice.

Sir John Perott being this Year called Home out of Ireland, delivered up his Charge, leaving all things in a peaceable Condition, to Sir William Fitz Williams, having first brought in such as were any way suspected, to deliver Hostages for their Fidelity, and that out of hand, lest, if they took Deliberation, they might seem to study a Revolt: the most suspicious of all he providently apprehended and committed to custody, and put the rest in mind of their Allegeance towards their Prince in these doubtfull Times; who, because of his Love towards the Irish Nation, readily and willingly hearkned unto him therein.

Till this time (that I may digress a little) the English-men had very easie Wars in Ireland, eight hundred Foot and three hundred Horse were holden an invincible Army. Randolph with 600 English easily discomfited O-Neal with 4,000 Irish. Colier in the Year 1571 with his one single Company defeated a thousand Hebridians in Connaught. 300 Horse overthrew the Butlers with a great Multitude of Rebels. And (to omit other like Instances) two Companies of Foot wone in one day above 20 Castles from the Irish. But after that they were by Perrott's Command exercised daily at Home, taught to use their Weapons, and to discharge their Guns at a Mark, that so they might be the more ready for Service against the Hebridians, and had afterwards been bred up in the Netherland Wars, and learned the ways of Fortifications; they then troubled the English (as we shall after see) with a more difficult War.

XV

The One and Thirtieth Year of Her Reign, Anno Domini 1588

Now we are come to the Year of Christ One thousand five hundred eighty and eight, which an Astronomer of Koningsberg, above an hundred years before, foretold would be an Admirable Year, and the German Chronologers presaged would be the Climacterical Year of the World. The Rumours of Wars, which before were but slight and small, began now to grow greater daily and greater: and now the Reports were no longer uncertain, but the universal and unanimous Belief of all men carried it for certain Truth, that a most invincible Armada was rigged and prepared in Spain against England, and that the famousest Captains and expertest Leaders and old Souldiers were sent for out of Italy, Sicily, yea and out of America, into Spain.

For the Bishop of Rome, some Religious persons in Spain, and several English Fugitives, had of late called back the Spaniard to his former Design for the Conquest of England, which had been interrupted by the space of ten Years before by the Portugal Wars; earnestly exhorting him,

> That seeing God had blessed him with such exceeding great Blessings and Benefits, Portugal with the East-Indies and many rich Islands being laid of late to his Dominions, he in like manner would perform somewhat which might be pleasing and acceptable to God the Giver of so great Good things, and beseeming the Grandeur and Majesty of the Catholick King. But nothing could there be more acceptable to God, or more beseeming him, than to propagate and enlarge the Church of God. That

the Church of God could not be more gloriously nor more mer-
itoriously propagated, than by the Conquest of England, and
replanting the Catholick Roman Religion, and abolishing Heresie
there. This War (they said) would be most just, not onely because it was necessary, but also because it was for the Maintenance
of Christ's Religion: in regard that the Queen of England, being
Excommunicated, persisted contumacious against the Church of
Rome, supported his Rebels in the Netherlands, annoyed the
Spaniards by continual Depredations, surprised and sacked his
Towns in Spain and America, and had very lately put the Queen
of Scots to Death, violating thereby the Majesty of all Kings.
And no less profitable would this War be than it was just. For so
should he lay unto his Empire those flourishing Kingdoms, ex-
tinguish the Rebellion in the Low-countries, which was kept alive
as it were by the Breath it had from England, secure his Voiages
to and from both Indies, and lessen his yearly Expences for Con-
voying his Indian Fleets forward and backward. And for a ready
Proof hereof, they suggested, That the English Navy was neither
for Number nor Bigness of Vessels, nor for Strength, comparable
to that of Spain, especially the Portugal Fleet being now added
to it: That England had no Forts nor Defences; that it was unprovided of Commanders, Souldiers, Cavalry and Munitions, bare
of Wealth and Friends; that there were many in all parts of the
Realm addicted to the Romish Religion, who would presently
joyn their Forces with his. Briefly, that so great was the Strength
of the Spaniard both by Sea and Land, and so unmatchable the
Valour of the Spaniards, that no man durst oppose him; so that
they did confidently assure themselves of his Victory. Moreover,
that now an Opportunity was as it were offered him by God
himself, whilst he had no ground to fear any thing either from
the Turk, having lately concluded a Truce with him, or from the
French, who were now imbroiled in a Civil War. They made
him believe also, that England was easier to be conquered than
the Netherlands; in respect it was a shorter and convenienter Cut
from Spain to England, namely by a free and open Sea; but to
the Netherlands a longer and more difficult, by a Sea for a great
part of it narrow and pent, and lying over against England.
Also, that the Low-Countries were as it were a continued Bulwark, fortified every-where with so many Cities and Castles; but
England with none at all: so that it was an easie matter for them
to pierce presently into the very Bowels of the Land, as well as
they had done of late into Portugal. And, lastly, out of that

military Axiome, That it is not good leaving an Enemy at our Back, That the English therefore, being inveterate Enemies to the Spaniards, must necessarily be first conquered, upon whose Assistance the Netherlanders relying had so long a time sustained the Burthen of the War, and without whom they could not longer subsist. So as England being once conquered, the Low-Countries must of necessity be subdued.

These things being thus disposed, and the Business resolved on, they enter into serious Consultation about the best way and manner of Invading England. Don Alvares Bassano, Marquess of Sancta Cruce, to whom was committed the principal Charge and Conduct of the Armada, was of Opinion, that first of all some Port-towns in Holland or Zeland should unawares be surprized by the Prince of Parma's Land-forces and some Spanish Ships sent beforehand, where the Spanish Fleet might have safe Harbour and a Place of Retreat, and from whence it might conveniently attempt the Invasion; considering that the Fleet could not ride safely in the unquiet British Sea, where the Winds often changed, and wherein the Tides were specially to be observed. With him agreed in Opinion the Prince of Parma, who urged this Expedition tooth and nail. Others disliked this Project, as being a thing difficult, full of Danger, requiring long Time, much Labour, great Expence, and the Success thereof like to be uncertain; adding that it could neither be done secretly nor at unawares, but would easily be prevented by the English. These men were of Opinion, that England might easilier be wone with the same Charge; and that the Victory would be certain and sure, if a well-provided Army from Spain and the Low-Countries were landed by a powerfull Navy at the Thames Mouth, and London, the chief City, surprized by a sudden Assault. This seemed to them very easie to be effected, and therefore all concurred in this Opinion, that it was forthwith to be put in Execution. Of these notwithstanding some thought it meet that War should be first proclaimed by an Herald, and that to good and wise purpose, as they thought; both to remove Suspicion and Jealousie out of the neighbour-Princes Minds, and also to force the Queen to call in foreign Forces to her Assistence; hoping that they (according to the usual Insolency of Mercenaries) would mutiny, and spoil the Countrey, and that she thereby would procure the Ill will of her

Subjects, and all things would run into Confusion in England. But this was not hearkned to by those who were puffed up and eager with Confidence of their own Strength; for they held it sufficient to recommend the Cause, the Armada and Army to the Bishop of Rome, and to the Prayers of the Catholicks to God and the Saints, and to set forth a Book in print for a Terrour, wherein the whole Preparation was particularly set down: which verily was so vast throughout all Spain, Italy and Sicily, that the Spaniards themselves were amazed at it, and named it The invincible Armada.

The Prince of Parma also in the Netherlands, by the King of Spain's Command, built Ships, and many flat-bottomed Boats, each of them big enough to carry 30 Horse, with Bridges fitted to them: Mariners he hired from the Eastern parts of Germany, prepared Piles sharpened at the neather End, armed with Iron, and hooked on the Sides, and provided twenty thousand Barrels, and an infinite number of Faggots; and in the Sea-towns of Flanders he had an Army in readiness of 103 Companies of Foot, and 4,000 Horse, amongst which were 700 English Fugitives, who of all others were least esteemed. Neither was Stanley, who had the Command of them, nor Westmorland, nor others who offered their Service and Counsel, once heard, but for their Unnaturalness to their Countrey they were debarred from all Access, and as most inauspicious persons worthily and with Detestation rejected. Sixtus Quintus also, Bishop of Rome, that he might not seem to be wanting to the Cause, sending Cardinal Allen, an English-man, into the Low-Countries, renewed the Bulls declaratory of Pius Quintus and Gregory the Thirteenth, excommunicated the Queen, dethroned her, absolved her Subjects from all Allegeance, and published his Croisado in print, as it were against Turks and Infidels, wherein out of the Treasury of the Church he granted plenary Indulgences to all that gave their Help and Assistence. Whereupon the Marquess of Burgoew of the House of Austria, the Duke of Pastrana, Amadæus of Savoy, Vespasian Gonzaga, John de Medicis, and many Noblemen from all Parts, listed themselves voluntarily for this Enterprise and Expedition.

Queen Elizabeth on the other side, that she might not be taken unprovided, prepared with all Diligence imaginable as strong a

Fleet as she could, and all things necessary for War. And she herself (who was of a quick Judgment in discerning mens Natures and Dispositions, and ever then most happy when she made her own free Choice, and trusted not to the Recommendations of others,) assigned most excellent men to every particular Place and Charge. The Command of the whole Fleet she gave to Charles Lord Howard of Effingham, Lord Admiral of England; of whose fortunate Conduct she had a very great Perswasion, and whom she knew, by his moderate and noble Carriage, to be skilfull in Sea-matters, wary and provident, valiant and courageous, industrious and active, and of great Authority and Esteem amongst the Sea-men of her Navy. Him she sent early to the Western Parts of England, where Drake, whom she appointed Vice-admiral joyned with him. The Lord Henry Seimour, second Son to the Duke of Somerset, she commanded to lie upon the Coast of the Low-Countries with 40 Ships, English and Netherlandish, and to take Care that the Prince of Parma came not out to Sea with his Forces. Though some there were who earnestly perswaded her to expect the Enemy's Coming, and to welcome him with a Land-battel, according as had been resolved in the Reign of Henry the Eighth, when the French with a strong Fleet threatned England.

For Land-service there were disposed along the Southern Coasts 20,000 men. Besides which two Armies were raised of choice well-disciplin'd and experienc'd men: the one under the Command of the Earl of Leicester, consisting of 1,000 Horse and 22,000 Foot; which incamped at Tilbury, not far from the Thames Mouth, (for the Enemy was fully resolved to set first upon London:) the other under the Leading of the Lord Hunsdon, consisting of 34,000 Foot and 2,000 Horse, to guard the Queen's Person.

Arthur Lord Grey, Sir Francis Knolles, Sir John Norris, Sir Richard Bingham, and Sir Roger Williams, Knights, and excellent Souldiers, were made choice of to consult about the best way of managing the War at Land. These men thought good, that the most convenient Landing-places for the Enemy, as well out of Spain as out of the Low-Countries, should be well manned and fortified; namely, Milford Haven, Falmouth, Plymouth, Portland, the Isle of Wight, Portsmouth, that open Coast of Kent which we call the Downs, the Thames Mouth, Harwich, Yar-

mouth, Hull, &c. And that the trained Bands all along the maritime Countries should meet in Arms upon a Signal given to defend the said Parts, and doe their best to prohibit the Enemy's
Landing. And if the Enemy did Land, to lay all the Countrey
waste round about, and to spoil all things that might be of any Use
to them, that so they might find no Food but what they brought
with them on their Shoulders. And to busie the Enemy night and
day with continual Alarms, so as to give them no Rest: but not to
put it to the Hazzard of a Battel, till more Commanders with
their Companies were come up to them. Of which Commanders
they nominated one in every Shire to have the chief Command
and Conduct. I list not to relate particularly what Mid-land Shires
they assigned to aid this and that Coast, what Numbers, what
Arms and what manner of Fight they agreed upon.

In this troublesome Season, some beat it many times into the
Queen's Head, that the Spaniards abroad were not so much to be
feared as the Papists at Home; for the Spaniards would not attempt any Hostility against England but upon Confidence of
Help from them: and that therefore, for better Security, the
Heads of that Party were upon some Pretence or other to be
taken off; alledging the Example of King Henry the Eighth,
when the Emperour and the French King, by the Instigation of
the Pope, were ready to invade England; for as soon as he had
put to Death the Marquess of Excester, the Baron Montacute,
Edward Nevil, and others, whom he suspected to favour their
Enterprise, their Expedition presently was dashed. But the
Queen, disliking this as cruel Counsel, thought it sufficient to
commit some of the Papists, and those not of the chief, to Custody at Wisbeach in the Fens. And having her Eyes and Mind
every way, she by frequent Letters excited and quickned the
Estates, who were not asleep the while. Sir William Fitz-Williams, Lord Deputy of Ireland, she directed what he should doe.
The King of Scots she put in mind by her Friends in Scotland,
and by Messengers, to be very wary of the Papists and the Spanish
Faction. But he, not ignorant how great a Tempest and Destruction hung over head, was of his own Accord forward and carefull, and, according to his continual good Affection to the true
Religion and the Queen, had already refused to give Audience to
the Bishop of Dumblane, (who was sent from the Bishop of

Rome,) and had procured a Confederacy to be entred into by the Protestants of Scotland for resisting the Spaniards: and he himself marching in Person with an Army into Annandale, forced Maxwell's Camp, who, contrary to his Faith given, was returned out of Spain into Scotland, and favoured the Spaniard's Designs, took him and threw him into Prison, declared the Spaniards Enemies, and made Preparation against them with great Chearfulness and Alacrity.

Amidst these great Preparations for War by both Parties, Projects for Peace were not quite laid aside. Two years before, when the Prince of Parma had considered with himself how difficult a matter it would be to bring the Low-country War to an Issue, as long as it was cherished with daily Supplies from the Queen, had dealt seriously by Letters, with the Help of Sir James a Croftes, one of the Privy Council, a man very desirous of Peace, Andrew Van Loe, a Netherlander, and others, that there might be a Treaty of Peace, he being impowered thereto by the King of Spain. The Queen fearing lest this were done politickly underhand to break off the Amity betwixt her and the Confederate Provinces, and to allure them cunningly to the Spaniard, deferred the matter a while. But now, to divert the War which threatened on both sides, she resolved to treat of Peace, but with the Sword in her Hand: neither indeed was the Prince of Parma against it.

In the month of February therefore Commissioners were sent into Flanders, viz. Henry Earl of Derby, William Brook Lord Cobham, Sir James a Croftes Controller of the Queen's Household, Valentine Dale and John Rogers Doctours of Law: who being received in the Prince's Name with all Courtesie and Civility, sent Dale presently to him, to understand his Mind about the Place of Meeting, and to see his Commission from the King of Spain. He appointed the place near Ostend, not in Ostend itself, which was now held by the English against the King: and as for his Commission, he promised it should be shewed them when they met. But he wished they would hasten the matter, lest any thing should happen in the mean time which might hinder the Treaty of Peace. But Richardot said plainly and expressly, "that he knew not what might be attempted in the mean time against England." Not long after Rogers was sent to the Prince by the Queen's express Command, to understand for certain whether there were any Design for Invading of England, as he and Richardot seemed of late to give Hints of. He affirmed, that he never had the least thought of Invading England, when he wished the matter might be hastened; and was somewhat angry with Richardot, who denied that any such words had fallen from him.

On the 12th day of April there met with the English Commissioners in Tents near Ostend, Count Aremberg, Champigny, Richardot, Maes a Doctour, and Garnier, sent as Commissioners from the Prince of Parma; who voluntarily gave the English Commissioners the Precedency and upper Hand both in going and sitting. They affirming that the Prince had sufficient Power and Commission to treat of a Peace, the English propounded, that a Truce might first be concluded on. The other denied it, because it would be damageable and prejudicial to the Spaniard, (who had been at the Charge of maintaining a strong Army for now full six Months,) in case a Peace should not be agreed upon. The English insisted, that a Truce was promised before they came into the Low-Countries. They on the other side acknowledged that a Truce was promised six Months before, but not accepted; and that it was not in the Queen's Power to make a Truce for the Hollanders and Zelanders, who daily attempted Acts of Hostility. The English urged that the Truce might be general, for all the Queen's Dominions and the Kingdom of Scotland. They refused to grant it for any more than four Towns onely in the Netherlands which were in the Queen's Hands, that is to say, Ostend, Flushing, Bergen-op Zome, and Briell; and that onely during the Treaty and twenty days after; and upon such Terms, as it should be lawfull in the mean time for the Queen of England to invade Spain, and for the Spaniard to invade England out of Spain and the Low-Countries.

Whilst the time was spent and squandered away from day to day in arguing about the Truce and the Place of Treaty, which at length was appointed to be at Borbourg, Sir James a Croftes, out of his singular Affection to Peace, made a Journey to Bruxells without acquainting the rest of the Commissioners, and there propounded certain Articles in private; for which he was afterwards upon Leicester's Accusation imprisoned, though in the Judgment of the rest of the Commissioners the said Articles were not to be misliked: but Commissioners must not pass the Limits of their Commission. At last, when the English Commissioners could by no means get from them that there should be an absolute Cessation of Arms, nor see the the Prince of Parma's Commission to treat of Peace, they proposed these things following.

That the ancient Leagues betwixt the Kings of England and the Dukes of Burgundy might be renewed and confirmed. That all the Netherlanders might fully enjoy their Privileges, and serve God with Freedom of Conscience. That the Spaniards and foreign Souldiers might be removed out of the Netherlands, so as neither the Netherlanders nor the bordering Countries might have cause to fear them. Which things if they might be granted, the Queen would condescend to reasonable Conditions concerning those Towns in the Netherlands which she then had in Possession, (that it might appear that it was not for her own Advantage, but for the necessary Defence as well of the Netherlands as of herself, that she had taken up Arms,) provided the Money which was due to her from thence might be repayed. They answered, That there would be no Difficulty in renewing the ancient Leagues, when they should once come to a friendly Conference together about the same. That there was no Reason why foreign Princes should take Care of the Netherlanders Privileges, which were most freely and bountifully granted not onely to the Provinces and Towns that were reconciled, but even to those also which were reduced by Force of Arms. And for foreign Souldiers, they were retained upon urgent Necessity, as long as Holland, England and France were in Arms. As for those four Towns which had been taken from the King, and the Repayment of the Money which the Queen had expended, the Spaniard might in reason demand as many thousands of Ducats to be repayed him by the Queen, as he had disbursed upon the Low-Countrey War from the time that she first supported the revolting Netherlanders, and took them into her Protection.

About this time Dale by the Queen's Command went to the Prince of Parma, and mildly expostulated with him about a Book lately set forth by Cardinal Allen an English-man, wherein he exhorted the Nobility and People of England and Ireland to joyn with the Spanish Forces under the Conduct of the Prince of Parma, to execute the Sentence of Sixtus Quintus Bishop of Rome, published already by Bull against the Queen of England, whereby she was declared an Heretick, Illegitimate, and taxed of

Cruelty against Mary Queen of Scots, &c. and her Subjects commanded to aid the Prince of Parma against her. (And indeed there were a great number of these Bulls and Books printed at Antwerp, to be dispersed all over England). The Duke denied "that ever he saw any such Book or Bull, neither did he undertake any thing upon the Bishop of Rome's Account; but his own Prince he must obey. As for the Queen of England, he had so high an Esteem of her for her Royal Vertues, that next to the King his Master he honoured her above all, and desired to doe her Service. That he had perswaded his King to condescend to this Treaty of Peace, which would be more advantageous for the English than for the Spaniards. For if the Spaniards be overcome, they will soon repair their Loss; but if you (said he) be once vanquished, your Kingdom is quite lost by it." To whom Dale replied, "Our Queen is provided of Strength sufficient to defend her Kingdom; and you yourself in your Wisedom may judge, that a Kingdom cannot easily be wone by the Fortune of one Battel, seeing the King of Spain hath not yet been able after so long a War to recover his ancient Inheritance in the Netherlands." "Be is so (said the Duke,) these things are in the Hand and Disposal of the Almighty."

The Commissioners continued their Proposals, Answers and Replies to one another, and still spun as it were the same Thread over again. The English urging that a Toleration of Religion might be granted to the Confederate Provinces, at least for two years; it was answered, "As the Spaniard demanded it not for the English Catholicks, so they hoped the Queen was so prudent as not to desire any thing which should be against the Honour, Oath and Conscience of the Spaniard." When they demanded the Money due from the Estates of Brabant; they answered, "That it was lent without the King's Knowledge or Leave: but when the Accounts were cast up, how much the said Money was, and how much the King had disbursed about the War, it would soon be known who had most due to them." With such Answers as these they dallied with the English, till the Spanish Fleet was come upon the Coast of England, and the Thundering of the Ordnance was heard from the Sea. And then they received a safe Conduct from the Prince of Parma, (who had in the mean time drawn down all his Forces to the Sea-side,) and were honourably conducted by his Commissioners to the Borders near Calice. Thus came this Treaty to nothing, which at first was begun by the Queen (as the wiser sort have thought) to divert the Spanish Fleet; and continued by the Spaniard, purposely to surprize England at unawares and unprovided. So as they seemed on both sides to sow the Foxe's Skin to the Lion's.

The said Spanish Fleet, being the best furnished with Men, Munition, and all manner of Provision, of any that ever the Ocean saw, and called by the arrogant name of Invincible, consisted of 130 Ships: In which were 19,290 Souldiers, 8,350 Mariners, 2,080 Galley-slaves, 2,630 great Ordnance.

Don Alphonso Perez de Gusman, Duke of Medina Sidonia, had the principal Command thereof; (for Don Antonio Columna, Duke of Paliano, and the Marquess of Sancta Cruce, to whom this Command was formerly designed, died both of them while the Fleet was Rigging;) and under him John Martinez de Recalde, an experienced Sea-man.

On the 29th of May the Fleet set sail out of the River Tayo, and while it bent its Course towards the Groign in Gallicia it was totally scattered and dispersed by an hideous Tempest, so that with much ado it met again together some few days after at the Groign and other Harbours thereabouts; three Gallies being conveyed into France by the Policy of David Gwinn an English Slave, and the Treachery of the Turkish Rowers. It was reported to be so weather-beaten and distressed, that the Queen was verily perswaded that this Fleet was not to be looked for this Year; and Secretary Walsingham wrote to the Lord Admiral to send back four of the biggest Ships, as if the War were now at an end. The Lord Admiral did not easily believe it, and therefore humbly desired that nothing might be rashly credited in so weighty a matter, and that he might retain the Ships with him, though it were at his own Cost and Charges. And taking the Benefit of a favourable Wind, he set sail toward Spain, to surprize the Enemy's weather-beaten Ships in their Harbours. When he was not far from the Coast of Spain, the Wind came about into the South, and he thereupon (who was commanded to defend the Coast of England, fearing lest with the same Wind they might arrive in England undiscovered,) returned to Plymouth.

With the same Wind the Duke of Medina set Sail with his

whole Fleet from the Groign the 12th day of July according to the Account of the Julian Year: and after a day or two he sent Roderico Telie before into the Low-Countries, to advertise the Prince of Parma of the coming of the Fleet, and to tell him what was best to be done. For he had Orders to joyn with the Prince of Parma's Forces and Shipping, and to conduct them under the Protection of his Fleet into England, and withall to set the Land-forces on Shoar at the Thames Mouth. And now will I give a brief Account, out of the most credible Relations as well of the Spaniards as of our own Countreymen, what was done every day in this Expedition, that the Truth may the more plainly appear.

On the 16th day there was a great Calm, and a thick Fog till Noon: then the North east-Wind blew very strongly, and presently after the West-Wind, till Midnight, and then the East-south-east-Wind; insomuch as the Spanish Fleet being dispersed thereby was hardly gathered together again till it came within Sight of England on the 19th day. Upon which day the Lord Admiral of England, being certainly informed by Flemming, the Captain of a Pinnace, that the Spanish Fleet was entred into the Brittish Sea, (which the Sea-men ordinarily call the Channell,) and was seen near the Point called the Lizard, towed the English Fleet forth into the main Sea, not without great Difficulty, the Wind blowing stifly into the Haven, but indeed with singular Diligence and Industry, and with admirable Alacrity of the Sea-men, whom he encouraged at their Halser-work, assisting them and the common Souldiers in the doing of it in person.

The next day the English discovered the Spanish Fleet with lofty Turrets like Castles, in Front like a Half-moon, the Wings thereof spreading out about the length of seven Miles, sailing very slowly, though with full Sails, the Winds being as it were tired with carrying them, and the Ocean groaning under the Weight of them; which they willingly suffered to pass by, that they might chase them in the Rere with a fore right Wind.

On the 21st of July the Lord Admiral of England, sending a Pinnace before called the *Defiance*, denounced War by discharging her Ordnance; and presently his own Ship, called the *Ark-royal*, thundered thick and furiously upon the Admiral (as he thought) of the Spaniards, (but it was Alphonso de Leva's Ship). Soon after Drake, Hawkins and Forbisher played stoutly with their Ordnance upon the hindmost Squadron, which was commanded by Recalde, who laboured all he could to stay his men from flying to the main Fleet, till such time as his own Ship being much battered with Shot, and now grown unserviceable, he was fain himself with much adoe to retreat thither also. At which time the Duke of Medina gathered together his Fleet which was scattered this way and that way, and, hoising more Sail, held on his Course with what speed he could. Neither could he doe any other, seeing both the Wind favoured the English, and their Ships would turn about with incredible Celerity and Nimbleness which way soever they pleased, to charge, wind, and tack about again. And now had they maintained a smart Fight for the space of two Hours, when the Lord Admiral thought not good to continue it any longer, because 40 of his Ships were not yet come in, being scarce got out of the Haven.

The next Night following the *Saint Catharine*, a Spanish Ship, having been much torn and battered in the Fight, was taken into the midst of the Fleet to be repaired. And an huge Ship of Biscay, which was Oquenda's wherein was the King's Treasurer, began to flame all of a light Fire, by means of the Gun-powder, which was fired on purpose by a Netherland Gunner who had been mis-used by them. Yet was the Fire soon quenched by Ships sent in to help her: amongst which the Gallion of Don Pedro de Valdez, falling foul of another Ship, brake her Fore-mast or Boresprit, and being left behind, since no man (the Sea being tempestuous and the Night dark) could come to rescue her, fell into Drake's Hands as good Prize; who sent Valdez to Dartmouth, and left the Money to be rifled by his men. Drake was commanded to carry a Lantern that night, but neglected it, having five great Hulks in Chace belonging to some Merchants of Germany, whom he thought to be Enemies: by means whereof he caused almost the whole English Fleet to lie still, in regard the Night-light was no-where to be seen. Neither did he and the rest of the Fleet till towards Night the next day recover Sight of the Lord Admiral, who all the Night before, with two Ships, the *Bear* and the *Mary-rose*, followed the Spanish Fleet. All this day the Duke was employed undisturbed in setting his Fleet in Order. Alphonso de Leva he ordered to joyn the first and the last Squadron together: to every Ship he assigned his Station to ride in, according to the

Form resolved on in Spain, upon pain of Death to those that should abandon their Station: Glich, an Ensign, he sent to the Prince of Parma, to tell him in what Condition he was: and the aforesaid Biscain Ship of Oquenda's he turned loose to the Waves, having first shipped the King's Money and the men into other Ships. Which Ship fell the same day into the English-mens Hands, with about 50 Mariners and Souldiers pitifully maimed and half burnt, and was brought into the Haven of Weymouth.

On the 23d day of the month, betimes in the morning, the Spaniards, taking the Opportunity of a Northerly Wind, tacked about against the English, who for their Advantage soon turned aside towards the West. And after they had for some time striven to get the Wind one of another, they prepared themselves on both sides to fight: and fight they did confusedly and with variable Fortune, whilst on the one side the English manfully rescued some Ships of London that were hemmed in by the Spaniards; and on the other side the Spaniards as stoutly rescued Recalde when he was in Danger. Never was there heard greater Thundering of Ordnance on both sides; notwithstanding which the Spaniards Shot flew for the most part over the English without Harm doing; onely Cock an English-man died with Honour in the midst of the Enemies in a small Ship of his. For the English Ships, being far lesser than theirs, charged the Enemy with wonderfull Agility and Nimbleness, and having given their Broadsides, presently stood off at a distance from them, and levelled their Shot directly without missing at those great Ships of the Spaniards, which were heavy and altogether unwieldy. Neither did the Lord Admiral think good to adventure Grappling with them, as some unadvisedly perswaded him. For the Enemy had a strong Army in his Fleet, but he had none: their Ships were far more for number, of bigger Burthen, stronger, and higher built; so as their men fighting from those lofty Hatches, must inevitably destroy those who should charge them from beneath. And he foresaw that an Overthrow in that case would endamage him much more than a Victory would advantage him. For if he were vanquished, he should very much endanger all England; and if he were Conquerour, he should onely gain a little Honour for overthrowing the Fleet, and beating the Enemy. On the 24th day of the month they forbore fighting on both Sides. The Lord Ad-

miral sent some of his smaller Ships to the next Coasts of England, to fetch Powder and other Provision for Fight; and divided the whole Fleet into four Squadrons: whereof the first he
commanded himself, the second he committed to Drake, the
third to Hawkins, and the fourth to Forbisher; and appointed out
of every Squadron certain small Vessels to give the Onset and
attack the Enemy on all sides at once in the dead of the Night:
but being becalmed, his Design took not Effect.

On the 25th which was Saint James his day, the *Saint Anne*,
a Galleon of Portugal, which could not keep up with the rest, was
set upon by some small English Ships; to whose Rescue came Leva
and Don Diego Telles Enriques with three Galleasses: whom
the Lord Admiral himself, and the Lord Thomas Howard in the
Golden Lion, towing their Ships with their Boats, (so great was
the Calm,) charged so furiously with their Ordnance, that much
adoe they had, but not without Loss, to free the Galleon; and
from that time no Galleasses would venture to engage. The Spaniards report, "That the English at the same time battered the
Spanish Admiral then in the Rere of the Fleet with their great
Ordnance, coming up closer to her than before, and, having slain
many of her men, shot down her main Mast: but Mexia and
Recalde in good time beat the English off. That then the Spanish
Admiral, assisted by Recalde and others, set upon the English
Admiral, and that the English Admiral escaped by means of the
Wind turning. That the Spaniards from that time gave over the
Pursuit, and, holding on their Course, dispatched a fresh Messenger to Parma, desiring him to joyn his Fleet as soon as possible
with the King's Armada, and withall to send some great Shot
for the Spanish Fleet." These things were unknown to the English, who write, "That from one of the Spanish Ships they rent
the Lantern, and from another the Beak-head, and did much
hurt to the third. That the *Non-Parile* and the *Mary-rose* fought
a while with the Spaniards: and that other Ships rescued the *Triumph* which was in Danger." Thus as to the Account and Particulars of the Engagements they who were present at them do not
report the same thing, whilst on both Sides every man relates
what he himself observed.

The next day the Lord Admiral Knighted the Lord Thomas
Howard, the Lord Sheffield, Roger Townsend, John Hawkins,

and Martin Forbisher, for their Valour. And it was resolved, from thenceforth to fall upon the Enemy no more till they came to the Brittish Frith or Strait of Calice, where the Lord Henry Seimour and Sir William Winter waited for their coming. So with a fair Etesian Gale (which in our Skie bloweth for the most part from the South-west and by South clear and fair) the Spanish Fleet sailed forward, the English Fleet following it close at the Heels. But so far was it from terrifying the Sea-coasts with its Name of Invincible, or with its dreadfull Show, that the young Gentry of England with incredible Chearfulness and Alacrity, (leaving their Parents, Wives, Children, Cousins and Friends at Home,) out of their hearty Love to their Countrey, hired Ships from all Parts at their own private Charges, and joyned with the Fleet in great numbers: amongst others the Earls of Oxford, Northumberland, Cumberland, Thomas and Robert Cecyl, Henry Brooke, Charles Blunt, Walter Raleigh, William Hatton, Robert Cary, Ambrose Willoughby, Thomas Gerard, Arthur Gorges, and others of good Quality.

On the twenty-seventh day of this Month towards Night the Spaniards came to an Anchor before Calice, having Notice by their Pilots, that if they proceeded any farther, it was to be feared they might be driven by force of the Tide into the Northern Ocean. Near unto them also rode at Anchor the Lord Admiral with his Ships, within Cannon shot of them; with whom Seimour and Winter joyned their Squadrons. And now were there in the English Fleet 140 Sail, all of them Ships fit for Fight, good Sailers, and nimble and tight for tacking about which way they would: yet were there not above fifteen of them which did in a manner sustain and repell the whole Brunt of the Fight. The Spaniards forthwith, as they had done many times before, urged the Duke of Parma by Messengers dispatched one after another to send 40 Fly-Boats, that is, light Vessels, without which he could not well fight with the English, by reason of the Overgreatness and Sluggishness of the Spanish Ships, and the notable Agility of the English: they also earnestly prayed him to put to Sea with his Army, which the Spanish Fleet would protect, as it were under her Wings, (for so it had been resolved,) till it were landed in England. But he, being not yet ready, could not come at their Call; his flat-bottomed Boats for the shallow

Chanels leaked, his Provision of Victuals was not yet gotten, and his Mariners, who had been kept together hitherto against their Wills, had many of them withdrawn themselves and slunk away. There lay watching also at the Mouth of the Havens of Dunkirk and Newport, from whence he was to put forth to Sea, the Men of War of the Hollanders and Zelanders, so strongly provided of great Ordnance and Musketiers, that he could not put from Shoar, unless he would wilfully thrust himself and his upon imminent and certain Destruction. And yet he (being an expert and industrious Souldier) seemed to omit nothing that lay in his Power, through the ardent Desire he had to the Conquest of England.

But Queen Elizabeth's prudent Foresight prevented both his Diligence, and the credulous Hope of the Spaniards: for by her Command, the next day after the Spaniards had cast Anchour, the Lord Admiral made ready eight of his worst Ships, besmeared them with Wild-fire, Pitch and Rosin, and filled them with Brimstone and other combustible matter, and sent them down the Wind in the dead of the Night, under the Command of Young and Prowse, amongst the Spanish Fleet. Which when the Spaniards espied approaching towards them, the whole Sea glittering and shining with the Flame thereof, supposing that those Fireships, besides the Danger of the Fire, were also provided of deadly Engines and murthering Inventions, they raised a sad Outcry, weighed Anchour, cut their Cables, and in a terrible Panick Fear with great Haste and Confusion put to Sea. One of their Fleet, being a great Galleasse, having broken her Rudder, floated up and down, and the next day in great Fear making towards Calice, ran upon the Sands, and was after a smart and for a long time dubious Fight taken by Amias Preston, Thomas Gerard, and Harvy, Don Hugo de Moncada, the Captain of it, being first slain, and the Souldiers and Rowers either drowned or put to the Sword. A great quantity of Gold which she had on board was pillaged by the English: The Ship and Ordnance fell to the Governour of Calice.

The Spaniards report that the Duke, when those Fire-ships approached, commanded the whole Fleet to weigh Anchour and stand to Sea; yet so as, having avoided the Danger, every Ship should return to his former Station. And indeed he returned himself, giving a Sign to the rest to doe the like, by discharging a great Piece; which notwithstanding was heard but by a few, because they were so scattered all about and driven for Fear, some of them into the wide Ocean, and some upon the Shallows of Flanders.

In the mean time Drake and Fenner played fiercely with their Ordnance upon the Spanish Fleet as it was gathering together again over against Graveling; with whom presently after joyned Fenton, Southwell, Beeston, Cross, Riman, and soon after the Lord Admiral himself, the Lord Thomas Howard, and the Lord Sheffield. The Duke Leva, Oquenda, Recalde, and the rest, with much adoe got clear of the Shallows, and endured the Charge as well as they could, insomuch as most of their Ships were very much shattered and shot through and through. The Galleon *Saint* Matthew, under the Command of Don Diego Piementelli, coming to assist Don Francisco de Toledo in the *St. Philip*, which was soar battered with many great Shot by Seimour and Winter, driven near Ostend, and again shot through and through by the Zelanders, and taken by the Flushingers, was likewise herself taken, and the whole Spanish Fleet grievously distressed and put to it all the day long.

On the last day of the Month betimes in the morning the West-north-west Wind blew hard, and the Spanish Fleet endeavouring to recover the narrow Strait, was forced toward Zeland. The English gave over the Chace, because (as the Spaniards think) they saw them carried so fast to their Ruine: for the West-north-west Wind blowing, they could not but run upon the Sands and Shallows near Zeland. But the Wind turning presently into the South-west and by West, they sailed before the Wind, and being got clear of the Shallows, in the Evening they held a Council what to doe: and it was unanimously resolved to return into Spain by the Northern Ocean, in regard they wanted many Necessaries, especially great Shot, their Ships were torn and shattered, and no Hope there was that the Prince of Parma could bring out his Fleet to joyn with them.

Wherefore having now recovered into the main Ocean, they steered their Course Northward, the English Fleet having them in Chace; against which now and then they turned and made Head. And whereas most men thought they would tack about again and come back, the Queen with a masculine Spirit came and took a View of her Army and Camp at Tilbury, and riding about through the Ranks of Armed men drawn up on both sides her, with a Leader's Truncheon in her Hand, sometimes with a martial Pace, another while gently like a Woman, incredible it is how much she encouraged the Hearts of her Captains and Souldiers by her Presence and Speech to them.

The same day that the last Fight was the Prince of Parma, after he had made his Prayers to our Lady of Hall, came somewhat late to Dunkirk, where he was welcomed with opprobrious and reproachfull Speeches by the Spaniards, as if in Favour of Queen Elizabeth he had lost them so fair an Opportunity of doing noble Exploits. The Duke, to give them some kind of Satisfaction, punished the Purveyors of Victuals; laughing meanwhile in his Sleeve at the Insolency and Boasting of the Spaniards, whom he had heard vapouring, that whither-soever they turned themselves they carried assured Victory along with them; and that the English would not once dare to look them in the Face. And verily Don Bernardine de Mendoza foolishly and with ridiculous Falsity printed a Poem in France containing a Triumph before the Victory. However, that Parma might not come forth from Dunkirk, the Lord Admiral commanded the Lord Henry Seimour and the Hollanders to have a strict Eye upon the Coast of Flanders, while he himself chased the Spaniards till they were gone past Edenborough Frith in Scotland, anciently called Bodotria. For some there were that feared they would have Recourse to the King of Scots, who was already exasperated for his Mother's Death. Certainly Ashbey, the Queen's Embassadour in Scotland, to pacifie his Mind, this Month made him large Offers, to wit, the Title of a Duke in England, a yearly Pension of 5,000 Pounds, a Guard to be maintained at the Queen's Charge, and some other matters; whether of his own Head, or by Command of others, I cannot tell, nor do I list to be curious in examining: but upon him the Blame fell, and the Offers were never made good to him.

But the Spaniards having now thrown off all Design and Hope of coming back again, and placing their whole Safety in their Flight, made no stay any-where. And thus this great Armada, which had been three complete Years in rigging and preparing with infinite Expense, was within one Month's space many times fought with, and at the last overthrown, with the Slaughter of many men, not an hundred of the English being missing, nor any Ship lost, save onely that small one of Cock's: (for all the Shot from the tall Spanish ships flew quite over the English:) and after it had been driven round about all Britain by Scotland, the Orcades and Ireland, grievously tossed, and very much distressed, impaired and mangled by Storms and Wrecks, and endured all manner of Miseries, at length returned Home with Shame and Dishonour. Whereupon several Moneys were coined, some in Memory of the Victory, with a Fleet flying with full Sails, and this Inscription, *Venit, vidit, fugit,* that is, It came, it saw, it fled; others in Honour of the Queen, with Fire-ships and a Fleet all in Confusion, inscribed, *Dux Fœmina facti,* that is, A Woman was Conductour in the Exploit. In their Flight sure it is that many of their Ships were cast away upon the Coasts of Scotland and Ireland, and above 700 Souldiers and Sea men cast on Shoar in Scotland; who, at the Intercession of the Prince of Parma to the King of Scots, and by Permission of Queen Elizabeth, were a year after sent over into the Low-Countries. But more unmercifully were those miserable Wretches dealt withall whose Hap it was to be driven by Tempests into Ireland: For they were slain some of them by the wild Irish, and others put to the Sword by Command of the Lord Deputy. For he, fearing lest they would joyn with the Irish Rebels, and seeing that Bingham, Governour of Connaught, whom he had once or twice commanded to shew Rigour towards them as they yielded themselves, had refused to doe it, sent Fowl Deputy-marshal, who drew them out of their Lurking-holes and Hiding-places, and beheaded about 200 of them. This Carriage the Queen condemned from her Heart, as savouring of too great Cruelty. Herewith the rest being terrified, sick and starved as they were, they committed themselves to the Sea in their broken and tattered Vessels, and many of them swallowed up of the Waves.

The Spaniards that got Home imputed their Misfortune to the Prince of Parma's Negligence, and their own too obsequious Prudence, who thought it a great Crime not punctually to observe their Instructions. For by their Instructions they were strictly commanded not to attempt any thing before such time as the Prince of Parma had joyned his Forces with theirs, and they were not at all left to their own Judgment and Discretion as Occasion should serve. Otherwise they bragged that they could very easily have surprized the English Fleet in their Havens. And martial men warmly disputed the Case, whether Instructions were not religiously to be observed and kept to, whatsoever should fall out, lest through Neglect of Obedience all Authority and Command should be violated; or whether they might not upon urgent Necessity correct and enlarge their Instructions, and accommodate them to the present Occasion, according as new matter should arise, lest weighty Importances and Opportunities of doing considerable Service might otherwise be let slip and lost.

The Spanish King himself bare the Overthrow very patiently, as received from God, and gave, and commanded to be given all over Spain, Thanks to God and the Saints that it was no greater; and shewed singular Pity and Commiseration in relieving the distressed Souldiers and Mariners.

Queen Elizabeth in like sort commanded publick Prayers and Thanksgiving to be used throughout all the Churches of England: and she herself, as it were going in Triumph, went with a very gallant Train of Noblemen through the Streets of London, which were all hung with blew Cloath, (the several Companies of the Citie standing on both Sides the Way with their Banners in decent and gallant Order,) being carried in a Chariot drawn with two Horses, (for Coaches were not then so much in use amongst Princes as now they are amongst private men,) to Paul's Church (where the Banners taken from the Enemy were hung up to be seen,) gave most hearty Thanks to God, and heard a Sermon, wherein the Glory was given to God alone. On the Lord Admiral she conferred a certain Revenue for his happy Service, and many times commended him and the Captains of her Ships, as men born for the Preservation of their Countrey. The rest she gratiously saluted by Name as oft as she saw them, as men that had so well merited of her and the Commonwealth, (wherewith they esteemed themselves well rewarded;) and those that were wounded and indigent she relieved with noble Pensions. The Learned men, both at Home and abroad, congratulating the Victory with Hearts transported for Joy, wrote Triumphal Poems in all Languages upon this Subject.

This publick Joy did Sir Robert Sidney augment, who (returning out of Scotland) assured the Queen that the King of Scots
was firm and constant in his Amity with her, that he sincerely
embraced the true Religion, and would defend the same. This Sir
Robert Sidney was sent unto him while the Spanish Fleet lay yet
hovering up on the Coast of Britain, to congratulate his Kindness towards the Queen, and acknowledge the same with
Thanks, to commend his chearfull Readiness for the Defence
of the common Interest, and to promise him like Assistence from
her, if the Spaniards should attempt to land in Scotland: and
moreover to put him in mind how greedily the Spaniard gaped
after the swallowing of all Britain, urging the Bishop of Rome
to excommunicate him, by that means both to deprive him of
the Kingdom of Scotland, and to exclude him from the Succession in England: as also to advertise him what threatning
Speeches Mendoza and the Pope's Nuncio had given out against
him; and that therefore he was to have a circumspect care of
himself for fear of the Papists in Scotland. At which time the
King (that I may take notice of it by the way) said merrily,
"That he looked for no other Favour from the Spaniard than
what Polyphemus promised Ulysses, namely, that after all the
rest were devoured, he should be swallowed the last."

Neither was the publick Joy any thing abated by Leicester's
Death, (though the Queen took it much to heart,) who about
this time, namely on the 4th day of September, died of a continual Fever upon the Way as he went towards Killingworth.
He was fifth Son to John Duke of Northumberland; one of King
Edward's Privy-chamber; under Queen Mary, who restored him,
his Brethren and Sisters in Bloud, Master of the English Munition at the Siege of Saint Quintin's; and under Queen Elizabeth,
(to whom by reason of a certain Conjunction and Affinity of
their Minds, and that haply through a hidden Conspiracy and
Consent of their Stars, [which the Greek Astrologers term
Synastria] he was most dear,) he was Master of the Horse,
chosen into the Orders of Saint George and Saint Michael, of the
Queen's Privy Council, Lord Steward of her Houshold, Chancellour of the University of Oxford, Justicer of the Forests on
this side the River of Trent, Lieutenant and Captain-general of
the English Forces in the Low-Countries, Governour and Cap-

tain-general of the United Provinces in the Netherlands, and this Year General of the English Army against the Spaniards: and now, in the very Period of his Life, began to entertain new Hope of Honour and Power, by being put into the high Authority of Lieutenancy under the Queen in the Government of England and Ireland. Which indeed he had obtained, the Letters Patents being drawn, had not Burghley and Hatton prevented it, and the Queen in time foreseen the Danger of trusting too great a Power in one man's Hand. He was esteemed a most accomplished Courtier, spruce and neat, free and bountifull to Souldiers and Students, a cunning Time-server and Respecter of his own Advantages, of a Disposition ready and apt to please, crafty and subtile towards his Adversaries, much given formerly to Women, and in his latter days doating extremely upon Marriage. But whilst he Preferred Power and Greatness, which is subject to be envied, before solid Vertue, his detracting Emulatours found large matter to speak reproachfully of him, and even when he was in his most flourishing Condition spared not disgracefully to defame him by Libels, not without mixture of some Untruths. In a word, people talked openly in his Commendation, but privately he was ill spoken of by the greater part. But whereas he was in the Queen's Debt, his Goods were sold at a publick Outcry: for the Queen, though in other things she were favourable enough, yet seldom or never did she remit the Debts owing to her Treasury.

The Prince of Parma, though he were now frustrate of his Design for Invading of England, yet to win some Reputation against the English with that puissant Army which had been provided against England, and withall to open a Way into Zeland, and preserve Brabant free from Incursions, besieged Bergen upon the River Zome, a Town of Brabant, both strong by its natural Situation, and fortified also with Works round about, wherein the most part of the Garrison were English. But this his Enterprise was also disappointed by the Providence of the Lord Willoughby, and the Valour of the Garrison. For though during the Heat of the Siege there grew a hot Dissension amongst them, whilst some favoured Sir William Drury, whom the Lord Willoughby, General of the English, had made Governour of the Town, and some favoured Morgan, to whom the

Queen had by her Letters given the Place: nevertheless they all agreed for the common Defence and Safety, and behaved themselves manfully; and by their frequent Sallies and military Strategems so employed the Enemy, that after 400 of them were slain, taken prisoners, or drowned, (whom Grimston and Redhead, feigning themselves Fugitives, had with great Promises, Protestations and deep Oaths, drawn into a Bulwark of the Town,) the Prince of Parma being now out of all Hopes of blocking up the Haven and carrying the Town, Winter also coming on, and Victuals failing, brake up the Siege after two months continuance. And the Lord Willoughby, to reward military Valour, Knighted Sir Francis Vere, who now began to grow famous, Sir Thomas Knolles, Sir Nicholas Parker and Sir John Pooly, for their courageous Behaviour.

As England was at this time troubled with Enemies abroad, so was it pestered this Year also with Schism at Home: (for Schism usually springeth up most rankly in the Heat of War). And certainly never did contumacious Impudency and contumelious Malapertness against Ecclesiastical Magistrates shew it self more bold and insolent. For when the Queen (who was Always the same) would not give Ear to Innovatours in Religion, who designed (as she thought) to cut in sunder the very Sinews of the Ecclesiastical Government and her Royal Prerogative at once, some of those men who were great Admirers of the Discipline of the Church of Geneva thought there was no better way to be taken for establishing the same in England, than by Inveighing and Railing against the English Hierarchy, and stirring up the People to a Dislike and Hatred of the Bishops and Prelacy. These men therefore set forth scandalous Books against both the Church-government and the Prelates, the Titles whereof were *Martin Marre-Prelate, Minerals, Diotrephes, A Demonstration of Discipline,* &c. In these Libels they belched forth most virulent Calumnies and opprobrious Taunts and Reproaches in such a scurrilous manner, that the Authours might seem to have been rather Scullions out of the Kitchen, than pious and godly men. Yet were the Authours thereof (forsooth) Penry and Udal, Ministers of the Word, and Job Throckmorton, a learned man, and of a facetious and gybing Tongue. Their Favourers and upholders were Richard

Knightley and Wigston Knights, men otherwise good, grave and sober, but drawn in by certain Ministers, who aimed at some private Respects of their own. For which the said Knights had smarted by a heavy Fine laid upon them in the Star-Chamber, had not the Archbishop of Canterbury (such was his Mildness and good Nature) with much adoe requested and obtained a Remission thereof from the Queen.

Whilst these men by their Calumnies made way for the aforesaid Discipline, others that were Confederates with them began to exercise the same in Corners in despight of the Authority of the Laws, holding Synods and Classes in several places, and forming Presbyteries. And for this cause Thomas Cartwright, Edmund Snape, Andrew King, Proudlow, Payne, and some other Ministers of the Word were called in Question; whom some over-Zealous people conspired to deliver out of the Magistrates Hands. But how extravagant the petulant Impudence of these Ministers was, which notwithstanding the Archbishop by his Prudence and Patience overcame, I leave to the Ecclesiastical Historian, to whom it properly belongeth.

Now was that hideous Tempest blown over which so thundered and threatened out of Spain: Nevertheless there brake forth some blustering Storms, as it were the Relicks thereof, in Ireland and Scotland; but a more violent Tempest fell upon Spain out of England, as I will shew afterward. For in Ireland, whilst the Lord Deputy Sir William Fitz-Williams searched after and rigorously demanded the Spaniards Goods that were shipwrecked and cast on Land, and on that respect imprisoned some as Favourers of the Spaniards, amongst other things Occasion was given and taken of those turbulent Commotions which afterward brake forth.

Daniel Rogers, who was some time since sent into Denmark to condole the Death of Frederick the Second, and confirm the former Amity with his Son and Successour, now dealt with the Trustees or Guardians of the Realm, "That no Danes might serve under the Enemy against the Queen of England; That Arrests of Ships might not be granted in the Strait of Denmark, called the Sound for private mens miscarriages; That the Fishing of Ireland, the Liberty whereof was by the ancient League to be renewed every seven years, might not be voided by new Pretences and Devices; That Custome might not be payed in the said Sound by the English but at their Return from the Baltick Sea, and that in the usual Money of Denmark; That the Owners of Ships might not suffer Prejudice for any Frauds committed by the Masters or Pilots; That the Packs of Cloaths might be free from payment of Impositions; And that the Custome called *Lastgelt* might be remitted to the English." But in regard of the King's Minority these things were put off till another time. For the Danes were somewhat unsatisfied with the English, because they sailed now into Russia, not by that Strait of Denmark, but by the Coasts of Norway, Finmark, Lapland, Scricsinnia and Biarmia. But Boris Theodorides, who was chosen Successour in the Empire of Russia to Theodore Joannides, that died about the beginning of this Year, omitted no means of helping and cherishing the English, seriously applying himself by all kind and good Offices to procure the Amity of the Queen.

Bibliography

Works of William Camden
(Not all editions of each work are listed)

Britannia sive florentissimorum Regnorum Angliae, Scotiae, Hiberniae et Insularum adjacentium ex intima antiquitate Chorographica Descriptio. London, 1586, 1587, 1590, 1594, 1600, 1607; Frankfort, 1590, 1616; Amsterdam, 1617, 1639. Translation by Philemon Holland. London, 1610, 1637. Translation by Edmund Gibson. London, 1695, 1722, 1753, and with some corrections by George Scott, 1772. Translation by Richard Gough. London, 1789, 1806.

Institutio Graecae grammatices compendiaria in usum Scholae Westmonasteriensis. London, 1595, 1604, 1608, and over ten editions by 1700.

Reges, Reginae, Nobiles, et alii in ecclesia collegiata B. Petri Westmonasterii sepulti. London, 1600, 1603, 1606.

Anglica, Normanica, Hibernica, a veteribus scripta. London, 1603.

Remains concerning Britain. London, 1605, and seven editions by 1700.

Actio in Henricum Garnetum Societatis Jesuiticae in Angliae Superiorem et caeteros. London, 1607. (A translation of the government's official pamphlet on the Gunpowder Plot.)

Annales rerum Anglicarum et Hibernicarum regnante Elizabetha. First part (to 1588). London, 1615. Second part with first. Leyden, 1625. Second part alone. London, 1627. Whole work. Leyden, 1639, 1677. Edited with corrections from Camden's manuscripts by Thomas Hearne. London, 1717. Translation (French) of first part. London, 1624. Translation (French) of whole work. Paris, 1627. Translation (English) of first part, by Abraham Darcy. London, 1625. Translation (English) of second part, by Thomas Browne. London, 1629. Translation (English) of whole work, by Richard Norton. London, 1630, 1635. Anonymous translation (English). London, 1675, 1688.

Included in White Kennett, *A Complete History of England: with the lives of all the Kings and Queens thereof.* 3 vols. London, 1706. Vols. 1 and 2 were actually collected by John Hughes; the translation of Camden, by a "Mr. Davis," is included in vol. 2. It is customary to cite the work by White Kennett's name although he was the author of only the third volume. Included in this work is Camden's fragmentary *Annals of James I.*

For a late seventeenth-century life of Camden and for many of Camden's letters as well as some minor pieces of his work such as the criticisms of Thuanus' account of Mary of Scots and his own fragmentary annals of James I, see Thomas Smith, *V. Cl. Camdeni et illustrium virorum ad G. Camdenum epistolae. Cum appendice varii argumenti. Accesserunt Annalium Regni Regis Jacobis I apparatus et commentarius de Antiquitate Dignitate et Officio Comitis Marescalli Angliae. Praemittitur G. Camdeni vita* (London, 1691).

Additional Reading on Camden and Contemporary Historical Writing

There is no full-scale biography or study of Camden. The only life is Smith's Latin one, published in 1691. Aside from the *Dictionary of National Biography* article by Sir Edward Maunde-Thompson, the most useful biographical account is Edmund Gibson's, printed as part of the preface to his edition of *Britannia.* (For fuller details on biographical material see footnote 1, above.) There is an appreciative essay on Camden by Stuart Piggott, "William Camden and the Britannia," in *Proceedings of the British Academy,* vol. 37 (1951).

There has not been much modern writing about the Tudor historians. But there are two good general accounts, F. S. Fussner, *The Historical Revolution, 1570–1640* (London, 1962), and F. J. Levy, *Tudor Historical Thought* (San Marino, Calif., 1967). The latter surveys the entire Tudor century. The later development of the historical tradition pioneered by Camden is studied in D. C. Douglas, *English Scholars*, 2d ed. (London, 1951). There is a good account of the quarrels over Brutus and Arthur in T. D. Kendrick, *British Antiquity* (London, 1950).

The origins of the Society of Antiquaries are discussed in Joan Evans, *A History of the Society of Antiquaries* (Oxford, 1956).

Index

Gray, Patrick, Master of Gray, 181–82, 195, 198, 253, 272
Greenland, visited by Davis, 211
Greville, Sir Fulke, xiii, 131
Grey, Arthur, Baron Grey de Wilton, 48, 240, 247, 291, 294, 312
Grey, Henry, Earl of Kent, 239, 247, 284, 285, 286, 288
Grey, Lady Katharine, 24
Grey, Lord John of Pyrgo, 15, 31
Grey, William, Baron Grey de Wilton, 24, 42, 47, 49
Grindall, Edmund, Bishop of London, Archbishop of York, Archbishop of Canterbury, 15, 21, 33; obituary, 161
Guest, Edmund, Bishop of Rochester, 21, 33
Guise family, 38, 39, 47, 48, 61, 90, 101, 178, 193, 195, 220, 254, 275, 277, 278, 282, 288, 299
Guise, Henry, Duke of, 144, 145, 155, 175, 177, 278, 280, 285
Guzman de Silva, Don Diego de, 86

Hakluyt, Richard, 301
Hall, Edward, xxv
Hamburg, shift of Merchant Adventurers there 1569, 106
Hamilton, James, Duke of Chatelherault, 40, 44, 45, 48, 62, 71, 99, 109
Hamilton, James, Earl of Arran, 51, 62
Hampton. See Southampton
Harding, Thomas, 85
Harrison, Richard, separatist, 163
Hastings, Francis, Earl of Huntingdon, 59
Hastings, Henry, Earl of Huntingdon, 59, 99, 121, 150
Hatton, Sir Christopher, Vice-Chamberlain, Lord Chancellor,

132, 135, 189, 195, 231, 240, 247, 258, 279, 296, 306, 330
Hawkins, Sir John, 86, 319, 322
Heath, Nicholas, Archbishop of York, 9, 10, 17, 19, 31
Heneage, Sir Thomas, Vice-Chamberlain, 215
Henry II, King of France, 12, 24–25, 37, 38
Henry III, King of France, Duke of Anjou to 1573, 86, 100, 114, 131, 133, 134, 145, 146, 151, 155, 186, 195, 203, 238, 275, 277, 280, 282, 285, 299
Henry VIII, King of England, 58
Hepburn, James, Earl of Bothwell, 62, 65, 67, 68, 69, 70, 72, 94, 95, 129
Herbert, Henry, Earl of Pembroke, 239, 247
Herbert, William, Earl of Pembroke, 10, 106, 111, 113, 114, 115, 118
Herodotus of Halicarnassus (Halicarnassaeus), 6
Herries (Heris), Maxwell, Baron Harries, 87, 89, 91
Hertford, Earl of. See Seymour, Edward
Hodgkin, John, Suffragan of Bedford, 33
Hohenlohe (Hollock), Count (Grave), 216
Hooker, John, xvii
Horne, Robert, Bishop of Winchester, 21, 33
Hospitall. See l'Hôpital
Howard, Charles, Baron of Effingham, Lord Admiral, 38, 142, 212, 219, 239, 312, 318, 319, 320, 321–22, 323, 325, 326
Howard, Henry, xxxvi, 31, 172, 232
Howard, Philip, Earl of Arundel, 131, 171, 219, 229, 249, 250; his attempt to flee, imprisonment, 192–93

Stafford, William, conspirator, 278, 279
Stanley, Edward, Earl of Derby, 10
Stanley, Henry, Earl of Derby, 182, 239, 247, 259, 284, 314
Stanley, Sir William, 218, 301, 302, 311
Statutes: Treason (25 Edward III), 176, 238
——1559 session: Elizabeth's title, 18; Supremacy, 19; Tenths and First-Fruits, Uniformity, Episcopal leases, 30
——1571 session, treason trials procedure, 176, 259, 269
——1582 session, penal acts against Papists extended, 142
——1585 session: Association, 190–91; Jesuits and seminary priests, 191–92, 238
Stewart, Francis, Earl of Bothwell, 197, 222
Stewart, Henry, Lord Darnley. See Darnley
Stewart, James, Earl of Moray, Regent of Scotland, xxxvii, 40, 44, 49, 60, 61, 62, 64, 65, 66, 67, 68, 69, 71, 72, 87, 91, 92, 93, 94, 95, 97, 98, 99, 109, 110, 111, 112, 113, 116, 117
Stewart, John, Earl of Athol, 71, 96
Stewart, Margaret, Countess of Lenox, 63, 91
Stewart, Matthew, Earl of Lenox, 67, 71, 99, 110
Story, John, 106
Stourton, John, Baron Stourton, 240
Stow, John, xvii
Strabo, xvi, xxii
Stuart, Esmé, Seigneur d'Aubigny, Duke of Lennox, 127, 128, 145, 153, 155

Stuart, James, Earl of Arran, 145, 156, 170, 196, 197, 198–99
Stuart, William, Colonel, 155, 168, 199
Stubbs, John, publishes *The Gulf* opposing Anjou marriage, 137, 138
Sussex, Earl of. See Radcliffe, Thomas

Tacitus, 7
Talbot, Francis, Earl of Shrewsbury, 10, 20, 43
Talbot, George, Earl of Shrewsbury, 43, 99, 100, 114, 121, 153, 177–82, 183, 239, 258, 284
Talbot, Robert, xvii
Theodore, Czar of Russia, 159
Thirlby (Thurlby), Thomas, Bishop of Ely, 12, 20, 25, 32
Thou, Jacques Auguste de, (Thuanus), xxv
Throckmorton, Francis, 171, 173, 175–76, 193, 194, 259
Throckmorton, Job, 331
Throckmorton, Sir Nicholas, 38, 56, 68, 69, 70, 71, 72, 96, 106, 112–13, 115, 117, 118, 147
Tichburne, Chidiock, conspirator, 229, 230, 233, 234, 237, 259
Tilney, Charles, conspirator, 229, 230, 237, 259
Tobacco, first importation into England, 210–11
Trappes, M. de, 278, 279
Travers, John, 229, 235, 237
Troyes, Treaty of, 74–75
Tunstall, Cuthbert, Bishop of Durham, 27, 31
Turberville, James, Bishop of Exeter, 20, 32
Tyrone (Tir-Oen), Earl of. See O'Neal, Hugh